Gard Granerød
Abraham and Melchizedek

Beihefte zur Zeitschrift für die alttestamentliche Wissenschaft

Herausgegeben von
John Barton · Reinhard G. Kratz
Choon-Leong Seow · Markus Witte

Band 406

De Gruyter

Gard Granerød

Abraham and Melchizedek

Scribal Activity of Second Temple Times
in Genesis 14 and Psalm 110

De Gruyter

G

ISBN 978-3-11-022345-3
e-ISBN 978-3-11-022346-0
ISSN 0934-2575

Library of Congress Cataloging-in-Publication Data

Granerød, Gard
    Abraham and Melchizedek : scribal activity of Second Temple times in Genesis 14 and Psalm 110 / Gard Granerød.
        p. cm. − (Beihefte zur Zeitschrift für die alttestamentliche Wissenschaft ; Bd. 406)
    Originally presented as the author's thesis (Ph. D.) − MF Norwegian Lutheran School of Theology, 2008.
    Includes bibliographical references and index.
    ISBN 978-3-11-022345-3 (23 × 15,5 cm : alk. paper)
    1. Bible. O.T. Genesis XIV − Criticism, Redaction.   2. Bible. O.T. Psalms CX − Criticism, Redaction.   3. Bible. O.T. Genesis − Relation to Psalms.   4. Bible. O.T. Psalms − Relation to Genesis.   5. Intertextuality in the Bible.   6. Abraham (Biblical patriarch)   7. Melchizedek, King of Salem.   I. Title.
    BS1235.52.G73   2010
    221'.066 − dc22

                                        2010002468

Bibliographic information published by the Deutsche Nationalbibliothek

The Deutsche Nationalbibliothek lists this publication in the Deutsche Nationalbibliografie; detailed bibliographic data are available in the Internet at http://dnb.d-nb.de.

Printing: Hubert & Co. GmbH & Co. KG, Göttingen
∞ Printed on acid-free paper

Printed in Germany

www.degruyter.com

Preface

This work was submitted to MF Norwegian School of Theology (henceforth MF) in June 2008 as partial fulfilment of the requirements for the degree *Philosophiae doctor* (Ph.D.) and was defended in a public disputation on December 11, 2008. In connection with the publication it has been revised at selected points. In addition, indices on sources and names have been included.

The work has been made possible thanks to a Ph.D. scholarship with a duration of three years, granted by The Research Council of Norway, and by an additional half-year extension offered by MF.

I am indebted to the two doctoral supervisors I have had: Prof. Dr. Terje Stordalen (now at Faculty of Theology, University of Oslo) and Prof. Dr. Karl William Weyde. Prof. Stordalen helped me greatly in the process of applying for a Ph.D. scholarship, and with his help I overcame many obstacles in the first half of my period as a Ph.D. student. Moreover, I trace much of my interest in 'scribal activity' to a series of lectures on inner-biblical exegesis that Prof. Weyde gave when I was a graduate student. And as doctoral supervisor, he has been invaluable as a critical reader and dialogue partner. I would also like to thank Dr. Nils Aksel Røsæg, Director of Research at MF, who shared of his great experience with Ph.D. projects.

Moreover, I would like to thank my good colleagues at or affiliated with the Department for Old Testament Studies: Prof. Dr. Corinna Körting, Associate Prof. Dr. Hanne Løland, Assistant Prof. Andrew D. Wergeland, Associate Prof. Kristin Moen Saxegaard, and Ph.D. student Jørn Varhaug. I also thank Prof. Dr. Kåre Berge (NLA School of Religion, Education and Intercultural Studies, Bergen) who more than once gave valuable critique to papers and drafts. In many ways, my colleagues have been a source of comfort in my sometimes lonesome 'wandering in the wilderness'. I have also been fortunate to have had the opportunity to presents drafts of various chapters at almost every annual meeting of the German–Nordic OTSEM network (Old Testament Studies: Epistemologies and Methods), funded by the Nordic research board NordForsk. I also send warm thoughts to the librarians at MF, who always offer excellent service: Elna Oline Strandheim, Mette Angell Røkke, Bente Røren, Hanne Rakel Løvaas, and Inger Johanne Gillebo.

Further, I would like to thank the members of the committee that examined me at the public defence of my dissertation for giving me instructive tips for improvements: Prof. Dr. Reinhard G. Kratz (Göttingen), Prof. Dr. Magnar Kartveit (Stavanger), and—once again—Prof. Corinna Körting. I am nevertheless responsible for the work, including the weaknesses and misunderstandings it possibly contains.

Finally, I am indebted to Walter de Gruyter and to the editors of the series Beihefte zur Zeitschrift für die alttestamentliche Wissenschaft for having expeditiously and cordially accepted this work for publication. Paul Kobelski and Maurya Horgan at the HK Scriptorium in Denver, Colorado, have with professional skills undertaken the job of copyediting, typesetting, and preparing the indices of this work.

To a large extent, this work has been a family enterprise. During the process of writing my wife, Antone, gave me much freedom and space. I dedicate this book to her and to our four children, of whom two were born when this work was in progress and of whom the youngest was born just a couple of months after the public defence of the dissertation: Berge (b. 2002), Ansgar (b. 2004), Bror (b./d. 2007), and Eira (b. 2009).

Stokke, near the town of Tønsberg
September 2009

Gard Granerød

Contents

Part I: Introduction

1. Background, Method, Aim, and Overview

1.1 Genesis 14: A Late Work of a Scribe's Desk, Made on the Basis of Early Traditions?

Es bleibt dann nur ein methodisch sicherer Zugang [zu Genesis 14], der traditionsgeschichtliche.[1]

One can answer the question of the origin and setting of Gen. 14 only by making *appropriate distinctions*. None of the constituent parts grew out of the patriarchal period itself; only personal names . . . and some individual elements (use of certain words) were taken from the patriarchal story already assembled in the Pentateuch. *The narrative 14:12–24 (without the name Abraham) originated in the period of the judges* and comes from a cycle of savior narratives. When Abraham becomes the subject of the story, he acquires the importance of a savior hero, analogous [*sic*] to the figures in Judges. *The addition (vv. 18–20) very probably arose in the time of David*; an experience of Abraham is narrated with the purpose of legitimating cultic innovations in that period. *The report of the campaign (vv. 1–11) with its many names is certainly of extra-Israelite origin*; it follows in style and structure the royal inscriptions of Assyrian-Babylonian kings. It cannot be traced back to a definite historical event in the form in which it is preserved. The manner of presentation is unhistorical despite the acknowledgment of a historical campaign in a clumsy way. *The composite text of vv. 1–11 and 12–24 is the work of a scribe's desk from the late postexilic period*, to be compared with other late Jewish writings.[2]

The two quotations summarize Claus Westermann's method for solving the question of the origin and setting of Genesis 14—an enigmatic text that some have argued somehow renders history or tradition from the second millennium or first part of the first millennium BCE,[3] and others

---

1 Claus Westermann, *Genesis 12–50* (EdF 48; Darmstadt: Wissenschaftliche Buchgesellschaft, 1975), 41.

2 Claus Westermann, *Genesis 12–36* (trans. John J. Scullion; Minneapolis, MN: Augsburg, 1985), 192–93 (my emphasis).

3 See, e.g., Friedrich Cornelius, 'Genesis XIV', *ZAW* 72 (1960): 1–7; J. R. Kirkland, 'The Incident at Salem: A Re-examination of Genesis 14:18–20', *Studia Biblica et Theologica* 7 (1977): 3–23; Niels-Erik Andreasen, 'Genesis 14 in Its Near Eastern Context', in *Scripture in Context: Essays on the Comparative Method* (ed. Carl D. Evans, William W. Hallo and John B. White; PTMS 34; Pittsburgh, PA: Pickwick, 1980), 59–77; Benjamin Mazar, 'The Historical Background of the Book of Genesis', in idem, *The Early*

have labelled a late midrash or given comparable designations indicating a very late date of origin,[4] whereas still others have analyzed it from the perspective of philosophy and ethics.[5] Moreover, Westermann's conclusion seems to be taken as state of the discipline with respect to this enigmatic text—at least in European scholarship. On the one hand Genesis 14 is seen as one of the latest additions to the compositional growth of the Abraham narratives (Genesis 12–25). On the other hand, although the composition as such is often taken to be late, the textual

---

Biblical Period: Historical Studies (ed. Shmuel Ahitub and Baruch A. Levine; trans. Ruth and Elisheva Rigbi; Jerusalem: Israel Exploration Society, 1986), 49–62; Gordon J. Wenham, *Genesis 1–15* (WBC 1; Waco, TX: Word, 1987), 306–7 (cf. xlii–xlv), 318–320; Nahum M. Sarna, *Genesis: The Traditional Hebrew Text with the New JPS Translation: Commentary by Nahum M. Sarna* (JPS Torah Commentary; Philadelphia: Jewish Publication Society, 1989), 102; Victor P. Hamilton, *The Book of Genesis: Chapters 1–17* (NICOT; Grand Rapids, MI: Eerdmans, 1990), 398–401; Chaim Cohen, 'Genesis 14—An Early Israelite Chronographic Source', in *The Biblical Canon in Comparative Perspective* (ed. K. Lawson Younger, William W. Hallo, and Bernard Frank Batto; Scripture in Context 4; Ancient Near Eastern Texts and Studies 11; Lewiston, NY: Edwin Mellen, 1991), 67–107; Kenneth A. Kitchen, 'Genesis 1–50 in the Near Eastern World', in *He Swore an Oath: Biblical Themes from Genesis 12–50* (ed. Richard S. Hess, Gordon J. Wenham, and Philip E. Satterthwaite; 2d ed.; Carlisle, PA: Paternoster, 1994), 67–92; Francis I. Andersen, 'Genesis 14: An Enigma', in *Pomegranates and Golden Bells: Studies in Biblical, Jewish, and Near Eastern Ritual, Law, and Literature in Honor of Jacob Milgrom* (ed. D. P. Wright et al.; Winona Lake, IN: Eisenbrauns, 1995), 497–508; idem, 'The Enigma of Genesis 14 Revisited', *Buried History: Quarterly Journal of the Australian Institute of Archaeology* 35, nos. 2–3 (1999): 62; Othniel Margalith, 'The Riddle of Genesis 14 and Melchizedek', *ZAW* 112 (2000): 501–8; Amos Frumkin and Yoel Elitzur, 'The Rise and Fall of the Dead Sea', *BARev* (Nov./Dec., 2001): 42–50; and Dominique Charpin, '"Ein umherziehender Aramäer was mein Vater": Abraham in Lichte der Quellen aus Mari', in *"Abraham, unser Vater": Die gemeinsamen Wurzeln von Judentum, Christentum und Islam* (ed. Reinhard Gregor Kratz and Tilman Nagel; Göttingen: Wallstein, 2003), 40–52.

4 See, e.g., Abraham Kuenen, *An Historico-Critical Inquiry into the Origin and Composition of the Hexateuch (Pentateuch and Book of Joshua)* (trans. Philip A. Wicksteed; London: Macmillan, 1886), 139, 143 n. 4, 324 n. 12; Julius Wellhausen, *Die Composition des Hexateuchs und der historischen Bücher des Alten Testaments* (4th unrev. ed.; Berlin: W. de Gruyter, 1963 [= 3d rev. ed., 1899]), 24–25, 311–13; H. Holzinger, *Genesis* (KHC 1; Freiburg i. B.: Mohr, 1898), 146–47; P. Asmussen, 'Gen 14, ein politisches Flugblatt', *ZAW* 34 (1914): 36–41; Hermann Gunkel, *Genesis* (4th ed.; HKAT, Abteilung 1: Die historischen Bücher 1; Göttingen: Vandenhoeck & Ruprecht, 1917), 288; Roland de Vaux, 'Les Hurrites de l'Histoire et les Horites de la Bible', *RB* 74, (1967): 481–503 (503); and Reinhard Gregor Kratz, *The Composition of the Narrative Books of the Old Testament* (trans. John Bowden; London: T. & T. Clark, 2005), 273–74. See also Otto Eißfeldt, *Einleitung in das Alte Testament under Einschluß der Apokryphen und Pseudepigraphen sowie der apokryphen- und pseudepigrapenartigen Qumrān-Schriften* (3d rev. ed.; Neue theologische Grundrisse; Tübingen: J. C. B. Mohr [Paul Siebeck], 1964), 281.

5 See, e.g., Harold Brodsky, 'Did Abram wage a Just War?', *JBQ* 31.3 (2003): 167–73.

parts that one assumes Genesis 14 is composed of are thought to be traditions stemming from much earlier periods than the time a redactor combined them and added the resulting composition to the rest of the Abraham narratives.

Admittedly, Westermann was neither the first nor the last to approach Genesis 14 or parts thereof (particularly the so-called Melchizedek episode) by means of traditio-historical method.[6] Rather, he explicitly built on previous traditio-historically oriented research, with John A. Emerton and Werner Schatz as his most recent predecessors.[7]

The stress on the traditio-historical method as the adequate approach to Genesis 14 evident in the works of Westermann and his predecessors did not emerge in a scholarly vacuum. On the contrary, it was dependent on several factors. First, the textual integrity of Genesis 14 had already been questioned. Gerhard von Rad proposed that the chapter was a composition of no less than three parts.[8]

Second, Westermann worked within a traditio-historical paradigm. Various guises of tradition history were in vogue.[9] Form criticism had

---

6   See, e.g., H. S. Nyberg, 'Studien zum Religionskampf im Alten Testament', *ARW* 35 (1938): 329–87; H. Schmid, 'Jahwe und die Kulttraditionen von Jerusalem', *ZAW* 67 (1955): 168–97; H. W. Hertzberg, 'Die Melkisedek-Tradition', in idem, *Beiträge zur Traditionsgeschichte und Theologie des Alten Testaments* (Göttingen: Vandenhoeck & Ruprecht, 1962), 36–44; J. G. Gammie, 'Loci of the Melchizedek Tradition of Genesis 14:18–20', *JBL* 90 (1971): 385–96; M. Delcor, 'Melchizedek from Genesis to the Qumran Texts and the Epistle to the Hebrews', *JSJ* 2 (1971): 115–35; N. Habel, '"Yahweh, Maker of Heaven and Earth": A Study in Tradition Criticism', *JBL* 91 (1972): 321–37; K. Baltzer, 'Jerusalem in den Erzväter-Geschichten der Genesis? Traditionsgeschichtliche Erwägungen zu Gen 14 und 22', in *Die hebräische Bibel und ihrer zweifache Nachgeschichte* (ed. Erhard Blum and Rolf Rendtorff; FS R. Rendtorff; Neukirchen-Vluyn: Neukirchener Verlag, 1990), 3–12; F. L. Horton, *The Melchizedek Tradition: A Critical Examination of the Sources to the Fifth Century A.D. and in the Epistle to the Hebrews* (SNTSMS 30; Cambridge: Cambridge University Press, 1976); and P. J. Nel, 'Psalm 110 and the Melchizedek Tradition', *JNSL* 22 (1996): 1–14.

7   See Westermann's outline of the history of exegesis and in particular, the section devoted to the 'question of the unity and composition' of Genesis 14, in idem, *Genesis 12–36*, 189–90. Moreover, see John A. Emerton, 'Some False Clues in the Study of Genesis XIV', *VT* 21 (1971): 24–47, idem, 'The Riddle of Genesis XIV', *VT* 21 (1971): 403–39; and Werner Schatz, *Genesis 14: Eine Untersuchung* (Europäische Hochschuleschriften 23/2; Bern: Herbert Lang; Frankfurt am Main: Peter Lang, 1972).

8   See Gerhard von Rad, *Das erste Buch Mose: Genesis* (9th ed.; ATD 2/4; Göttingen: Vandenhoeck & Ruprecht, 1972), 137; and 2.2.2 below, Genesis 14*: A Compound Narrative?

9   Admittedly, there were different 'schools'. Westermann did strongly attempt to anchor the origin of patriarchal traditions in historical figures, even though he is unable to say *when* they lived. To him, it was impossible that all the patriarchal stories were invented. Nevertheless, he argued that the elements of oral tradition are something

already been established as a method and had reoriented Old Testament scholarship away from source criticism as the sole approach to the Pentateuch. Whereas Julius Wellhausen had focused on the sources of the Pentateuch and by doing that stressed the *literary* character of the biblical narratives,[10] Hermann Gunkel was more interested in the *oral* stages of the origin and transmission of the narratives prior to the literary fixation; the opening clause in Gunkel's Genesis commentary was accordingly 'Genesis ist eine Sammelung von Sagen.'[11] As Westermann puts it, it had already been acknowledged that each individual narrative had its distinct tradition history *before* it was incorporated into a written document.[12] Once the textual integrity of Genesis 14 had been questioned, then it was appropriate to seek the possible preliteral background for each of the textual units of which the chapter was assumed to have been composed.

A third factor, in light of which one should understand the stress on tradition history, is the question of the possible historical authenticity of Genesis 14. As a consequence of the accelerating number of ancient Near East cuneiform inscriptions that were discovered and published in the nineteenth century and later, the question of the identity of the kings with whom Abram waged war, according to Genesis 14, was put on the agenda.[13] The traditio-historical approach to Genesis 14 came in part as a response to the deadlock represented by philological and historical discussions. The goal of these discussions was to identify King Amraphel of Shinar, King Arioch of Ellasar, King Chedorlaomer of Elam, and King Tidal of Goiim (see Gen. 14:1) with historical figures known from cuneiform inscriptions. The ultimate goal was to give an answer to the question of *when* a four-king alliance under the leadership of Elam, similar to the alliance described in Genesis 14 (see vv. 5, 17), could have been

different from history. According to him, the question about the historicity of the patriarchal stories and figures is 'a question wrongly put'; cf. Westermann, *Genesis 12–36*, 43. However, on the other side, scholars such as Ivan Engnell, a leading figure of the so-called Uppsala school, argued that oral transmission prior to the literary fixation was a *reliable* process, also with regard to the question of the historicity of the narratives. See Engnell, 'Traditionshistorisk metod', in *SBU*, cols. 1254–64. For a brief orientation, see Klaus Koch, *Was ist Formgeschichte? Methoden der Bibelexegese* (5th and rev. ed.; Neukirchen-Vluyn: Neukirchener Verlag, 1989), 67–71, 97–106; Douglas A. Knight, 'Tradition History', *ABD* 6:633–38; and Martin Rösel, 'Traditionskritik/Traditionsgeschichte: I. Altes Testament', *TRE* 33:732–43.

10   See Wellhausen, *Composition*, 1–2.
11   Gunkel, *Genesis*, vii.
12   Westermann, *Genesis 12–50*, 20.
13   For a history of research on Genesis 14, see Schatz, *Genesis 14*, 13–62; and Westermann, *Genesis 12–36*, 187–90.

a historical reality in the second millennium. One can understand that such identifications were intriguing. In case of a positive identification between one or even several of the members of the four-king alliance in Genesis 14 and one or more kings mentioned in the cuneiform texts, the consequences for biblical scholarship would be tremendous. By identifying the kings that Abram fought with in Genesis 14, it would be possible—on the basis of extrabiblical sources—to answer *when* the so-called patriarchal period actually was. However, traditio-historical oriented scholars did not find this approach to be convincing.[14]

1.2 Brief Outline of Westermann's Results and My Objections

However, a traditio-historical approach can be problematic in many ways. *First*, from a methodological point of view, one can raise objections against its lack of control. I by no means reject that quite a few biblical texts have an oral, preliterate origin. In other words, in many cases biblical texts probably originated and were transmitted orally before they were eventually written down. Nevertheless, as soon as we are left to ourselves with no literary sources, we can at best make conjectures that are speculative.

Second, I question an important presupposition shared by scholars who have approached Genesis 14 by way of the traditio-historical method. Their axiom that more or less every patriarchal narrative stems from an originally self-contained oral tradition is beyond control. The presupposition has had a great influence of the prevailing view about Genesis 14, in particular with respect to its assumed lack of textual integrity. Even though I will discuss this later,[15] I find it necessary to anticipate the discussion already at this point: Within the paradigm of tradition history (here represented by Westermann), Genesis 14 is explained as the result of an amalgamation of three narrative parts:

a. an annalistic-styled campaign report (roughly Gen. 14:1–11),
b. a hero story about the patriarch (roughly vv. 12–17, 21–24), and
c. a story about Abram's meeting with the pre-Israelite priest-king Melchizedek, which builds on pre-Israelite, Canaanite traditions (vv. 18–20).

---

14 See, in particular, Emerton, 'Some False Clues in the Study of Genesis XIV', 24–47.
15 See 2.2.4 below, The Textual Integrity of Genesis 14*: A Unified and Internally Consistent Narrative.

The hero story about Abram's rescue of his kin Lot (b) is taken by Westermann and others to be the earliest one, and assumed to be dated to the premonarchic period. Subsequently, in the (early) monarchic period, this hero story was augmented by the story about the patriarch's meeting with Melchizedek, the priest of El Elyon and king of Salem (c). Finally, Westermann and other traditio-historically oriented scholars assume that the campaign report (a) was put at the beginning of the entire chapter, either shortly before or even during the Babylonian exile.

As for me, I am sceptical about the possibilities of doing research on the preliterary stages of biblical texts in general. Such research is done with few or meagre sources. In addition, I am not convinced that Genesis 14 lacks textual integrity. On the contrary, Genesis 14 is, according to my reading, an internally consistent narrative—however, with one important exception: I find that there are strong literary-critical arguments for the proposal that the so-called Melchizedek episode (vv. 18–20) is a secondary interpolation.[16] Contrary to Westermann and others, however, I find it unlikely that the assumed hero story about Abram's rescue of Lot (Gen. 14:12–17, 21–24) originally had a life of its own, independent of and earlier than the alleged annalistic-styled campaign report (Gen. 14:1–11), which introduces chapter 14 in the received biblical text.[17] Finally, I question the idea (often unarticulated) that the story about Abram's meeting with Melchizedek reflects cultic traditions in pre-Israelite Jerusalem/Jebus.[18]

Third, Westermann and other traditio-historically oriented scholars have not satisfactorily accounted for the immanent features in Genesis 14 that make this chapter so characteristic vis-à-vis the rest of the patriarchal narratives. Again, I find it necessary to anticipate some of my observations: The narrative framework of Genesis 14 resembles stories found in Joshua, Judges, 1–2 Samuel, and 1–2 Kings much more than any other story about Abraham, Isaac, and Jacob. Moreover, the author of Genesis 14 seems to have drawn much of his geographical information from the Table of Nations (Genesis 10). In addition, there are several similarities

---

16   See 2.2.3 below, Critical Examination of the Theory of a Tripartite Division; and 2.2.4, The Textual Integrity of Genesis 14*: A Unified and Internally Consistent Narrative.

17   See 2.2.1 below, The Melchizedek Episode (= ME) in Genesis 14:18–20: A Secondary Interpolation; and 8.6, Preliminary Conclusion and Point of Departure: The ME—A Doubly Late Interpolation.

18   See 8.4 below, The Terms and Concepts in the ME: Inconclusive with Respect to the Date of the Episode.

between Genesis 14 and the wilderness wandering narratives (Numbers 10–21; Deuteronomy 1–3) that need an explanation.[19]

1.3 Why a Study on Genesis 14?
A Brief Epistemological Consideration

Why is there a need for a new study of Genesis 14 or, for that matter, any other part of the Bible? Have they not been subject to research before? In the following I will briefly discuss this fundamental epistemological question.

In general, there are several things that can cause scholars to question earlier research and formulate new hypotheses. The easiest explanation is that (1) scholars are able to disprove the argumentation and/or results of previous research and point to a lack of logical reasoning and lack of coherence.

Moreover, (2) scholars' perceptions of the sources that were used in previous research may lead them to formulate new hypotheses. In the eyes of 'younger' scholars, previous research has left out sources/ material that they consider relevant for the particular issue in question. Consequently, although previous works, strictly speaking, are coherent and reached legitimate results when evaluated solely on the background of the premises and sources that they explicitly build upon, 'younger' researchers nevertheless consider these works to be insufficient because sources that, to their estimation, are relevant, have been left out. The weaknesses in the premises (e.g., the sources used) continue in the results.

Further, (3) the publication of new sources that somehow are relevant to the problem may open up possibilities for formulating new hypotheses. For instance, research on biblical hermeneutics in late Second Temple period Israel that was published *before* the discovery of the Dead Sea scrolls must necessarily be considered unsatisfactory today. The obvious reason is that the early research was ignorant of these important sources.

Eventually, (4) younger generations of scholars may prefer other methods, ask other questions, have other focuses, or work within paradigms that are different from those of earlier generations.[20]

---

19 See chapter 6, The Literary Building Blocks of the Author of Genesis 14*; and chapter 19, The Addition of Genesis 14 to the Torah in the Light of Second Temple Period Book Production.

20 Throughout the history of research, there are dozens of examples. The post-Enlightenment questioning of the received Judeo-Christian concept of a Mosaic authorship for

In the case of the enigmatic Genesis 14, I am not able to prove that previous tradition-historically oriented research on Genesis 14 suffers from lack of internal coherence or has other shortages in terms of reasoning (see 1 above). Neither can I point to new relevant primary sources that have been published after the emergence of Westermann's Genesis commentary or any other traditio-historically oriented contribution to Genesis 14 (see 3).

However, the reason why I intend to approach Genesis 14 with a new hypothesis is

- in part related to how I evaluate earlier research, in particular my scepticism to the methodological underpinnings of the traditio-historical method,[21]
- in part because I believe that previous traditio-historically oriented approaches have left out biblical texts that I believe are relevant for explaining the origin of Genesis 14,[22] and
- in part a result of my own affinity with the model for the growth of many biblical texts that underlies concepts such as 'inner-biblical interpretation', 'inner-biblical intertextuality', and *Fortschreibung*.[23]

From an argumentative viewpoint I can summarize the results of previous research under the lemma X. Although it no doubt is an over-simplification to subsume the results of previous research, I nevertheless do it for the sake of clarity in order to put on display how I justify the present study. Correspondingly, the conclusions I will draw in the discussions in subsequent chapters can to a large extent be called *non-X*.[24]

However, proving the weaknesses of earlier theses does not prove my own hypothesis. If I summarize my own hypothesis under the

---

the Pentateuch is but one example. In the seventeenth century Baruch (later: Benedictus) Spinoza abandoned the Mosaic authorship all together, and a century later Jean Astruc attempted to identify the sources that he thought Moses used when composing the Pentateuch. Despite the lack of consensus concerning the questions of the origin, textual integrity, possible sources, etc. of the received Pentateuch, no one today seriously any longer argues that Moses composed it. See Joseph Blenkinsopp, *The Pentateuch: An Introduction to the First Five Books of the Bible* (AB Reference Library; New York: Doubleday, 1992), 2–4.

21   See iv above and 2.2.4 below, The Textual Integrity of Genesis 14*: A Unified and Internally Consistent Narrative; and my reference to John Van Seters' critique there.

22   See ii above and chapter 6 below, The Literary 'Building Blocks' of the Author of Genesis 14*.

23   See 1.4, The Emergence of the Paradigm of Diachronic, Inner-Biblical Intertextuality.

24   See 2.2 below, The Textual Integrity of Genesis 14; chapter 4, Genesis 14* and the Composition History of the Abraham Narratives; and chapter 5, Why Was Genesis 14* Composed and Inserted into the Abraham Narrative? An Attempt at a Literary Answer.

lemma Y, I can not infer that Y is correct on the basis of the conclusion that X is *not* correct (*non-X*). Y and *(non-)X* are *incommensurable entities*.

Nevertheless, pointing out the weaknesses of earlier theses is a sufficient reason for testing out a new hypothesis. My hypothesis—to which I shall return below—will be formulated partly on the basis of observations I and others have made about Genesis 14 and partly on the basis of my affinity with scholarly works in general done within a distinct paradigm I find promising.[25]

As is evident so far, there is a circular movement between my a priori presuppositions and the results of my investigations. This epistemological reality is, as I see it, representative of how knowledge is acquired within most, if not every, study within the field of humanities. Because it is unavoidable, the best thing that I can do is try to make the nature and grounds of the results of the present study as transparent as possible. In that way I hope to make as clear as possible the limits of the results.[26] In the end, it is my hope that the validity of the study will benefit from such transparency.

1.4 The Emergence of the Paradigm of Diachronic, Inner-Biblical Intertextuality in Recent Research

In the last few decades there seems to have been a trend in Hebrew Bible/Old Testament scholarship to focus on *inner-biblical interpretation*— in a broad sense.[27] Although there have been voices calling for a methodological and terminological refinement,[28] various contributions share the

---

25 See 1.4 below, The Emergence of the Paradigm of Diachronic, Inner-Biblical Intertextuality in Recent Research; and 1.5, The Paradigm of Diachronic, Inner-Biblical Intertextuality: A Promising Paradigm for Exploring the Background, Origin and Purpose of Genesis 14.

26 See Hans-Georg Gadamer, *Gesammelte Werke. II Hermeneutik II: Wahrheit und Methode* (UTB 2115; J. C. B. Mohr [Paul Siebeck]: Tübingen, 1986/1993), 57–65.

27 Konrad Schmid opens his outline of the history of research on this issue by stating 'Das Thema innerbiblischer Schriftauslegung hat gegenwärtig Konjunktur in der alttestamentliche Wissenschaft'; cf. idem, ‚Innerbiblische Schriftauslegung: Aspekte der Forschungsgeschichte', in *Schriftauslegung in der Schrift: Festschrift für Odil Hannes Steck zu seinem 65. Geburtstag* (ed. Reinhard Gregor Kratz, Thomas Krüger, and Konrad Schmid; BZAW 300; Berlin: W. de Gruyter, 2000), 1–22 (1).

28 See, e.g., Benjamin D. Sommer, 'Exegesis, Allusion and Intertextuality in the Hebrew Bible: A Response to Lyle Eslinger', *VT* 46 (1996): 479–89; and Karl-William Weyde, 'Inner-Biblical Interpretation: Methodological Reflections on the Relationship between Texts in the Hebrew Bible', *SEÅ* 70 (2005): 287–300.

position that the origin and purpose of relatively late biblical passages or even entire books can be explained as either a *literary response to,* a *comment on,* or even a *continuation of* relatively earlier biblical texts.

1.4.1 In the Field of Prophetic Literature

In recent German-speaking biblical scholarship, one often finds the term *Fortschreibung* used, particularly in connection with the growth of the prophetic literature.[29] For instance, with respect to the history of the composition of the prophetic books, one can—at least in principle—distinguish between two types of redactional phenomena, the *Erstverschriftung* ('original codification, initial literary fixation', however not to be confused with the *ipsissima verba* of the prophet!) and the chronologically later *Fortschreibung* ('continual writing'). This distinction is not only useful in distinguishing between material of different ages. On the contrary, it says something about the value attributed to the earlier composition that someone found it worthy of commenting on. The *Fortschreibung* of a book and its redaction history is at the same time part of the history of interpretation. Whereas one can understand the *Erstverschriftung* as a written interpretation of the prophet's *oral* preaching, the *Fortschreibung* for its part continues or interprets the already-written text.

1.4.2 In the Field of Pentateuchal Studies

Moreover, recent study on the Pentateuch has been enriched by different types of *supplemental models,* all somehow challenging the now classic Documentary Hypothesis and its idea that the Pentateuch is a composition of four individual sources.[30] The growth of the Pentateuch

---

29   See, e.g., Reinhard Gregor Kratz, ‚Die Redaktion der Prophetenbücher', in *Rezeption und Auslegung im Alten Testament und in seinem Umfeld: ein Symposium aus Anlass des 60. Geburtstags von Odil Hannes Steck* (ed. Reinhard Gregor Kratz and Thomas Krüger, and Odil Hannes Steck; OBO 153; Freiburg: Universitätsverlag, 1997), 9–28. For a large-scale application of such a model, see Burkard M. Zapff, *Redaktionsgeschichtliche Studien zum Michabuch im Kontext des Dodekapropheton* (BZAW 256; Berlin: W. de Gruyter, 1997).

30   The classic scholarly model attempting to account for the disunity in the Pentateuch has been the so-called Documentary Hypothesis, a term coined by Julius Wellhausen in *Composition.* According to this model, the Pentateuch represents a composition (or perhaps better *collocation*) of four sources: in chronological order, the Yahwist, the Elohist, Deuteronomy, and the Priestly Writer (Wellhausen: 'Q', from 'quatuor' = 'book of four covenants'). However, this model has been under critique from many sides,

is explained in a way comparable to the *Fortschreibung* model for the growth of the prophetic literature: The assumed late layers in the Pentateuch are explained as supplements to earlier texts in the Pentateuch.[31]

1.4.3 . . . and in General

Finally, besides the obvious term 'inner-biblical interpretation', other terms such as 'allusion', 'echo', *'relecture'*, and '(biblical) intertextuality'[32] are often found in recent scholarship, as is also reflected in the titles of several books and articles.[33] This supports the assumption expressed above—that is, at least when they are used in a diachronic sense, meaning

---

above all for its lack of clarity about the literary role and function of the 'redactor' who—somehow—must have combined/collocated the sources. See John Van Seters, *The Pentateuch: A Social-Science Commentary* (Trajectories 1; Sheffield: Sheffield Academic Press, 1999), 41.

31 Different kinds of *supplemental models* have been proposed by Rolf Rendtorff, *Das überlieferungsgeschichtliche Problem des Pentateuch* (BZAW 147; Berlin: W. de Gruyter, 1976); Erhard Blum, *Die Kompostion der Vätergeschichte* (WMANT 57; Neukirchen-Vluyn: Neukirchener Verlag, 1984); idem, *Studien zur Komposition des Pentateuch* (BZAW 189; Berlin: W. de Gruyter, 1990); and Kratz, *Composition*.

32 For a brief discussion of how I use the term 'intertextuality', which was first introduced by Julia Kristeva, see also 13.1 below, The 'Abrahamic' Interpretation of Psalm 110 and Other Cases of Early Intertextual Readings of Genesis 14 and Psalm 110.

33 Perhaps serving as a door opener for a wider academic audience was Michael Fishbane, *Biblical Interpretation in Ancient Israel* (Oxford: Clarendon, 1985). See also idem, 'Inner-Biblical Exegesis', in *HBOT* 1:33–48; and idem, 'Types of Biblical Intertextuality', in *Congress Volume Oslo 1998* (ed. André Lemaire and Magne Sæbø; VTSup 80; Leiden: E. J. Brill, 2000), 39–44. Moreover, see John Barton, 'Intertextuality and the "Final Form"', in *Congress Volume Oslo 1998*, 33–37; David Carr, 'Intratextuality and Intertextuality—Joining Transmission History and Interpretation History in the Study of Genesis', in *Bibel und Midrasch: zur Bedeutung der rabbinischen Exegese für die Bibelwissenschaft* (ed. Gerhard Bodendorfer and Matthias Millard; FAT 22; Tübingen: Mohr Siebeck, 1998), 97–112; Reinhard Gregor Kratz, 'Innerbiblische Exegese und Redaktionsgeschichte im Lichte empirischer Evidenz', in *Das Judentum im Zeitalter des Zweiten Tempels* (ed. Reinhard Gregor Kratz; FAT 42; Tübingen: Mohr Siebeck, 2004), 126–56; Esther Menn, 'Inner-Biblical Exegesis in the Tanak', in *A History of Biblical Interpretation* (ed. Alan J. Hauser and Duane F. Watson; Grand Rapids, MI: Eerdmans, 2003–), 55–79; Kirsten Nielsen, 'Intertextuality and Hebrew Bible', in *Congress Volume Oslo 1998*, 17–31; Paul R. Noble, 'Esau, Tamar, and Joseph: Criteria for Identifying Inner-Biblical Allusions', *VT* 52 (2002): 219–252; Sommer, 'Exegesis, Allusion and Intertextuality in the Hebrew Bible', 479–89; Jeffrey H. Tigay, 'An Early Technique of Aggadic Exegesis', in *History, Historiography and Interpretation: Studies in Biblical and Cuneiform Literatures* (ed. H. Tadmor and M. Weinfeld; Jerusalem: Magnes, 1984), 169–89; Raymond Jacques Tournay, 'Les relectures du Psaume 110 (109) et l'allusion à Gédéon', *RB* 105 (1998): 321–31; and Weyde, 'Inner-Biblical Interpretation', 287–300.

that a late text somehow relates to a chronologically earlier one. It is my impression that the terms in biblical scholarship are used within a framework where the chronological order of the biblical texts is important—irrespective of the fact that the chronological order between the texts is questioned from time to time.

1.4.4 Common Denominators: Diachrony and Inner-Biblical Intertextuality

It is my assertion that all the approaches outlined above work within a common theoretical framework. I tentatively propose to subsume these approaches under the following name: *the paradigm of diachronic, inner-biblical intertextuality*.

Characteristic of this trend is that the Bible is addressed as a *written text* and the compositional history of passages and even books in the Bible is accordingly modelled as a *literary process*. This process took place in a community that already used and cherished earlier versions of the same biblical books. In some cases, the later passages or books can be interpretations of earlier texts. In other cases, the earlier texts may in various ways have provided templates for those who composed the later texts.[34]

The paradigm of diachronic, inner-biblical intertextuality represents another paradigm that differs from the traditio-historical one represented by Westermann, among others, which focuses more on the pre-literal oral origin and transmission of the biblical texts.

By 'intertextuality' I mean that texts belonging to different chronological stages in the growth of the biblical textual corpus are in dialogue with one another, or to be more precise, that later texts are in different ways in dialogue with earlier ones.[35] Moreover, a salient feature for all the approaches outlined above is that they have a diachronic component.

Finally, in all these approaches, the authors of the later texts seem to have intentionally related to earlier works. In some cases the purpose may have been to interpret the earlier text, that is, intending to impose a certain meaning on it. In other cases, the intention may not have been to interpret but rather to compose an entirely new and meaningful text

---

34   See also 19.4 below, Echoes of Earlier Texts in Genesis 14 and the Role of Literary Templates for the Production of New Texts.

35   For instance, late portions of the *Dodekapropheton* may have been conceived as *literary continuations* [German: *Fortschreibungen*] of chronologically earlier portions.

for its own sake, while using the literary building blocks/templates provided by earlier texts.

1.5 The Paradigm of Diachronic, Inner-Biblical Intertextuality: A Promising Paradigm for Exploring the Background, Origin, and Purpose of Genesis 14

I have attempted to show that objections can be raised against both the traditio-historical method in general and the traditio-historical approach to Genesis 14. Moreover, I have argued that such a critique opens up the opportunity for testing out a new hypothesis.

Further, I have attempted to show that one perhaps can argue that a paradigm shift has taken place during the last few decades. If the term 'paradigm shift' is too strong, then at least one can definitely observe that issues pertaining to 'inner-biblical interpretation' (in a broad sense) have been emphasized much more in recent research than in earlier contributions to Old Testament scholarship.

Therefore, it is reasonable to hypothesize that the background, origin, and purpose of the enigmatic and troublesome text Genesis 14 can be investigated within the paradigm of diachronic, inner-biblical intertextuality.

1.6 Aim, Scope, and Fundamental Hypothesis

This investigation focuses on the enigmatic text Genesis 14 in particular and seeks to discuss

- *when* the text was composed,
- *how* and *why* it was done,
- *who* did it, and
- *what* meaning the author may have intended.

In light of the discussion above I will seek to fulfil the task within the paradigm of diachronic, inner-biblical intertextuality. The fundamental hypothesis is that the author (or authors) of Genesis 14 composed the text somehow in relation to an already-existing text, either as a commentary or as a literary continuation.

1.7 Overview of Part II, Part III, and Part IV

For the sake of clarity, I will outline the body of the present study (part II to IV). By doing so, I hope to clarify to the reader the progress of the argument from one chapter to the next.

1.7.1 Ad Part II: Genesis 14*

In chapter 2 I will

- discuss the characteristics of Genesis 14* vis-à-vis the other patriarchal narratives and other texts (see 2.1),
- discuss the textual integrity of Genesis 14 (see 2.2),
- account for some text-critical issues related to the narrative (see 2.3), and
- formulate a more concrete hypothesis to be tested out in the rest of part II (see 2.4).

An important point is that Genesis 14, on the one hand, contains features that are not typical of the rest of the patriarchal narratives but, on the other hand, are typical of other types of biblical literature. This observation gives an important impetus for formulating a general hypothesis about the origin of Genesis 14* (for the meaning of the asterisk, see the following paragraph): The easiest explanation for what seems to be an accumulation of literary borrowings in the text is that Genesis 14 is the work of a scribe's desk (German: *Schreibtischarbeit*), composed by someone who is versed in the Scriptures — and not merely an editor who puts together assumed ancient traditions.

The conclusion drawn from the discussion about the textual integrity of Genesis 14 will be important for the outline of the entire present investigation, namely, that the so-called Melchizedek episode (Gen. 14:18–20) is a secondary interpolation. Unlike Westermann and others, however, I conclude that the rest of Genesis 14 is a unified and internally consistent narrative. Henceforth, I will refer to this text as 'Genesis 14*' (i.e., the narrative with the exception of the Melchizedek episode). Correspondingly, most of part II will be devoted to Genesis 14*, whereas part III will be devoted to the secondary interpolation in vv. 18–20 (the Melchizedek episode).

In chapter 3 I will briefly touch on the discussion concerning the age and growth of the Abraham tradition. It will be argued that the Abraham tradition probably represents a relatively late development. The relevance for this study is that a late origin for the Abraham tradition as such weakens the probability of earlier proposals, namely, that Genesis 14 somehow renders a very old tradition.

In chapter 4 I will discuss the compositional growth of the Abraham narratives. The focus will, in particular, be on the block Genesis 14–17 that appears as a wedge between an assumedly more original and immediate connection between Genesis 13 and 18. Moreover, an important conclusion will be that Genesis 14* appears to have been part of the composition of the Abraham narratives in one of its latest stages. There are least two reasons for this. First, Genesis 14* is part of the interrupting block Genesis 14–17 that in itself is late (although not the work of a single hand). Second, the narrative is neither referred to nor presupposed later on in the Abraham composition.

In chapter 5 I will attempt to explain *why* Genesis 14* was composed. Among other things, I will point to the fact that the author of the Aramaic *Genesis Apocryphon* from Qumran (1Q20) already recognized a *Leerstelle* after Gen. 13:17–18 in his *Vorlage*. I propose that Genesis 14* is composed for its present position in the Abraham narratives in response to that which its author considered to be a *Leerstelle* after Genesis 13. Following immediately after Gen. 13:14–18, Genesis 14* plays on Abram's failure to comply with Yahweh's command to walk through the length and breadth of the land by making the invading kings the first ones to actually fulfil the act of taking possession of it. However, Abram eventually defeats the invaders and completes the walk through the land.

In chapter 6 I will attempt to argue for the thesis that Genesis 14* is a product of literary activity. I argue that it, among other things, appears to contain several literary borrowings from other biblical texts (in particular from 1 Samuel 30, the Table of Nations [Genesis 10], and the wilderness wandering narratives [Deuteronomy 1–3; Numbers 10–21]). However, I will also argue that the author got some of the names occurring only in Genesis 14* (some of the names of the members of the four-king alliance and some of their kingdoms) from another, nonbiblical, source. This latter source may not necessarily have been a written document. On the contrary, the source may have been oral communications from the Elamite and other diaspora communities living in Second Temple period Samaria (see Ezra 4) and stems from their (quasi-) historical and (quasi-) geographical knowledge. In sum, I will discuss *how* Genesis 14* was composed.

In chapter 7, which completes part II, I will discuss the historical meaning of Genesis 14* and the ideology of its author. A prerequisite for this is to determine a date of composition for Genesis 14*. Therefore, I first synthesize the data from the various approaches to Genesis 14* that are relevant for establishing a *terminus a quo* and a *terminus ante quem*. I argue that it cannot have been composed much before the fifth century and not later than the first half of the second century BCE. On the basis of the time frame thus established and certain trends and conceptions that one can infer, based on other sources, to have been current among Jews in the Persian and early Hellenistic periods, I conclude part II with a historically qualified conjecture about the historical meaning of Genesis 14*. My proposal is that the author wanted to plea for the restoration of the land under the control of Abraham's children.

1.7.2 Ad Part III: The Melchizedek Episode (= ME) in Genesis 14:18–20

In part III I will address the questions of the origin and purpose of the Melchizedek episode (= 'ME', Gen. 14:18–20).

In chapter 8 I will offer a brief orientation on previous research on the ME and Psalm 110. As briefly touched upon above, I hold the ME to be late in a double sense (both in terms of date of interpolation into Genesis 14* and date of composition; see 8.6, Preliminary Conclusion and Point of Departure: The ME—A Doubly Late Interpolation; see also 2.2.1, The Melchizedek Episode (= ME) in Genesis 14:18–20: A Secondary Interpolation). Because the ME is dependent upon the narrative in Genesis 14*, it has probably never had a 'life of its own' independent of Genesis 14*. Therefore, contrary to what is often implied—in particular in works on the history of Israelite religion—the ME has a limited value (if any at all) for the early history of the religion of Israel and/or pre-Israelite Jerusalem.

In chapter 9 I formulate a hypothesis for the origin of the Melchizedek episode on the basis of the paradigm of diachronic, inner-biblical intertextuality, which is, as mentioned, fundamental for the present study. According to the model I propose for *why* the ME was composed and interpolated into the narrative, the episode is the result of an assimilation between two texts: Genesis 14* on the one hand and Psalm 110 on the other (see chapters 11, 13, and 14).

The first hypothesis I will formulate in chapter 9 is that at some point in the Second Temple period, Psalm 110 was read historiographically, that is, it was connected to an assumed historical event. Consequently, the psalm was read as a poetic version of the narrative found in Genesis 14* about Abram's war with the four kings. Moreover, in chapter 13 I attempt to substantiate this hypothesis. On the basis of cases from the early rabbinic literature and the early Jewish hermeneutics of intertextuality, I will argue that the intertextual connection between Psalm 110 and Genesis 14 started before the Melchizedek episode was composed and interpolated into the latter narrative.

The second hypothesis I formulate in chapter 9 is that the assumed similarities between Genesis 14* and Psalm 110—which assumedly were identified by the Second Temple period readers who interpreted Psalm 110 as a historiographic psalm spoken to Abraham—functioned as a catalyst for an additional assimilation. In chapter 11 I attempt to substantiate this hypothesis by showing that there are analogies in the Bible to the phenomenon of assimilation. Moreover, in chapter 14 I propose that the concrete result of the additional assimilation was the Melchizedek episode itself.

At first glance, chapter 10 and chapter 12 seem to fall outside the sequence of thought in part III. However, I consider both discussions to be necessary in order to substantiate the assimilation model I propose for the origin of the ME. In chapter 10 I focus on Psalm 110, attempting in particular to discuss and indentify the characters speaking and being spoken to, attempting to account for certain issues in the history of research of this particular psalm that are relevant in this context, and, finally, arguing that one probably should date its composition to the monarchic period. Moreover, in chapter 12, I will discuss the troublesome and enigmatic half verse Ps. 110:4b אַתָּה־כֹהֵן לְעוֹלָם עַל־דִּבְרָתִי מַלְכִּי־צֶדֶק. I argue that Psalm 110 was interpreted in a different way in the Second Temple period (and when the ME, I argue, was composed and interpolated into Genesis 14*) compared to how it appears to have been read around the time of its composition in the monarchic period. In short, in chapter 12 I argue that the Hebrew *hapax legomenon* עַל־דִּבְרָתִי (Ps. 110:4b) probably originally (i.e., in monarchic period) had a causal sense and that מַלְכִּי־צֶדֶק (Ps. 110:4b) probably originally was a nominal clause. Consequently, the English translation 'after the order of Melchizedek' that is traditionally found (so the NRSV etc.) renders more closely the late LXX translation κατὰ τὴν τάξιν Μελχισεδεκ (LXX Ps. 109:4b) than it renders the Hebrew עַל־דִּבְרָתִי מַלְכִּי־צֶדֶק. The LXX version evident in LXX Ps 109:4b probably presupposes knowledge of the ME and the biographical data about the priest-king Melchizedek offered there.

In chapter 15 I build on the conclusions of the previous chapters and address the question of the origin of the figure Melchizedek whom we meet in the ME. I argue that the priest-king Melchizedek who appears in the ME probably is the result of a personification of the words מַלְכִּי־צֶדֶק in Ps. 110:4. In other words, the Melchizedek figure appearing in the ME is probably an invented literary character (see also 12.6, The Two Words מַלְכִּי־צֶדֶק in Psalm 110:4b). However, because I cannot entirely exclude the possibility that מַלְכִּי־צֶדֶק was a personal name in the monarchic Psalm 110 from the outset, I consider another possibility as well. According to this alternative explanation, in the ME we have a situation in which an originally marginal biblical figure (the Melchizedek of Psalm 110, otherwise not mentioned in the biblical literature) has been given a secondary legendary biography. According to the alternative model on the origin of the Melchizedek figure, the Melchizedek episode deals with the originally marginal Melchizedek figure in a way comparable to how the late Enoch literature dealt with the originally marginal Enoch figure (see 15.2, Alternative Explanation: Creation of Legendary Biographies and New Narrative Roles). Finally, discussing genre, I tentatively propose that the ME represents an early example of an aggadah that has been incorporated into the biblical text itself (see 15.4, Assimilation—In Form of an Aggadah?).

In chapter 16 I will synthesize the information from previous chapters that are relevant for proposing the date of composition and date of interpolation of the ME. I will argue that several texts from the last centuries BCE seem to betray knowledge of the ME. Therefore, given that they indirectly attest to the existence of the ME, these texts also provide valuable clues for the *terminus ante quem*. Yet, because the episode probably is dependent on Genesis 14*, the date of composition of Genesis 14* serves as *terminus a quo*. So, I will argue that it is possible to establish a relative chronology. Although I lack absolute dates, I will nonetheless argue for a qualified guess: We should probably seek the date of composition of the ME around the middle of the Second Temple period or perhaps earlier.

In chapter 17 I will finish part III with a critical assessment of the assimilation model I have developed for explaining the origin of the ME.

1.7.3 Ad Part IV: The Addition of Genesis 14*
and the Melchizedek Episode in Perspective

In the final, and relatively brief, part IV I will seek to put in perspective the conclusions drawn in part II and part III concerning Genesis 14* and the addition of the Melchizedek episode respectively.

First, in 19.2, The Technical Aspect, I will discuss how Genesis 14* and, subsequently, the Melchizedek episode may have become part of the biblical text from a technical viewpoint. Therefore, I will seek to relate the assumption that Genesis 14* and the ME are late additions to the book of Genesis to the available knowledge about how books were produced in the Second Temple period (writing material, book format, the division into textual units, etc.). I will conclude that the likeliest explanation is that Genesis 14* was added in connection with the production of a new copy.

Moreover, this leads to the question of whether the author is identical with the copyist. Because it is not possible to answer this question, the focus will instead be on the milieu of the authors of Genesis 14* and the ME (see 19.3, The Milieu of the Authors and Copyists). Depending on recent contributions to the issue of literacy in ancient Israel, I assume that the centre of Jewish literary culture in the Second Temple period was the Jerusalem Temple itself. Therefore, one may assume that the authors in some way belonged to the priestly circles (see 19.3.1, The Centre of Jewish Literary Culture in the Second Temple Period).

Furthermore, I will attempt to explore what the implications are for the understanding of Genesis 14* and the ME in that they were both probably authored by priests. Here, I, *inter alia,* indicate possible implications relating to the rivalry between the different priestly lines we can infer must have taken place throughout the Second Temple period (see 19.3.2, Priestly Provenance: Implications for Understanding the ME?).

Then, I briefly account for recent works that emphasize the interplay of orality and textuality as a backdrop for how biblical books were shaped. In particular, I exemplify David M. Carr's proposal that Israelite authors had been trained to write new texts by building on literary templates provided by earlier texts (see 19.4, Echoes of Earlier Texts in Genesis 14 and the Role of Literary Templates for the Production of New Texts).

Finally, I conclude the study with a brief, though fundamental, discussion about reworkings and additions as a sign of the status of the text reworked: The high estimation of a given text is probably one of the factors that explain why it—in some cases, again and again—was reworked and expanded (see 19.5, Expansion and Reworking: Sign of the High Estimation of the Text Reworked).

Part II: Genesis 14*

2. Genesis 14:
Characteristics, Textual Integrity, and Textual Criticism. Preliminary Discussion and Hypotheses

The present chapter will open with a preliminary discussion of the features that are unique to Genesis 14 and that make the narrative stand out from the rest of the patriarchal narratives. Then I will discuss the textual integrity of Genesis 14. I will conclude that the Melchizedek episode (Gen. 14:18–20) is a secondary insertion. On the basis of this, most of the discussion concerning the Melchizedek episode will be postponed to a separate part of this thesis.[1] As for the remaining part of Genesis 14 (henceforth labelled 'Genesis 14*'), I will argue that it represents an internally consistent narrative that probably is not the result of a combination of two originally independent narratives. Furthermore, after a text-critical orientation, I will propose a hypothesis regarding the origin of Genesis 14 and its integration into the Abraham composition.

2.1 Features Unique to Genesis 14 in the Context of the Patriarchal Narratives

2.1.1 Abram on the International Political Scene

Genesis 14 stands out from the surrounding patriarchal narratives because of its contents and its form. Nowhere else in the Pentateuch is there talk of a comparable military conflict involving rebelling suzerains and coalitions of international powers quelling revolts. Elsewhere, Abraham, Isaac, and Jacob are *patres familias,* and the narratives centre around family issues. Now, family matters are also present in Genesis 14—Abram rescues his kin Lot. However, outside Genesis 14* the patriarchs do not face putatively historically identifiable figures such as King Chedorlaomer of Elam, King Tidal of Goiim, King Amraphel of Shinar,

---

1   See Part III: The Melchizedek Episode (=ME) in Genesis 14:18–20.

and King Arioch of Ellasar. This way of connecting events in a patriarch's life to the larger world history is unique within the patriarchal
narratives (see 2.1.3, Detailed Itineraries, Chronological Specifications,
and Abundance of Names). The closest parallels in the patriarchal narratives to seemingly historical allusions are the references to Abimelech,
king of Gerar (Genesis 20–21), to the Philistines (Genesis 26), and to Pharaoh (Genesis 12; 37–50). The problem, however, is that the latter is but
the throne name of many rulers of Egypt over millennia and does not
provide any chronological help, neither internally in the patriarchal narratives nor externally in the extrabiblical sources. Similarly, also the former — Abimelech — is possibly a throne name used by all kings of Gerar.[2]

2.1.2 Absence of Metaphysical Explanations in Genesis 14*

Genesis 14* differs from the rest of the patriarchal narratives in its apparent absence of a metaphysical explanation for, for example, Abram's
miraculous victory. Needless to say, in general God/Yahweh plays an
important role in the patriarchal narratives. He neither appears as a pup-
peteer nor as a distant, retired deity. On the contrary, he intervenes in
history when the different characters account for their own deeds and
misdeeds. God's intervention happens by means of auditions (Gen. 12:1;
17:3, 9, 15, 19; 18:13, 20, 26; 20:6; 21:12; 24:12; 25:23; 31:3, 11; 35:1, 10–11)
and revelations (Gen. 12:7; 17:1; 18:1; 26:2, 24; 35:9; 46:29). In addition,
God/Yahweh is explained as the one who gives success (Gen. 27:20) and
the ultimate ground behind certain realities (45:8).

In Genesis 14*, however, there is no divine power explicitly present.
In light of the fact that warfare is an important ingredient in this text,
and in addition, in light of the fact that the patriarch Abram pursues and
overcomes the four invading kings only with the help of 318 men (again,
no divine auxiliary is reported), this absence is particularly intriguing.

The insertion of the so-called Melchizedek episode (vv. 18–20)
changes the impression of 'profanity' that the war narrative in Genesis
14* creates. Melchizedek's bringing forth of bread and wine is accom-
panied by religious speech-acts, that is, blessings. Moreover, his second
blessing functions as a theological interpretation of the events in Genesis 14*. The relative clause in v. 20 ('And blessed be El Elyon who has
delivered your enemies into your hand') in fact alters the picture of the

---

2   In addition, the reference to Abimelech suffers from the fact that the Sea People
     (among them the biblical 'Philistines') migrated to the Near East first around the
     twelfth century BCE. So Victor H. Matthews, 'Abimelech', *ABD* 1:20–21.

course of events. According to the priest-king Melchizedek, Abram's victory over the four kings and his salvaging of the captured people and possessions were basically nothing but the work of El Elyon, creator of heaven and earth. By means of the insertion of vv. 18–20 and Melchizedek's interpretation of historical events presented there, Abram's pursuit and victory turn out to be a holy war.[3]

2.1.3 Detailed Itineraries, Chronological Specifications, and Abundance of Names

Some stylistic features make Genesis 14* stand out from the rest of the patriarchal narratives. One of the distinctive features is its abundance of names and its detailed itineraries (vv. 14–16 and especially vv. [3]4–7).

All in all, the chapter counts some 460 words, of which 288 are used only once in the chapter. Ninety of these 288 words are names of persons or places.[4] In other words, nearly one third of the chapter's vocabulary is made up of names. The 'proper name quotient' (Cohen[5]) is much higher here than in any other text of similar size in the patriarchal narratives. Admittedly, itineraries as such are frequently found in the patriarchal narratives. The narratives in Genesis 12–50 as a whole are both framed by itineraries (see Gen. 11:27–32; 50:7–14)—and so connected with the preceding primeval history and the subsequent exodus narrative—and, in addition, to a certain extent internally bound together by itineraries. The many small, often self-contained stories about the patriarchs are often connected by means of different kinds of wanderings (e.g., Gen. 12:4–9; 13:1–4, 18; 28:1–5, 10–11; 29:1, etc.). However, none of these itineraries in Genesis 12–50 are elaborated as extensively as those in Genesis 14, especially vv. 4–7.

On the other hand, the itineraries in Genesis 14 are comparable to texts found in the so-called historical books in the Hebrew Bible. Though not elaborated to the same extent, texts such as 1 Kgs. 15:20; 2 Kgs. 15:29; 2 Chr. 13:19; 26:6; and 28:18 are all itineraries that resemble those of our chapter in that they are itineraries of expeditions and conquests.[6]

---

3   Compare v. 20aβ אֲשֶׁר־מִגֵּן צָרֶיךָ בְּיָדֶךָ and the proclamation of the ban frequently found in the books of Joshua, Judges, 1–2 Kings, and 1–2 Samuel; cf. Gerhard von Rad, *Der Heilige Krieg im alten Israel* (4th ed.; Göttingen: Vandenhoeck & Ruprecht, 1965), 7–8. Moreover, see 8.4.1.3, '. . . Who Delivered Your Enemies into Your Hands'.

4   According to Westermann, *Genesis 12–50*, 41.

5   Cohen, 'Genesis 14—An Early Israelite Chronographic Source', 67–107.

6   Yohanan Aharoni lists 'itineraries of expeditions and conquests' as one of three main types of geographical documents in the Bible. The other two are 'historical-geographical

Furthermore, yet another feature that is distinctive of Genesis 14 in comparison with other patriarchal narratives is the chronological specifications. The chapter opens with dating the narrated events to a putative particular period (Gen. 14:1).

וַיְהִי בִּימֵי אַמְרָפֶל מֶלֶךְ־שִׁנְעָר אַרְיוֹךְ מֶלֶךְ אֶלָּסָר כְּדָרְלָעֹמֶר מֶלֶךְ עֵילָם וְתִדְעָל מֶלֶךְ גּוֹיִם

And it came to pass in the days of Amraphel king of Shinar, Arioch king of Ellasar, Chedorlaomer king of Elam, and Tidal king of Goiim. . . .

This way of connecting events in the life of the patriarchs to the larger world history is unique within the patriarchal narratives. This is also the reason why the chapter sometimes has played an important role in attempts to establish a historically fixed point for the 'patriarchal period'.[7]

A recent example of this has been offered by Kenneth A. Kitchen. He uses the mention of the four-king alliance in Gen. 14:1 as a means to identify the alleged 'real background' of the narrative in Genesis 14. Whereas '[t]his racy narrative of alliances and wars of eastern kings' in his eyes 'has been discussed *ad nauseam* by biblical scholars, most of whom are unaware of its real background',[8] Kitchen for his part argues on the assumption that *he* knows this background. Arguing historically, he claims that alliances such as that in Genesis 14 proliferated at the beginning of the second millennium, between 2000 and 1700 BCE. Moreover, according to Kitchen, this was also the only period when Elam was involved in international politics west of Babylonia and Assyria proper. In other words, the 'real background' of Gen. 14:1 should be sought in the political situation in this period, which is described in texts such as the letter to King Zimri-Lim of Mari.[9]

Kitchen's argumentative strategy, however, which is part of a wider defence of the historicity and accuracy of the patriarchal narratives all together, focuses not so much on the biblical texts as it does on the his-

---

descriptions' and 'territorial administrative lists'. However, he holds Genesis 14 to be a very ancient example of the main type of itineraries of expeditions and conquests—a conviction not shared by the author of this thesis. See Aharoni, *The Land of the Bible: A Historical Geography* (trans. A. F. Rainey; rev. ed.; Philadelphia: Westminster, 1979), 83–92, 140–42.

7   See, e.g., Franz Marius Theodor de Liagre Böhl, 'Das Zeitalter Abrahams', in Böhl, *Opera Minora: Studies en bijdragen op assyrologisch en oudtestamentisch terrein* (Groningen and Djakarta: J. B. Wolters, 1953), 26–49, 476–79; idem, 'Amraphel', *RGG*[3] 1, cols. 332–33; and Jan Hendrik Kroeze, *Genesis veertien: een exegetisch-historische studie* (Hilversum: J. Schipper Jr., 1937). Moreover, see chapter 9, The Problem of Historicity and Genesis 14, in Thomas L. Thompson, *The Historicity of the Patriarchal Narratives: The Quest for the Historical Abraham* (BZAW 133; Berlin: W. de Gruyter, 1974), 187–95.

8   Kitchen, 'Genesis 1–50 in the Near Eastern World', 67–92 (71).

9   See *ANET*, 628.

torical events and situations that the texts allegedly refer to. In doing that, Kitchen abandons the methodological autonomy of biblical studies and does not account for the biblical texts on the basis of the texts' own premises, such as their compositional history, characteristics, etc.

Normally, the chronological order of the events appears from the internal connectives[10] in the patriarchal narratives. For instance, in Gen. 13:14 we read 'And Yahweh said to Abram, *after* Lot had separated from him' and in 13:10, '. . . *before* Yahweh's destroying of Sodom and Gomorrah'.[11] Moreover, the composers of the patriarchal narratives do not seem to have been guided by chronology alone but have made the composition rather plot oriented.[12] An example of the lack of chronology is found in connection with Sarah's age. Whereas Sarah is an old woman in Genesis 18 and 21, she probably is a young, marriageable woman in Genesis 20.

However, in Gen. 14:1 the narrator uses a construction similar to that found in, for example, Isa. 7:1; Esther 1:1; and Ruth 1:1. In these three cases, the construction . . . וַיְהִי בִּימֵי (*wayyiqtol* of היה, followed by the preposition ב and a plural construct form of יום and *nomen/-ina rectum/-a*) clearly introduces a new pericope. This new pericope narrates an event that takes place at an assumed dateable time. In the two latter cases, the construction even functions as a book opening.[13]

---

10 By 'connective' I mean words or cluster of words whose function is to connect groups of clauses or paragraphs to even more complex narrative structures. Moreover, see Hubert Cancik, *Grundzüge der hethitischen und alttestamentlichen Geschichtsschreibung* (Abhandlungen des Deutschen Palästinavereins; Wiesbaden: Otto Harrassowitz, 1976), § 3.2 (pp. 20–23) and § 15.3 (pp. 188–90).

11 Similarly, e.g., Gen. 15:1; 22:1, 20.

12 T. L. Thompson, 'Israelite Historiography', *ABD* 3:206–12 (209).

13 Isa. 7:1a:

וַיְהִי בִּימֵי אָחָז בֶּן־יוֹתָם בֶּן־עֻזִּיָּהוּ מֶלֶךְ יְהוּדָה עָלָה רְצִין

מֶלֶךְ־אֲרָם וּפֶקַח בֶּן־רְמַלְיָהוּ מֶלֶךְ־יִשְׂרָאֵל יְרוּשָׁלַם לַמִּלְחָמָה

עָלֶיהָ

And it happened in the days of Ahaz son of Jotham son of Uzziah, king of Judah, Rezin . . . and Pekah . . . went up to Jerusalem for war. . .

Ruth 1:1a:

וַיְהִי בִּימֵי שְׁפֹט הַשֹּׁפְטִים וַיְהִי רָעָב בָּאָרֶץ

And it happened when the judges ruled, and there was a famine in the land . . .

Esth. 1:1:

וַיְהִי בִּימֵי אֲחַשְׁוֵרוֹשׁ הוּא אֲחַשְׁוֵרוֹשׁ הַמֹּלֵךְ מֵהֹדּוּ וְעַד־כּוּשׁ

שֶׁבַע וְעֶשְׂרִים וּמֵאָה מְדִינָה

And it happened in the days of Ahasuerus, that is Ahasuerus who reigned over hundered and twenty-seven provinces from India to Cush.

Further, the chronological specifications in Gen. 14:4–5 are not typical in the context of the patriarchal narratives:

שְׁתֵּים עֶשְׂרֵה שָׁנָה עָבְדוּ אֶת־כְּדָרְלָעֹמֶר וּשְׁלֹשׁ־עֶשְׂרֵה שָׁנָה מָרָדוּ ⁵ וּבְאַרְבַּע עֶשְׂרֵה שָׁנָה בָּא כְדָרְלָעֹמֶר וְהַמְּלָכִים אֲשֶׁר אִתּוֹ וַיַּכּוּ אֶת־רְפָאִים בְּעַשְׁתְּרֹת קַרְנַיִם וְאֶת־הַזּוּזִים בְּהָם אֵת הָאֵימִים בְּשָׁוֵה קִרְיָתָיִם

Chronological references by means of the noun שָׁנָה, 'year', do of course occur elsewhere in the patriarchal narratives. In the majority of cases, שָׁנָה is used in order to indicate the age of the patriarchs (e.g., Gen. 17:1 וַיְהִי אַבְרָם בֶּן־תִּשְׁעִים שָׁנָה וְתֵשַׁע שָׁנִים וַיֵּרָא יְהוָה אֶל־אַבְרָם ..., 'And it happened, Abram was ninety-nine years old. And Yahweh appeared to Abram . . .'). In addition, chronology may be an integral part of the narrative itself. For instance, the noun שָׁנָה occurs several times in Genesis 29 for the purpose of indicating how long Jacob had to serve in order to marry Laban's daughters. However, nowhere in the patriarchal narratives does the noun שָׁנָה occur in order to indicate the duration of verbs denoting political or military activities, such as עבד, 'to serve', מלך, 'to rule', מרד, 'to rebel', נכה, 'to beat', and לחם, 'to wage war'. In contrast, such annalistic-styled chronological specifications are frequently found in the so-called historical books.[14]

In sum, because of both its content and many of its characteristic features, Genesis 14 stands out from the rest of the patriarchal narratives.

2.2 The Textual Integrity of Genesis 14

In the history of research, there has been no consensus about the question of the textual integrity of Genesis 14. On the contrary, there have, roughly speaking, been two different positions. On the one hand there have been those who plea for a single authorship for the entire chapter (sometimes including the Melchizedek episode in vv. 18–20, sometimes not). On the other hand, there have been those who argue that Genesis 14 is a composition of two or three narratives and/or traditions that originally were independent of each other. It follows that the latter position

---

Moreover, see Adele Berlin, 'On the Use of Traditional Jewish Exegesis in the Modern Literary Study of the Bible', in *Tehilla le-Moshe: Biblical and Judaic Studies in Honor of Moshe Greenberg* (ed. Mordechai Cogan, Barry L. Eichler and Jeffrey H. Tigay; Winona Lake, IN: Eisenbrauns, 1997), 173–83 (181).

14 See, e.g., Judg. 3:8, 14; 1 Sam. 13:1; 2 Sam. 2:10–11; 5:4–5; 11:1; 15:7; 1 Kgs. 2:11, 39; 6:1; 9:10; 11:42; 14:20–21, 25; 15:1–2, 9–10, 25, 28, 33; 16:8, 10, 15, 23, 29; 22:1–2, 41–42, 52; 2 Kgs. 1:17; 3:1; 8:3, 16–17, 25–26; 9:29; 10:36; 11:3–4; 12:1–2, 7; 13:1, 10; 14:1–2, 17, 21, 23; 15:1–2, 8, 13, 17, 23, 27, 30, 32–33; 16:1–2; 17:1, 4–6; 18:1–2, 9–10, 13; 21:1, 19; 22:1, 3; 23:23, 31, 36; 24:1, 8, 12, 18; 25:1–2, 8, 27.

implies a more complex model for the literary history of the growth of the chapter and the tradition-historical background for each of the assumed parts than the former.

In the following, I will address the question of the textual integrity of Genesis 14. In my estimation, *subtraction* is the only transparent and in part, controllable, method for describing the possible growth or supplementation of a narrative. Consequently, I will have as a starting point the whole narrative in Genesis 14 as it has been received. Then I will subtract narrative units that one can easily delimit and give reasonable arguments for their being secondary.

The discussion will give two results: first, that the Melchizedek episode in Gen. 14:18–20 (henceforth 'ME') is secondarily inserted into its narrative framework, and second, that the rest of Genesis 14 ('Genesis 14*', that is, *without* the ME) is a unified text with a single author when considered as a narrative. (However, the following must be pointed out: Although I argue that the narrative is unified *qua* narrative, I will, nevertheless, in a separate chapter below argue that the author borrowed literary building blocks from different types of biblical literature.[15] In other words, I argue that many literary building blocks were used to compose a unified narrative.)

2.2.1 The Melchizedek Episode (= ME) in Genesis 14:18–20: A Secondary Interpolation

For a long time many scholars have recognized that the dialogue between Abram the Hebrew (who has returned after having beaten King Chedorlaomer and his allies) and the unnamed king of Sodom appears to have been interrupted by the ME.[16] In Gen. 14:17, the king of Sodom is reported to have gone out to meet Abram at the Valley of Shaveh. Suddenly, in vv. 18–20 a new figure appears who has not been introduced earlier in the narrative: King Melchizedek of Salem. After bringing out bread and wine and then blessing Abram and El Elyon, Melchizedek again disappears as suddenly as he first appeared. Then, in Gen. 14:21 the king of Sodom again speaks to Abram, apparently unaffected by the Melchizedek intermezzo. Neither here nor later in Genesis 14 are there any references to Melchizedek.

---

15 See chapter 6, The Literary Building Blocks of the Author of Genesis 14*.
16 An exception is Gordon J. Wenham, who does not think the ME is an insertion into the narrative. See Wenham, *Genesis 1–15*, 305–7, 315–8.

Therefore, one can make an argument from a potential continuity and state that the ME interrupts the narrative. Originally, probably nothing interrupted the dialogue between Abram and the king of Sodom. The idea that there is a fracture between the ME and the narrative framework is supported by the way Genesis 14* has been treated in early examples of its reception history. In both the Aramaic *Genesis Apocryphon* from Qumran (1Q20/1QapGen[ar]) and the pseudepigraphical book of *Jubilees,* the narrative unevenness shown above has been smoothed out; both ancient texts render the meeting between the king of Sodom and Abram in a single, uninterrupted paragraph. In the *Genesis Apocryphon* the account follows immediately after Abram's meeting with Melchizedek (1Q20 22:18–26); while in the book of *Jubilees* the ME is missing and instead there is a law of the tithes; see *Jub.* 13:28–29. So, both the *Genesis Apocryphon* and *Jubilees* offer proof that the impression of the ME interrupting the narrative flow is not only a modern sentiment.

Moreover, the ME is probably secondarily inserted into the narrative. The other possibility, namely, that the narrative has been composed secondarily around the ME, is unlikely because the narrative frame does not seem to be dependent on the ME. On the contrary, the ME is dependent on the narrative context. This is evident in Melchizedek's second blessing: 'blessed be God Most High, who has delivered your enemies into your hand!' (Gen. 14:20b). The phrase אֲשֶׁר־מִגֵּן צָרֶיךָ בְּיָדֶךָ only makes sense as a reference to Abram's victory in Gen. 14:14–16.

The identification of Yahweh with El Elyon in Abram's oath (Gen. 14:22) is attested only in the MT. The identification must be discussed in particular because it is occasionally used as an argument that the ME was originally not a secondary interpolation but an integral part of the narrative.[17] In the MT Abram swears (lit.: 'I raise my hand') to 'Yahweh, El Elyon, maker of heaven and earth.' Of the textual witnesses, only the MT identifies Yahweh with El Elyon:

הֲרִימֹתִי יָדִי אֶל־יְהוָה אֵל עֶלְיוֹן קֹנֵה שָׁמַיִם וָאָרֶץ

However, neither the ancient textual witnesses nor the ancient rewritten Bibles reflect such an identification. The *Genesis Apocryphon,*[18] the LXX,[19] the Vulgate,[20] and the Peshitta[21] all lack 'Yahweh', whereas the Samaritan Pentateuch instead reads האלהים אל עליון.

---

17   For instance, Gordon J. Wenham argues that Abram's oath to El Elyon is inexplicable
     without the ME. See Wenham, *Genesis 1–15,* 306–7.

18   אל עליון מרה שמיא וארעא

19   θεὸν τὸν ὕψιστον ὃς ἔκτισεν τὸν οὐρανὸν καὶ τὴν γῆν

20   'Dominum Deum excelsum possessorem caeli et terrae'.

21   ʾlhʾmrymʾ

These data have been evaluated differently. J. A. Emerton suggests that the missing reference to Yahweh in the LXX may be due to a homoioteleuton: '[The omission] may have been influenced by the proximity of the preposition *ʾel* to the noun *ʾel* in the phrase *ʾel yhwh ʾel*'. On the contrary, J. A. Fitzmyer argues that 'Yahweh' in MT Gen. 14:22 is a later gloss. He discusses the parallel text in the *Genesis Apocryphon* (1Q20 22:21) and its *Vorlage* thus:

> In translating Gen 14:22 . . . the author of [the *Apocryphon*] has either omitted the tetragrammaton or more likely translated merely what was in his text of Genesis. At first sight the omission might seem to be owing to reverence for the sacred name, especially since it is known that Qumran scribes used many substitutes for the name יהוה. . . . However, because the omission in this text agrees with the LXX . . . and the Peshitta against the Targums, it is more likely that יהוה in the MT of Gen. 14:22 is a later gloss introduced into MSS of biblical tradition.[22]

Fitzmyer is probably correct in seeing the reference to Yahweh in MT Gen. 14:22 as a late gloss.[23] Being attested only in the MT, the easiest explanation is that יהוה was inserted as a gloss into an early manuscript in the Masoretic branch of the textual transmission. Because almost all textual witnesses reflect knowledge of the ME whereas only the MT reflects the identification of Yahweh and El Elyon in Gen. 14:22, we can conclude that the insertion of the gloss 'Yahweh' in MT 14:22 probably took place *after* the ME had been interpolated. Consequently, the LXX reflects the original reading of Gen. 14:22, according to which Abram took an oath only in the name of El Elyon.

This conclusion will be decisive for the rest of the present study. In the rest of part II I will focus on Genesis 14*. I will focus in particular on the ME in part III.

2.2.2 Genesis 14*: A Compound Narrative?

Having subtracted the secondarily interpolated Melchizedek episode, the question arises whether Genesis 14* for its part is an integrated and unified narrative. In modern times, the scholars who have answered this question can be divided into two schools. The first school's answer is *no*: leaving the ME aside, Genesis 14 is made up of two originally

---

22 Joseph A. Fitzmyer, *The Genesis Apocryphon of Qumran Cave 1 (1Q20)* (3d ed.; BibOr 18/B; Rome: Editrice Pontificio Istituto Biblico, 2004), 251.

23 Also Michael Fishbane argues that Abram originally swore by El Elyon in Gen. 14:22. In his view, later scribes are responsible for revising the text by prefixing the Tetragram to the divine name El Elyon. See Fishbane, *Biblical Interpretation in Ancient Israel*, 545.

independent narratives that subsequently were combined. The fracture between the two parts is then usually located somewhere between v. 11 and v. 13, resulting in a story about the revolt and punishment in vv. 1–11 and about Abram's rescue mission and successful return in vv. 12–17, 21–24. Nevertheless, the other school's answer is *yes*: Genesis 14* is an integrated, unified text (and some will also count the above mentioned ME as part of the unified text).

Gerhard von Rad was probably the first to question the textual integrity of Genesis 14; in addition, he sought to identify the components of which it was composed.[24] He argued that the chapter had grown together from two main components of very different origin and character. The first, vv. 1–11, was probably a fragment of an old Canaanite epos and was not originally a story about Abraham. However, the other, vv. 12–17, 21–24, was originally a story about the patriarch. Von Rad found support for this position in the alleged suture between v. 11 and v. 12: 'Vor V. 12 ist also eine Bruchstelle, an der sich die beiden Erzählungsstoffe scheiden.'[25] Later, in the period of the united monarchy, the ME was interpolated into the narrative about the meeting between Abram and the king of Sodom.[26]

John A. Emerton developed von Rad's proposal further. He argued that the most convincing argument for Genesis 14* being a combination of two originally separate parts is the difference in character between them.[27] From a traditio-historical point of view, he distinguished between two types of material in the chapter that he argued were of different provenance. According to Emerton, the earliest material consisted of a popular tradition about the heroic and noble doings of Abram, a 'hero story' (approximately Gen. 14:12–17, 21–24). Moreover, the first part of the chapter (approximately Gen. 14:1–11) was of an annalistic type, written in a style reminiscent of the historical books of the OT. According to

---

24   Earlier, John Skinner was open to the possibility that a cuneiform document could have come into the possession of a postexilic Jew. Partly on the basis of this cuneiform document the postexilic author wrote a quasi-historical account blending fact and fiction. However, Skinner considered the extent of the historical document to be undetermined. In connection with the question about the possible historical trustworthiness of Genesis 14, he wrote: 'The fallacy lies in treating the chapter as a homogenous and indivisible unity: it is like discussing whether the climate in Asia is hot or cold on conflicting evidence drawn from opposite extremes of the continent.' See John Skinner, *A Critical and Exegetical Commentary on Genesis* (2d ed.; ICC; Edinburgh: T. & T. Clark, 1930), 276. Nevertheless, he did not develop any model for the growth of the composition of Genesis 14.
25   Von Rad, *Das erste Buch Mose*, 137.
26   Von Rad, *Das erste Buch Mose*, 138–39.
27   Emerton, 'The Riddle of Genesis XIV', 403–39 (431–32).

Emerton, this first part of an annalistic type was of a later date than the hero story about the patriarch.

As for the growth of the text, Emerton argued that the ME was added to the early hero story about Abram's heroic deeds (which originally was transmitted orally) in the early monarchic period. Eventually, the annalistic-like story about King Chedorlaomer and his allies was added to the Abram-Melchizedek composition no earlier than in the seventh century BCE.[28]

Shortly after Emerton's article 'The Riddle of Genesis XIV' was published, Werner Schatz published his detailed study on Genesis 14.[29] Independently of Emerton, Schatz argued for a model of the literary growth of Genesis 14 that in its basic outline was quite similar to that of Emerton.[30] Also Schatz's argument was based on traditio-historical assumptions[31] and the assertion that a mixture of styles ('Stilmischung') was evident in Genesis 14.[32] Consequently, also according to Schatz, the growth of the chapter started with an oral report about Abram's rescue of his kinsman Lot and his refusal of the king of Sodom's offer (that is, Gen. 14:13–17, 21–24). Schatz admitted that this originally oral report did not have the same beginning as now appears in Genesis 14. Therefore, it is in his view no longer possible to reconstruct it (Emerton does not touch on this problem).[33] However, Schatz assumed that the oral report originally contained more detailed information about both the enemy defeated by Abram and the location of the battleground where Abram triumphed. This crucial information is lacking in Gen. 14:13–17, 21–24. Moreover, the ME was added to the oral report about Abram around the time of David. This composition, which Schatz termed the *basis* (*Grundlage*) for Genesis 14, was then incorporated into the Yahwistic traditions. Subsequently, around 550 BCE, this *Grundlage* was subject to a thorough Deuteronomistic reworking. The Deuteronomists were responsible for combining the *Grundlage* with a tradition about four eastern kings and their invasion of Canaan (i.e., Gen. 14:1–11).

Schatz suggested that the tradition about the eastern kings was associated with a widespread tradition about a sacrilege that failed. Following Michael C. Astour, Schatz supposed that this tradition—independently

---

28 John A. Emerton, 'Some Problems in Genesis XIV', in *Studies in the Pentateuch* (ed. John A. Emerton; VTSup 41; Leiden: E. J. Brill, 1990), 73–102 (102).

29 Schatz, *Genesis 14: Eine Untersuchung* (Europäische Hochschuleschriften, 23/2; Bern: Herbert Lang; Frankfurt am Main: Peter Lang, 1972).

30 Schatz, *Genesis 14*, 81–83, 301–2, and 321–4.

31 See Schatz, *Genesis 14*, 263–80.

32 See Schatz, *Genesis 14*, 291–302.

33 Schatz, *Genesis 14*, 322.

of Genesis 14—was also reflected in the so-called Chedorlaomer-texts from the Spartoli tablets of the British Museum (dated to the second century BCE; see 6.3.1.1, Earlier Attempts to Identify the Names) and also in Herodotus *Histories* and the OT pseudepigrapha.[34]

In his commentary on Genesis, Claus Westermann explicitly followed Schatz and, in particular, Emerton. In his estimation, the most important result of previous research was the recognition of the composite character of the chapter and the original independence of its three constituent parts, vv. 1–11; 12–17; and 21–24; 18–20.[35] To begin with, there was a hero story from the time of the judges (approx. vv. 12–17, 21–24). Unlike his predecessors, Westermann suggested that the hero story originally was *not* about Abraham. On the contrary, only later on was it connected to the patriarch. Nonetheless, in the time of David, the ME was added to the hero story that at that time had already been related to the patriarch. Eventually, in the late postexilic period, this composition was further expanded by the addition of vv. 1–11.

In summary, von Rad, Emerton, Schatz, and Westermann all agree on a tripartite division of Genesis 14: an annalistic-style account (approx. vv. 1–11), a hero story about Abram's rescue (approx. vv. 12–17, 21–24), and the ME (vv. 18–20). However, they disagree about their chronological order. Von Rad argued that the annalistic account represented the earliest part (fragment of a Canaanite epos) that subsequently was combined with a story about the patriarch. Eventually, the ME was added in the monarchic period. The other three argue that the hero story about Abram's rescue represents the earliest part to which first the ME, and later the annalistic account in vv. 1–11, were added shortly before or during the exile.

2.2.3 Critical Examination of the Theory of a Tripartite Division

Objections can be raised to both models outlined above. As to the proposal of Emerton, Schatz, and Westermann, an important argument *against* the idea that an originally independent hero story about Abram was the earliest part has been offered by Schatz himself. When Gen. 14:12–17, 21–24 are read without the introduction in vv. 1–11, the hero story does not have any beginning. First, without any information about the identity of the defeated enemies,[36] and second, without any informa-

---

34 Schatz, *Genesis 14*, 277, 320, refers to 2 Macc. 3; 4 Macc. 4:1–14; 3 Macc. 1:8–2:24, and Herodotus, *Histories*, 8.35ff.

35 Westermann, *Genesis 12–36*, 189–93.

36 According to the model of Schatz and Emerton, the mentioning of Chedorlaomer in 14:17 must be secondarily inserted in connection with the later addition of vv. 1–11.

tion about what had previously happened to Lot, which resulted in him being taken captive,[37] the story simply does not make sense.[38]

Were we with Emerton (and Westermann) to imagine an independent, oral popular tradition about Abram's heroic deeds, then we would have to postulate decisive background information. For instance, there would be a need for an identification of persons to whom the pronominal suffixes in v. 15 were referring ('He divided his forces against *them* by night . . . and routed *them* and pursued *them* . . .'). Additionally, there would be a need for information about the background of the capture of Lot: what had happened previously?

The model developed by Emerton and Schatz, and refined by Westermann, namely, that the earliest part of Genesis 14 is a hero story about Abram, is not convincing. The story in Gen. 14:12–17, 21–24 needs the information provided in the first part of the chapter to make sense.

Moreover, von Rad's model is also unlikely. Admittedly, it does not suffer the same problems as that of Emerton, Schatz, and Westermann. According to it, the assumed fragment of a Canaanite epos reflected in the account of the invasion of the four kings (Gen. 14:1–11) comes chronologically *before* the story about Abram. So, if the assumed hero story about Abram in the latter part of the chapter should have been secondarily combined with the fragment, then there is no problem regarding the background for Abram's actions. However, the proposal raises several historical challenges. Where in ancient Israel should such a cultural transfer from the ancient Canaanites to the Hebrews be located? And what kind of institution in ancient Israel took care of this epos and brought it in connection with its own patriarchal tradition? Why does the biblical tradition probably not contain additional fragments of such Canaanite epics? And who were these Canaanites, and did they really write epic literature? Except for the alleged fragment in Gen. 14:1–11 none are known.

In addition, scholars who argue for a tripartite division of Genesis 14 all build on *aesthetic* arguments. Emerton says,

> The distinction between A [i.e., the campaign of Chedorlaomer and the kings who were with him] and B [i.e., the story about Abram the noble hero and the king of Sodom] . . . is based primarily on the difference in character between the two passages.[39]

---

37   Lot is mentioned by name in vv. 12, 16 and referred to as 'his kin' (אָחִיו) in v. 14.
38   Contrary to, e.g., Emerton, who says that '[t]he story of Abram [i.e., Gen. 14:12–17, 21–24] makes sense as a story on its own'; cf. Emerton, 'Some Problems in Genesis XIV', 73–102 (79).
39   Emerton, 'Some Problems in Genesis XIV', 73–102 (79).

In order to be convincing, such an argument based on aesthetics needs to be supported by additional arguments. However, as I have demonstrated above, none of the advocates for a tripartite division succeed. Von Rad's proposal causes more problems than it solves. Moreover, if the proposal of Emerton, Schatz, and Westermann is taken literally, then it is clear that the allegedly earliest and most original part of the chapter, the story about Abram's heroic deeds, is *not* self-contained.

2.2.4 The Textual Integrity of Genesis 14*: A Unified and Internally Consistent Narrative

So, my examination of the arguments put forward by those who argue for a tripartite division of Genesis 14 shows that it is *not possible to delimit and subtract any substantial narrative part except for the ME*. Although there is an internal division in the narrative (approximately between vv. 11 and 12), this division reflects shift of scenes in the unfolding narrative and cannot be used as an argument for diachronic growth as long as additional arguments do not support this. The conclusion, then, is that we should take as a starting point the assumption that there is a *fundamental internal consistency* in the story told.

The assumption that Genesis 14 is a consistent story does in principle not exclude the possibility of the existence of secondary explications in the narrative. The manifold, slightly varying references to Lot in the chapter make it legitimate to ask whether they might have been subject to secondary reworking. Lot is mentioned three times: vv. 12, 14a, and 16.

Verse 11–12 reads:

וַיִּקְחוּ אֶת־כָּל־רְכֻשׁ סְדֹם וַעֲמֹרָה וְאֶת־כָּל־אָכְלָם וַיֵּלֵכוּ ¹² וַיִּקְחוּ אֶת־לוֹט וְאֶת־רְכֻשׁוֹ בֶּן־אֲחִי
אַבְרָם וַיֵּלֵכוּ וְהוּא יֹשֵׁב בִּסְדֹם

And they took all the goods of Sodom and Gomorrah and all their food and they went. ¹² And they took Lot and his goods, the son of Abram's brother, and they went. And he was living in Sodom.

Verse 14a reads:

וַיִּשְׁמַע אַבְרָם כִּי נִשְׁבָּה אָחִיו

And Abram heard that his brother had been taken captive.

Verse 16 reads:

וַיָּשֶׁב אֵת כָּל־הָרְכֻשׁ וְגַם אֶת־לוֹט אָחִיו וּרְכֻשׁוֹ הֵשִׁיב וְגַם אֶת־הַנָּשִׁים וְאֶת־הָעָם

And he brought back all the goods, and even Lot, his brother, and his goods he brought back, and even the women and the people.

One problem arises: the exact relation between Abram and Lot. Is the latter the former person's nephew (v. 12) or his brother/kin (vv. 14a, 16)? There is a semantic flux in the meaning of the noun אָח. The grammar of the received text does perhaps show signs of secondary reworking. In v. 12, the phrase בֶּן־אֲחִי אַבְרָם appears somehow displaced in the clause. Normally, one would expect such information to have come immediately after the mention of Lot. This gives rise to the suspicion that the phrase בֶּן־אֲחִי אַבְרָם is a gloss.

Moreover, the reference to Lot found in Gen. 14:16 also appears to be awkward from a syntactic point of view. The MT seems to offer an extra clause (underlined in the above quotation). The last part of the entire sentence seems to be governed by the initial *wayyiqtol* form (וַיָּשֶׁב) and not by the *qatal* (הֵשִׁיב) that concludes the assumed secondary clause. One can therefore consider the possibility that the clause וְגַם אֶת־לוֹט אָחִיו וּרְכֻשׁוֹ הֵשִׁיב has been secondarily inserted into Gen. 14:16 in order to make it even clearer that the rescue by Abram included Lot *also*.

The ambiguity concerning the relation between Abram and Lot is evident in the preceding Abraham narratives as well. Genesis 12:5 says that Lot is the son of Abram's brother (בֶּן־אָחִיו). However, in Gen. 13:8 Abram says to Lot, 'Let there be no strife . . . for we are brothers/ kindred' (כִּי־אֲנָשִׁים אַחִים אֲנָחְנוּ).

The references to Lot in vv. 12, 14, and 16, then, might very well be part of the original narrative. However, the phrase בֶּן־אֲחִי אַבְרָם (v. 12) and the clause וְגַם אֶת־לוֹט אָחִיו וּרְכֻשׁוֹ הֵשִׁיב can be explained as glosses, yet stemming from two different hands, one with the information from Gen. 12:5 in mind, the other with information from Gen. 13:8.

Now, the fundamental unity of Genesis 14—sometimes with the ME, sometimes without—has also been previously defended by scholars such as Hermann Gunkel,[40] and, more recently, by John Van Seters,[41] Gordon J. Wenham,[42] Walter Zimmerli,[43] Erhard Blum,[44] and J. Gordon

---

40 Gunkel, *Genesis*. With the exception of vv. 18–20, Gunkel finds no traces for the assumption that the chapter is composed by different sources (p. 290).

41 John Van Seters, *Abraham in History and Tradition* (New Haven, CT: Yale University Press, 1975).

42 Wenham, *Genesis 1–15*.

43 Walter Zimmerli, 'Abraham und Melchisedek', in *Das nahe und das ferne Wort* (ed. Fritz Maaß; FS Leonard Rost; BZAW 105; Berlin: W. de Gruyter, 1967), 255–64; Zimmerli, *1. Mose 12–25: Abraham* (ZB 1.2; Zurich: Theologischer Verlag, 1976).

44 Erhard Blum, *Die Komposition der Vätergeschichte* (WMANT 57; Neukirchen-Vluyn: Neukirchener Verlag, 1984), 462 n. 5.

McConville.[45] For instance, Blum has recognized the unevenness in Gen. 14:12 (repeating v. 11) and the difference in character between Gen. 14:1–11 ('Bericht') and 14:12–24 ('Erzählung'). However, in his view, this could have been intended by the author. Moreover, any theory about the parts stemming from originally independent traditions is questionable from his point of view because then one needs to postulate larger additions to each part.[46]

Van Seters has made an important observation about the presuppositions with which one approaches Genesis 14:

> Presuppositions about the traditions behind this chapter have a great deal of influence on views regarding its unity and the sources upon which it drew. Thus, the decision about how one proceeds with the analysis is most important.[47]

An a priori belief that all the patriarchal stories originally were made up of self-contained oral traditions is evident in the argumentation of Emerton, Schatz, and Westermann. For instance, Emerton explicitly writes: 'We can *imagine* a popular oral tradition about the heroic and noble doings of Abram.'[48] For Emerton, Schatz, and Westermann, this a priori conception of early patriarchal traditions—matched with the observation of differences in character between different part of Genesis 14—results in a hypothesis of a preliterary oral tradition that originally was self-contained. Yet, such a hypothesis raises more questions than it answers. Therefore, there is no compelling reason to question the fundamental internal consistency of the narrative in Genesis 14*.

I argued above that the Melchizedek episode (vv. 18–20) is a secondary interpolation in Genesis 14*. Moreover, I argued that the narrative in Genesis 14* is internally consistent, which suggests a common authorship for the entire narrative. Below, in chapter 6, The Literary Building Blocks of the Author of Genesis 14*, I will argue that the author of Genesis 14* borrowed words, constellations of names, and motifs from different types of biblical literature.

---

45   J. Gordon McConville, 'Abraham and Melchizedek: Horizons in Genesis 14', in *He Swore an Oath: Biblical Themes from Genesis 12–50* (ed. Richard S. Hess, Gordon J. Wenham, and Philip E. Satterthwaite; Carlisle, PA: Paternoster, 1994), 93–118.

46   See Blum, *Die Komposition der Vätergeschichte*, 462 n. 5; and, in addition, Van Seters, *Abraham in History and Tradition*, 301.

47   Van Seters, *Abraham in History and Tradition*, 296.

48   Emerton, 'The Riddle of Genesis XIV', 403–39 (431, my emphasis).

2.3 Genesis 14 and Textual Criticism

From a text-critical point of view, Genesis 14 does not represent any major challenge. By this, I mean to say that the received text (the MT), for the most part, is attested by other important textual witnesses, namely, the LXX and the Samaritan Pentateuch, in addition to the other ancient versions, that is, the Peshitta, the Vulgate, and the Targums. All of the textual witnesses offer basically an identical text or, in the case of the ancient translations, reflect a Hebrew *Vorlage* similar to the MT.

The goal of the text-critical discussion is to collect data on the differences between the textual witnesses. Moreover, in those cases where they offer differing texts, they will be evaluated with the purpose of identifying the putative original reading of Genesis 14*.[49]

Despite the general textual consensus among the witnesses, there are some differences. I will attempt to systemize and account for most of them below. In addition, in each case I will evaluate the differing data and discuss which reading probably best reflects the *Urtext*. By *Urtext* I refer to the putative result of the literary growth that has led up to the composition of Genesis 14 and that was the basis for the subsequent textual transmission. However, in the case of Genesis 14, a text I argue has been composed at a relatively late stage to fill out a *Leerstelle*,[50] I do not find it reasonable to speak of several pristine forms of the text. In the case of Genesis 14* it is more reasonable to assume that the original work of the author is identical with the *Urtext*.[51]

Initially I will also make clear that I use the apocryphal book of *Jubilees* and the Aramaic *Genesis Apocryphon* from Qumran only very cautiously when the goal is a text-critical one (that is, to describe a putative *Urtext*). First, neither *Jubilees* nor the *Genesis Apocryphon* is a translation but, on the contrary, is an example of the genre of 'rewritten Bible'.[52] Moreover, *Jubilees*, in particular, suffers from the fact that it is preserved in a Geez translation of a Greek text that for its part is probably a translation of a Hebrew text. Being in Aramaic, and both linguistically and

---

49   For a broad discussion about textual criticism and the Hebrew Bible, see Emanuel Tov, *Textual Criticism of the Hebrew Bible* (2d rev. ed.; Minneapolis MN: Fortress Press, 2001), 85–86.

50   See in particular chapter 5, Why Was Genesis 14* Composed and Inserted into the Abraham Narrative? An Attempt at a Literary Answer; and 7.1 below, The Date of Composition: A Synthesis of the Different Approaches.

51   For a discussion of this, see Tov, *Textual Criticism of the Hebrew Bible*, 171–77.

52   See Philip S. Alexander, 'Retelling the Old Testament', in *It Is Written: Scripture Citing Scripture: Essays in Honour of Barnabas Lindars* (ed. D. A. Carson and H. G. M. Williamson; Cambridge: Cambridge University Press, 1988), 99–121.

chronologically closer to its biblical *Vorlage*, the *Genesis Apocryphon* is more important. However, this also is not a translation but an important example of the early reception history of the book of Genesis. So, when biblical material is lacking in *Jubilees* or the *Genesis Apocryphon*, then such an absence does not necessarily suggest that the material was not present in the biblical *Vorlage*. On the contrary, the reason for the silence can in many cases be found in the agenda the authors had when rewriting the biblical text. Nonetheless, because it probably is linguistically close to its Hebrew *Vorlage*, the Aramaic *Genesis Apocryphon* should be given weight in questions regarding the orthography of the biblical text.[53]

2.3.1 Differences in the Rendition of Names

As mentioned, despite the basic textual consensus among the textual witnesses, there are nevertheless some differences among them. One recurring type of difference seems to be closely connected with one of the characteristics of Genesis 14: the abundance of names—especially ethnic and topographic but also personal. In some textual witnesses names sometimes appear as totally different from the corresponding name in the MT. To mention but a few examples: Gen. 14:1 in both the MT and the LXX speak of Arioch as 'king of Ellasar'. However, in the Vulgate and in Symmachus he is king of Pontus. And, including the Aramaic *Genesis Apocryphon* from Qumran among the textual witnesses, Arioch is made king of Cappadocia. Moreover, whereas the MT speaks of an otherwise unknown עֵמֶק הַשִּׂדִּים, 'Valley of Siddim'(?), the LXX renders it 'the salt valley'. Further, in Gen. 14:5 the LXX speaks of 'the giants' (τοὺς γίγαντας) and the 'strong nations with them' (ἔθνη ἰσχυρὰ ἅμα αὐτοῖς), where the MT reads 'the Rephaim' (רְפָאִים) and 'the Zuzim in Ham' (הַזּוּזִים בְּהָם) respectively. As for the latter, the Vulgate also has a phrase similar to the LXX 'with them' (*cum eis*), whereas other witnesses have a preposition + a place name (some Samaritan мss: בהם; *Targ. Onq.*: בהמתה, 'in Chemta'; *Targ. Ps.-J.*: בהמתא, 'in Hametha'; *Genesis Apocryphon*: בעמן, 'in Ammon'). The latter problem in v. 5 indicates that the witnesses' respective *Vorlagen* either have had a consonantal text different from the MT (ח instead of ה) or that the consonant cluster בהם has been vocalized

---

53   Benjamin Ziemer has a different approach to the *Genesis Apocryphon* as a source to questions concerning textual criticism and the composition history of the Pentateuch; see Ziemer, *Abram – Abraham: Kompositionsgeschichtliche Untersuchung zu Genesis 14, 15 und 17* (BZAW 350; Berlin: W. de Gruyter, 2005). However, for my critique of Ziemer's approach, see 5.1.2 below, Benjamin Ziemer: Genesis 14—a Midrash to Genesis 15.

differently (either as preposition + pronominal suffix or preposition + the possible place name Ham). Nevertheless, in those cases where one apparently cannot explain the differences as the result of errors in the textual transmission or differing vocalizations, one should probably explain the variant readings as *actualizing interpretations* of the *Vorlage*.[54]

Therefore, when the MT, the Samaritan Pentateuch, and the LXX offer the same reading of names, one should give their reading priority over the reading of the other textual witnesses. This is almost always the case.

However, as for the name of one of Abram's Amorite allies—Aner (Gen. 14:13, 24)—the MT, the Samaritan Pentateuch, and the LXX, and in addition, the early Aramaic *Genesis Apocryphon*, disagree. The MT reads עָנֵר; the Samaritan Pentateuch ענרם; the LXX Αυναν; and the *Genesis Apocryphon* reads ארנם.[55] In this case, it is not possible to establish the earliest reading by means of textual criticism. Below (see 6.2.4, Abram the Hebrew and His Amorite Allies) I propose that the name is a personification of a place name, as is the case with Mamre and Eschol. It is possible, then, that the name originally was Arnon (אַרְנֹון/אַרְנֹן), after the stream that functions as a border between Moab and the Amorites.

2.3.2 Differences Caused during the Copying and Transmission of the Text or by Differing Vocalization

Moreover, in three cases the LXX indirectly confirms the MT despite differing readings. In Gen. 14:11, the MT reads that King Chedorlaomer and the kings who were with him 'took all the goods [רְכֻשׁ] of Sodom and Gomorrah. . .'. The LXX reads instead that they took 'all the horses [ἵππον]. . .'. This same phenomenon is also evident in vv. 16 and 21. The LXX translators must have read the noun רֶכֶשׁ 'horses, team of horses, baggage horses', which has the same consonants but a different vocalization. Furthermore, in 14:16 in the MT, the noun רְכֻשׁ occurs twice. In the last case, the LXX remarkably does not render it 'horses' but correctly

---

54   For instance, according to Symmachus, Chedorlaomer was king of the Scythians (Σκυθῶν); cf. Gen. 14:1, 9. The term 'Scythian' first appears in written history in the annals of Esarhaddon (681–668 BCE) and then continues to be mentioned in Babylonian, Persian, and Greek texts in the latter part of the first millennium BCE. Then, in the first centuries CE the Scythians fade from history. Symmachus is dated to the late-second or early-third century CE; see Jennifer M. Dines, *The Septuagint* (Understanding the Bible and Its World; London: T. & T. Clark, 2004), 89. So, he might have connected the story in Genesis 14 to peoples in an immediate past.

55   Moreover, Josephus reads Ἔννηρος (*Ant.* 1.182).

translates it as 'his possessions' (τὰ ὑπάρχοντα αὐτοῦ). In this case, the particular noun must have had a *mater lectionis* in the LXX translator's *Vorlage* similar to that attested by the Samaritan Pentateuch (ורכושו), making a vocalization like רְכֻשׁ ('horses') impossible.

Moreover, a classic example of the interchange of similar letters is evident in Gen. 14:14. According to the MT, Abram 'emptied out' (וַיָּרֶק, perhaps an otherwise unknown military technical term) his retainers (possible translation of חֲנִיךְ[56]). Here, the Samaritan Pentateuch reads וידק. This is possibly a form of the root דוק, which perhaps means 'to look closely at' or 'to muster [troops]'.[57] The LXX for its part reads ἠρίθμησεν 'count, number' (in the meaning 'muster'), and *Targ. Onq.* reads זיר, 'to strengthen, to make active and ready, to instigate'.[58] Now, although the Samaritan reading is equally as difficult to understand as the MT, it seems clear that either the ר has been graphically mistaken to be a ד or vice versa. However, which one is the original is less certain. No matter what the original reading is, the meaning in the context is fairly clear.

In addition, a difference between the textual witnesses obscures the exact understanding of the chronological specifications in Gen. 14:4–5.[59] In these two verses, two cardinal numbers (שְׁתֵּים עֶשְׂרֵה 'twelve' and שְׁלֹשׁ־עֶשְׂרֵה 'thirteen' in v. 4) and one ordinal number (i.e., preposition + cardinal number, בְּאַרְבַּע עֶשְׂרֵה 'in the fourteenth [year]' in v. 5) occur. However, as for שְׁלֹשׁ־עֶשְׂרֵה in v. 4, all the textual witnesses have an ordinal reading, only with the exception of the MT and *Targ. Onq.*[60] Because the Samaritan Pentateuch and the LXX, plausibly independently of each other, agree against the MT reading, one should therefore assume that the preposition ב has been accidentally omitted in the Masoretic tradition.[61]

A similar case where all the textual witnesses offer a similar reading differing from the received text is found in Gen. 14:6. Here, the MT reads that Chedorlaomer and the kings who were with him beat 'the Horites in *their* mountain Seir [בְּהַרְרָם שֵׂעִיר] whereas all the other textual witnesses

---

56   A *hapax legomenon* according to HALOT 1, s.v. חֲנִיךְ, 333.

57   See Schatz, *Genesis 14*, 69.

58   See Jastrow, 412.

59   These chronological specifications are also difficult because of the uncertainty of the time references of the verbal form(s) עבדו (and possibly מרדו). Should one translate with the perfect tense ('they *served*') or rather the past perfect tense ('they *had served*')?

60   LXX: τῷ δὲ τρισκαιδεκάτῳ; the Vulgate: tertiodecimo anno [sg. abl.]; Sam.: עשרה שלש; Peshitta: *bdtltʿsrʾ*; *Targ. Onq.*: תלת עסרי; *Targ. Ps.-J.*: בתיליסרי; GenAp: בשנת תלת עשרה.

61   Though it has been suggested that the MT שְׁלֹשׁ־עֶשְׂרֵה is an accusative of time. According to Chaim Cohen, Ibn Ezra, who found a similar phenomenon in Exod. 20:11, was the first to propose this; see Cohen, 'Genesis 14—An Early Israelite Chronographic Source', 67–107 (75). On the accusative of time in general, see J–M, § 126i (pp. 458–59).

read 'in the mountains [the Samaritan Pentateuch: בהררי; the LXX: ἐν τοῖς ὄρεσιν; the Vulgate: in montibus; *Targ. Onq.*: בטוריא; *Genesis Apocryphon*: בטורי] of Seir'. The latter reading should be preferred because it is broadly attested in textual witnesses that for the most part are independent of one another. It is also attested in the early *Genesis Apocryphon* and is syntactically better than the MT. The final ם that appears in the MT must have been added to the Masoretic textual branch either accidentally or for an otherwise unknown reason.[62]

Finally, in MT Gen. 14:22, Abram swears an oath in which he identifies Yahweh with El Elyon, whereas according to all the other witnesses Abram swears by El Elyon only. Above, in 2.2.1, The Melchizedek Episode (= ME) in Genesis 14:18–20: A Secondary Interpolation, I have argued that the biblical text originally did not read 'Yahweh' and that the identification of El Elyon with Yahweh represents an inner-Masoretic development.

2.3.3 Differences Owing to Subsequent Stylistic Improvements

In Gen. 14:19, the MT reads 'and he [Melchizedek] blessed *him*' (וַיְבָרְכֵהוּ) whereas the Samaritan Pentateuch and the LXX both read 'and he blessed *Abram*' (אֶת אברם/τὸν Αβραμ). In the context of the previous clause in v. 18b ('and he [וְהוּא] was priest of El Elyon') the pronominal suffix in the MT וַיְבָרְכֵהוּ could potentially continue to refer to Melchizedek because no new subject is introduced in between. However, in light of the context, it is likely that it is Melchizedek who utters the blessing. Therefore, the LXX and Samaritan readings may represent secondary clarifications or harmonizations of the narrative,[63] replacing the suffix by the name Abram.

2.4 Hypothesis

As will be discussed more thoroughly below in 4.3.6, Did Genesis 15 Originally Continue Genesis 13 or Genesis 14?, there are reasons to assume that the covenant text in Genesis 15 was composed as a continuation of the story about the separation between Abram and Lot and

---

62 However, William Foxwell Albright suggests it is an antique enclitic ם that appears in the middle of a construct chain and renders the clause 'mountains of Seir'; see Albright, *Yahweh and the Gods of Canaan: A Historical Analysis of Two Contrasting Faiths* (London: Athlone, 1968), 39.

63 See Tov, *Textual Criticism of the Hebrew Bible*, 85–86.

Yahweh's promise of land to Abram and his descendants in Genesis 13. Both Genesis 13 and Genesis 15 are promise texts. In addition to these overall similarities in content, there is above all apparently a close connection between Abram's words in 15:3aβ, 'You have *given me no offspring* [הֵן לִי לֹא נָתַתָּה זָרַע], and Yahweh's promise in Gen. 13:15, 'For everything that you see I will give *to you and your descendants* [לְךָ אֶתְּנֶנָּה וּלְזַרְעֲךָ] for ever'. Abram's utterance links immediately to Yahweh's promise.[64]

In light of the preliminary discussion above I will argue that Genesis 14 appears as a wedge between Genesis 13 on the one side and Genesis 15 on the other. The discussion above suggests that Genesis 14 has been secondarily inserted between these chapters. Moreover, the discussion in 2.1, Features Unique to Genesis 14 in the Context of the Patriarchal Narratives, indicates a separate provenance for Genesis 14.

The preliminary observations justify the following hypotheses regarding Genesis 14*:

- Genesis 14* (that is, Genesis 14 before the Melchizedek episode was interpolated), is the late work of a scribe's desk (German: *Schreibtisch-arbeit*). Its author is a scribe well versed in different parts of the collection of Scriptures we today refer to as the Hebrew Bible. When composing Genesis 14*, he used and/or borrowed literary building blocks (literary templates) from several of these texts. When arguing that Genesis 14 is the late work of a scribe's desk I do not use the term as Westermann does, referring to the editorial collocation of assumed ancient traditions. On the contrary, here the term refers to how the very narrative and its constituent parts originated.

- Moreover, if one succeeds in identifying these 'building blocks' and the sources from which they have been borrowed, then one also has a basis for determining a *terminus a quo* for the date of composition of Genesis 14*. As a *terminus ante quem*, the earliest documented cases of reception history of Genesis 14* serve.

- Finally, when one has framed in a limited period for the date of composition of the text, then one also has a better basis for making historically qualified conjectures about the historical meaning of Genesis 14*.

---

64   For additional arguments supporting the thesis that Genesis 15 was composed in order to continue Genesis 13, see below, 4.3.6, Did Genesis 15 Originally Continue Genesis 13 or Genesis 14?

3. Genesis 14* and the Abraham Tradition

3.1 Point of Departure: A People Named after the Most Prominent Patriarch's Grandson

There are reasons to assume that the elevated position of the patriarch Abraham as the forebear of the people of Israel represents a relatively late development in the self-comprehension of the people of Israel. In the following I will attempt to survey the texts outside of the Pentateuch that mention Abraham. The purpose will be a negative one: to establish a historical context that weakens proposals suggesting that Genesis 14* reflects (very) old traditions about the patriarch.

As a point of departure we should consider the name of the chosen people: 'Israel' (יִשְׂרָאֵל) and 'sons of Israel' (בְּנֵי יִשְׂרָאֵל). Whereas the name Israel, according to the biblical chronology, was first given to the *person* Jacob (Genesis 32), it was transformed into the name of a *nation*. This semantic flux is evident in the opening verses of the book of Exodus. In v. 1 the narrator sets forth to list the names of the 'sons of Israel' who came to Egypt 'together with Jacob'. Moreover, in v. 6 we are told that the whole generation of the twelve sons of Jacob died. However, in v. 7 we are nevertheless told that the 'sons of Israel' were fruitful and pro-lific. Moreover, in v. 8 the new pharaoh in Egypt utters his fear that 'the people of the sons of Israel' (עַם בְּנֵי יִשְׂרָאֵל) were more numerous and pow-erful than the Egyptians. In additon, already in the book of Genesis there are examples of the anachronistic use of the term 'Israel', where the term signifies a *nation* and not the *person* Jacob.[1]

Nevertheless, in Exodus 1, as in most other biblical tradition, the *people* is normally designated by the name of the patriarch *Jacob*, whose alias after the fight with God at Peniel in Genesis 32 is *Israel* (see, e.g.,

---

1 See, e.g., Gen. 34:7 'And the *sons of Jacob* came in from the field. When they heard the men felt hurt and became very angry. For he had done a disgrace *in Israel* [בְּיִשְׂרָאֵל] by lying with *Jacob's* daughter. Such a thing should truely not be done!' Moreover, 'Israel' may stand for both an individual and a collective within a single verse, Gen. 47:27: 'And Israel settled [singular: וַיֵּשֶׁב יִשְׂרָאֵל] in the land of Egypt, in the land of Goshen. And they became settled in it, they were fruitful and they became very many [plural: וַיֵּאָחֲזוּ בָהּ וַיִּפְרוּ וַיִּרְבּוּ מְאֹד]'.

Hos. 12:3 [Eng. trans., 2]; Isa. 9:7; 14:1; etc.). So, in light of the status given to Abraham in the present patriarchal narratives in Genesis 12–50, it is remarkable that the people of whom he is the ancestor did not name itself after him but, on the contrary, after his grandson Jacob/Israel.

This suggests that the present biblical genealogy of the patriarchs—according to which Abraham is Jacob's grandfather and thereby also the real forefather of the people of Israel—is not original. On the contrary, the genealogy has to stem from a time after the people's identity irrevocably had been coined as 'Israel'. Therefore, we may either assume that Israel/Jacob originally enjoined greater veneration than did Abraham, or, alternatively, we may assume that Israel/Jacob already played the role of the forebear of the people when the Abraham traditions first entered the scene. As Wellhausen once put it, Abraham is perhaps the youngest figure in the company, and it was probably at a comparatively late period that he was put before his son Isaac.[2]

3.2 References to Abraham outside the Pentateuch

Moreover, Abraham plays a remarkably insignificant role in the biblical texts outside the Pentateuch. In Genesis 12–25 he is the main character. Because Abraham is the (fore)father of the other patriarchs one gets the impression that he is not only the first of the patriarchs in terms of chronology but also the most prominent: It was he who was called to leave Ur-Kasidim and go to the land Yahweh promised to him and his descendants. Despite this, Abraham is seldom referred to in the Hebrew Bible. Outside the Pentateuch, אַבְרָהָם and אַבְרָם occur in only twenty-three verses: Josh. 24:2–3; 1 Kgs. 18:36; 2 Kgs. 13:23; 1 Chr. 1:27–28, 32, 34; 16:16; 29:18; 2 Chr. 20:7; 30:6; Neh. 9:7; Ps. 47:10; 105:6, 9, 42; Isa. 29:22; 41:8; 51:2; 63:16; Jer. 33:26; Ezek. 33:24; and Mic. 7:20.

3.2.1 Abraham in the Historical Literature

In the historical narratives, different themes are hinted at when Abraham is referred to. Sometimes his name is merely part of the formula 'Yahweh, God of Abraham, Isaac, and Israel' (1 Kgs. 18:36; 2 Chr. 29:18; 30:6). However, in one case, this formula occurs in connection with a reference to a certain covenant: 2 Kgs. 13:23, 'But Yahweh was gracious

---

2   Julius Wellhausen, *Prolegomena zur Geschichte Israels* (6th ed.; Berlin: W. de Gruyter, 2001), 317.

to them [Israel, that is, the northern kingdom] and had compassion on them and he turned toward them. Because of his covenant with Abraham, Isaac, and Jacob he did not want to destroy them. . .'.

Moreover, in the opening chapter of the first book of Chronicles, Abraham is part of the great genealogy covering the period from Adam to the descendants of David and Solomon down to the Babylonian exile (1 Chronicles 1–3). The Chronicler obviously has knowledge of the changing of his name from Abram to Abraham (1 Chr. 1:27; cf. Genesis 17). Moreover, the Chronicler presupposes an Abraham story in which Abra(ha)m is the son of Terah, the father of Isaac, the grandfather of Israel/Jacob and the great grandfather of Israel's twelve sons. In other words, the Chronicler seems to have a patriarchal narrative as a source whose basic genealogical structure is identical with Genesis 12–50.

In Joshua 24, Abraham occurs in a retrospective speech on the occasion of the covenant renewal at Shechem.[3] Through Joshua, Yahweh outlines the salvation history of the people, starting with Terah, Abraham, and Nahor, who lived 'on the other side of the Euphrates'. There, they were polytheists (Josh. 24:2)—a piece of information not found anywhere else in the Hebrew Bible. From Mesopotamia, Yahweh led Abraham to the land of Canaan and made his offspring many. Moreover, Abraham had the son Isaac, who had the sons Esau and Jacob. Whereas the former inhabited the hill country of Seir, the latter and his sons went down to Egypt. Then Yahweh sent Moses and Aaron, defeated the Egyptians, brought the people out, and led them into the wilderness. After a long time in the wilderness, Yahweh brought them to the land of the Amorites, where the people took possession of the land (Josh. 24:2–8). From this we may assume that the historian behind Joshua 24 had a quite elaborate tradition about the history of the people at his disposal. Not only is the historian acquainted with Abraham's Mesopotamian background, but he also seems to have known that Yahweh made Abraham's descendants many. Moreover, Abraham appears as the patriarch of the patriarchs.

Now, of particular importance in dating the historical résumé in Joshua 24 is the fact that the patriarchal narrative—in which Abraham, Isaac, Jacob, and Jacob's sons are all included—is connected to the story about Israel in Egypt and its subsequent exodus from there under the leadership of Moses and Aaron. The combination of these two differing traditions about the origin of Israel suggests that Joshua 24 is a quite

---

3   For an orientation in the history of research, see Ed Noort, *Das Buch Joshua: Forschungsgeschichte und Problemfelder* (EdF 292; Darmstadt: Wissenschaftliche Buchgesellschaft, 1998), 205–22.

late text.[4] According to Konrad Schmid, the combination of the two independent traditions about the origin of Israel (the story of the patriarchs and the exodus story), which is evident in, for example, Joshua 24, reflects the overall picture in the Hexateuch ('das hexateuchische Gesamtbild'), which arranges the book of Genesis before the book of Exodus. This combination Schmid ascribes to a post-Priestly redaction.[5]

Moreover, in Nehemiah 9 there is a similarly styled résumé of the salvation history. However, unlike Joshua 24, the author of Nehemiah 9 has his point of departure in Yahweh's creation of the heavens and earth (Neh. 9:6). According to Nehemiah, this deity is identical with the God who chose Abram, brought him out of Ur-Kassidim and gave him the name Abraham (Neh. 9:7; cf. Gen. 11:28; 17:5). Moreover, the author knew that Abraham was faithful before Yahweh and that Yahweh made with him a covenant to give to his descendants 'the land of the Canaanite, the Hittite, the Amorite, the Perizzite, the Jebusite, and the Girgashite' (Neh. 9:8; cf. Gen. 15:6, 18–20). Then the résumé says that Yahweh saw the distress of the Israelites in Egypt and heard their cry at the Sea of Reeds (Neh. 9:9; cf. Exodus 3), and performed signs and wonders against Pharaoh (Neh. 9:10; cf. Exodus 4–11). Moreover, he divided the sea before them and threw those who pursued them into the depths (Neh. 9:11–12; cf. Exod. 14:15–31). Furthermore, what is unique for Nehemiah 9 vis-à-vis Joshua 24 is that the former résumé contains numerous references to the giving of the law at Sinai (Neh. 9:13–14; cf. Exodus 12; 13; and Exodus 19–Numbers 10). After the wilderness wandering and the events there, the résumé continues with the conquest of the land, the driving out of the Canaanite inhabitants, the apostasy and unwillingness to comply with the law, Yahweh's giving them over to their enemies and subsequent appointment of saviours who saved them, and his admonitions through the prophets until the days of Ezra (Neh. 9:15–32).

The résumé in Nehemiah 9 appears to refer to a more complete history of salvation than Joshua 24 does. That is, the Nehemiah text begins in Genesis 1 and continues beyond the period of monarchy, exile, and subsequent restoration. As for the status of Abraham, it is important to note that out of all the patriarchs the Nehemiah résumé mentions only

---

4   See also Blum, *Die Kompostion der Vätergeschichte*, 52.
5   See Konrad Schmid, *Erzväter und Exodus: Untersuchungen zur doppelten Begründung der Ursprünge Israels innerhalb der Geschichtsbücher des Alten Testaments* (WMANT 81; Neukirchen-Vluyn: Neukirchener Verlag, 1999), 358, and further references there. See also R. G. Kratz, 'Der vor- und nachpriesterschriftliche Hexateuch', in *Abschied vom Jahwisten: Die Komposition des Hexateuch in der jüngsten Diskussion* (ed. Jan Christian Gertz, Konrad Schmid, and Markus Witte; BZAW 315; Berlin: W. de Gruyter, 2002), 295–323 (299–307).

him by name. All in all, the author mentions only a handful of individuals besides Abraham: Pharaoh (v. 10), Moses (v. 14), Sihon king of Heshbon, and Og king of Bashan (v. 22).

In summing up the historical texts referring to Abraham discussed so far, it is reasonable to assume that these texts are in general late. That is evidently the case with Nehemiah 9, which must have been written at a time when the canonical history of salvation as we now have it in the Hebrew Bible was existent. The genealogy in 1 Chronicles 1–3 must be of approximately the same date. However, Joshua 24 may be earlier than Nehemiah 9, for it fails to mention the revelation of the law at Sinai as Nehemiah does. Nonetheless, because of the elaborate history of salvation that it presupposes, it is probably a relatively late composition.

Furthermore, the reference to Abraham, Isaac, and Jacob in 2 Kgs. 13:23 is part of a Deuteronomistic interpretation of the historical information given in the preceding v. 22: 'And King Hazael of Aram oppressed Israel all the days of Jehoahaz'. The notification in v. 23 that Yahweh 'had not yet [עַד־עַתָּה] thrown them [= Israel, meaning the northern kingdom] away' reveals that the author knows that Yahweh will throw them away later. That suggests a date after 722 BCE.

Nevertheless, the texts referring to Abraham found in the so-called Deuteronomistic literature are composed earlier than the texts found in the Chronistic history. The Deuteronomistic references let Abraham, together with Isaac and Jacob, help in identifying God as 'Yahweh, God of Abraham, Isaac, and Jacob' (1 Kgs. 18:36). Moreover, Abraham and Isaac and Jacob are those with whom Yahweh made a covenant (2 Kgs. 13:23). And Abraham is the one who was called to go to Canaan, where Yahweh made his descendants many (Josh. 24:2–3).

3.2.2 Abraham in the Poetic Literature

With the exception of Psalms 47 and 105, Abraham is totally absent from the poetic literature. In Psalm 47, normally taken to be an enthronement hymn celebrating God's kingship, Abraham is referred to in Ps. 47:10a [Eng. trans., 9a], 'The noblemen of the peoples are gathered [*with*[6]] the people of the God of Abraham.' Different dates for this particular psalm have been suggested, depending on how the idea of an enthronement

---

6 The MT does not have the preposition עם. However, since the LXX reads μετὰ τοῦ θεοῦ Αβρααμ '*with* the God of Abraham', one may assume that the MT reading is caused by a haplography.

of Yahweh is understood.[7] According to one theory, the enthronement of the deity was celebrated in the pre-Israelite cult in Jerusalem and was incorporated into the later Israelite cult of Yahweh. According to another theory, the motif of the enthronement of the deity is of Mesopotamian origin and was imported to Jerusalem. According to yet another theory, the motif may simply be a reflection of a human enthronement ritual. Finally, it has also been suggested that the whole motif of יְהוָה מָלָךְ presupposes and literarily depends on Isa. 52:7.[8]

I do not intend to discuss the possible migration of the motif of the enthronement of the deity in the ancient Near East. Rather, I pursue another path for dating the psalm. We observe that the psalm uses the divine names Yahweh, Elyon (עֶלְיוֹן), God (אֱלֹהִים), and the God of Abraham (אֱלֹהֵי אַבְרָהָם). Proceeding from the premise that the Priestly source of the Pentateuch was the first to identify the God of Abraham with Yahweh (as is evident in Exod. 3:6), then we may perhaps have established a *terminus a quo* identical with the date of P, regardless of the absolute date of P. Moreover, we see that the psalm uses the noun אֱלֹהִים as a divine name, not as an appellative. Albert de Pury has suggested that this particular use of the noun can help to date texts in the Pentateuch. His thesis is that the author of the Priestly source was the one who first 'invented' the use of אֱלֹהִים as a proper name (no longer merely a common noun) for the divinity also known as Yahweh.[9] So, the use of אֱלֹהִים as a proper name suggests that Psalm 47 is not older than the Priestly source.[10]

We are probably on more solid ground when dating Psalm 105 (= 1 Chronicles 16) than we are with Psalm 47. Psalm 105 knows of Yahweh's covenant with and promise of land to the patriarchs ('Abraham' and 'Isaac', vv. 7–11); it perhaps echoes the wanderings and deeds of the patriarchs in the land (vv. 12–15), definitely echoes the Joseph story

---

7   See, e.g., Hans-Joachim Kraus, *Psalmen. I Psalmen 1–59* (5th ed.; BKAT 15.1; Neukirchen-Vluyn: Neukirchener Verlag, 1978), 504; and R. G. Kratz, *Reste hebräischen Heidentums am Beispiel der Psalmen* (Nachrichten der Akademie der Wissenschaften zu Göttingen. I. Philologisch-historische Klasse; Göttingen: Vandenhoeck & Ruprecht, 2004), 17–20.

8   Quoted after the NRSV: 'How beautiful upon the mountains are the feet of the messenger who announces peace, who brings good news, who announces salvation, who says to Zion, "Your God reigns [מָלַךְ אֱלֹהָיִךְ]"'.

9   Albert de Pury, 'Gottesname, Gottesbezeichnung und Gottesbegriff. *'elohim* als Indiz zur Entstehungsgeschichte des Pentateuch', in Gertz, Schmid, and Witte, eds., *Abschied vom Jahwisten*, 25–47.

10   On the basis of form critical observations Hermann Spieckermann argues that Psalms 47, 96–99 cannot be dated earlier than the exilic period; see Spieckermann, *Heilsgegenwart: Eine Theologie der Psalmen* (FRLANT 148; Göttingen: Vandenhoeck & Ruprecht, 1989), 181 n. 5.

(vv. 16–22), the wandering of the Israelites into Egypt and their multiplication there (vv. 23–25), the sending of Moses and Aaron and the wandering out of Egypt under their command (vv. 26–38), and the miraculous wilderness wandering (vv. 39–41). The psalmist explains the entire exodus out of Egypt and also the miraculous wilderness wandering by referring to the covenant (בְּרִית, see vv. 8–9) he made with Abraham:

> Psalm 105:42–45 (NRSV): [42] For he remembered his holy word, [and] Abraham, his servant. [43] And he brought his people out with joy. . . . [44]And he gave them the lands of the peoples; the labour of the nations they took in possession [45] that they can observe his statutes and watch over his laws. Hallelujah!

The accumulation of biblical traditions referred to in Psalm 105 clearly suggests a late date. The combination of the tradition about the patriarchs on the one hand and the exodus tradition on the other suggests that the psalm does not antedate the Priestly source of the Pentateuch.[11] Moreover, depending on N. Lohfink, Hans-Joachim Kraus states that the psalm probably presupposes a Pentateuch that is already 'built together' ('zusammengebaut').[12] In any case, Psalm 105 does not give us any evidence for, say, a preexilic veneration of Abraham as the most prominent patriarch.

3.2.3 Abraham in the Prophetic Literature

In the prophetic literature Abraham occurs only seven times (Isa. 29.22; 41:8; 51:2; 63:16; Jer. 33:26; Ezek. 33:24; Mic. 7:20).

3.2.3.1 The Book of Isaiah

As for the four references to Abraham in Isaiah, three are located in those parts of the book that conventionally are called Deutero- (and Trito-) Isaiah (Isaiah 40–66). Therefore, because of their literary context, we can at the outset establish as working theories that Isa. 41:8; 51:2; and 63:16 are postexilic.

(1) In Isa. 63:16 *Abraham's* fathership is contrasted to *Yahweh's* fathership: 'You are our father, for Abraham does not know us and Israel does not acknowledge us. You are our father. . .'. The statement critical of

---

11   See 3.2.1 below, Abraham in the Historical Literature, and the reference to Konrad Schmid there.

12   Kraus, *Psalmen. II Psalmen 60–150* (5th ed.; BKAT 15.2; Neukirchen-Vluyn: Neukirchener Verlag, 1978), 892.

the patriarch is part of a literary unit unambiguously presupposing the destruction of the temple (see v. 18, 'For a little while your holy people took possession but our adversaries trampled down your sanctuary [מִקְדָּשׁ]'). When the author of Isaiah 63 refers to a tradition about Israel and Abraham as fathers of the people—though in a negative way—it means that these traditions are already known at the time of composition of the text. Moreover, the negative attitude toward the patriarchs provides a contrast to the more positive assessments found in the references to them both within and outside the Pentateuch.

(2) The reference to Abraham in Isa. 41:8 is part of a speech addressed to Israel, alias Jacob, alias the offspring of Abraham (Isa. 41:8–13 [16]):

> Isa. 41:8–9 (NRSV): But you, Israel, my servant, Jacob, whom I have chosen, the offspring of Abraham, my friend; [9] you whom I took from the ends of the earth, and called from its farthest corners, saying to you, 'You are my servant, I have chosen you and not cast you off'.

The speech itself is difficult to date because it lacks unambiguous references to dateable events or persons. However, the addressees seem to live in anxiety and distress, threatened by otherwise unidentified enemies. These text internal observations, together with the observation that the message of the unit is in accordance with the very opening of the so-called Deutero-Isaiah (Isa. 40:1, '"Comfort, comfort my people," says your God'), makes a preexilic date for this text unlikely.

Formally, Abraham seems to disrupt an otherwise perfect parallelism between Israel and Jacob. For instance, in Isa. 41:14a only Israel and Jacob occur as addressees: 'Do not fear, you worm Jacob, you men of Israel!' This raises the question as to whether the reference to Abraham in 41:8 is an original part of the speech. The lack of symmetry speaks against this. Nevertheless, independent of this, Isa. 41:8–9 reflects Yahweh's act of election. However, it is *Jacob* who is explicitly chosen (יַעֲקֹב אֲשֶׁר בְּחַרְתִּיךָ 'Jacob, whom I have chosen'). Consequently, it is probably of Jacob that Yahweh says in v. 9, 'I seized you from the ends of the earth and from her remotest parts I called you and I said to you "You are my servant, I have chosen you [בְּחַרְתִּיךָ] and I shall not reject you"'.

So, the Abraham tradition as reflected in Isa. 41:8 does conceive of him as a forebear, as is evident in the phrase זֶרַע אַבְרָהָם 'seed of Abraham'. Moreover, to this phrase the suffixed participle אֹהֲבִי is attached. Nevertheless, it should be pointed out that although the theme of Yahweh's election plays a great role in this particular verse, it is still *Jacob* who explicitly is called the chosen one, and *not* Abraham. In this text, which at the earliest should be dated to the exilic period, the reference to the seed of Abraham appears to have been interpolated secondarily. Even if it is an original part of the text, then it is still Jacob that is the subject of Yahweh's election.

(3) Moreover, in Isa. 51:2, Abraham appears together with Sarah: 'Look to Abraham your father and to Sarah who brought you forth! While being one I called him, and I blessed him and made him many'.

Isa. 51:2 is part of 51:1–3. From 51:3a it appears that Yahweh shall comfort Zion and all her ruins: 'For Yahweh will comfort Zion, he will comfort all her ruins and make her wilderness like Eden and her deserts like the garden of Yahweh. . .'. The comfort motif and the explicit mention of ruins not yet rebuilt enable us to establish the Babylonian exile as *terminus a quo*.

The Abraham tradition recalled here seems to be in accordance with parts of Gen. 12:1–3. Abraham is 'called' (Gen. 12:1a) and 'blessed and made many' through Sarah (Gen. 12:2). However, no promise of land is given to Abraham according to Isa. 51:2. Furthermore, it is relevant for the description of the nature of the author's source that he refers to Eden and the garden of Yahweh (Isa. 51:3). This may suggest that he knew the Yahwistic creation account now found in Genesis 2 and/or the narrative about the separation of Abraham and Lot (see Gen. 13:10). In addition, the rhetorics of Isa. 51:1–3 demonstrates that the people spoken to already conceive of Abraham and Sarah as their forebears.

(4) Finally, Abraham is also mentioned in a fourth passage in Isaiah:

Isa. 29:22: Therefore, thus says Yahweh, God[13] of the house of Jacob, he who ransomed [פָּדָה] Abraham: 'No longer shall Jacob be ashamed. . .'.

If the verb פָּדָה hints at a particular event in the life of the patriarch where Yahweh ransomed Abraham, none of the narratives that have been transmitted to us in the Pentateuch are likely candidates. The book of Genesis does not know any story about Abraham being enslaved. Nowhere is Abraham taken captive and subsequently ransomed by anyone. Alternatively, the verb could be used figuratively and signify God's acts of salvation toward him. For instance, one can speculate that it may refer to Abraham and Sarah's stay in Egypt (Gen. 12:10–20) or perhaps to an idea that Abraham is the firstborn of the people of the covenant.

In light of the general tenor of Isa. 29:22–24 (salvation), and in particular because the concept of Yahweh's redemption of Israel seems to be a favourite topos in the Deutero-Isaianic preaching,[14] it is probable

---

13   The phrase אֶל־בֵּית יַעֲקֹב can also be rendered 'to the house of Jacob'.

14   Besides the occurrence of פדה in Isa. 29:22, the root פדה and the synonym root גאל do (with derivations) occur in the following places in the book of Isaiah: 1:27; 35:9; 41:14; 43:1, 14; 44:6, 22ff.; 47:4; 48:17, 20; 49:7, 26; 50:2; 51:10; 52:3, 9; 54:5, 8; 59:20; 60:16; 62:12; 63:4, 9, 16.

that Isa. 29:22 also stems from the same redaction and/or reworking with Isaianic material as the so-called Deutero-Isaiah.[15]

3.2.3.2 Micah 7:20

Abraham is mentioned in the very last verse of the book of Micah:

> Micah 7:20 (NRSV): You will show faithfulness to Jacob and unswerving loyalty to Abraham, as you have sworn to our ancestors from the days of old.

The verse is part of a hymn in Mic. 7:18–20 about Yahweh's compassion. The hymn combines a spiritualized reference to the exodus[16] with references to Jacob and Abraham. In addition, a group is referenced that is not further defined except for being called 'our fathers' (אֲבֹתֵינוּ). This latter group is not identical with Jacob and Abraham. Nevertheless, 'Jacob' and 'Abraham' seem to stand collectively for a group contemporary with the author and do not represent two single individuals. They function as representatives for the speaking corporate entity.

It is accepted among most commentators of the book of Micah that the last hymns attached to the book are postexilic and not composed by the prophet Michah of Moresheth, who has given his name to the book.[17] Therefore, the corporate speaking evident behind the phrase 'our fathers' refers to the postexilic people of Israel.

3.2.3.3 Jeremiah 33:26

In the saying in Jer. 33:26, Yahweh assures the people that he will bring back the captives of 'the seed of Abraham, Isaac, and Jacob'. The saying is part of a word of Yahweh to Jeremiah in which the rejection of both

---

15 So Knud Jeppesen, *Jesajas Bog fortolket* (Copenhagen: Det danske Bibelselskap, 1988), 166.

16 See Mic. 7:19b, 'You will cast all our sins into the depths [בִּמְצֻלוֹת] of the sea', and Exod. 15:5, 'The floods covered them [i.e. Pharaoh's chariots, his army and his chariot fighters]; they went down into the depths [בִּמְצוֹלֹת] like a stone'.

17 See in particular 7.2.1, Abram in Genesis 14*—A Model Figure, for references to secondary literature supporting this. In addition to the position of B. M. Zapff, which will be presented there, it can also be noted that Wilhelm Rudolph calls Mic. 7:18–20 a postexilic liturgy; see Rudolph, *Micha, Nahum, Habakuk, Zephanja* (KAT 13.3; Gütersloh: Gütersloher Verlagshaus Gerd Mohn, 1975), 121. Moreover, both James Luther Mays, *Micah: A Commentary* (OTL; Philadelphia: Westminster, 1976), 167; and H. W. Wolff, *Dodekapropheton 4: Micha* (BKAT 14.4; Neukirchen-Vluyn: Neukirchener Verlag, 1982), xxxiv, 193, date the composition and insertion of the text into the book of Micah to the postexilic period. Furthermore, even Delbert R. Hillers, who is explicitly critical of diachronic approaches to the book of Micah, is open to a possible later date for this particular psalm; see Hillers, *Micah: A Commentary on the Book of the Prophet Micah* (Hermeneia; Philadelphia: Fortress, 1984).

Israel and Judah is taken as a matter of fact (see Jer. 33:24, 'The two families that Yahweh chose have been rejected by him'). Consequently, this text cannot be dated earlier than the Babylonian exile. It is the people that Yahweh will have mercy upon (cf. 33:26b) that is called 'the seed of Abraham, Isaac, and Jacob'. Therefore, in this exilic or postexilic text 'Abraham' and the other two patriarchs function as identity markers.

3.2.3.4 Ezekiel 33:24

The last prophetic text to be discussed here that mentions Abraham is Ezek. 33:24. The verse is part of a literary unit where God speaks in a form of disputation (Ezek. 33:23–29). It appears from the speech that the deportation to Babylon is not yet known. On the contrary, according to vv. 24 and 27 there are people who live in ruins (חֳרָבָּה) and in open field (פְּנֵי הַשָּׂדֶה) when the words are spoken. Therefore, with Matthias Köckert we can assume that the saying presupposes only the first conquest of Jerusalem in 598/597 BCE, not the collapse that took place a decade later in 587 BCE.[18] Moreover, Yahweh's announcement in Ezek 33:28 of a further and complete destruction supports this relatively narrow chronological setting: 'I will make the land a desolation and a waste, and its proud might shall come to an end; and the mountains of Israel shall be so desolate that no one will pass through' (NRSV). According to Köckert, Ezek. 33:24 is probably the earliest of all the prophetic references to Abraham.

The reference to Abraham in Ezek. 33:24 appears in a context in which the prophet quotes Yahweh's defaming of the inhabitants of 'these ruins in the land of Israel'. They keep saying:

אֶחָד הָיָה אַבְרָהָם וַיִּירַשׁ אֶת־הָאָרֶץ וַאֲנַחְנוּ רַבִּים לָנוּ נִתְּנָה הָאָרֶץ לְמוֹרָשָׁה

Ezek. 33:24aβ.b (NRSV): Abraham was only one man, yet he got possession of the land; but we are many; the land is surely given us to possess.

So, it seems that the survivors of the first conquest of Jerusalem in 598/597 comforted themselves by quoting these words. The content of the quotation is twofold: first, that Abraham was only one person, and second, that he got possession of (ירשׁ) the land. On this basis, the inhabitants infer that because they are many, they have received the land as their possession.

The inhabitants reached this particular conclusion (which they comforted themselves with) by using the hermeneutical technique

---

18 Matthias Köckert, 'Die Geschichte der Abrahamüberlieferung', in *Congress Volume: Leiden 2004* (ed. André Lemaire; VTSup 109; Leiden: E. J. Brill, 2006), 103–28.

qal wahomer, that is, inferring from the smaller to the larger (*a minori ad maius*).[19] Based on the fact that Abraham got possession of the land although he was only one, they infer that they, being many, will definitely be given the land.

However, against this particular interpretation of the inhabitants, Yahweh puts their failure to fulfill the law (Ezek. 33:25–26, '. . . you eat flesh with the blood, and lift up your eyes to your idols, and shed blood . . . you commit abominations, and each of you defiles his neighbor's wife . . .') and their confidence in their own strength rather than in God (Ezek 33:26aα, 'You support yourself on your swords'). Then Yahweh asks rhetorically (Ezek. 33:26b) 'shall you then possess the land?'

As for the nature of this reference to Abraham, some remarks can be made. First, the reference to Abraham from Yahweh's perspective appears to be ambiguous. Whether Yahweh is critical of the inhabitants because of their reference to the patriarch or because of the *a minori ad maius* derivation that they make on the basis of it is not evident. Second, the reference provides positive evidence for the existence of a preexilic Abraham tradition. Third, this tradition seems to have been known by the people of Judah. Fourth, it connects Abraham to the possession of the land. In contrast, Ezekiel 20 connects the possession to the exodus out of Egypt.[20] Furthermore, fifth, Ezek. 33:24 speaks of Abraham as a single individual. The point made by the Judeans, namely, that they in contrast to Abraham are many, may indirectly reveal that the Abraham tradition known by the Judeans also included the motif of the blessing and multiplication of Abraham.

3.2.4 Summing up Abraham outside the Pentateuch

Summing up the discussion about the references to Abraham in the poetic and prophetic literature, nearly all references to Abraham outside the Pentateuch stem from the postexilic period. The earliest reference to Abraham is probably the one found in Ezek. 33:24, a saying probably associated with Judah that should be dated to the period between 598/597 and 587/586 BCE. Moreover, I have initially noted how remarkable it is

---

19   See Fishbane, *Biblical Interpretation in Ancient Israel*, 420.

20   The precise meaning of the verb וַיִּירְשׁוּ in Ezek. 33:24 is not entirely clear, however. ירשׁ in qal may indicate that the possession of something is given to someone who passively inherits, e.g., as in Gen. 15:3, 'one of my household will be my heir'. But it may also involve activity from the side of the grammatical subject, as, e.g., Deut. 1:8, 'Go and take possession [בֹאוּ וּרְשׁוּ] of the land . . .'. The context in which the verb is used in Ezekiel 33 does not help us to determine the meaning here.

that the people are named after Abraham's grandson and not Abraham himself. All in all, this suggests that Abraham's current status as the first and most venerable of the patriarchs represents a late development in the growth of the biblical traditions.[21] Although there must have been some kind of a preexilic Abraham tradition, at least in preexilic Judah, as is evident in Ezekiel 33, it seems that it was after the Babylonian exile that Abraham first had a 'successful career' as the forebear of the people.

Therefore, the extrapentateuchal references to Abraham do not indicate that the Abraham tradition was widespread and well established in the monarchic period. Although this does not exclude the possibility that certain Abraham traditions are preexilic, the extrapentateuchal references do not, at least, provide external support for proposing that Genesis 14* reflects very old traditions about the patriarch.

---

21 The references to patriarchal traditions in the book of Hosea point in the same direction. Regardless of whether the references to patriarchal traditons in Hosea 12 are authentic Hoseanic or not, it is remarkable that it is *Jacob* who is mentioned, not Abraham. According to Roman Vielhauer, the historical retrospects in, among others, Hosea 12 are literary continuations (*'Fortschreibungen'*) that cannot be earlier than the exilic period; see Vielhauer, *Das Werden des Buches Hosea: Eine redaktionsgeschichtliche Untersuchung* (BZAW 349; Berlin: W. de Gruyter, 2007), 178–82.

4. Genesis 14* and the Composition History of the Abraham Narratives

4.1 Introduction

In this chapter I will discuss the literary growth leading up to the Abraham composition that is found in the received book of Genesis. In particular, I will discuss at what stage Genesis 14* became part of the Abraham narratives in Genesis.

The question of the place of Genesis 14, in particular, in the composition about Abraham has been touched upon in earlier contributions to the history of composition of Genesis—however, with a varying degree of argumentation offered. For instance, without further ado, Reinhard G. Kratz simply characterizes Genesis 14 a 'midrash-like addition.'[1] He does not pay attention to the question of *when* it was added, neither in terms of relative or absolute chronology.

Moreover, Claus Westermann brackets Genesis 14 as the latest insertion to Genesis 12–25.[2] In his view, it is the work of 'a scribe's desk from the late postexilic period.'[3] According to Westermann, the scribe used three different types of earlier material. The three constituent parts, he argues, stem from the period of the judges (vv. 12–17, 21–24), the time of David (vv. 18–20), and the Assyrian-Babylonian period (vv. 1–11).

Finally, it should be noted that Erhard Blum excludes Genesis 14 from the model of the history of the composition of the patriarchal stories that he develops. In a two-page footnote he offers two explicit reasons why. First, none of the lines and connections that he finds in the Abraham composition and reworkings of it lead, in his opinion, to Genesis 14. Second, Blum considers the results of previous research on the transmission history to be hypothetical. (I agree with Blum at this point. However, I do not see its argumentative value for excluding Genesis 14 from the history of composition.) Despite these two reasons, Blum, nonetheless, argues that the Melchizedek episode is a secondary insertion

---

1   Kratz, *Composition*, 273–74.
2   Westermann, *Genesis 12–36*, 128.
3   Westermann, *Genesis 12–36*, 192–93.

into the chapter. Moreover, he *de facto* includes Genesis 14 in the history of composition: in his estimation, Genesis 14—at least in its present form—seems to have been created (German: *gestaltet*) with regard to its present position between Genesis 13 and Genesis 15.[4]

The section attributed to Abraham in the patriarchal narratives in the book of Genesis embraces, roughly speaking, Genesis 12–25. In contrast to the Jacob section and, in particular, the Joseph novella, the Abraham section is characterized by its many more or less independent, apparently episodic, events.[5] Although it could be argued that the promises of land and offspring bind the episodes together and that they drive the course of events, most of the episodes in the Abraham narratives appear as self-contained stories. Nevertheless, despite this, the Abraham stories are after all part of a larger composition.[6]

---

4   Blum, *Die Komposition der Vätergeschichte*, 462–64 n. 5.
5   See, e.g., Alexander Rofé, *Introduction to the Composition of the Pentateuch* (Biblical Seminar 58; Sheffield: Sheffield Academic Press, 1999), 90.
6   With regard to the premise that the Abraham narratives appear as a chain of episodic events, counter voices have been raised advocating a more intricate compositional structure. A good representative of this is Gary Rendsburg, *The Redaction of Genesis* (Winona Lake, IN: Eisenbrauns, 1986), 27–52 (for a critical review, see Anthony Abela, 'The Genesis Genesis', *Melita Theologica* 39 [1988]: 155–85).
      Building upon Cassuto, Rendburg argues that the so-called Abraham cycle consists of ten 'trials or ordeals which Abraham undergoes.' The first five trials (labelled A, B, C, D, E), he argues, relate concentrically to the last five (correspondingly labelled E', D', C', B', A'), thus forming a chiasm. The chiastic parallelism between each of the first five trials and their alleged respective counterparts in the five last trials is expressed by means of so-called theme words. In addition, each one of the trials A, B, C, etc. is connected to the neighbouring trial by means of catchwords (A with B, B with C, etc.). Moreover, according to Rendsburg's chiastic model, the Abraham cycle 'pivots' around Gen. 17:1–5. Two controls, he argues, confirm the fact that these verses actually represent the focal point of the chiastic parallelism: the use of the divine name 'Elohim' and the 'new' name 'Abraham' (not 'Abram'). In the Abraham cycle, the use of 'Elohim' is used for the first time in Genesis 17 and thereafter. Moreover, whereas the patriarch is called 'Abram' in the first five trials in Genesis 12–16, he is likewise called 'Abraham' from Genesis 17 and thereafter.
      According to Rendsburg's model, Genesis 14 represents Abram's fourth trial (labelled D and summarized 'Abram comes to the rescue of Sodom and Lot'). The corresponding trial at the other side of the assumed focal point is then Gen. 18:16–19:38 (labelled D' and summarized 'Abraham comes to the rescue of Sodom and Lot').
      In Rendsburg's view, the preponderance of correspondences in terms of so-called theme words between the alleged corresponding trials, *and* the many catchwords that bind together neighbouring units all in all leave an impression of a conscious redactional structuring of the Abraham cycle. Moreover, he concludes that this redactional structuring undermines the relevance of the use of the divine name Elohim and/or Yahweh for Pentateuchal source criticism. For source criticism, the different theophores in the Abraham cycle is a sign of lack of unity. However, in Rendsburg's eyes,

In the following, I will discuss the compositional context of Genesis 14*. In particular, I will concentrate on the text block Genesis 14–17, which I, like many others, argue is interrupting a more original connection between Genesis 13 and Genesis 18.[7] After having proposed a model of the literary growth of the block Genesis 14–17 where the Priestly material function as a fix point, I will conclude that Genesis 14* must represent the latest addition to the block that interrupts the connection between Genesis 13 and Genesis 18.

4.2 Fractures in the Proximate Compositional Context of Genesis 14*

There are several indications to suggest that Genesis 14–17 represents a text block that interrupts an original and immediate narrative transition from Genesis 13 to Genesis 18. I will argue that the text block made up of Genesis 14–17 in the received text has been secondarily inserted into an earlier narrative about Abraham and Lot.

The first indication supporting this theory is the recognition of a potential continuation between Genesis 13 and Genesis 18. To put it differently, Gen. 18:1 appears to continue where Gen. 13:18 ends:

> Gen. 13:18: And Abram moved his tent, and came and settled by the oaks of Mamre, which are at Hebron, and there he built an altar to Yahweh.

> Gen. 18:1: And Yahweh appeared to him[8] by the oaks of Mamre while he was sitting at the entrance of the tent in the heat of the day.

---

it—together with the shift from Abram to Abraham—is an indication of a redactional structure.

    However, if one proceeds from the premise that Rendsburg actually is correct when arguing for a redactional structuring of the Abraham narratives that has resulted in a large-scale chiastic parallelism, such a structure principally does not exclude the possibility for diachronic growth in the Abraham narratives. Rendsburg himself concludes that '[t]he presence of these devices in the narrative betokens a well-conceived blueprint expertly executed by the individual responsible for bringing together the various traditions surrounding Israel's first patriarch' (p. 52). However, an easier explanation is that a redactor—probably the last one in a succession of many—modified and perhaps even expanded *an already existing composition*. A chiastic structure might already have been present in the redactor's *Vorlage* This structure, then, he developed further.

7   As for the view that Genesis 13 was followed by Genesis 18, see, e.g., Westermann, *Genesis 12–36*, 125–30; Kratz, *Composition*, 271–74; and Blum, who states that Genesis 13, 18–19 constitute the 'compositional nucleus' of the Abraham stories; see Blum, *Die Komposition der Vätergeschichte*, 273.

8   Many modern translations slur over the fact that the Hebrew text has a third person pronominal suffix (וַיֵּרָא אֵלָיו יְהוָה) by instead offering the personal name 'Abraham'.

Abram's itinerary in Genesis 13 ends בְּאֵלֹנֵי מַמְרֵא, 'by the oaks of Mamre', which in addition is identified with Hebron. This place is identical with the place in Genesis 18 where Yahweh appears to Abraham/the three men who visit him.

One has to support the argument made from potential continuity by additional arguments.[9] An additional argument is connected to the already mentioned name 'Mamre'. In both Gen. 13:18 and 18:1, 'Mamre' is most probably a place name. However, this particular noun also occurs twice in the text block Genesis 14–17, which interrupts a presumptively more original Abraham–Lot narrative. In these two cases, namely, in Gen. 14:13 and 14:24, 'Mamre' is the name of a person—an Amorite allied with Abraham. This difference in the use of the name suggests a different provenance for Genesis 14* than for the assumed more original Abraham–Lot narrative.[10]

A second indication in support of an original connection between Gen. 13:18 and 18:1 is provided by the word pair 'to tent'/'a tent'. In 13:18, Abram is reported to be 'tenting' (וַיֶּאֱהַל). Moreover, in 18:1 he is sitting at the entrance of 'the tent' (הָאֹהֶל). Nowhere in between these two verses do we find these words. On the contrary, Abram's situation described in Gen. 13:18 as having moved his tent and settled seems to find its natural continuation in the clause . . . וְהוּא יֹשֵׁב פֶּתַח־הָאֹהֶל, 'while he was sitting at the entrance of the tent [. . .]' in Gen. 18:1bβ.

A third indication in support of the view that Genesis 14–17 has been secondarily inserted into an earlier Abraham–Lot narrative is related to the protagonists in the narratives. In Genesis 13, the story revolves around the separation between Lot and Abram; the former chooses the well-watered plain of Jordan (Gen. 13:11) while Abram settles in Canaan (Gen. 13:12). Both Lot and Abram are active characters in the narrative. Lot does not appear again as an active agent until *after* the closure of the assumed secondary block Genesis 14–17. Whereas Abraham, as already mentioned, was sitting at the entrance of the tent in Gen. 18:1aβ (וְהוּא יֹשֵׁב פֶּתַח־הָאֹהֶל כְּחֹם הַיּוֹם), Lot is reported to be sitting in the gateway of Sodom in Gen. 19:1aβ (וְלוֹט יֹשֵׁב בְּשַׁעַר־סְדֹם). Therefore, in Genesis 19, Lot appears as an active and speaking character who follows his own agenda, just as he did in Genesis 13. In contrast, in Genesis 14–17 Lot

---

9   See David M. Carr, *Reading the Fractures of Genesis: Historical and Literary Approaches* (Louisville, KY: Westminster John Knox, 1998), 32–33.

10   A comparable case where the same name shifts between functioning as a place name and as a personal name is found in the transition in Gen. 11:27–32 from the primeval history to the patriarchal history in connection with the name Haran. Most commentators argue that this transition text is of a composite nature, partly on the basis of this shift of semantic value.

does not appear as an active character in any of the narratives. Although he is mentioned twice in Genesis 14*, he appears only as a passive character, as one who plays the role of an extra. He does not act on his own, but is only the subject of other people's actions (see v. 12: Chedorlaomer and his allies; and v. 16: Abram).

Summing up the argument so far, we are on solid ground in concluding that the texts in the block Genesis 14–17 cuts off an immediate and more original narrative connection between Genesis 13 and 18. In the following, I will focus on the literary, diachronic stratification within these four chapters.

4.3 The Literary Growth of the Text Block Genesis 14–17

4.3.1 Doublets and Contradictions

Having argued that Genesis 14–17 is a block that breaks off an original narrative that continues from Genesis 13 to Genesis 18, I do not, however, imply that all the texts in these four chapters come from the same hand. On the contrary, I will argue that it is to a certain degree possible to trace the growth of the composition within this block.

What has been said above about the Abraham narratives in general, namely, that they appear episodic, does, of course, also apply to the block Genesis 14–17. Yet, there are some particular features that strongly suggest a different provenance for the various texts in this block. Among the most striking features is the double covenant ritual, first the one in Genesis 15, and then a second one in Genesis 17. As for the first covenant text, Gen. 15:18 says that Yahweh made a covenant with Abram on that day, promising to give the land to his descendants. In the second covenant text in Genesis 17, El Shadday makes a covenant again, now with Abram and his descendants after him throughout generations (see 17:9, 13).

Moreover, in Genesis 16, we can observe a contradiction as to the person who names Ishmael. According to Gen. 16:11bα, 'you shall call [וְקָרָאת, spoken to Hagar] him Ishmael', the name giver was Hagar. However, according to Gen. 16:15b, it was Abram: 'And Abram named his son, whom Hagar bore, Ishmael.'

Further, the oracle spoken to Abram in Gen. 15.(12) 13–16 appears secondary. This is likely for two reasons. First, the double time designation (see v. 12, 'And the sun was about to set . . .' and v. 17, 'And the sun had set . . .') signals that the text in between has been secondarily added. By means of this device, called resumptive repetition or *epanalepsis*, the editor who inserted vv. (12) 13–16 into an already existing text signals that he returns to the flow of the narrative.[11] Second, whereas Gen. 15:12 tells that a deep sleep fell on Abram, the scenery in Gen. 15:17 seems to be identical to that in Gen. 15:7–11. Nowhere in Gen. 15:17–21, or the subsequent narrative, is there any talk of him waking up again from the deep sleep that fell on him according to Gen. 15:12.

In summary, although the block Genesis 14–17 interrupts an original connection between Genesis 13 and Genesis 18 (that is, an earlier Abraham–Lot composition), this interruption is nonetheless the result of a diachronic process in which several authors have been involved.

4.3.2 Identifying and Subtracting the Priestly Material

When attempting to outline the diachronic growth of the Pentateuch and, in particular, the book of Genesis, David M. Carr and, more recently, Reinhard G. Kratz, have made convincing pleas for the literary-critical method of subtraction. This method presupposes that at least two things are already known: first, the final text, which of course is the result of the growth of the composition, and second, that at least one of the textual components of which the final text is composed is known.

Now, as to the final result, the received Abraham composition in Genesis is evident. All known textual witnesses testify with one voice that the composition evident in the MT is not challenged by competing compositions with regard to length, order of texts, etc., in any of the different ancient witnesses to the biblical text. Therefore, we may infer that the received Abraham composition was authorized earlier than,

---

11　For another case of resumptive repetition, see Exodus 6. In Exod. 6:12 Moses is quoted saying,

הֵן בְּנֵי־יִשְׂרָאֵל לֹא־שָׁמְעוּ אֵלַי וְאֵיךְ יִשְׁמָעֵנִי פַרְעֹה וַאֲנִי עֲרַל שְׂפָתָיִם

See! The sons of Israel do not listen to me; how then shall Pharaoh listen to me, who am of uncircumcised lips?

Moreover, in Exod. 6:30 the clause reappears, but in reverse order:

הֵן אֲנִי עֲרַל שְׂפָתַיִם וְאֵיךְ יִשְׁמַע אֵלַי פַּרְעֹה

See! I am of uncircumcised lips, how then shall Pharaoh listen to me?

In between these two verses the received biblical text presents a genealogy of Moses and Aaron. The fact that this genealogy has another *form* than the surrounding narrative and *also* the resumptive repetition of Exod. 6:12 found in Exod. 6:30, i.e., *after the end of the genealogy*, all suggest that the genealogy has been secondarily inserted. See Richard Friedman and Shawna Overton, 'Pentateuch', in *EncJud* 15:730–53 (741).

for example, compositions belonging to that part of the Hebrew Bible subsumed under the heading the Prophets.

The reason for this latter inference is evident when we compare the MT and the LXX. Whereas both textual witnesses agree about both the extent of and the order of the narratives in the Abraham composition in the book of Genesis, they differ when it comes to those texts that in the MT are counted among the Prophets. For instance, in the case of the book of Jeremiah, the textual evidence proof that there are two literary strata: one (according to Emanuel Tov, *later*) reflected in the MT and also the Targums, the Peshitta and the Vulgate, and another (Tov: *earlier*) reflected in the LXX and more recently in the Qumran discoveries. These two textual traditions differ both in terms of length (the LXX is nearly 20% shorter than the rest) and the order of the text.[12]

Moreover, as to the second point, namely, that one in advance has to know at least one of the components of which the final text is composed, there is today a high degree of consensus among biblical scholars concerning the Priestly material. Most assume that there is a distinction between Priestly and non-Priestly material. Further, there is likewise a consensus about the demarcation of this Priestly material within the Pentateuch.[13] Therefore, in order to describe the literary growth of the block Genesis 14–17, the best method will be to start with an identification and subsequent subtraction of the Priestly material.

The identification of the Priestly material is not, as mentioned, problematic. In the ancestral history (Genesis 12–50), the backbone of the Priestly source is made up of promise texts: Genesis 17; 26:34–35; 27:46–28:9; 35:9–15; and 48:3–6. These texts have close links to one another. Not only are they promises; in addition, they all use the divine name אֵל שַׁדַּי (except Gen. 26:34–35), the name by which Yahweh made himself known before eventually revealing the four-letter name to Moses (see Exod. 6:3).

Because the block Genesis 14–17 is in focus here, Genesis 17 is, of course, particularly interesting. The chapter prescribes circumcision as a sign of the covenant (אוֹת בְּרִית) between God and Abraham and his descendants. The phrase אוֹת בְּרִית in Gen. 17:11 recalls the previous sign of a covenant that God made, namely, the one between himself and Noah, his descendants, and every living creature in Gen. 9:1–17. The

---

12   See Tov, *Textual Criticism of the Hebrew Bible*, 313–50, for more details on Jeremiah and for further examples of how different readings among textual witnesses may be explained by means of literary criticism rather than by textual criticism.

13   The disagreement is more about where to locate the end of the Priestly material: within the Pentateuch, beyond it in the book of Joshua or even further? For a large-scale application of using the Priestly writing as a certain basis for unfolding the compositional history of the Pentateuch, see Kratz, *Composition*, in particular, pp. 3–4.

story about God's revelation of the commandments of the postdiluvian world to Noah and the covenant making with him in Genesis 9 is likewise Priestly. In addition, Genesis 9 echoes the first creation account in Gen. 1:1–2:3, which—needless to say—is Priestly.

Therefore, we can identify Genesis 17 as a Priestly part of the block Genesis 14–17 because of the use of the divine name El Shadday and because of its 'Priestly' concern with laws (in this case circumcision). In addition, the Priestly interest in the exact chronological framework of the patriarchal narratives is evident both in Genesis 17 and beyond. According to Gen. 17:1, 24–25, the covenant was made when Abram was ninety-nine years old; his son Ishmael was thirteen when he was circumcised. However, chronological notes of this kind are also found in the previous chapter Genesis 16 about the birth of Ishmael. The final verse Gen. 16:16 seems Priestly, indeed: 'Abram was eighty-six when Hagar bore Abram Ishmael.' Moreover, the preceding verse Gen. 16:15 does not appear to be integrated in the narrative, as well. The information that Abram gave the name Ishmael to the son whom Hagar bore for him contradicts Gen. 16:11. We can therefore infer that this verse represents the Priestly summary of the non-P story about the birth of Ishmael.[14] Further, the chronological note in Gen. 16:3 ('after Abram had lived in the land of Canaan ten years') should be reckoned as Priestly. All in all, this and all the other chronological notes form a coherent timeline along which, among other things, the events in Abram's/Abraham's life were placed: Abram was seventy-five years old when he went out of Haran (Gen. 12:4) and, after having lived ten years in Canaan (Gen. 16:3), he got Ishmael at the age of eighty-six[15] (Gen. 16:16). At the age of ninety-nine, Yahweh/God appeared to him (Gen. 17:1); Ishmael was thirteen years old the same day (Gen. 17:25).

One should probably also add Gen. 16:1a to P: 'And Sarai, Abram's wife, bore him no [children].' This clause might pick up the information given in Gen. 11:30 ('Now Sarai was barren. She had no child') which is part of the genealogy in 11:28–30. Westermann takes the latter genealogy

---

14   Admittedly, it could be argued that since Genesis 16 does not have any report about the actual birth of Ishmael except the note in Gen. 16:15, then this particular verse is an integral part of the narrative. However, it still remains that there is a contradiction between verses 11 and 16. One explanation is that no report about Hagar's giving birth to Ishmael is necessary, since it is a promise text and an aetiology. It could also be considered whether the Priestly editor who combined the P and non-P replaced the non-P account of Hagar's giving birth to Ishmael by the P version in Gen. 16:15.

15   The number 86 (and not 85 as one could expect) comes as a result of so-called inclusive reckoning; cf. the NT: Jesus was crucified on Good Friday and resurrected on the *third* day, that is, the first day of the week, Sunday.

to be Yahwistic and thus in his view pre-Priestly.[16] However, Kratz argues that Gen. 11:28–20 represents a post-Priestly addition to P.[17]

4.3.3 Material Dependent on the Priestly Material

Having identified the Priestly material in the block Genesis 14–17 — but before I continue discussing the pre-Priestly material in the block — I first have to discuss whether there are any insertions that clearly are dependent on the Priestly material. In other words, I have to focus on potential post-Priestly material. Now, the Priestly chronological notes are not alluded to anywhere in the narratives themselves except in Gen. 17:17 in a narrative that is Priestly at the outset. Therefore, it appears that no post-Priestly author has used the Priestly chronology. Moreover, neither are there any allusions to the (Priestly) concern with circumcision evident in the Priestly covenant text Genesis 17. In the context of Genesis 14–17, the only text that one may consider potentially dependent on Genesis 17 is the covenant text in Genesis 15, especially the last part in Gen. 15:7–21. Given that these two covenant texts actually are doublets, then the questions arise: Does one of them depend on the other, and moreover, which one is the source and consequently the earlier version, and which one is the dependent and later text?

These questions have been previously discussed. Here, I will attempt to render and evaluate two recent discussions that have come to different conclusions with regard to the question of the relation between Genesis 15 and 17: those of David M. Carr[18] and Christoph Levin.[19]

David M. Carr has argued that the Priestly author of Genesis 17 presupposes Genesis 15. According to his model of the growth of the Abraham composition, Genesis 15 is a later addition to what he refers to as the non-P, promise-centred Genesis composition. Carr temporarily situates the revision process that Genesis 15 was part of between the earliest composition of non-P Genesis in the late preexilic or the early exilic period on the one side and early postexilic Priestly writing counter to that tradition on the other. In other words, Carr argues that Genesis 15 was added in the exilic or early postexilic period. The period of the revision of which he argues Genesis 15 was a part is concurrent with the period in

---

16   Westermann, *Genesis 12–36*, 123–30.

17   Kratz, *Composition*, 238, 259, 262, 272.

18   David M. Carr, *Reading the Fractures of Genesis: Historical and Literary Approaches* (Louisville, KY: Westminster John Knox, 1998).

19   Christoph Levin, 'Jahwe und Abraham im Dialog: Genesis 15', in *Gott und Mensch im Dialog: Festschrift für Otto Kaiser zum 80. Geburtstag* (ed. Markus Witte; BZAW 345; Berlin: W. de Gruyter, 2004), 237–57.

which the Deuteronomistic history was retouched in a way that it came to include more references to the patriarchs.[20] Consequently, Carr conceives of Genesis 15 as part of what he calls the 'semi-Deuteronomistic revisions of both the Pentateuch and the Deuteronomistic history'.[21]

However, Christoph Levin has argued for another model for the relation between Genesis 15 and Genesis 17. In his view, Genesis 15 is a post-Priestly, redactional text composed for a context that originally consisted of Genesis 13 and 16 (and not yet Genesis 14). The two dialogues that Genesis 15 comprises (vv. 1–6* and vv. 7–21*) do not stem from the same hand. In his estimation, the latter dialogue is composed as a supplement to the former. However, he still argues that both show borrowings from Priestly writing (in addition to borrowings and echoes from the Deuteronomistic literature and the book of Ezekiel respectively).[22]

Levin's conclusion that Genesis 15 is post-Priestly (i.e., later than Genesis 17)[23] comes as the result of a rather complex chain of arguments. Decisive is his assumption that the opening verse in Genesis 15, especially the talk about a 'very great reward' (שְׂכָרְךָ הַרְבֵּה מְאֹד), connects with Genesis 13, a chapter that for its part has experienced growth over time.[24] To be more precise, Genesis 15 and, in particular, the talk about a 'very great reward' (see Gen. 15:1) responds to Yahweh's promise of land in Gen. 13:14–15a:

> And Yahweh said to Abram, after Lot had separated from him,
>
> 'Raise your eyes and look from the place where you are, northward and southward and eastward and westward! [15] For all the land that you see I will give to you. . .'.

In order to establish a relative date of composition for this promise, Levin stresses the statement of location that occurs three times: in Gen. 12:8; Gen. 13:3; and Gen. 13:14.

Abram's raising of his eyes in the promise text in Gen. 13:14–15 takes place 'from the place where you are' (מִן־הַמָּקוֹם אֲשֶׁר־אַתָּה שָׁם, Gen. 13:14aβ). However, this statement does not specify the place and must therefore refer back to the place described explicitly in Gen. 13:3: 'the place where

---

20 Carr, *Reading the Fractures of Genesis*, 173–74.

21 Carr, *Reading the Fractures of Genesis*, 173.

22 Levin, 'Jahwe und Abraham im Dialog: Genesis 15', 237–57 (256). Moreover, among others, Jan Christian Gertz argues that Genesis 15 is a postpriestly text; see Gertz, 'Abraham, Mose und der Exodus: Beobachtungen zur Redaktionsgeschichte von Gen 15', in *Abschied vom Jahwisten: Die Komposition des Hexateuch in der jüngsten Diskussion* (ed. Jan Christian Gertz, Konrad Schmid, and Markus Witte; BZAW 315; Berlin: W. de Gruyter, 2002), 63–81.

23 Levin, 'Jahwe und Abraham im Dialog', 237–57 (241).

24 In other words, the talk about a 'very great reward' in Gen. 15:1 does not refer to Abram's rejection of the offer of the king of Sodom in Gen. 14:21–24 but comes as a response to Yahweh's promise in Genesis 13.

his tent had been from the beginning, between Bethel and Ai'. Moreover, this statement of place explicitly refers farther back, namely, to the place where Abram pitched his tent earlier (Gen. 12:8a.bβ: 'And he moved from there to the mountain on the east of Bethel and pitched his tent, with Bethel on the west and Ai on the east . . .').

Referring to Wellhausen, Levin argues that Abram's return in Gen. 13:3 to this particular place where he already was in Gen. 12:8 would not have been necessary if the story about the endangerment of the ancestress in Egypt (Gen. 12:10–20) had been an original part of the composition.[25] On the contrary, he argues that this story about the ancestor and ancestress in Egypt is a secondary excursus. The story in Gen. 12:10–20 is an excursus in which Abram and Sarah's wandering into and out of Egypt functions as a typological anticipation of the Israelites' wandering into and out of Egypt (as told in the Joseph story and Exodus).

Now, Levin explicitly identifies Exod. 11:1–3 as part of the *Vorlage* on the basis of which the author of the endangerment of the ancestress story (Gen. 12:10–20) composed his text. In this *Vorlage*—and this is what is relevant for the dating of Genesis 15—both Priestly and non-Priestly narrative threads have been combined. On this basis, it follows that the story about Abram and Sarah in Egypt in Gen. 12:10–20 must be post-Priestly. Therefore, the resumptions of the place where Abram is dwelling that are evident in both Gen. 13:3 and Gen. 13:14–15a must also be later than the Priestly writing.[26] Now, as I initially mentioned, Genesis 15 probably responds to the promise text at the closure of Genesis 13. From this, one can infer that Genesis 15 must also be later than the Priestly material, as is also its catalyst, the promise text in Genesis 13.

It should be pointed out that Levin reckons with a growth within the Priestly material. As for the Priestly covenant text in Genesis 17, in his view only a part of it belongs to the Priestly *Grundschrift*, which he designates P^G.[27]

Despite its complexity, I find Levin's model for the relationship between Genesis 15 and 17 (Genesis 15 being post-Priestly and thus later than and dependent on Genesis 17) more convincing than Carr's model (Genesis 15 being pre-Priestly and thus earlier than Genesis 17).

To conclude, then, by subscribing to Levin's conclusion, I have at the same time argued that Genesis 15 represents material in the textual block Genesis 14–17 that is dependent on the Priestly material (above all, Genesis 17).

---

25   See Wellhausen, *Composition*, 23.
26   Levin, 'Jahwe und Abraham im Dialog', 237–57 (240–41).
27   See Levin, 'Jahwe und Abraham im Dialog', 237–57 (241 n. 18).

4.3.4 Pre-Priestly Material in the Block Genesis 14–17
on Which the Priestly Material Is Dependent

Having identified the Priestly material (4.3.2, Identifying and Subtracting the Priestly Material) dependent on the Priestly material (4.3.3, Material Dependent on the Priestly Material), I will follow up by discussing the pre-Priestly material on which the Priestly material appears to be dependent.

It is evident from the Priestly covenant text in Genesis 17 that its Priestly author was familiar with a tradition about Ishmael as Abraham's son (see Gen. 17:18, 20, 23, 25–26). Although Hagar is not mentioned by name in Genesis 17, it is nonetheless evident that the Priestly author did not conceive of Abraham's wife Sarah as Ishmael's mother. The Priestly notes in Gen. 16:1a, 3, 15–16 support this.[28]

Therefore, we may infer that the Priestly author knew the story about the birth of Ishmael in Genesis 16* (i.e., the core of the narrative without the Priestly additions). Consequently, we can identify the Ishmael–Hagar story in Genesis 16* as part of the pre-Priestly material on which the Priestly material is dependent.

4.3.5 The Growth of the Block Genesis 14–17:
A Preliminary Synthesis

So far, I have not discussed when the narrative about Abram's war with the eastern kings in Genesis 14* was positioned between the earlier Abraham–Lot composition, which is characterized by an immediate connection between Genesis 13 and Genesis 18. Summarizing the results thus far regarding the growth of the block Genesis 14–17, it is possible to identify the Priestly material within Genesis 14–17. The Priestly material

---

28   The Priestly version of the birth of Ishmael in Genesis 16 is as follows:

[16:1a] וְשָׂרַי אֵשֶׁת אַבְרָם לֹא יָלְדָה לוֹ

[16:3] וַתִּקַּח שָׂרַי אֵשֶׁת־אַבְרָם אֶת־הָגָר הַמִּצְרִית שִׁפְחָתָהּ מִקֵּץ עֶשֶׂר שָׁנִים לְשֶׁבֶת אַבְרָם בְּאֶרֶץ כְּנָעַן וַתִּתֵּן אֹתָהּ לְאַבְרָם אִישָׁהּ לוֹ לְאִשָּׁה

[16:15] וַתֵּלֶד הָגָר לְאַבְרָם בֵּן וַיִּקְרָא אַבְרָם שֶׁם־בְּנוֹ אֲשֶׁר־יָלְדָה הָגָר יִשְׁמָעֵאל

[16:16] וְאַבְרָם בֶּן־שְׁמֹנִים שָׁנָה וְשֵׁשׁ שָׁנִים בְּלֶדֶת־הָגָר אֶת־יִשְׁמָעֵאל לְאַבְרָם

[16:1a] And Sarai, Abram's wife, did not bear him [a child]. [16:3] And Sarai, Abram's wife, took Hagar the Egyptian, her maidservant, after Abram had lived in the land of Canaan ten years, and she gave her to Abram, her husband, for him as wife. [16:15] And Hagar bore for Abram a son, and Abram gave his son that Hagar bore him the name Ishmael. [16:16] And Abram was 86 years when Hagar bore Ishamel for Abram.

comprises Gen. 16:1a, 3, 15–16; and 17:1–27. Moreover, the Priestly material is dependent on a narrative about Hagar and the birth of Ishmael.
We can infer, then, that the Priestly author knew Genesis 16*. Finally, I
have concluded that Genesis 15 is post-Priestly; it is a text that continues
and responds to Genesis 13, especially 13:14–15a.

According to the previous discussion, it was Genesis 16* that first
broke off the original and immediate connection between Gen. 13:18 and
Gen. 18:1*. It is impossible to know for sure the intention of the interpolator in adding the Hagar–Ishmael narrative. However, we see that the
theme 'birth of a son' is present in both the promise of land and descendants in Genesis 13 (cf. vv. 15–16) and in Genesis 16*. It is suggested that
the intention is connected to that.

Moreover, the particular version of Genesis 16* that first discon-
nected Gen. 13:18 from Gen. 18:1 must have had another and more
original opening than now. For, given that 16:1a, 'And Sarah, Abram's
wife bore him no children', is a Priestly note (see 4.3.2, Identifying and
Subtracting the Priestly Material), then the narrative lacks an introduction of Sarai. Genesis 16:1b reads וְלָהּ שִׁפְחָה מִצְרִית וּשְׁמָהּ הָגָר, 'And she had an
Egyptian maidservant and her name was Hagar'. This cannot have been
the original opening because it presupposes an identification of the third
person feminine singular pronominal suffix –āh with Sarai.

Subsequently, the Priestly material was added, namely, the brief P
version of the Hagar–Ishmael story (Gen. 16:1a, 3, 15–16) and Genesis 17,
which includes a promise of a son by Sarah. Genesis 17 was the Priestly
author's response to the previous promises of a son for Abraham at the
same time as it was a corrective vis-à-vis the story about the birth of
Ishmael in Genesis 16*. Here, as elsewhere in the Pentateuch, the Priestly
material forms a consecutive narrative. In general, although the Priestly
material is dependent on its non-Priestly *Vorlage*, it still forms a consecutive, complete narrative thread.[29] This is, of course, also the case with the
Priestly material in the text block Genesis 14–17.[30]

Later on, after the Priestly material had been added to Genesis 16*,
the post-Priestly covenant text in Genesis 15 was added to the block (see
4.3.3, Material Dependent on the Priestly Material).

However, one question has still not been dealt with: At what stage in
the growth of the text block interrupting Genesis 13 and Genesis 18 did
Genesis 14* enter the scene? I believe the answer is found when one has

---

29   See Kratz, *Composition*, 244.
30   See note 28 above.

scrutinized even more thoroughly a question already touched upon:[31] Did Genesis 15 originally continue Genesis 14* or Genesis 13?

4.3.6 Did Genesis 15 Originally Continue Genesis 13 or Genesis 14?

In scholarly literature, one will occasionally find statements suggesting that Genesis 14 finds its continuation in Genesis 15. To be more precise, it is argued that Genesis 15 presupposes Genesis 14. A logical consequence of this assumption is that either Genesis 14 and Genesis 15 was inserted into the patriarchal narratives at the same time or that Genesis 15 was composed later than Genesis 14.

Several scholars argue that there are many phrases in Genesis 15 alluding to the preceding chapter, Genesis 14.[32] To begin with, Gen. 15:1 opens by reading 'After these things the word of Yahweh came to Abram in a vision' (v. 1a). In the present context, the phrase אַחַר הַדְּבָרִים הָאֵלֶּה— a phrase that occurs with slight variations in Gen. 22:1, 20; 39:1; and 40:1—relates the events that take place in Genesis 15 chronologically after those in Genesis 14. Moreover, interpreters attempt to use the formula of encouragement and the associated reason and assurance in Gen. 15:1b to strengthen the assumption that Genesis 14 also originally preceded Genesis 15: 'Fear not, Abram! I am a shield to you. Your reward shall be very great'. The encouragement formula addressed to Abram is then thought to have its background in his war activity in the previous chapter 14. Moreover, the noun מָגֵן ('shield') is conceived of as an allusion to the verb מִגֵּן ('to deliver'), which Melchizedek uses in his blessing of Abram (Gen. 14:19–20). In addition, the clause that Abram's reward shall be very great (שְׂכָרְךָ הַרְבֵּה מְאֹד) is explained as God's response to Abram's renouncing his legal claim to the goods that the eastern kings had taken as booty from the king of Sodom (see Gen. 14:11, 21–24).

In addition, there have been attempts to identify other allusions in Abram's utterance in Gen. 15:2b. This half verse, which escapes any agreed-upon translation because of its unintelligible and probably corrupt syntax, contains the names Damascus and Eliezer. As for Damascus, the place name also occurs in Gen. 14:15 as a geographical point to

---

31　See Levin's argumentation for Genesis 15 being a post-Priestly text above in 4.3.3, Material Dependent on the Priestly Material.

32　So, e.g., Wenham, *Genesis 1–15*, 387; Carr, *Reading the Fractures of Genesis*, 164; and Schmid, *Erzväter und Exodus*, 176–77. For further references and a critical examination of them, see Levin, 'Jahwe und Abraham im Dialog', 237–57 (in particular, p. 239).

locate Hobah, the place where Abram gave up his pursuit of the eastern
kings. The fact that the place name is found only twice in the Pentateuch,
it is thought, connects these two chapters. Moreover, the name Eliezer
is thought to be somehow related to the number of the men that Abram
mustered according to Gen. 14:14, שְׁמֹנָה עָשָׂר וּשְׁלֹשׁ מֵאוֹת ('three hundred and
eighteen'). This identification relies on an arithmetical hermeneutical
technique, a *gematria* called *mispar hekhrehi* ('absolute value'). Accordingly, when one sums up the numerical value of the consonants in the
name אֱלִיעֶזֶר the result is 318.[33]

However, there are difficulties connected to each of the proposed
allusions in Genesis 15 to Genesis 14. The weakest cases are found in
Gen. 15:2b. The clause [אֱלִיעֶזֶר] הוּא דַּמֶּשֶׂק (whether אֱלִיעֶזֶר belongs to the
clause or not is difficult to say because of the problematic syntax) is probably secondary. This phrase is introduced by the deictic element הוּא. In
addition, the phrase is syntactically awkward in the second half of v. 2.
These circumstances indicate that we may be dealing with an explicative
gloss,[34] a secondary comment that the glossator introduced to clarify
the sense of Gen. 15:2. (However, we as today's readers may very well
question whether it really was a success as long as the received text now
is even more obscure. . . .) Therefore, proceeding from the premise that
the reference to Damascus in Gen. 15:2b is part of a secondary gloss, then
the terminological connection between Genesis 14 and Genesis 15 established by these two chapters' exclusive use of the name 'Damascus' can
be explained as the result of secondary redactional activity.

Moreover, no matter whether the personal name אֱלִיעֶזֶר is part of the
gloss or originally belongs to the text that has been glossed, the possible
connection between 318, the number of Abram's men in Gen. 14:14, on
the one hand, and the name Eliezer in Gen. 15:2, on the other, escapes
any verification. Although *gematria* as such was introduced to the Jews
as early as in the Second Temple period,[35] such a historical observation does not prove that there is an intentional connection between the

---

33   See David Derovan, Gershom Scholem, and Moshe Idel, 'Gematria', in *EncJud* 7:424–
27. See also S. Gevirtz, 'Abram's 318', *IEJ* 19, no. 2 (1969): 110–13; and Tigay, 'An Early
Technique of Aggadic Exegesis', 169–89 (179). According to Tigay, the use of letters of
the alphabet as numeral signs was a relatively late practice among Semites and was
borrowed from the Greeks. He refers to coins from the Hasmonaean period that—if I
read him correctly—are representative of the earliest evidence of the practice among
the Jews. Nevertheless, he also refers to a Phoenician from the fourth century that also
used letters as numeral signs (p. 179 n. 30).
34   See Fishbane, *Biblical Interpretation in Ancient Israel*, 44–46.
35   See note 33 above.

number and the name.[36] Moreover, even if there actually is an intended connection between them, this connection can likewise be secondary. As noted above, the name 'Eliezer' might also be part of the gloss. Consequently, the possible connection established by means of *gematria* can also be explained as the result of secondary redactional activity.

Furthermore, although there is no etymological relationship between the noun מָגֵן ('shield', Gen. 15:1bα) and the verb מִגֵּן (third person singular piel of the verb מגן, 'to deliver', Gen. 14:20aβ) there is definitely both assonance and consonance in the two words.[37] But again, as I and quite a number of other biblical scholars have argued, the part of Genesis 14 in which the verb מִגֵּן occurs is a secondary insertion: The Melchizedek episode in Gen. 14:18–20 is an interpolation dependent on, and consequently later than, its narrative framework in Genesis 14*. Therefore, if the assonance and consonance are intended, the similarity reflects the intention of an editor who wanted to integrate Genesis 14 and 15 closer to each other. The easiest identification of this editor is that he is the author of the Melchizedek episode: When composing and interpolating the Melchizedek episode into Genesis 14*, his version of the patriarchal narratives was a composition in which Genesis 14* was followed by Genesis 15. From the latter chapter he borrowed Yahweh's word of encouragement to Abram (see Gen. 15:1, '. . . Fear not, Abram! I am your shield [מָגֵן]') when composing Melchizedek's blessing of El Elyon (see Gen. 14:20, 'blessed be El Elyon who delivered [מִגֵּן] your enemies into your hand!').

The only two remaining candidates among the possible allusions in Genesis 15 to the preceding chapter 14 are the formula of encouragement, 'Fear not, Abram!', and the assurance, 'Your reward shall be very great', both found in Gen. 15:1b. However, it is unlikely that the rationale for the encouragement 'Fear not' can be found in Genesis 14. After all, the encouragement comes *after* Abram's hostilities with Chedorlaomer and his allies have ceased (see 14:15–16). Why should Abram be encouraged shortly after having won a military victory over a coalition of four kings? On the contrary, the context of Yahweh's encouragement of Abram is a different one.

---

36 Moreover, even if there should be an intended connection, this could be secondary; as noted above, the name Eliezer might be part of the gloss so that it represents a secondary attempt to connect the two neighbouring chapters.

37 Admittedly, there is a possibility that the vocalization of these two words was different in the Second Temple period, that is, when the Melchizedek episode was composed and interpolated into Genesis 14*. Consequently, the *assonance* can possibly be the result of a causal phonetic development. Nevertheless, the consonants in both words must have been constant so that the *consonance* has been present from the outset, i.e., the moment the Melchizedek episode was inserted into Genesis 14*.

The clause 'Your rewards shall be very great' does not allude to Abram's renouncement in Gen. 14:21–24 of the king of Sodom's offer. On the contrary, in the context of the dialogue between Yahweh and Abram in Genesis 15, the phrase 'your reward' (שְׂכָרְךָ) gives Abram reason to call attention to two facts: first, that he is childless (Gen. 15:2a) and, second, that Yahweh has not given him any offspring so that a slave will be his heir (Gen. 15:3: 'And Abram said: "Since you have given me no offspring, one borne in my household will be my heir"'). Moreover, Abram's words in Gen. 15:3 (הֵן לִי לֹא נָתַתָּה זָרַע) appear as a bold reversal of Yahweh's promise in Gen. 13:15 ('For everything that you see I will give to you and your descendants [לְךָ אֶתְּנֶנָּה וּלְזַרְעֲךָ] for ever').[38]

Furthermore, we can observe an escalation from the dust of the earth to the stars above in Yahweh's promise in Genesis 15 vis-à-vis the one in Genesis 13. First, in Gen. 13:16 Yahweh promises that he will make Abram's offspring 'like the dust of the earth' and continues, 'If a man is able to number [אִם־יוּכַל אִישׁ לִמְנוֹת] the dust of the earth, then your offspring too can be numbered'. However, in Gen. 15:5 he brings Abram 'outside' and says: 'Look toward heaven and count the stars, if you are able to count them [אִם־תּוּכַל לִסְפֹּר]'.

Therefore, in light of the discussion above, I conclude that none of the alleged allusions in Genesis 15 to Genesis 14 can support the proposal that Genesis 15 continued Genesis 14 from the outset. On the contrary, a more likely conclusion is that Genesis 15 initially responded to and continued Genesis 13. Above, I have argued that Genesis 15 is a post-Priestly text. From this we can infer that the placing (and probably also the composition) of Genesis 14* in between Genesis 13 and the post-Priestly covenant text Genesis 15 must have taken place even later: after the composition of Genesis 15. In other words, at the time of the composition of Genesis 15, Genesis 14 was not yet part of the block interrupting the original narrative thread from Genesis 13 to 18.

4.4 Summary and Conclusion

Above, I have attempted to answer the question about when the particular stage Genesis 14* was added to the growing Abraham composition in the book of Genesis. I have proceeded from the premise that Genesis 14–17 interrupts an earlier Abraham–Lot composition (i.e., originally Gen. 18:1

---

38   'Der Wortlaut "du hast mir nicht *gegeben* (לֹא נָתַתָּה)" greift wörtlich auf die vorangegangene Verheißung zurück. Damit sind Anlaß und Stellung von Gen 15 hinreichend erklärt.' Levin, 'Jahwe und Abraham im Dialog', 237–57 (240).

followed immediately after Gen. 13:18). This interrupting block does not stem from one hand. On the contrary, the final result that we know in the received text as Genesis 14–17 is itself the result of a literary growth.

I have attempted to outline the growth of the composition of the block Genesis 14–17 by means of the redaction-critical method of subtraction. In general, in order to subtract, one needs to know at least one of the textual components of which the final text is constructed. In this particular case, the Priestly material has served this purpose. After having identified the Priestly material in the block Genesis 14–17, I have continued by identifying material that is dependent on the Priestly material and material that the Priestly material itself depends on.

Two important conclusions on the way to identify the stage at which Genesis 14* was added to the growing block in between Genesis 13 and Genesis 18 have been, first, that Genesis 15 is post-Priestly and, second, that Genesis 15 from the outset responds to and continues Genesis 13 (and not Genesis 14*!).

Therefore, to conclude, these two insights above allow us to infer that the placing (and, as I will argue more thoroughly below, the very composition) of Genesis 14* between Genesis 13 on the one side and Genesis 15 on the other took place even later, that is, after the composition of Genesis 15. This conclusion excludes the idea expressed by, for example, Gordon J. Wenham, that Genesis 14 is an 'indispensable stepping stone' between Genesis 13 and Genesis 18 and *eo ipso* part of the larger and original "Lot–Abraham cycle."'[39]

Now, having concluded that Genesis 14* represents the latest addition to the text block that secondarily interrupts the more original Abraham–Lot composition, I cannot, however, on the basis of the discussion above conclude that the date of interpolation of Genesis 14* into the book of Genesis is identical with the date of composition of Genesis 14*.

Proceeding from the premise that Genesis 14* is a unified narrative (and not a combination of two traditions of different provenance, as Westermann, Schatz, Emerton, etc. have argued; see 2.2, The Textual Integrity of Genesis 14), then there are three possibilities as to the origin and date of composition of this enigmatic text.

First, there is the possibility that the story about King Chedorlaomer, his allies, and Abram the Hebrew was originally part of another biblical composition and that it subsequently was relocated to the place it has in the present composition. Second, another possibility is that the story had already existed for some time, either orally or in writing (albeit not in any protobiblical composition) before it eventually was incorporated into the

---

39   Wenham, *Genesis 1–15*, 306–7.

Abraham narratives in the book of Genesis. Finally, a third possibility is that the story was composed for its present position in the Abraham narratives. In the case of Genesis 14*, however, both the first and the second possibilities are unlikely.

As to the first, if the story actually initially belonged to another compositional context and then subsequently was relocated, it seems reasonable to assume that a relocation would have left the original compositional context with a gap. However, as far as I can see, no such gaps exist, particularly in the context of the (other) patriarchal narratives in Genesis where one first would have to look for it.

As to the second possibility, in particular, the characteristic features of Genesis 14* necessitate another explanation. Above, in chapter 2, Genesis 14: Characteristics, Textual Integrity, and Textual Criticism: Preliminary Discussion and Hypotheses, I focused (on a preliminary basis) on these features. On the basis of them I argued that Genesis 14* seems to be the product of literary activity and that it appears to presuppose and depend on other, and consequently earlier, biblical traditions. Moreover, below in chapter 6, The Literary Building Blocks of the Author of Genesis 14*, I will attempt to substantiate this thesis even further. Nevertheless, this thesis implies a relatively late date for Genesis 14* and also implies that one has to explain the story's coming into being 'inner-biblically', that is within the paradigm of so-called diachronic, inner-biblical intertextuality.

Therefore, the third possibility is most plausible: Genesis 14* was composed for its present place in the Abraham narratives at the outset.

In the following chapter, I will pursue this approach further. There I will argue that modern as well as ancient readers can/could claim to see a *Leerstelle* between Yahweh's command in Gen. 13:17 and Abram's failure to comply fully with it in Gen. 13:18. I will argue that Genesis 14* was composed to fill out this *Leerstelle*.

5. Why Was Genesis 14* Composed and Inserted into the Abraham Narrative? An Attempt at a Literary Answer

We can approach the question in the heading above in different ways. In particular, two approaches stand out: a historical one and a literal one. As for the former, one can discuss possible historical circumstances that in different ways may have caused the author to compose his text or that at least may have had an impact on the way he composed it. Such historical discussions presuppose that one has established a date of composition for the text in question. Moreover, it presupposes a discussion of several historical questions concerning the (historical) horizon of the author. I will discuss all these questions in a subsequent chapter.[1] In the present chapter, however, I will focus on the literary approach. Now, despite my mentioned distinction between the historical and the literary approach, I am not suggesting that a literary approach to the question of why Genesis 14* was composed is not historical. On the contrary, I do not think that any text is without a historical context, be it the context of its composition, transmission, or reception. Nevertheless, because below I will argue that the composition of Genesis 14* in part can be explained as a response to that which the author of Genesis 14* understood to be a *Leerstelle* in the biblical text, I find this distinction useful and appropriate here.

5.1 Introduction

My thesis about a relatively late date of composition for Genesis 14* is not in itself unique in light of the history of research. On the contrary, it seems to have been accepted wisdom in parts of the scholarly community that the narrative is a very late text, perhaps even the latest in the Pentateuch.[2] Although I also agree with those who date Genesis 14*

---

1   See chapter 7, The Historical Motivation for the Author of Genesis 14* and the Text's Historical Meaning.

2   See note 4 in chap. 1.

late, I nevertheless find the 'received knowledge' regarding the late date of Genesis 14 generally to be poorly argued. For instance, R. G. Kratz calls Genesis 14 a 'late midrash' that, however, can be assumed to rest on an earlier 'special tradition'.[3] Nowhere, however, does he account for these particular characteristics of the text. On the contrary, Kratz is representative of a number of exegetes who share the use of such terms as 'late midrash', etc. to describe Genesis 14, but who do not (or in some cases not thoroughly) account for *why* Genesis 14 was composed and *how* it was done.

At the end of the nineteenth century, Abraham Kuenen[4] argued that the postexilic redactor of the Pentateuch in this chapter offered a postexilic midrash of Abram's life, comparable to those the Chronicler had at his disposal. In the same period, Julius Wellhausen,[5] H. Holzinger[6] and Hermann Gunkel,[7] while opposing suggestions that the chapter was part of either the P, J, or E source, argued that it was the product of postexilic, Jewish *Schriftgelehrtsamkeit* (so Wellhausen [pp. 24, 312], and Holzinger [p. 147]; Gunkel: *gelehrte Dichtung* and *legende aus der Zeit des Judentums*, whose tradition about the four Babylonian kings the author got—directly or indirectly—from Babylon itself; see pp. 288–90). Later, Otto Eißfeldt, assuming that the narrative of Genesis 14 presupposed a complete compilation of L (lay source), J, E, B (*Bundesbuch*), D, H (*Heiligkeitsgesetz*), and P, indicated that a Jew in the late postexilic period had at his disposal a couple of traditions about certain war activities in the distant past and about the pre-Israelite priesthood in Jerusalem. These extra-Pentateuchal traditions he moulded to a narrative glorifying Abraham and the Jerusalemite priesthood, respectively.[8] Even later, Roland de Vaux also eventually characterized Genesis 14 as a midrash.[9]

In recent times, there have been attempts by scholars who date Genesis 14 relatively late to explain *why* and *how* it was composed given its present position in the compositon of the Abraham narrative. Here, I will

---

3   Kratz, *Composition*, 260, 272.
4   Kuenen, *An Historico-Critical Inquiry*, 139, 143 n. 4, 324 n. 12.
5   Wellhausen, *Composition*, 24–25, 311–13.
6   Holzinger, *Genesis*, 146–47.
7   Gunkel, *Genesis*, 288.
8   Eißfeldt, *Einleitung in das Alte Testament*, 281.
9   See Roland de Vaux, 'Les Hurrites de l'Histoire et les Horites de la Bible', 481–503 (503) where he argues that Genesis 14 more of an enigma than a help for the historian. However, earlier in *Die hebräischen Patriarchen und die modernen Entdeckungen* (Düsseldorf: Patmos, 1961), 42, de Vaux argued that Genesis 14 was based on a document or tradition dating back to the time of the patriarchs.

discuss the—to my knowledge—most recent proposals, namely, those put forward by David M. Carr and Benjamin Ziemer.

5.1.1 David M. Carr: Genesis 14 Unfolds the Curse of Canaan and the Blessing on Shem

David M. Carr, who though he does not belong among those who date Genesis 14 very late in the Second Temple period, holds the insertion of Genesis 14–15 to be part of a relatively late, albeit pre-Priestly, revision of the non-Priestly proto-Genesis. In Carr's opinion, the earliest part of Genesis 14 and crucial parts of Genesis 15 predated their use in this part of the Abraham story. Genesis 14 originated in large part from an independent source. As they now stand, the chapters add a new focus to the pre-Priestly proto-Genesis in that they link Abraham with both the primeval history and the story of the exodus and conquest.[10] Carr, following D. Steinmetz, argues that Genesis 14–15 continues themes already seen in Gen. 9:18–27 and 10:16–18a. Carr argues that the curse of Canaan is evident in Genesis 14 where five Canaanite kings are enslaved by certain descendants of Shem, Ham, and Yaphet (Carr puts forward Gen. 10:9 as a cross reference to Gen. 14:1–4) and are defeated when they attempt to rebel (Gen. 14:5–12). At this point Abraham conquers the conquerors, an act that, according to Carr, 'hints at [Abraham's] supremacy over the others who descended from Noah and at his appropriation of the blessing on Shem that was given by Noah'.[11]

However, the continuation of themes from Genesis 9 to the subsequent chapter Genesis 14 is not as evident as Carr would argue. First, it is not obvious that the kings of the Pentapolis actually were Canaanites. On the contrary, from the narrative about the separation of Lot and Abram in Genesis 13, one gets the impression that Abram remained in Canaan, whereas Lot, who settled in the cities of the Plain and moved his tents toward Sodom (see Gen. 13:12–13), in fact left Canaan. Moreover, the description of the Canaanite territory in Gen. 10:19 does indeed refer to Sodom, Gomorrah, Admah, and Zeboiim, however, not in an inclusive way: 'And the territory of the Canaanites extended from Sidon . . . and *in the direction of* [בֹּאֲכָה] Sodom, Gomorrah, Admah, and Zeboiim, as far as Lasha'. Second, Carr's statement that the kings of the Pentapolis are enslaved 'by certain descendants of Shem, Yaphet, and Ham' (p. 164) simply does not make sense because Canaan is the descendant of Ham

---

10   Carr, *Reading the Fractures of Genesis*, 163–66.
11   Carr, *Reading the Fractures of Genesis*, 264.

(Gen. 10:6) and because Carr's cross reference Gen. 10:9 is about Nimrod, the mighty hunter. Third, Abram's victory in Genesis 14 cannot hint at his 'appropriation of the blessing on Shem that was given by Noah' (p. 164) because Noah nowhere blesses Shem. In Gen. 9:25–27 it is surely said that Canaan will be a slave to his brothers. Gen. 9:26 reads:

וַיֹּאמֶר בָּרוּךְ יְהוָה אֱלֹהֵי שֵׁם וִיהִי כְנַעַן עֶבֶד לָמוֹ

> And he said: Blessed be Yahweh, the God of Shem, and may Canaan be his/their slave.[12]

If Carr thinks of the phrase 'And may Canaan be his/their slave' as the blessing on Shem, then one can reply: Where in Genesis 14 is that hinted? It cannot be Abram's victory over the eastern kings. Moreover, the kings of the Pentapolis, even if they, after all, should be counted as Canaanites, do not appear as Abram's slaves in the chapter. On the contrary, Abram and the king of Sodom appear to be on equal footing in the dialogue in Gen. 14:17, 21–24.

Consequently, Carr's proposal cannot be sustained. The positive arguments for the insertion of Genesis 14–15 (which he holds together when it comes to their insertion in the Abraham composition) are not convincing. In addition, Carr's model of the growth of the Abraham composition is not convincing when it comes to Genesis 14 and the relative date for its insertion into the composition. Above, in chapter 4, Genesis 14* and the Composition History of the Abraham Narratives, I have argued that Genesis 14 is the latest of the texts belonging to the block Genesis 14–17, a block that interrupts the more original continuity between Genesis 13 and 18.

5.1.2 Benjamin Ziemer: Genesis 14 a Midrash to Genesis 15

Another proposal for why Genesis 14 was placed exactly at its present position is offered by Benjamin Ziemer. Ziemer argues that the conditions (*Bedingungen*) for the insertion of the core (*Grundschicht*) of Genesis 14 into the ancestral history were twofold. First, in the *Grundschicht* of Genesis 14 there was fundamental agreement on the basic data of the Abraham–Lot tradition. Second, was a feeling that the narrative *Leerstellen* were closed by its insertion. Although the *Grundschicht* in Ziemer's view originally was an independent document before it got

---

12 The rendering of Gen. 9:26 in the NRSV is not in touch with the Hebrew text: 'He also said, "Blessed *by the* LORD *my God be Shem*; and let Canaan be his slave"' (my emphasis).

its present position in the context, the text can now be understood as a midrash to Gen. 15:1–2. The *Grundschicht* of Genesis 14 probably originated at the same time as other traditions about Abraham and Jacob—traditions that for their part have remained apocryphal and have never became part of the canonical text. Ziemer argues that there are several reasons why this tradition, in particular, was included in the canon, in contrast to these other contemporary traditions:

> Einerseits füllt es einige Leerstellen in Gen 15, indem die offen gebliebene Beziehung zum Ostjordanland geklärt, die Privilegierung Jerusalems begründet und ein konkreter Anlass für die Gottesrede von Gen 15,1 gegeben wird. Und andererseits stellt es in einer, gerade im Vergleich zu anderen, 'apokryph' gebliebenen Traditionen, nahezu perfekten historischen Fiktion die israelitische Vorgeschichte in den Kontext der Weltgeschichte. . . . Die Einfügung vollzieht sich noch vor der Endkomposition des Pentateuch. Doch hat das Kapitel selbst keine kompositionsprägende Kraft entwickelt, was sich darin zeigt, dass die redaktionelle Angleichung an den Kontext stärker innerhalb von Gen 14 stattfindet als außerhalb.[13]

Pivotal for Ziemer's study of Genesis 14 is the *Grundschicht* that he establishes in a synopsis by comparing the MT with the Aramaic *Genesis Apocryphon* from Qumran. The 'largest common text' (*der grösste gemeinsame Text*) attested in both textual witnesses is what he characterizes as the *Grundschicht*. As an analogy to this method, he refers to the two-source hypothesis about the origin of the New Testament Gospels.[14] In his opinion, the *Grundschicht* was a Hebrew text that originally existed independent from its present context (*eigenständiges Dokument*).[15] The *Grundschicht* was not literarily dependent on the proto-Masoretic or proto-Samaritan textual tradition. On the contrary, it served as *Vorlage* for all subsequent textual traditions.

However, there are strong arguments against the pivotal idea posited by Ziemer of a *Grundschicht* for Genesis 14. Most important, the status Ziemer apparently gives both the MT and the Aramaic *Genesis Apocryphon*, namely, as textual witnesses on equal footing, is dubious. The *Genesis Apocryphon* is an example of a rewritten Bible. Therefore, we should expect that the responsible rewriter followed a certain agenda when rewriting the *Vorlage*. In order to reach this goal we may, contrary to what Ziemer argues,[16] be open for his also leaving out certain details,

---

13 Ziemer, *Abram—Abraham*, 88.
14 Ziemer, *Abram—Abraham*, 46.
15 Ziemer, *Abram—Abraham*, 70–72.
16 Ziemer, *Abram—Abraham*, 41: 'Gegen bewusste Auslassungen im Genesis-Apokryphon spricht dessen Detailverliebtheit bis zur Redundanz das starke geographische Interesse sowie die Tendenz zum Ausgleich mit dem Kontext'.

such as what the Chronicler does in his reworking of older sources. Moreover, its language, Aramaic, speaks against giving the *Genesis Apocryphon* the status as a textual witness on an equal footing with the MT. Ziemer does not think the *Genesis Apocryphon* is a direct translation of the assumed *Vorlage* in Hebrew from which both the MT and the *Apocryphon* stem. Rather, he posits that the *Genesis Apocryphon*, for this particular text, uses as *Vorlage* an Aramaic text that is an almost literal translation of the assumed Hebrew *Grundschicht*. So, between the assumed *Grundschicht* and the Aramaic *Genesis Apocryphon*, Ziemer hypothesizes a literal translation of the *Grundschicht* into Aramaic. Even if there was such a missing link, it is not possible, however, to determine whether this Aramaic translation was literal or not.

Therefore, the arguments Ziemer gives for his thesis that the canonical Genesis 14 stems from an originally independent document, the *Grundschicht*, are not convincing. Moreover, because of that, the reasons Ziemer proposes for why this document was incorporated into the already canonical Abraham composition, namely, to fill out *Leerstellen* in Genesis 15, cannot be sustained. Even less convincing is the idea that Genesis 15 in some way refers to a privileged Jerusalem. It is difficult to determine where this *Leerstelle* regarding the Holy City is located in Genesis 15. Moreover, the proposal that Genesis 14 provides an occasion for the divine speech in Genesis 15 is not likely. Christoph Levin[17] has made a better case for his thesis that Genesis 15 originally continued the promise in the latter part of Genesis 13, which also is suggested by Abram's resumption in chapter 15 of God's promise of land and descendants from Genesis 13 (see 4.3.3, Material Dependent on the Priestly Material).

5.2 A *Leerstelle* in the Conclusion of Genesis 13

Although I do not follow Ziemer, I nevertheless agree with him that the key word for explaining why Genesis 14* has been positioned between Genesis 13 and 15 is *Leerstelle*. However, the *Leerstelle* that the one who composed and inserted Genesis 14* intended to fill out is not primarily to be sought in Genesis 15. By paying attention to the early reception history of the canonical Abraham composition in the Aramaic *Genesis Apocryphon*, we will see that the author of the *Genesis Apocryphon* located a problematic spot — a *Leerstelle* — at the end of Genesis 13, where Yahweh promises land to Abram and his descendants. So, the *Genesis Apocryphon*

---

17   Levin, 'Jahwe und Abraham im Dialog', 237–57.

may give us a first-hand glimpse into how ancient Jewish scribes worked in order to fill out what they saw as a *Leerstelle*.[18]

By the term *Leerstelle* I refer to a gap in the narrative. In literary criticism in general, the term is part of the vocabulary of reader–response criticism, focusing on the readers and their experience of a literary work, and was to my knowledge, first coined by Wolfgang Iser.[19] Also here, I focus on the readers' experience with a literary work. However, the readers who are interesting in this context are historical ones, namely, the readers of the not-yet-complete and still-growing Abraham narratives in the Second Temple period. Therefore, a *Leerstelle* is that which, according to the readers' experience with the text, was felt to be a gap in the narrative. In the Second Temple period the identification of a *Leerstelle* had to be done on the basis of subjective criteria—as is still the situation today. Consequently, it is not important to determine if such a gap from the outset was an author-intended literary device or if it was the accidental result of editorial activity in which two or more narratives were combined or interwoven.

5.2.1 Genesis 13:14–18

In Gen. 13:14–16 Yahweh calls Abram to view the land that he promises to give to Abram and his offspring as an eternal possession. In the following v. 17, Yahweh commands Abram to carry out a concrete action, namely, to walk through the length and breadth of the land, and gives the reason that he will give it to him.

> Gen. 13:14–17 (NRSV): [14] The LORD said to Abram, after Lot had separated from him, 'Raise your eyes now, and look from the place where you are,

---

18   Carr, 'Intratextuality and Intertextuality—Joining Transmission History and Interpretation History in the Study of Genesis', 97–112 (99), has outlined how ancient Jewish interpreters often can confirm the presence of certain problems in the biblical text, even if they used a different interpretive framework to exploit these problems as interpretational opprortunities. He concludes,

> '[t]he above survey suggests that close readers of Genesis not in search of particular diachronic problems ran up against three main types of fractures left in the final form of the book: fractures causes by the combination of P and non-P . . . , fractures caused by the incorporation into non-P materials of various, independent earlier traditions . . . , and fractures possibly caused by either juxtaposition of earlier traditions or redactional/compositional extension of a given written context . . .' (109).

19   Wolfgang Iser, *Der Akt des Lesens: Theorie ästhetischer Wirkung* (Uni-Taschenbücher 636; Munich: Fink, 1976).

northward and southward and eastward and westward; [15] for all the land
that you see I will give to you and to your offspring forever. [16] I will make
your offspring like the dust of the earth; so that if one can count the dust of
the earth, your offspring also can be counted. [17] Rise up, walk through the
length and the breadth of the land, for I will give it to you'.

The command, however, does not seem to be carried out. On the contrary, v. 18 merely reports as follows:

> Gen. 13:18 (NRSV): [18] So Abram moved his tent, and came and settled
> [וַיֶּאֱהַל אַבְרָם וַיָּבֹא וַיֵּשֶׁב] by the oaks of Mamre, which are at Hebron; and there he
> built an altar to the LORD.

No mention is made of the expedition that one could expect as a response
to the command Yahweh gives in v. 17.[20] The only verb of motion in Gen.
13:18 that potentially could function as Abram's compliance with Yahweh's command to walk through the land in Gen. 13:17 is the וַיֶּאֱהַל.

However, the verb אהל does not encompass the notion of walking
through the length and breadth of the land, קוּם הִתְהַלֵּךְ בָּאָרֶץ לְאָרְכָּהּ וּלְרָחְבָּהּ.
The verb, which is a denominative of the noun אֹהֶל, occurs only three
times in biblical literature (Gen. 13:12, 18; Isa. 13:20). In Gen. 13:12 it
is used in connection with the particle עַד: 'Lot עַד־סְדֹם וַיֶּאֱהַל (pitched his
tent[s] [continuously]) until [he reached] Sodom'. In this context the
iterative notion is evident because of the particle עַד (see Gen. 12:6 where
the same is observed in connection with the verb עבר). Moreover, in Isa.
13:20b the verb is used in a parallelism: 'Arabs will not pitch [their] tent
[יַהֵל > *יְאַהֵל[21]] there; shepherds will not make flocks lie down [יַרְבִּצוּ] there'.
In this case, the verb seems to have a punctual aspect. Therefore, no iterative notion is attached semantically to the verb אהל. A possible iterative
notion is probably present only when the verb and the particle עַד are
juxtaposed. Therefore, it is legitimate to doubt whether Abram in Gen.
13:18 really fulfils Yahweh's command in Gen. 13:17.

The idea that there is a discrepancy at the conclusion of Genesis 13 is
not without parallel in the Hebrew Bible, as one should expect in such a
compilation of different texts and traditions. Just to mention a few other
examples: one can compare the discrepancies between the two creation
accounts in Genesis 1 and Genesis 2–3, respectively. Another example is
the name of the God that the patriarchs invoked. According to Gen. 13:4,
Abram called on the name of Yahweh already when journeying around

---

20   Some translations fail to render the discrepancy between vv. 17 and 18. For instance,
     the Norwegian NO 78/85 translation smoothes it out by rendering וַיֶּאֱהַל אַבְרָם by a phrase
     with an *iterative* notion ('Så flyttet Abram *omkring* med sine telt' [my emphasis]).
21   So *HALOT* 1, *s.v.* אהל, 18–19.

the Promised Land. However, according to Exod. 6.3 the same Yahweh says to Moses,

> I appeared to Abraham, Isaac, and Jacob as El Elyon, but by my name Yahweh I did not make myself known to them.

A final example in the context of the Abraham narratives is found in Genesis 18. In this story the number and identity of *dramatis personae* are not clear. In the one moment, Yahweh appears to the patriarch. However, in the next, three men visit him.

In particular, the assumption that there is a fracture between Gen. 13:14–17 on the one side and the succeeding v. 18 on the other[22] is strengthened by a comparison with another formally identical promise text, namely, Gen. 12:1–4. In Gen. 12:1 Yahweh commands Abram to go (לֶךְ־לְךָ) from his country and his kindred and his father's house to the land Yahweh will give him. After the description of the promises in Gen. 12:2–3, v. 4aα continues by stating as follows:

וַיֵּלֶךְ אַבְרָם כַּאֲשֶׁר דִּבֶּר אֵלָיו יְהוָה

And Abram went as Yahweh had told him.

Here, in Gen. 12:1–4, it is evident that Abram complies with the command given to him. Moreover, Abram's failure in Gen. 13:18 to fulfil the command has been noticed by the Talmud.[23] Modern commentators too have noted that Genesis 13 lacks a report of the actual execution similar to that in Gen. 12:4a.[24] Early on, Julius Wellhausen considered the promise to Abram in Gen. 13:14–17 to be a late insertion into a J tradition. According to him, the original J tradition was about the separation between Abram and Lot and, consequently, how the former became the sole lawful proprietor of the land because the latter renounced it.[25] A slightly different explanation has been proposed by Gerhard von Rad. Although noting the fracture in the narrative, he argued that vv. 14–17 are indeed old, ascribing them to J, but that this promise nonetheless is drawn from a tradition different from that of Abram and Lot, which makes up the core of the remaining chapter 13.[26] Unlike most others,[27]

---

22 Thus against Wenham, *Genesis 1–15*, 298–99.

23 See *b. B. Bat.* 15b and *b. Sanh.* 111a.

24 For instance, Sarna, *Genesis*, 101; Westermann, *Genesis 12–36*, 179 and Zimmerli, *1. Mose 12–25*, 32.

25 Wellhausen, *Composition*, 23–24. Thus also Gunkel, *Genesis*, 175–76; Benno Jacob, *Das erste Buch der Tora: Genesis* (Berlin: Schocken, 1934), 973; and Westermann, *Genesis 12–36*, 1985), 172.

26 Von Rad, *Das erste Buch Mose*, 132.

27 An exception is Gunkel, who also renders the verb in v. 14a with a 'past in the past'. Nevertheless, Gunkel interprets the chapter with a literary critical approach. Accord-

Alter offers a translation in which Yahweh's speech in 13:14a is given
a past-perfect time reference.[28] Thus Yahweh spoke to Abram *immediately after* Lot separated from him (v. 11b), not at a time when Abram
had already been living in Canaan for a while and Lot had moved his
tents close to Sodom. The consequence of this translation is that the contrast between vv. 14–17 and v. 18 weakens. Nevertheless, despite Alter's
translation, v. 18 still lacks an explicit execution of the command given
in v. 17.

5.2.2 The Parallel to MT Genesis 13:14–18
in the Aramaic *Genesis Apocryphon*

As already anticipated above, I assert that the Aramaic *Genesis Apocryphon* illustrates that early readers of Genesis 13 found a *Leerstelle* between
Gen. 13:17 and 18. According to Joseph A. Fitzmyer, who follows E. Y.
Kutscher, the Aramaic *Genesis Apocryphon* was probably composed
sometime in the first century BCE.[29] The literary genre of this Qumran
manuscript has been discussed. Fitzmyer says it is a 'good example of the
so-called rewritten bible'.[30] However, the parallel to MT Genesis 14 differs from the rest of the Apocryphon. First, whereas the rest of the Apocryphon is written in first person and thus is autobiographical, Abram is
referred to in the third person in the narrative in 1Q20 21:23–22:26, the
section corresponding to Genesis 14. Moreover, the literal translation of
the Hebrew text of Genesis abounds in 1Q20 21:23–22:26. The translation of Genesis 14 in the *Genesis Apocryphon* resembles the literal translations found in the Qumran Targums, whereas the rest of the *Genesis
Apocryphon* does not.[31] Nevertheless, the rest of the *Genesis Apocryphon* is

---

ingly, the purpose of the promise is, in Gunkel's opinion, more to motivate Abram's
sole acquisition of Canaan than the fact that Lot renounces it.

28 Robert Alter, *Genesis* (New York: Norton, 1996), 56: 'And the Lord *had said* [וַיהוָה אָמַר] to
Abram after Lot parted from him' (my emphasis), i.e., pluperfect, allegedly because of
the word order (subject + verb) and the use of the suffix tense.

29 So according to E. Y. Kutscher, who dates on the basis of linguistic criteria; see Kutscher, 'Dating the Language of the Genesis Apocryphon', *JBL* 76 (1957): 288–92. Fitzmyer discusses Kutscher's proposal together with other proposals as to the date of
composition that are based on, e.g., aesthetic arguments (Geza Vermes), the use of עליון
in the text (Wacholder), and assumed historical allusions (F. Altheim and R. Stiehl).
He does not find any of them convincing except for Kutscher's dating based on philological arguments. See Fitzmyer, *Genesis Apocryphon*, 26–28.

30 Fitzmyer, *Genesis Apocryphon*, 20.

31 Fitzmyer, *Genesis Apocryphon*, 17, 20.

still closely dependent on the biblical stories of Genesis. 'The essentials of these stories are generally preserved in this text, even though they are frequently expanded by the addition of details either imaginative or derived from some other biblical or non-biblical source'.[32]

A synopsis of MT of Gen. 13:14–18 and the Aramaic *Genesis Apocryphon* shows the additional material in the latter:

Genesis 13:14–18 (NRSV)	1Q20 21:8–22:26 (translation of Florentino García Martínez and Eibert J. C. Tigchelaar[33])
[14] The LORD said to Abram, after Lot had separated from him,	[8] God appeared to me in a night vision and said to me: Go up to Ramat Hazor, which is to the North of [9] Bethel, the place where you are living;
'Raise your eyes now, and look from the place where you are, northward and southward and eastward and westward;	raise your eyes and look to the East, to the West to the South and to the north.
[15] for all the land that you see I will give to you and to your offspring forever.	Look at all [10] this land, which I am giving you and your descendants for ever. The following morning I went up to Ramat Hazor and looked at the land from [11] that height, from the River of Egypt up to Lebanon and Senir, and from the Great Sea up to Hauran, and all the land of Gebel up to Qadesh, and all the [12] Great Desert which there is to the East of Hauran and Senir as far as the Euphrates. And he said to me: I shall give all this land to your descendants and they will inherit it forever.
[16] I will make your offspring like the dust of the earth; so that if one can count the dust of the earth, your offspring also can be counted.	[13] I will multiply your descendants like the dust of the earth which no-one can count. In the same way, your descendants will be innumerable.

---

32 Fitzmyer, *Genesis Apocryphon*, 16–17.
33 Florentino García Martínez and Eibert J. C. Tigchelaar, eds., *The Dead Sea Scrolls Study Edition. I 1Q1–4Q273* (Leiden: E. J. Brill, 1997), 44–45.

¹⁷ Rise up, walk through the length and
the breadth of the land, for I will give
it to you'.

Get up, walk and go, ¹⁴ and see how
great is its length and how great is its
width. For I shall give it to you,
to you and to your descendants after
you, for all the ages.
¹⁵ I, Abram went out to traverse and
see the land. I began the traverse at the
River Gihon. I went along the shore of
the sea until ¹⁶ I reached the mountain
of the Bull. I walked from the sh[ore]
of this Great Sea of Salt, skirting the
mountain of the Bull towards the East,
through the breadth of the land, ¹⁷
until I reached the River Euphrates. I
proceeded towards the East along the
bank of the Euphrates, until reaching
the Red Sea. I continued walking along
the shore ¹⁸ of the Red Sea until arriv-
ing at the branch of the Sea of Reeds
which issues from the Red Sea, and
continued towards the South until
I reached the ¹⁹ River Gihon. Then I
turned back and arrived at my house
in peace and found my people well.

¹⁸ So Abram moved his tent, and came
and settled by the oaks of Mamre,
which are at Hebron;
and there he built an altar to the Lord.

I went and settled at the oaks of
Mamre, at Hebron, ²⁰ to the North-east
of Hebron.
There I built an altar,
and upon i[t] I offered a holocaust
and an offering to the God Most High.
And I ate and drank there, ²¹ I and all
the people of my household. I invited
Mamre, Arnem and Eshkol, the three
Amorite brothers, my friends, and
they ate together ²² with me and drank
with me.

In the synopsis above, one easily sees that the author of the *Apocryphon*
offers five lines of additional material in 1Q20 21:15–19. These lines follow immediately after Yahweh's command to walk through the land
(1Q20 21:13b–14, cf. Gen. 13:17).[34]

---

34   Another case where a narrative in the Hebrew Bible has been left unfulfilled is found
     in Gen. 28:22. Here, Jacob vows to tithe all of his possessions. This vow is, however,

Why, then, does the author of the *Apocryphon* add these lines? The only probable explanation is that he recognized that something was missing in his Hebrew *Vorlage* in comparison to Gen. 12:4aα, which states that Abram 'went as Yahweh had told him'.[35] In other words, the Hebrew phrase וַיֶּאֱהַל אַבְרָם וַיָּבֹא וַיֵּשֶׁב (cf. Gen. 13:18) that the author probably found in his *Vorlage* did not, in his eyes, present Abram as obedient *enough* with regard to the command to 'walk through the land in its length and breadth'. Therefore, the author assimilated this passage to the one found earlier in Gen. 12:1–4.[36]

5.2.3 Excursus: The Extent of the Promised Land and the Territories of the Invading Kings in the *Genesis Apocryphon*

The *Genesis Apocryphon* offers a detailed itinerary in 1Q20 21:15–19 describing the route Abram took upon receiving Yahweh's command. First, Abram set out from the River Gihon (ניחון נהרא) and then went along the shore of the sea (ליד ימא) until he reached the mountain of the Bull (טור תורא). From the shore of the Great Sea of Salt (ימא רבא דן די מלחא) along the mountain of the Bull he walked 'through the breath of the land' (לפותי ארעא) until he reached the River Euphrates (פורת נהרא). Travelling east along the River Euphrates he came to the Red Sea (ימא שמוקא), along the shore of which he continued walking until he arrived at the branch of the Sea of Reeds (לשן ים סוף). From there, he continued toward the South (דרומא) until he reached the River Gihon (גחון נהרא).

All these geographical points can be identified.[37] The River Gihon, one of the rivers flowing out of Eden according to Gen. 2:13, is the Nile, as is evident from both *Jub.* 8:15 (indirectly) and Josephus, *Ant.* 1.39 (explicitly). Moreover, the mountain of the Bull—borrowed from the Greek name Ταῦρος ὄρος—is identical with the Taurus (Turkish: Toros)

---

    unfulfilled in the Hebrew Bible. According to Robert A. Kugler, this gap has been filled out in the pseudepigaphic *Aramaic Levi Document* 9; see Kugler, *From Patriarch to Priest: The Levi-Priestly Tradition from Aramaic Levi to Testament of Levi* (SBLEJL 9; Atlanta: Scholars Press, 1996), 90.

35   Unfortunately, the lines in the *Genesis Apocryphon* that correspond to the beginning of the Abram story are not known. However, the lost six lines at the beginning of column 19 probably corresponded to Gen. 12:1–7; see Fitzmyer, *Genesis Apocryphon*, 179.

36   See also James L. Kugel, *Traditions of the Bible: A Guide to the Bible as It Was at the Start of the Common Era* (Cambridge, MA: Harvard University Press, 1998), 287: 'Since it was obvious [to the author of the *Genesis Apocryphon*] that Abraham must have done as he was bidden [i.e., in Gen. 13:17] this author simply filled out the details [i.e., in 1Q20 21:15–19].

37   For the discussion of each of these names, see Fitzmyer, *Genesis Apocryphon*, 224–27.

mountain range, or, more precisely, the part called Mount Amanus north of the Gulf of Alexandretta (Turkish: Iskenderun). This mountain plays an important role in several Jewish texts discussing the extent of *ha-ʾareṣ*.[38] According to the Mishnah, Amanus is the northern border of the land given to Abram (*Šeb.* 6:1). Likewise, in the Tosefta it plays a role as northern border of the land:

> What is [considered] the Land [of Israel] and what is considered outside the Land [of Israel]? All that slopes down from the Mountains of Amanus [טור אמנון] and inward . . . (*t. Ter.* 2:12).[39]

Further, in the context of the *Genesis Apocryphon*, the Sea and the Great Sea of Salt must be the Mediterranean. The Red Sea (ימא שמוקא) does not, however, correspond to the modern meaning of the Red Sea, that is, the sea between Asia and Africa, especially between the Arabian peninsula and the Horn of Africa. According to M. Copisarow,[40] the term 'the Red Sea' (Ἐρυθρὴ θάλασσα) originated among Greek mariners in antiquity. Whereas it first designated only the sea between Asia and Africa, it was gradually extended to include the Indian Ocean and eventually the Persian Gulf. Therefore, the ancient historians spoke of the Ἐρυθρὴ θάλασσα, the 'Red' or 'Erythraean Sea' as the sea into which the Euphrates and the Tigris emptied.[41] Moreover, 'the branch of the Sea of Reeds' is the modern Gulf of Suez. The *Genesis Apocryphon* refers to it as distinct from but still connected with (נפק, 'issues from', 'goes forth from') the Red Sea (also in *Jub.* 8:14 this gulf is referred to as 'branch'/'tongue').

In sum, the geographical points in the *Genesis Apocryphon* itinerary make the land Abram traversed through enormous. The land given to Abram according to the *Apocryphon's* version of the itinerary encompasses the whole fertile crescent, the Arabian and the Sinai peninsulas and the land east of the Nile.

---

38 Its name occurs in several variants: אמנה, אמנון, אמנוס, etc. See Jastrow, 78.

39 Translation of Alan J. Avery-Peck, in *Tosefta. I First Division: Zeraim (The Order of Agriculture)* (ed. Jacob Neusner and Richard S. Sarason; New York: Ktav, 1986). The southern border is the Brook of Egypt (נחלי מצרים; see *t. Ter.* 2:12). Nevertheless, the determination of the land is a question of uttermost importance for the observance of the laws of the land, such as the law of the offering of the first fruits (Lev. 23:10 NRSV), 'Speak to the people of Israel and say to them: When you enter the land that I am giving you and you reap its harvest, you shall bring the sheaf of the first fruits of your harvest to the priest', and the law of the sabbatical year (Lev. 25:2 NRSV), 'Speak to the people of Israel and say to them: When you enter the land that I am giving you, then the land shall observe a sabbath for the LORD'.

40 Referred to by Fitzmyer, *Genesis Apocryphon of Qumran Cave 1*, 226.

41 Josephus, *Ant.* 1.39; Herodotus, *Histories* 1.180, etc.

However, I believe that there are links between the unique *Genesis Apocryphon* itinerary discussed above and the subsequent narrative about the invasion of the eastern kings. Whereas the four kings in the Hebrew text are called Amraphel, king of Shinar, Arioch, king of Ellasar, Chedorlaomer, king of Elam, and Tidal, king of Goiim (Gen. 14:1, 9), the invading kings in the *Genesis Apocryphon* are called Chedorlaomer, king of Elam (עילם), Amraphel, king of Babylon (בבל), Arioch, king of Cappadocia (כפתוך), and Tidal, king of Goiim, which is Mesopotamia (גוים די הוא בין נהרין; see 1Q20 21:23–24).

In two or perhaps three instances, the political entities found immediately outside the boundaries of Abram's walk through the land in the *Genesis Apocryphon* correspond to the lands of the invading kings in 1Q20 21:23–22:26 (corresponding to MT Genesis 14). Babylonia, the kingdom of Amraphel (1Q20 21:23), and even more so, Tidal's land Mesopotamia (literally 'between rivers', 1Q20 21:24), are found *east* of the River Euphrates. Mesopotamia has, of course, never been a separate kingdom, but simply a term for different kingdoms that have in common that their main territory is located between the Euphrates and the Tigris. Nevertheless, in the *Apocryphon* it is a political entity, east of the Euphrates, the river serving as the eastern border in Abram's traverse through the land given to him. Moreover, Cappadocia, the kingdom of Arioch (1Q20 21:23), is probably located immediately *north* of the land Abram staked out. The traditional southern and eastern borders of Cappadocia were the Taurus mountain range, of which the mountain of the Bull is a part, and the Euphrates, respectively.[42]

Therefore, it can be argued that the author of the *Genesis Apocryphon* intentionally linked Abram's itinerary to the subsequent narrative about the invasion of Chedorlaomer, Amraphel, Arioch, and Tidal.

5.2.4 Preliminary Conclusion

It is clear, then, that modern critical scholars are not the only ones who have found a *Leerstelle* at the conclusion of Genesis 13.[43] The author of the *Genesis Apocryphon* also found something to be missing in his *Vorlage*. In light of other minor and major discrepancies in the Hebrew Bible this is not unusual. Rather, fractures such as the one between the last two verses in Genesis 13 are something one must expect to discover in a biblical text that has grown over time.

---

42   Richard D. Sullivan, 'Cappadocia', *ABD* 1:870–72 (870).
43   See 5.2.1, Genesis 13:14–18.

Earlier, I argued that Genesis 14* has been secondarily inserted between Genesis 13 and 15.[44] We may assume that the transition between Gen. 13:17 and 13:18 is earlier than the insertion of Genesis 14*.

This raises some questions: Can the *Genesis Apocryphon* serve as an illustration of how Jewish scribes expanded a biblical text? Is Genesis 14*, as a whole, composed particularly for its present position *after* Genesis 13 in order to fill out and respond to that which its author thought of as a *Leerstelle*? Could the answer to the question 'Why was Genesis 14* composed' be found here?

If the answer is positive, then the author of the *Genesis Apocryphon* was not satisfied with Genesis 14 as an already existing attempt to fill out the *Leerstelle*. In the eyes of the apocryphal author, the biblical narrative in Genesis 14 did not present Abram as obedient as he should have been to Yahweh's command in Gen. 13:17.[45]

5.3 The Composition of Genesis 14* Triggered by the *Leerstelle* after Genesis 13:17

In what follows, I will argue that it makes sense to read Genesis 14* as the product of Jewish creativity in late-biblical time. Provoked by Abram's only partial fulfilment of the command to go through the land in order to take possession of it, the author of Genesis 14* created a narrative in which the promise of land to Abram at first appears to be endangered, but where Abram eventually complies with the command and restores the situation. This I will do, first, by testing the thesis of whether there is any kind of connection between Gen. 13:17 and Genesis 14*. Second, I will examine whether it is possible to read Genesis 14* as a response to this *Leerstelle*, particularly in light of the motif of the endangerment of the promise.

At different times commentators have interpreted the act of walking through the length and breadth of the land as a legal custom. According to Rabbi Eliezer, one who performs such an act acquires

---

44 See chapter 4, Genesis 14* and the Composition History of the Abraham Narratives.
45 For instance, see 1Q20 21:2–4 'Upon it [= the altar at Bethel] I offered holocaust and an offering to the God Most High and invoked the name of the Lord of the Universe there; I praised God's name and blessed God. I gave thanks there in God's presence for all the flocks and wealth which he had given me, because he had acted well towards me, and because he had returned me in peace to this land'. Compare the biblical parallel Gen. 13:4 (NRSV): 'to the place where he had made an altar at the first; and there Abram called on the name of the Lord'.

the affected field.[46] Rabbinic Hebrew terms this symbolic act *ḥazakah* (חֲזָקָה),[47] but there are different opinions among the rabbis as to whether merely traversing the land is a mode of acquisition.[48] David Daube saw Gen. 13:17 and 28:13 as examples of the idea of a man acquiring land by walking through the whole of it or stepping or lying on it.[49] More recently the same point has been made by Nahum M. Sarna, who also refers to Ruth 4:7–9; Deut. 11:24; and Josh. 1:3–4.[50] So, in this context, the bidden walk through the land in Gen. 13:17 does have a legal goal: transfer of ownership.[51]

However, in what comes after Gen. 13:17, it is not Abram who performs the legal rite referred to as *ḥazakah* in rabbinic Judaism. On the contrary, those who literally walk through the length and breadth of the land are the invading kings, Chedorlaomer, Arioch, Amraphel, and Tidal. Genesis 14:5–6 reports that they travelled southwards through Transjordanian territories. Then they came to En-mishpat, which is identified with Kadesh, and thereafter to Hazazon-tamar, which probably is an alternative name for Tamar, a geographical location in the southern boundary of the land according to Ezek. 47:19; 48:28. Eventually, they engaged the rebellious kings of the Pentapolis in the Valley of Siddim, which is identified with the Dead Sea (Gen. 14:7–8). One of the cities of the Pentapolis is Zoar, the alternative name for Bela (see Gen. 14:2bβ). Thereafter, the narrative gives no details of the route of the invading kings except that Abram pursued them as far as Dan. From there, he pursued them farther to Hobah, north of Damascus (Gen. 14:14–15).

It is remarkable that both Dan (Gen. 14:15) and Zoar (Gen. 14:2) mark the northern and southern borders respectively of the Promised Land in

---

46 *Y. Qid.* 59d (= 1:3). See also Benno Jacob, *The First Book of the Torah: Genesis* (Berlin: Schocken, 1934 [reprint, New York: Ktav, 1976]), 365.

47 Sarna, *Genesis*, 100, who also refers to *Targ. Ps.-J.*; *t. B. Bat.* 2:11; *b. B. Bat.* 100a; *Gen. R.* 41:13; and *Ruth R.* 7:10.

48 See *b. B. Bat.* 100a; and Shalom Albeck and Menachem Elon, 'Acquisition', in *EncJud* 1:359–63.

49 David Daube, *Studies in Biblical Law* (Cambridge: Cambridge University Press, 1947 [reprint New York: Ktav, 1969]), 37. He, however, also interprets the pointing out of the land ('fines demonstrare') in Gen. 13:14–15 as a legal act where the ownership is transferred; see pp. 25ff.

50 See note 47 above.

51 The motif of treading one's foot over something symbolizes person's legal rights over it. This motif is further evident in the metaphor of the (royal) footstool (i.e., Ps. 110:1; Isa. 66:1 and several ancient Near Eastern iconographic depictions). See Othmar Keel, *Die Welt der altorientalischen Bildsymbolik und das Alte Testament* (5th ed.; Göttingen: Vandenhoeck & Ruprecht, 1996), 233.

a text that clearly resembles Gen. 13:14–17, namely, the story about the death of Moses in Deuteronomy 34. In this text, Yahweh makes Moses see the land from the top of Mt. Nebo:

> Deut. 34:1–3 (NRSV): Then Moses went up from the plains of Moab to Mount Nebo, to the top of Pisgah, which is opposite Jericho, and the LORD showed him the whole land: Gilead as far as Dan, ² all Naphtali, the land of Ephraim and Manasseh, all the land of Judah as far as the Western Sea, ³ the Negeb, and the Plain—that is, the valley of Jericho, the city of palm trees—as far as Zoar.

Therefore, one can observe a movement through the length and the breadth of the land in Genesis 14*. However, whereas the eastern kings literally take the first steps, it is *Abram* who completes the traverse through the land. Abram, for his part, ends up as the beneficiary of the *ḥazakah* of the land because he eventually acts, after first having been passive. By pursuing and defeating the invaders, he appears as not only morally superior but also as the rightful owner of the land that Yahweh pointed out in Gen. 13:17 (see also 6.4, The Map Plotted in Genesis 14 and David's Empire According to 2 Samuel 8).

The second test is to examine Genesis 14* in light of the motif of the endangerment of the promise. Yahweh promises to Abram in Gen. 12:1, 3, 7 that he will get many descendants, a great name, blessing, and land. It is commonly agreed that the theme of promise plays an important role in the Abraham story and the patriarchal story as a whole. For instance, Yahweh reaffirms the promise of the land in Gen. 13:14–17; 15:18–21; 18:17–18; 22:15–18; 26:3–5, 24; 28:13–15; 32:13 [Eng. trans., 12]; 46:1–4. In general, the narratives develop with their basis in the promises, or the promises serve as indispensable background for the narratives. For instance, in this way the story about Abram and Sarai in Egypt (Gen. 12:10–20) may be understood as a story about endangerment of the ancestress and thus the promise of many descendants. In the story about Abraham's acquisition of a burying place in Machpelah for his wife Sarah (Genesis 23), it is stressed that the cave and its surroundings are bought for an appropriate price, and not repossessed for free from Ephron the Hittite. In light of the promise theme, Yahweh's status as giver of the land to the patriarch is not endangered through Abraham's eagerness to pay full price.

Read as a response to the *Leerstelle* at the end of Genesis 13, Genesis 14* does fit well into the recurring motif in the Abraham narratives about the multiple endangerments of Yahweh's promises. However, in Genesis 14, the promise of land is put at risk by two circumstances: (1) Abram's own passivity vis-à-vis the command to walk through the land in Gen. 13:17 (see Gen. 13:18) and (2) the invasion of the eastern kings (see Genesis 14*). The author of Genesis 14* has composed a narrative in which Abram's passivity and the invasion of the alliance of the four kings *together* jeopardize Yahweh's promise of land in Gen. 13:17.

Fortunately, Abram eventually responds and 'restores' the original promise by defeating the invaders at the same time as he continues and completes their walk through the land.

5.4 Summary and Conclusion

Above, I have demonstrated that ancient Jewish readers actually identified a *Leerstelle* after Gen. 13:17 (see the *Genesis Apocryphon*). Moreover, I have shown that there is an inner coherence between the ritual prescribed in the command in Gen. 13:17 (which I identify with the later rabbinic terminology *ḥazakah*), and what the invading kings and Abram actually do in the subsequent chapter (Genesis 14). In addition, I have shown that Genesis 14*, understood as a filling out of the *Leerstelle*, fits in with the motif of the endangerment of the promise that recurs in the rest of the Abraham narratives. On the basis of this, the following conclusion seems plausible: The composition of Genesis 14* is the result of Jewish creativity in late-biblical time which was triggered by the *Leerstelle* after the command to walk through the land in Gen. 13:17. By composing Genesis 14*, the author consequently filled out this *Leerstelle*.

An analogy from the late-biblical period to the phenomenon of filling out a *Leerstelle* is found in the book of *Jubilees*. In the received biblical text (Gen. 5:18–24) we learn about Enoch that he is the son of Jared, that he got his son Methuselah at the age of sixty-five, that he got other children, and that all his days were three-hundred-and-sixty-five years. Quite exceptional is what we read in v. 24: 'Enoch walked with הָאֱלֹהִים. And he was no more, because אֱלֹהִים took him'.

In *Jubilees* this short notice has been expanded with a story about Enoch's visit to heaven (*Jub.* 4:16–26). Besides being credited with being the first one to learn to write and being the first one to have written 'testimonies', Enoch is also reported to have experienced a unique communication with the angels of God 'for six jubilees of year'. During this period the angels of God showed him everything that is on the earth and in the heavens (*Jub.* 4:21–22). [52]

---

52 Moreover, see also 15.2, Alternative Explanation: Creation of Legendary Biographies and New Narrative Roles.

In the next chapter, I will argue that the relatively late author borrowed literary building blocks from earlier biblical texts as well as quasi-historical and quasi-geographical information from foreign diaspora communities in the vicinity of the province of Judah when composing Genesis 14*.

6. The Literary Building Blocks
of the Author of Genesis 14*

6.1 Introduction

Having argued that Genesis 14* represents a late addition to the Abraham narratives in Genesis 12–25[1] and that the composition of the text is the fruit of Jewish creativity in late-biblical time triggered by a *Leerstelle* thought to be evident after Genesis 13,[2] I will now focus on the information that the late author appears to have used when composing the narrative.

In this chapter, I will argue that the author of Genesis 14* to a large extent borrowed and reused larger and smaller themes and literary elements from different kinds of already existing biblical texts. The task, then, will be to identify and examine those literary building blocks that the author took over from other biblical texts and reused in Genesis 14* (narrative style and framework, certain clusters of names of places and nations, etc.). Moreover, the question of 'building blocks' that do not seem to have been borrowed from any known (biblical) source will also be addressed; in addition, I will discuss the other types of sources the author might have had at his disposal in these cases. These nonbiblical sources do not need to have been written documents (such as the so-called Chedorlaomer texts, as Michael C. Astour argues[3]). Instead, they may have been quasi-historical and quasi-geographical information that the author got from diaspora communities such as those reported to have been found in Samaria (Ezra 4).[4]

As for how texts in general were produced in late-biblical times, I follow David M. Carr's model. He suggests that (late) Israelite authors

---

1   See chapter 4, Genesis 14* and the Composition History of the Abraham Narratives.
2   See chapter 5, Why Was Genesis 14* Composed and Inserted into the Abraham Narrative? An Attempt at a Literary Answer.
3   See below, 6.3.1.1, Earlier Attempts to Identify the Names.
4   A comparable situation is present in Chronicles, which frequently offer special material vis-à-vis its biblical *Vorlage*. In these cases also one must ask where the special information comes from; see Kratz, *Composition*, 22–35; and Sara Japhet, *I & II Chronicles* (OTL; London: SCM, 1993), 14–23.

were trained from the outset to write new texts by building on templates provided by earlier ones.[5] Therefore, it is not surprising that quite a few biblical texts seem to 'echo' other (and earlier) texts. Whether we are dealing with 'marked' and 'author-intended intertextuality' is difficult to decide because in most cases, the authors do not make their intentions known.[6]

6.2 Literary Building Blocks Borrowed from Biblical Sources

6.2.1 The Narrative Framework

Michael C. Astour has argued that what he conceives of as the annalistic, official style of Genesis 14 is identical with the style of what he calls the Deuteronomist. As Gunkel did previously,[7] Astour points out several analogies in 2 Kings:

> 2 Kgs. 18:7b, 13 (NRSV): He [= Hezekiah] rebelled [מרד, see Gen. 14:4] against the king of Assyria and would not serve [עבד, see Gen. 14:4] him. . . . In the fourteenth year [see Gen. 14:5] of King Hezekiah, King Sennacherib of Assyria came up against all the fortified cities of Judah and captured them.

> 2 Kgs. 24:1, 10, 12b–13a (NRSV): In his days King Nebuchadnezzar of Babylon came up; Jehoiakim became his servant for three years; then he turned and rebelled [מרד, see Gen. 14:4] against him. . . . At that time the servants of King Nebuchadnezzar of Babylon came up to Jerusalem, and the city was besieged [see Gen. 14:5]. . . . The king of Babylon took him prisoner in the eighth year of his reign. He carried off all the treasures of the house of the LORD, and the treasures of the king's house . . . [see Gen. 14:11].

> 2 Kgs. 24:20b–25:1a (NRSV): Zedekiah rebelled against the king of Babylon [מרד, see Gen. 14:4]. And in the ninth year of his reign, in the tenth month, on the tenth day of the month, King Nebuchadnezzar of Babylon came with all his army against Jerusalem, and laid siege to it [see Gen. 14:5]. . . .

From this Astour concludes:

> The similarity is striking and leaves no doubt as to when and by whom Genesis 14 was written. What it describes is a typical situation of the period between the eighth and sixth centuries, many times experienced by Israel

---

5   See David M. Carr, *Writing on the Tablet of the Heart: Origins of Scripture and Literature* (Oxford: Oxford University Press, 2005), 159; and 19.4 below, Echoes of Earlier Texts in Genesis 14 and the Role of Literary Templates for the Production of New Texts.

6   See Nielsen, 'Intertextuality and Hebrew Bible', 17–31.

7   Gunkel, *Genesis*, 280.

and Judah and occurring with distressing monotony in the Assyrian royal inscriptions.[8]

Astour thinks that the chapter fits completely within the framework of the Deuteronomistic historiographic essays. Others have also noted similarities between Genesis 14 and texts from the historical books, in particular 1 Samuel 30.[9]

Attempting to strengthen Astour's proposal that Genesis 14 is influenced by the Deuteronomist, Gerhard P. J. Stoltz and A. P. B. Breytenbach demonstrate that there are striking similarities both in the broad outline of the narratives and on the word level between Genesis 14 and 1 Samuel 30, where David appears as a kinglike hero in fighting the Amalekites. Stolz and Breytenbach compare the outline of the chapters as follows:[10]

GENESIS 14		1 SAMUEL 30	
Vv.	Description	Vv.	Description
1–11	Foreign kings defeat the Pentapolis and take men and goods as spoil.	1–6	The Amalekites invade Ziklag and take men and goods as spoil.
12–16	Abraham defeats the kings with 300[11] [sic!] men and, rescues his nephew Lot and brings back men and spoil.	7–20	David defeats the Amalekites with 200[12] [sic!] men, rescues his women and brings back men and spoil.

---

8   Michael C. Astour, 'Political and Cosmic Symbolism in Genesis 14 and in Its Babylonian Sources', in *Biblical Motifs: Origins and Transformations* (ed. Alexander Altmann; Brandeis University Studies and Texts 3; Cambridge, MA: Harvard University Press, 1966), 65–112 (70).

9   Schatz, *Genesis 14*, 278; and Yochanan Muffs, 'Abraham the Noble Warrior', *JSJ* 33 (1982): 81–108. Moreover, Muffs refers to Moshe Weinfeld's Genesis commentary in Hebrew (Tel-Aviv, 1975, not consulted). Focusing mainly on the seemingly common set of deeds of both Abram and David in that both renounce any claim on the returned spoils, Muffs states that the resemblance between the two chapters is evident, irrespective of whether the patriarch *foreshadows* or *reflects* King David.

10   Gerhard P. J. Stoltz and A. P. B. Breytenbach, 'Genesis 14—'n redaksie-kritiese ondersoek', *Hervormde teologiese studies* 57, nos. 3–4 (2001): 1312–43 (1335).

11   So Stoltz and Breytenbach. The MT reads 318.

12   So Stoltz and Breytenbach. The MT says that David set out with six hundred men, of whom two hundred stayed behind because they were too exhausted to cross the wadi (1 Sam. 30:9–10).

| 17, 21–25 | Abraham takes no spoil for himself, gives them back to the king of Sodom. | 21–25 | After a quarrel David divides the spoil equally among those who went with him and the rear party. |
| 18–20 | Abraham is blessed by Melchizedek and gives him a tenth of the spoil. | 26–34 | David sends part of the spoil as gift to the elders of Judah. |

Furthermore, Stoltz and Breytenbach illustrate the similarities at the word word level:[13]

Word	Genesis 14	1 Samuel 30
וַיְהִי	1	1, 25
יוֹם	1	1, 12, 13, 25
עָשׂוּ	2	23
מִלְחָמָה	2, 8	24
עבד	4, 15	13
בוא	5, 7, 13	1, 3, 9, 21, 23, 26
נכה	5, 7, 15, 17	1, 17
שׁוב	7, 16, 17	12, 19
שׂדה	7	11
עֲמָלֵק	7	1, 13
ישׁב	7, 12	21, 24
יצא	8, 17, 18	21
שׁם	10	31
נוס	10	17
לקשׁ	11, 12, 21, 23, 24	11, 16, 18, 19, 20
אכל	11, 24	11, 12, 16
הלך	11, 12, 24	2, 9, 21, 22, 31
שׁמע	14	24
שׁבה	14	2, 3, 5
רדף	14, 15	8, 10
חלק	15, 24	24
לילה	15	12
אשׁה	16	2, 3, 5, 18, 22
עם	16	4, 6, 21, 22

---

13   Stoltz and Breytenbach, 'Genesis 14—'n redaksie-kritiese ondersoek', 1312–43.

קָרָא	17	21
אַחֲרֵי	17	8, 21
לֶחֶם	18	11, 12
כֹּהֵן	18	7
יָד	20, 22	15, 23
נתן	20, 21	11, 12, 22, 23
כֹּל	3, 7, 11, 16, 20, 23	6, 16, 18, 19, 20, 22, 23, 26
אמר	19, 21, 22, 23	6
נֶפֶשׁ	21	6
יהוה	22	6, 8, 23, 26
אִם	23	15, 17, 22
נער	24	13, 17
אִישׁ	24	1, 2, 3, 6, 9, 10, 11, 13, 17, 21, 22, 31

In light of the similarities on both the macro and the micro levels, Stoltz and Breytenbach, agreeing with Astour, assume that Genesis 14 is Deuteronomistic influenced. I hesitate to use the term Deuteronomistic. Nevertheless, I subscribe to their basic thesis. Below I will point out other literary building blocks that the author seems to have borrowed from other texts.

6.2.2 The Pentapolis

The five cities of Sodom, Gomorrah, Admah, Zeboiim, and Bela/Zoar constitute a coalition in Genesis 14*. Together they rebel and fight against the four invading kings. The apocryphal book of Wisdom refers to them as Πεντάπολις. According to Wis. 10:6, Abraham escaped when fire descended on the Pentapolis, not only on Sodom and Gomorrah as depicted in Genesis 19. This later text holds that all five cities shared the same destiny.

However, nowhere in the Hebrew Bible do these five cities occur together, except for Genesis 14*. Nevertheless, four of these cities constitute a Tetrapolis in two separate texts: Gen. 10:19 and Deut. 29:22 (Eng. trans. 23). In the first text, Sodom, Gomorrah, Admah, and Zeboiim apparently are neighbours and serve as border points for the description of the territory of Canaan.[14] Moreover, in Deut. 29:22 (Eng. trans. 23), the

---

14 Gen. 10:19 (NRSV): 'And the territory of the Canaanites extended from Sidon, in the direction of Gerar, as far as Gaza, and in the direction of Sodom, Gomorrah, Admah, and Zeboiim, as far as Lasha'.

destruction of these four cities functions as a paradigm for the destruction with which Yahweh will punish covenant disloyalty.[15] In this text, their common tragic end is stressed more than their location.

Except for the mentioned two texts (and in Genesis 14*), these four cities do not occur together. On the contrary, either Sodom appears alone,[16] or they appear as the two pairs 'Admah and Zeboiim' and 'Sodom and Gomorrah' respectively. The pair 'Admah and Zeboiim' is mentioned only in Hos. 11:8. In this text, the destruction of the two cities serves as a negative model in a Yahweh speech. More frequent is the pair 'Sodom and Gomorrah'. Outside Genesis 14* these two cities occur as a pair in Gen. 13:10; 18:20; 19:24, 28; Deut. 32:32; Isa. 1:9–10; 13:19; Jer. 23:14; 49:18; 50:40; Amos 4:11; and Zeph. 2:9. In addition, within Genesis 14*, only Sodom and Gomorrah and none of the other five cities are mentioned in Gen 14:10–11.

The accumulation of two pairs of cities of destruction is most easily explained as a subsequent and late development.[17] Deuteronomy 29:22 (Eng. trans. 23), one of the two texts presenting the two pairs of cities as a Tetrapolis, is probably exilic if not postexilic.[18] Deuteronomy 29 is part of the paraenetic epilogue and not part of the core of the book of Deuteronomy. Moreover, Gen. 10:19 is part of the Table of Nations in

---

15 Deut. 29:21–22 (Eng. trans., 22–23, NRSV): 'The next generation, your children who rise up after you, as well as the foreigner who comes from a distant country, will see the devastation of that land and the afflictions with which the LORD has afflicted it—all its soil burned out by sulfur and salt, nothing planted, nothing sprouting, unable to support any vegetation, like the destruction of Sodom and Gomorrah, Admah and Zeboiim, which the LORD destroyed in his fierce anger'.

16 Sodom alone: Gen. 13:12–13; 14:12, 17, 21–22; 18:16, 22, 26; 19:1, 4; Isa. 3:9; Lam. 4:6; Ezek. 16:46, 48–49, 53, 55–56 (in Ezekiel together with Samaria).

17 Only Hosea, who is of Northern provenance, speaks of the pairs Admah and Zeboiim, whereas the rest of the prophets, all of Judean origin, speak of Sodom and Gomorrah as a pair. According to Zimmerli, the combination of these two pairs represents a subsequent conflation of traditions, one northern and another southern; see Zimmerli, *1. Mose 12–25*, 36. Zimmerli, however, is not clear as to when and where these two traditions were conflated. Nevertheless, I believe it is correct to think of the tetrapolis Sodom, Gomorrah, Admah, and Zeboiim as a subsequent conflation of traditions.

18 Moshe Weinfeld argues that Deuteronomy 29 reflects the neo-Assyrian period; see Weinfeld, *Deuteronomy 1–11: A New Translation with Introduction and Commentary* (AB 5; New York: Doubleday, 1991), 13. However, according to Joseph Blenkinsopp, most commentators agree that the Moab covenant text in Deut. 28:69–32:47 (Eng. trans. 29:1–32:47) was either composed or greatly expanded after the mid-sixth century BCE. The reason is that it can best be explained as addressing the Babylonian diaspora after the fall of Jerusalem; see Blenkinsopp, *The Pentateuch*, 214. However, see also Wellhausen, *Composition*, 193; and Kratz, *Composition*, 129.

Genesis 10, which is a rather 'messy text'.[19] As Westermann puts it, 'Gen 10 gives a first impression of system and lack of system wonderfully interwoven'.[20] The redactor (Westermann: 'R') behind the text passed on the Priestly system of genealogies and expanded it in some places with Yahwistic material. According to Westermann, Gen. 10:19 is part of a Yahwistic expansion of the genealogy of Ham into a Priestly genealogical list (Gen. 10:6–7, 20). R has expanded this version with the Yahwistic material found in Gen. 10:8–19, that is, including the verse referring to the Tetrapolis.[21] Moreover, according to Westermann, Sodom and Gomorrah were the original border points in Gen. 10:19. Subsequently, Admah and Zeboiim were added as a parallel to the first pair.[22] He does not, however, give any proposals as to who added Admah and Zeboiim and when it was done.

Such a conflation must have probably taken place on a literary level after the fall of the Northern Kingdom (see note 17 above). Therefore, it is reasonable to assume that the Pentapolis of Genesis 14* represents an even later development than the Tetrapolis in Gen. 10:19 and Deut. 29:22 (Eng. trans. 23).

The author of Genesis 14* must have probably either known the two particular texts, Gen. 10:19 and Deut. 29:22 (Eng. trans., 23), or he must have been acquainted with a similar conflation of the two pairs of cities of destruction. However, he augmented the Tetrapolis with an additional city: 'Bela, that is Zoar'. As a place name, Bela is known only from Genesis 14*. A place Zoar, however, was mentioned already in Gen. 13:10 in connection with Lot's separation from Abram. Moreover, the same place turns up again in the story about the destruction of Sodom and Gomorrah as Lot's city of refuge (Gen. 19:22–23). So, although Zoar is apparently not affected by the sulphurous fire from heaven (Gen. 19:24), it is still the place where Lot's wife was turned into a pillar of salt (Gen. 19:26), a place where Lot does not dare to live (Gen. 19:30), and, moreover, a place that serves as a point of departure for the story about the incestuous conception of Moab and Ammon (Gen. 19:30–38).

It is perhaps because of Zoar's apparent proximity to the cities of destruction in both Genesis 13 and 19 that the author of Genesis 14* started to associate the city with the doomed Tetrapolis, and by doing

---

19 See also Wayne Horowitz, 'The Isles of the Nations: Genesis X and Babylonian Geography', in *Studies in the Pentateuch* (ed. John A. Emerton; VTSup 41; Leiden: E. J. Brill, 1990), 35–43; and Kratz, *Composition*, 237, 248–59, 273, 293, 310.

20 Claus Westermann, *Genesis 1–11* (trans. John J. Scullion; Minneapolis MN: Fortress, 1994), 498.

21 Westermann, *Genesis 1–11*, 499.

22 Westermann, *Genesis 1–11*, 524; and idem, *Genesis 12–36*, 194–95.

that eventually counted it as one of the cities of destruction. Moreover, an additional reason for including Zoar among the cities of destruction can be that the author of Genesis 14* was dependent on the extent of the land evident in Moses' farewell speech (Deuteronomy 34). In Deut. 34:1–3, Zoar functions as the southernmost geographical point whereas Dan functions as the corresponding northernmost point. With the exception of Deuteronomy 34, these two cities (i.e., Zoar and Dan) appear in the same context in the entire Bible only in Genesis 14*. (Furthermore, see 5.3 above, The Composition of Genesis 14* Triggered by the *Leerstelle* after Genesis 13:17).

6.2.3 People and Places Subdued by the Invading Kings and the Wilderness Wandering of the Israelites

After having served King Chedorlaomer of Elam for twelve years, the Pentapolis kings rebelled in[23] the thirteenth year (Gen. 14:4). Then, in the fourteenth year, King Chedorlaomer of Elam and 'the kings who were with him' (Gen. 14:5a) returned. The text gives a detailed description of the route they took:

> Gen. 14:5–7 (NRSV): In the fourteenth year Chedorlaomer and the kings who were with him came and subdued the Rephaim in Ashteroth-karnaim, the Zuzim in Ham, the Emim in Shaveh-kiriathaim, ⁶ and the Horites in the hill country of Seir as far as El-paran on the edge of the wilderness; ⁷ then they turned back and came to En-mishpat (that is, Kadesh), and subdued all the country of the Amalekites, and also the Amorites who lived in Hazazon-tamar.

This cluster of names occurs in the narrative about the Israelites' wandering in the wilderness after they left Sinai/Hebron. The wilderness wandering narrative appears in a longer version in Numbers 10–21 and a shorter (and later) résumé put in the mouth of Moses in Deuteronomy 1–3. The similarity appears most striking between the stations of the route of Chedorlaomer and his allies on the one hand and the stations of the wilderness wandering on the other hand, as offered in the opening chapters in Deuteronomy. As others have already observed, it turns out

---

23 Depending on whether the MT שָׁנָה עֶשְׂרֵה-וּשְׁלֹשׁ 'and thirteen years' is correct. The Samaritan Pentateuch reads עשרה בשלש '*in* the thirteenth. . . .' So also Peshitta (*bdtltʿsrʾ*); *Targ. Onq.* (עסרי תלת); *Targ. Ps.-J.* (בתליסרי); and the *Genesis Apocryphon* (עשרה תלת בשנת). However, the MT שְׁלֹשׁ-עֶשְׂרֵה could be an accusative of time. Thus Cohen, 'Genesis 14—An Early Israelite Chronographic Source', 67–107 (75). Cohen quotes Ibn Ezra as the first to have suggested this and as one who also found a similar phenomenon in Exod. 20:11. On the accusative of time in general, see J-M, § 126i.

that the stations along Chedorlaomer's route appear in reversed order[24] of the stations listed in Deuteronomy 1–3.[25]

The correspondence in terms of names and the sequence in which they appear (i.e., the opposite direction) suggest that the author of Genesis 14* borrowed them from the wilderness wandering narrative. With its basis in the summary of Moses in Deut. 1:6–3:22, the correspondence in terms of stations and the more or less consequent reversal of the order in which they appear in Gen. 14:5–7 is evident:

(a) According to Deut. 1:19–20, the Israelites reached *Kadesh-barnea* in the hill country of the Amorites after they set out from Horeb.[26] According to Gen. 14:7, Chedorlaomer and his allies came to En-mishpat, which is also called *Kadesh*, where they also subdued all the fields of the Amalekites and also the Amorites in Hazazon-tamar.

(b) Moreover, according to Deut. 2:1 the Israelites walked around *Mount Seir* (הַר־שֵׂעִיר) for a long time, and according to Deut. 2:22 Yahweh drove out the *Horites* (הַחֹרִי) from their land and handed it over to the descendants of Esau.[27] According to Gen. 14:6, Chedorlaomer and his allies subdued the *Horites* (הַחֹרִי) in the (or: their?) *hill country of Seir* (בְּהַרְרָם שֵׂעִיר[28]) as far as El-paran on the edge of the wilderness.

(c) After the Israelites passed by their kin, 'the descendants of Esau who live in Seir', they headed for the wilderness of Moab (Deut. 2:8). In this context, *Elath* (אֵילַת) appears as a geographical point (NRSV: 'leaving behind Elath and Ezion-geber'). The corresponding place in Chedorlaomer's itinerary is *El-paran* (אֵיל פָּארָן, Gen. 14:6). The corresponding element in both verses is the

---

24 Moshe Seidel has claimed that words in an older text may appear in reverse order in a later one; see Seidel, 'Parallels Between the Book of Isaiah and the Book of Psalms' [Hebr.], *Sînay* 38 (1956): 149–72; 229–40; 272–80 (150). However, this has been criticized by Sommer, 'Exegesis, Allusion and Intertextuality in the Hebrew Bible', 479–89 (485 n. 12), who holds the value of such an observation to be limited because the inversion does not help us recognize which text is the source and which the borrower.

25 Already S. R. Driver, *The Book of Genesis* (4th ed.; London: Methuen, 1905), 155, pointed to the similarities between Genesis 14 and Deuteronomy 1–3. According to him, the 'archaeological learning' implied in Gen. 14:1–3, 6–9 recalls the 'antiquarian notices' in Deut. 2:10–20, 20–23; 3:9, 11, 13b, 14. More important is the discussion of Moshe David (= Umberto) Cassuto, 'Berešit', '*Enṣiqlopediya miqra'it*, II (Jerusalem: Mosad Bialiq, 1954), 318–35 (328–29); and following him, Astour, 'Political and Cosmic Symbolism in Genesis 14 and in Its Babylonian Sources', 65–112 (73).

26 Deuteronomy also uses the shorter name Kadesh for the same place; see Deut. 1:46; 2:14.

27 In the list of clans and kings of Edom in Gen. 36:15–43, both 'Seir' and 'the Horites' appear. To make the picture even more complicated, in the list Seir appears both as a person and a place.

28 See above, 2.3.2, Differences Caused during the Copying and Transmitting of the Text or by Differing Vocalization.

word אַיִל, 'mighty tree.'[29] The place name Elath is a feminine derivation of the noun אַיִל.[30]

(d) According to Deut. 2:13–18, after Seir, the Israelites crossed the Wadi Zered and entered *Moab*. Moreover, according to a note already in Deut. 2:10, the previous inhabitants of Moab were the *Emim*. According to Gen. 14:5, Chedorlaomer subdued 'the *Emim* in Shaveh-kiriathaim'.[31] The assumption that the Kiriathaim of Gen. 14:5 is in Moab is confirmed by Jer. 48:1 and Ezek. 25:9.[32]

(e) According to Deut. 2:18–19, the Israelites skirted the *land of the Ammonites*, 'the descendants of *Lot*'. Moreover, Deut. 2:20 states that the land of the Ammonites is counted as a land of Rephaim, whom the Ammonites for their part called *Zamzummim*. According to Gen. 14:5, Chedorlaomer subdued הַזּוּזִים בְּהָם 'the *Zuzim* in *Ham*'. Here, in this case, the Hebrew text offers but an auditory similarity between the stations of Chedorlaomer's and the Israelites' routes. However, the *Genesis Apocryphon* demonstrates that the potential similarity has been tightened up. Its rendition זּוּ‏ל‏זמיא די עמן, 'the *Zu^mzumites* [?] of Ammon', demonstrates that 'Ham' has been identified with Ammon. Moreover, whereas its manuscript originally read זוזמיא, 'the Zuzimites[?]', a supralinear *mem* was subsequently inserted, as is evident in the present textual form זּוּ‏ל‏זמיא.[33]

(f) Finally, according to Deut. 2:24–3:11, the Israelites eventually crossed the Wadi Arnon and entered the land of the two Amorite kings Sihon and Og. The former reigned in Heshbon, and the latter, King Og of Bashan, reigned in Edrei (see Deut. 3:1) and in *Ashtaroth* (see Deut. 1:4). As for the route of Chedorlaomer, Gen. 14:5 reports that he subdued the *Rephaim* in *Ashteroth-karnaim* (עַשְׁתְּרֹת קַרְנַיִם).

In addition to the correspondences outlined above between the itinerary of Chedorlaomer's campaign and Deuteronomy 1–3, Genesis 14* also contains names that occur only in the longer wilderness wandering narrative in Numbers 10–21 and not in the résumé in Deuteronomy 1–3. The first case is represented by 'the fields of the Amalekites' (שְׂדֵה הָעֲמָלֵקִי, see Gen. 14:7). In the wilderness wandering narrative in Numbers, the Amalekites appear in two contexts. First, in the story about the spies sent out

---

29 The LXX renders Gen. 14:6 [ἕως] τῆς τερεμίνθου τῆς Φαραν, '[to] the terebinth of Paran'.

30 See *HALOT* 1, *s.v.* אֵילַת, 41. The alternative form אֵלוֹת (1 Kgs. 9:26; 2 Chr. 8:17; 26:2) has instead a feminine *plural* ending. The LXX renders Eilath by Αι/Ελανα and similar, which merely reflects the Aramaic feminine plural or the noun אַיִל, 'mighty tree'.

31 For שָׁוֵה, see below, 6.3.3, The Stations along Abram's Pursuit and Return.

32 The *Genesis Apocryphon* reads שוה הקריות. But even this reading points in the direction of Moab because a Moabite city named Kerioth appears in Amos 2:2 and probably Jer. 48:41.

33 1Q20 21:29, see also LXX Deut. 2:20 Ζομζομμιν.

from the Valley of Eshcol,[34] the spies report back, among other things, that the Amalekites live in the land of the Negeb (עֲמָלֵק יוֹשֵׁב בְּאֶרֶץ הַנֶּגֶב, Num. 13:29a). Moreover, they also appear in the subsequent narrative in which they are presented as too strong for the Israelites (see Num. 14:25, 43, 45). The second case is represented by 'Paran'. In addition to the already discussed correspondence between El-paran (אֵיל פָּארָן, Gen. 14:6) and Elath (אֵילַת, Deut. 2:8), the element Paran occurs in the longer version of the wilderness wandering in the collocation מִדְבַּר פָּארָן, 'the wilderness of Paran' (Num. 10:12; 12:16; 13:3, 26; cf. Deut. 1:1, etc.).

In addition, the place where the Pentapolis kings deploy their troops and where the battle with the four invading kings takes place is called *Valley of Siddim*, identified with the Dead Sea (Gen. 14:3, עֵמֶק הַשִּׂדִּים הוּא יָם הַמֶּלַח, cf. 14:8, 10). Siddim is not known from any other sources, and the ancient textual witnesses are not consistent in their rendition.[35] Whatever the meaning of this term might be (my proposal is 'stakes/[torturing] blocks'[36]), the very fact that Genesis 14* identifies it with the Dead Sea is more interesting. By identifying it with the Dead Sea, the author actually interprets the story of the destruction of Sodom and Gomorrah known from Genesis 19. Whereas these cities were burned out by sulfur and were associated with salt, according to Gen. 19:24–26, the author of Genesis 14* is the first known interpreter who articulated the idea that the Valley of Siddim was overflowing with water.[37] The author's interest in locating the Pentapolis, namely, by placing them at the bottom of the Dead Sea, conforms to his general geographical interest evident in the detailed itineraries.

6.2.4 Abram the Hebrew and His Amorite Allies

According to Gen. 14:13, Abram the Hebrew (אַבְרָם הָעִבְרִי) was living by the oaks of Mamre the Amorite (מַמְרֵא הָאֱמֹרִי), whose brothers were Eshcol (אֶשְׁכֹּל) and Aner (עָנֵר). Except for Genesis 14*, the names of two of the

---

34 See 6.2.4, Abram the Hebrew and His Amorite Allies.

35 The LXX: τὴν φάραγγα τὴν ἁλυκήν (14:3); ἡ δὲ κοιλὰς ἡ ἁλυκὴ (14:8, 10). The *Genesis Apocryphon*: עמקא די סדיא; the Peshitta: ʿwmqʾ dsdwmyʾ, etc.

36 This proposal is made on the basis of the *Genesis Apocryphon* reading סדיא, which is probably merely identical with MT הַשִּׂדִּים, except that שׂ is rendered by a ס and an Aramaic determined plural form is used. My assumption, then, is that MT הַשִּׂדִּים is a plural of שַׂד > סַד, meaning 'block, stake' (see *HALOT* 2, s.v. סַד, 743; and Jastrow, s.v. סַד, 956). One can imagine that the salt pillars surrounding the Dead Sea could be referred to as stocks to which someone's feet could be fastened with shackles; see Job 13:27; 33:11.

37 Astour, 'Siddim, Valley of', *ABD* 6:15–16.

three Amorite allies are always used as place names. Therefore, there is good reason to assume that the names of Abram's allies are personifications of toponyms.

The first, Mamre, appears in Gen. 13:18; 18:1; 23:17, 19; 25:9; 35:27; 49:30; and 50:13 as a name for a place that is sometimes also called Hebron and Kiriath-arba. Whereas Mamre is always used undisputably as a place name outside Genesis 14*, the fact that he is described as having brothers and appears as an ally of Abram demonstrates that Mamre is personified in Genesis 14*.

The name of Abram's second ally, Eshcol, appears in the phrase נַחַל אֶשְׁכֹּל ('Wadi Eshcol' or 'valley of a cluster [of grapes]') in the story about the twelve men Yahweh commanded Moses to send to spy out the land (Num. 13:23–24; cf. Num. 32:9; Deut. 1:24). This valley was located in the vicinity of Hebron (see Num. 13:22), which according to Gen. 13:18 is identical with the *place* Mamre. Moreover, the espionage of the land took place during the long wilderness wandering between the departure from Sinai/Horeb (Num. 10:11 and Deut. 1:6–7) on the one side and the victory over the Amorite kings Sihon and Og (Num. 21:21–35 and Deut. 2:26–3:11) with the subsequent division of Transjordan (Numbers 32 and Deut. 3:12–22) on the other. As argued above (see 6.2.3, People and Places Subdued by the Invading Kings and the Wilderness Wandering of the Israelites), the wilderness wandering has supplied the author of Genesis 14* with the stations of Chedorlaomer's itinerary. It is equally likely that the wilderness wandering narrative supplied the author with the personified Eshcol.

The name of Abram's third Amorite ally, Aner, is not known from any biblical narrative. Moreover, the textual witnesses do not render the name univocally.[38] Therefore, we can suspect that the MT does not render the original name. If Abram's Amorite ally Aner also is a personification of a place name such as Mamre or Eshcol, then a qualified conjecture as to where to look for the original place name would be the same literary context where both Mamre (alias Hebron) and Eshcol are found. This leads us to the narrative about the wilderness wandering — including the espionage of the land — and subsequent division of Transjordan. In this context we find the stream Arnon (אַרְנוֹן/אַרְנֹן), which functions as a border between Moab and the Amorites (Num. 21:13–14,

---

38   LXX: Αυναν; *Genesis Apocryphon*: ארנם; Samaritan Pentateuch: ענרם; Josephus, *Ant.* 1.182: Έννηρος.

26, 28; 22:36; cf. Deut. 2:24, 36; 3:8, 12, 16).[39] However, the proposed identification of Aner with the river Arnon lacks explicit evidence and is therefore conjectural.

Moreover, in Gen. 14:13, Abram is presented as the Hebrew (הָעִבְרִי) in context of (or in contrast to?) his Amorite allies. This is the first time the term Hebrew is used in the Bible, and surprisingly, it is not used often at all in the Bible. Later, it is used in the Joseph story,[40] in other stories that either serve as prelude to or part of the exodus narrative,[41] in a couple of laws,[42] and in a handful of places in 1 Samuel.[43] In addition, Jonah uses it as a (self-)designation when the seamen ask him about his country and people.[44]

Nevertheless, עִבְרִי is a gentilic form of the personal name Eber (עֵבֶר). According to the Table of Nations in Genesis 10, Eber, the eponymous father of the Hebrews, is the grandson of Shem (Gen. 10:21, 24–35; cf. Gen. 11:14–17). The Table of Nations also mentions the Amorites (Gen. 10:16), of whom nothing is heard until one Hebrew and three Amorites are said to be allies in Gen. 14:13.

Of course, the isolated fact that the terms Amorite and Eber (the father of the Hebrews) are found together in the Table of Nations does not alone allow us to assume that the author of Genesis 14* somehow reuses material from the geographical text in Genesis 10.[45] Yet, the fact that the term Amorites on the one hand and Eber/Hebrew on the other hand occur together in the same context only in Genesis 10 and 14 is yet another example of a possible close connection between the two texts. The discussion below about the names of the four invading kings and their kingdoms will make this assumption even more likely; see 6.3.1.2, My Proposal: Borrowings from the Table of Nations (Genesis 10).

---

39 Arnon functions as a border also in Deut. 4:48; Josh. 12:1–2; 13:9, 16; Judg. 11:13, 18, 22, 26; and 2 Kgs. 10:33. In Isa. 16:2 and Jer. 48:20 it is closely associated with Moab.
40 Gen. 39:14, 17; 40:15; 41:12; 43:32.
41 Exod. 1:15–16, 19, 22; 2:6–7, 11, 13; 3:18; 5:3; 7:16; 9:1, 13; 10:3.
42 Exod. 21:2; Deut. 15:12; cf. Jer. 34:9, 14.
43 1 Sam. 4:6, 9; 13:3, 7, 19; 14:11, 21; 29:3.
44 Jon. 1:9.
45 The two terms occur together in conjunction in another context, too: in the story about the revelation of the divine name in Exodus 3 (cf. vv. 17–18).

6.3 Literary Building Blocks Borrowed Partly from Biblical Sources, Borrowed Partly from Other Sources, or Invented by the Author

6.3.1 The Names of the Invading Kings and Their Kingdoms

The narrative in Genesis 14* starts with introducing the four invaders (v. 1): King Amraphel (אַמְרָפֶל[46]) of Shinar (שִׁנְעָר[47]), King Arioch (אַרְיוֹךְ) of Ellasar (אֶלָּסָר[48]), King Chedorlaomer (כְּדָרְלָעֹמֶר[49]) of Elam (עֵילָם[50]), and King Tidal (תִּדְעָל[51]) of Goiim (גּוֹיִם[52]). We find all four kings listed again in Gen. 14:9, but with Chedorlaomer at the head, followed by Tidal, Amraphel, and Arioch. Moreover, the four are subsumed under the single name 'Chedorlaomer' in Gen. 14:4 or under the phrase 'Chedorlaomer and the kings who were with him' in Gen. 14:5, 17.[53] Therefore, it is King Chedorlaomer of Elam who has the leading position. The fact that the introductory list in Gen. 14:1 has Chedorlaomer as number three instead of number one may be that this particular verse orders the kings' names alphabetically.

6.3.1.1 Earlier Attempts to Identify the Names

In the history of research, there have been many attempts to identify these kings and kingdoms with historically known kings and lands. However none have gained common acceptance. Recently, in view of some material published on Ugaritic literature, Othniel Margalith has proposed some identifications that to his estimation have not been sufficiently explored.[54] Margalith identifies Tidal with the thirteenth-century Hittite king Tudkhaliash III (1265–1240 BCE) and Amraphel with a number of Ugaritic kings, all bearing the name 'Ammurapi. Moreover, he suggests that the noun גּוֹיִם (Gen. 14:1, 9) refers to the peoples of the sea listed in Gen. 10:5, that Arioch could be a descendant of Zimrilim of Mari, that Ellasar could be identified with Alashiya, an ally of the Hittites

---

46   LXX: Αμαρφαλ.
47   *Targ. Onq.* and the *Genesis Apocryphon*: בבל; *Targ. Ps.-J.*: פונטוס.
48   Symmachus: Πόντου; the Vulgate: ponti; the *Peshitta*: dlsr; *Targ. Ps.-J.*: תלסר; the *Genesis Apocryphon*: כפתוך.
49   LXX: Χοδολλογομορ; the Samaritan Pentateuch: כדר לעמר; the *Peshitta*: krdlʿmr.
50   Symmachus: Σκυθῶν.
51   LXX: Θαργαλ; Peshitta: trʿl.
52   Symmachus: Παμφυλίας; the *Peshitta*: glyʾ; the *Genesis Apocryphon*: adds די הוא בין נהרין.
53   Gen. 14:17: כְּדָר־לָעֹמֶר in *two* words, joined by a *maqqeph*.
54   Margalith, 'The Riddle of Genesis 14 and Melchizedek', 501–8.

identified with Cyprus, or with a city in today's Lebanon called Ulassa. Margalith does not mention any proposals concerning King Chedorlaomer of Elam.

In light of the history of research, however, Margalith's proposals are, as far as I can see, not new. The name Tidal has already been associated with the Hittite name Tudkhaliash. At least five kings with this name are known.[55] Moreover, Margalith himself provides the most important argument against such detailed identifications (including his proposal to identify Amraphel with one of a number of kings of Ugarit called 'Ammurapi[56]). Because he holds Genesis 14 to be a 'hero-story' or a legend, Margalith does not expect to find any well-constructed plot, but rather a badly cobbled medley of episodes, dimly remembered from past traditions. This medley, which he calls a *para-mythe*,[57] includes both names that are ancient and names that are the invention of the narrator, whom he dates to the latter days of the first temple[58] because of the anachronism 'Dan' found in Gen. 14:14 (note 17, p. 505). Given that he is on the right track, then, it appears difficult to understand why Margalith seemingly insists on identifying the invaders of Genesis 14* with historical kings attested in ancient sources. In other words, if Genesis 14 indeed is a medley, then there is no need to identify the kings with historical persons. Nevertheless, I believe that he is on the right track when connecting the Goiim (גוים) of Genesis 14 with the coastland peoples in the Table of Nations (Genesis 10).[59]

In the history of research on Genesis 14, the so-called Chedorlaomer texts from the Spartoli tablets of the British Museum have been particularly influential. As the name suggests, they were thought to contain names found also in Genesis 14. In addition, certain common features in terms of content have been suggested. The texts were first published by Theophilus G. Pinches[60] but made available to a larger audience by

---

55 Jan Alberto Soggin, *Das Buch Genesis* (Darmstadt: Wissenschaftliche Buchgesellschaft, 1997), 230.

56 In addition, there is a linguistic problem: What do we do with the *l* in Amraphel? See Franz Marius Theodor de Liagre Böhl, 'Amraphel', in *RGG*[3] 1, cols. 332–33. Moreover, see Astour, 'Amraphel', *ABD* 1217–18; and Nahum M. Sarna, 'Amraphel', *EncJud* 2:106.

57 Margalith, 'The Riddle of Genesis 14 and Melchizedek', 501–8 (504).

58 The criterion is the anachronism 'Dan' in Gen. 14:14; see Margalith, 'The Riddle of Genesis 14 and Melchizedek', 501–8 (505 n. 17).

59 See 6.3.1.2 below, My Proposal: Borrowings from the Table of Nations (Genesis 10), where I argue that many of the names in Genesis 14* are borrowed from other biblical texts, including the Table of Nations (Genesis 10).

60 Theophilus G. Pinches, 'Certain Inscriptions and Records Referring to Babylonia and Elam and Their Ruler, and Other Matters', *Journal of the Transactions of the Victoria Institute* 29 (1897), 43–89.

Fritz Hommel.[61] Then, an improved transliteration and translation was published by Alfred Jeremias, who was also the first to name them the *so-called* Chedorlaomer texts (and not simply 'the Chedorlaomer texts').[62] Later, the texts were connected to Genesis 14 by William Foxwell Albright[63] and—several decades later—also by Michael C. Astour.[64] The so-called Chedorlaomer texts are very late tablets from the Parthian period (Jeremias: after 142 BCE; so also Astour[65]). However, it is assumed that they are copies of assumedly (early) Babylonian hero epics. According to Jeremias, the *terminus a quo* for their date of composition is the twelfth century BCE,[66] whereas according to Astour the composition took place in the mid-seventh century BCE.[67]

The so-called Chedorlaomer texts contain stories about the advances of four kings into Mesopotamia, their sacrilege there, and, eventually, the severe destiny the aggressors themselves experienced. As mentioned, scholars have attempted to identify names occurring in these texts with the names of the invading kings in Genesis 14. The most optimistic ones believed to find the name Chedorlaomer behind the logograms ^{m}KU .KU .KU .KU .MAL, king of Elam.[68] In addition, cognates to the biblical Arioch and Tidal have been found. The name of the *father* (*sic*) of one of the kings on one of the tablets is ^{m}ÌR-^{d}É-*a-ku*, which some scholars suggest resembles the name Arioch. Moreover, another of the kings on the tablets is ^{m}*Tu-ud-hul-a*, which some suggest resembles Tidal.

Hommel used the so-called Chedorlaomer texts as a means to verify the historicity of Genesis 14.[69] In constrast, Jeremias concluded that these texts have nothing to contribute to the question of the historicity

---

61   *Die altisraelitische Überlieferung in inschriftlicher Beleuchtung: Ein Einspruch gegen die Aufstellung der modernen Pentateuchkritik* (Munich: G. Franz'sche Hofbuchhandlung, 1897), 180–90.

62   Jeremias, 'Die sogenannten Kedorlaomer-Texte', *MVAeG* 21, no. 1 (1917): 69–97.

63   'The Historical Background of Genesis XIV', *JSOR* 10 (1926): 231–69 (see 236, 255, etc.).

64   Astour, 'Political and Cosmic Symbolism in Genesis 14 and in Its Babylonian Sources', 65–112, and repeated in several lexicon articles in *ABD*. See especially Astour, 'Chedorlaomer', *ABD* 1:893–95.

65   Astour, 'Chedorlaomer', *ABD* 1:893–95 (894).

66   See Jeremias, 'Die sogenannten Kedorlaomer-Texte', 69–97 (76 n. 2).

67   See Astour, 'Political and Cosmic Symbolism in Genesis 14 and in Its Babylonian Sources', 65–112 (81); and idem, 'Chedorlaomer', *ABD* 1:893–95 (894).

68   So Pinches, 'Certain Inscriptions and Records Referring to Babylonia and Elam and Their Rulers, and Other Matters', 43–90 (45, 48); and Hommel, *Die altisraelitische Überlieferung in inschriftlicher Beleuchtung*, 43–44, 180, 183 et al. This reading, however, was not followed by Alfred Jeremias, who instead translated 'Kuturnahunte'; see Jeremias, 'Die sogenannten Kedorlaomer-Texte', 69–97 (82 n. a, et al.).

69   For instance, see Hommel, *Die altisraelitische Überlieferung in inschriftlicher Beleuchtung*, 43–44, 190–202.

of Genesis 14. However, he proposed that both the Hebrew and the Babylonian authors created the names used in their respective historical accounts on the basis of a common source.[70] A similar proposal regarding the relationship with Genesis 14 was made by Michael C. Astour.[71] On the basis of the onomastic resemblance between the names in Genesis 14 and the Chedorlaomer texts, as well as the general tenor of the Chedorlaomer texts, Astour concluded that the author of Genesis 14 is very likely to have been acquainted with some earlier versions of these Chedorlaomer texts. According to him, a Jew in Babylon found, in an early version of the Chedorlaomer texts, certain things consistent with his own anti-Babylonian feelings and created a story consistent with Jewish/biblical themes and motifs.

However, Astour's conclusion is not convincing. First, one weakness is the fragile nature of the identification of names, particularly evident in the identification of the logograms ᵐKU .KU .KU .KU .MAL with Chedorlaomer. Second, the so-called Chedorlaomer texts do not synchronize the kings, which, in contrast, is the case in Genesis 14 where they make up an alliance. Third, the names are found on *different* tablets.[72] Fourth, the texts locate the kings' actions in Akkad/Babylon and not Palestine.

6.3.1.2 My Proposal: Borrowings from the Table of Nations (Genesis 10) and from the Foreign Population Living in the Diaspora

In the following I will argue that the Table of Nations in Genesis 10 also seems to be the source for the names of the kingdoms of the four invading kings in a way comparable to how the world map in Genesis 10 is reproduced in 1 Chronicles 1.[73]

However, as for the personal names of the four kings, I will propose that the author working in the Second Temple period himself compiled the names after having learned about them from other peoples living in the diaspora in his own part of the world.

---

70   Jeremias, 'Die sogenannten Kedorlaomer-Texte', 69–97 (97).
71   See Astour, 'Chedorlaomer', *ABD* 1:893–95 (894).
72   The so-called Chedorlaomer texts are written on *three* different tablets.
73   See Jürgen Kegler and Matthias Augustin, *Synopse zum Chronistischen Geschichtswerk* (Beiträge zur Erforschung des Alten Testaments und des antiken Judentums 1; Frankfurt am Main: Peter Lang, 1984), 74–76; and Magnar Kartveit, 'Names and Narratives: The Meaning of Their Combination in 1 Chronicles 1–9', in *Shai le-Sara Japhet: Studies in the Bible, Its Exegesis and Its Language* (ed. Moshe Bar-Asher et al.; Jerusalem: Bialik Institute, 2007), 59–80.

The names of the four invading kingdoms: First, I will start with the names of the four invading kingdoms. Three of these names are collocated in the Table of Nations in Genesis 10. A land of Shinar (שִׁנְעָר) occurs in Gen. 10:10 as a collective term for Babel, Erech, Accad, and Calneh.[74] Moreover, Elam (עֵילָם) occurs as one of Shem's descendants in Gen. 10:22. In addition, in Gen. 10:5 there is talk of אִיֵּי הַגּוֹיִם, 'the islands of the nations' (NJB) or 'coastland peoples' (NRSV)/'maritime nations' (JPS Tanakh).

An argument in support of an identification of the Goiim of Genesis 14* with the אִיֵּי הַגּוֹיִם in Genesis 10[75] is that Shinar and Elam are mentioned in the Table of Nations, as are also a Tetrapolis,[76] Eber (the father of the Hebrews), and the Amorites.[77]

Moreover, in light of this, there is also a good reason to discuss whether not the fourth invading kingdom, Ellasar (אֶלָּסָר), is also found in Genesis 10 and therefore reappears in Genesis 14*. Admittedly, a kingdom Ellasar is found in Genesis 14* only (vv. 1, 9). However, in the Table of Nations, a certain Elishah (אֱלִישָׁה) occurs as one of Javan's descendants together with Tarshish, Kittim, and Rodanim. Now, this Elishah is often identified with Alashiya in the scholarly literature, an ancient name often associated with Cyprus or a part of the island.[78]

The question of the location of Alashiya/Elishah is not relevant here. More important is whether the author of Genesis 14* may have used the Table of Nations in Genesis 10 and the reference there to Elishah as a source for the kingdom Ellasar, which he mentions in Gen. 14:1, 9. The first syllable (אֶל-) is identical, whereas the rest is not (Ellasar [-סָר/-יִשָׁה]).

As for the last letter in Ellasar and Elishah respectively, one could discuss whether an original *heh* has been misread as *resh*. Now, the Hebrew script did develop throughout the first millennium BCE and, in addition, there might have been different local styles. Moreover, we do not know at what time such a misreading possibly took place. The LXX, which

---

74 Given that כֻּלָּנֶה is *not* a misrepresentation of כל plus a pronominal suffix as suggested in the NRSV ('all of them').

75 In a list of kings that Joshua defeated west of the Jordan a 'king of Goiim in Galilee' (מֶלֶךְ־גּוֹיִם לְגִלְגָּל) appears (Josh. 12:23). The LXX renders βασιλέα Γωιμ τῆς Γαλιλαίας. Astour has suggested to compare Josh. 12:23 with Isa. 8:23 (Eng. trans., 9:1), where there is talk of גְּלִיל הַגּוֹיִם 'Galilee (lit. "district") of nations'; see Astour, 'Goiim', *ABD* 2:1057. Margalith connects this king with the coastland people mentioned in Gen. 10:5 and states that there were Aegaean settlements also in Canaan who fought the Israelite invasion under the מֶלֶךְ־גּוֹיִם mentioned in Josh. 12:23. See Margalith, 'The Riddle of Genesis 14 and Melchizedek', 501–8 (503).

76 See 6.2.2 The Pentapolis.

77 See 6.2.4 Abram the Hebrew and His Amorite Allies.

78 See Bustanay Oded, 'Cyprus: Ancient period', in *EncJud* 5:347–48. For other proposals as to the geographical location, see *HALOT* 1, *s.v.* אֱלִישָׁה, 56–57.

reads Ελλασαρ and thus agrees with the MT, could perhaps serve as a *terminus ante quem* (although we do not know exactly when the translation of the LXX took place).[79] Nevertheless, in, for instance, the paleo-Hebrew script used in an Exodus scroll fragment from the second century BCE, these two letters resemble each other (compare paleo-Hebrew *heh*: ꓱ and paleo-Hebrew *resh*: ꓱ). A downstroke characterizes both. Where *heh* has one vertical stroke combined with two lower horizontal bars, *resh* has a closed top made by a diagonal and a lower horizontal bar.[80]

> According to K. A. Mathews, the use of Paleo-Hebrew script in the Persian and early Hellenistic periods can be interpreted as a feature of Jewish nationalism. The Tennes rebellion against Persian domination (mid-fourth century BCE) in which Judah participated, created a climate which could account for the script's resurgence among the Jews during the late Persian period.[81]

If the misreading described above actually did take place, then the consonants -שׁ- in Elishah must have correspondingly at a certain point started to have been represented by a *samekh* as in Ellasar (אֶלָּסָר). An explanation along the lines drawn above seems more difficult. The consonants -שׁ- in paleo-Hebrew script would be something like wꓯ, whereas *samekh* in the same script perhaps would appear as ꓷ.[82]

The personal names of the four invading kings: Moreover, whereas it can be argued that the author of Genesis 14* borrowed the names of the four invading kingdoms from the Table of Nations, the same cannot be proposed for the personal names of the four invading kings: King Amraphel (אַמְרָפֶל) of Shinar, King Arioch (אַרְיוֹךְ) of Ellasar, King Chedorlaomer (כְּדָרְלָעֹמֶר) of Elam, and King Tidal (תִּדְעָל) of Goiim. One of these names occurs in another biblical text: Arioch. A person called Arioch appears in Dan. 2:14–15, 24–25 as the chief executioner of the royal household[83] and as king of the Elymeans, that is, the Elamites in the apocryphal book of

---

79   See the discussion concerning the translation of the Hebrew Bible into Greek in chapter 16, The Date of the Melchizedek Episode.

80   See Joseph Naveh, Solomon Birnbaum, David Diringer, Zvi Federbush, Jonathan Shunary, and Jacob Maimon, 'Alphabet, Hebrew', in *EncJud* 1:689–728.

81   See K. A. Mathews, 'The Background of the Paleo-Hebrew Texts at Qumran', in *The Word of the Lord Shall Go Forth: Essays in Honor of David Noel Freedman in Celebration of his Sixtieth Birthday* (ed. Carol L. Meyers, Michael Patrick O'Connor, and David Noel Freedman; American Schools of Oriental Research 1; Winona Lake, IN: Eisenbrauns, 1983), 549–68 (552).

82   *Samekh* is not attested in the second century BCE Exodus scroll fragment written in paleo-Hebrew. Therefore, I instead use as illustration a *samekh* type found in Hebrew seal inscriptions from the late-seventh/early-sixth century BCE. See Naveh et al., 'Alphabet, Hebrew', in *EncJud* 1:689–728 (694, fig. 10).

83   רַב־טַבָּחַיָּא דִּי מַלְכָּא. טַבָּח can also mean bodyguard.

Judith (see Jdt. 1:6).[84] However, the remaining three names are unknown in the rest of the Bible.

I propose that the author of Genesis 14* borrowed these names from other peoples with whom he was in contact or otherwise had knowledge about. Ezra 4 provides a good illustration of the ethnographic and geographic horizon that one may expect a Jew in the Second Temple period to have had. The Ezra text offers a summary of the opposition during the reigns of Darius, Xerxes, and Artaxerxes. The adversaries of the Jews who oppose the rebuilding of the walls of Jerusalem are people who are said to have been deported and settled in Samaria. Among them are *Persians*, people of *Erech* and *Babylonia* (both associated with Shinar according to the Table of Nations; see Gen. 10:10) and *Elamites* (see Ezra 4:9–10). Regardless of the historical authenticity of the details in this particular text, Ezra 4 does, nevertheless, prove that people in Judah may not have travelled far away to get in touch with other nations.

Chedorlaomer: King Chedorlaomer of Elam is, with the exception of Genesis 14*, mentioned neither in a biblical nor a nonbiblical source. However, in light of the cross-cultural contact in the Second Temple period, as described above, it is not necessarily strange that a Jewish author refers to an Elamite king with the Elamite name Chedorlaomer. Although the Persians took control of the traditional Elamite capital Susa in 539 BCE and by doing so put an end to Elam as an independent political power, Elam continued as a cultural entity.[85] The Elamite language continued as one of the official languages of the Persian empire,[86] and the former capital Susa continued as one of its capitals.[87]

Therefore, in the Second Temple period, the Elamite language was still used and even had an important position. Moreover, Ezra 4 testifies that there were Elamites among those who had been settled in Samaria. This circumstance may explain the fact that the author of Genesis 14* has King Chedorlaomer of Elam among the invading kings. One possible

---

84   In the quasi-historical book of Judith, a King Arioch of the Elymeans (Αριωχ βασιλέως Ἐλυμαίων), that is, the Elamites, figures as the only named vassal king among all the people of the hill country and those who live along the Euphrates, the Tigris, and the Hydaspes who rebel against King Nebuchadnezzar of the Assyrians (*sic*; see Jdt 1:7 Ναβουχοδονοσορ βασιλεὺς Ἀσσυρίων). The book of Judith may be dependent on Genesis 14. See below, 7.2.7, Fact and Fiction Interwoven in Quasi-Historical Narratives from the Persian and Hellenistic Periods.

85   See Acts 2:9.

86   Compare King Xerxes' trilingual foundation tablet from Persepolis in Akkadian, Persian, and Elamite in *ANET* 316–17.

87   In addition, Elam is also mentioned in Isa. 21:2; Jer. 25:25; 49:34–39; Ezek. 32:24; and Dan. 8:2.

explanation is that the author received knowledge about a historical figure with this name (but about whom nothing is known in the extra-biblical sources we know today) from the Elamites in the diaspora, such as those in Samaria. Another possibility is that he acquired linguistic competence enough to construct a perfect Elamite name from the same kind of diaspora group. For it is widely accepted that the first element, *Kutir/Kudur*, and the second, *Lagomar*, both reflect genuine Elamite words used to compose Elamite names,[88] although no collocation of Kutir/Kudur and Lagomar is known except for in Genesis 14*.[89] To my knowledge, the first element is found as late as the seventh century BCE in a royal name, namely, in the name Kutir-Nahhunte, an Elamite usurper ruling between 693 and 692 BCE.

Tidal and Amraphel: It is also possible to imagine why a Jewish author in the Second Temple period refers to King Tidal and King Amraphel using the same model as proposed above concerning Chedorlaomer. If the author had contact with foreign diaspora communities, he is also likely to have received some kind of information (cursory or more accurate) about their history. Now, contrary to the undoubtedly Elamite name Chedorlaomer and the Elamite diaspora in Samaria, I am less able to point at a *particular* people within the horizon of the Second Temple period author of Genesis 14* that nourished the memory of a King Tidal or a King Amraphel.

Nevertheless, as for Tidal in particular, no person with this name occurs elsewhere in the Bible.[90] However, the so-called Chedorlaomer texts from the Spartoli tablets of the British Museum referred to above (see 6.3.1.1, Earlier Attempts to Identify the Names) show beyond a doubt that people in the ancient Near East as late as in the Parthian period (ca. 238 BCE–224 CE!) were able to speak of a king *Tu-ud-hul-a*—a name mostly associated with the Hittite list of kings. Moreover, given that the Hebrew *Tidal* actually is a reflex of this name, it is not necessary to assume that the author of Genesis 14* used a *written* document as source. Further, it is not necessary to identify Tidal with a particular king (see 6.3.1.1, Earlier Attempts to Identify the Names). On the contrary, the author of Genesis 14* could have gotten the name through contact with people belonging

---

88 *Kutir* (rendered *Kudur* in Akkadian) means '(male or female) guarder, protector', and *Lagamar* is an Elamite goddess. See Schatz, *Genesis 14*, 87.

89 For instance, see Astour, 'Chedorlaomer', *ABD* 1:893–95.

90 See, e.g., note 55 above. Moreover, see *HALOT* 4, *s.v.* תִּדְעָל, 1689; and Astour, 'Tidal', *ABD* 6:551–52.

to foreign nations, perhaps such as those whom the Persians had settled in the former Northern Kingdom.[91]

Furthermore, as for Amraphel, there have been attempts in the history of research to identify him with persons known from history. As pointed out above, Margalith associated the name with a number of Ugaritic kings with the name 'Ammurapi. In addition, at the end of the nineteenth century, Amraphel was taken to be a Hebrew reflex of Hammurabi/Hammurapi, king of Babylon. Now, the latter identification was later rejected on historical and philological grounds. The historical counterargument is that Hammurabi never was active in the West.[92] Moreover, the philological counterarguments have been manifold. One problem is the vocalization. Which one was the original, the MT *Amraphel* or the LXX *Amarphal* (Αμαρφαλ)?[93] Another problem relates to the final *lamed* in Amraphel, which has no corresponding phoneme in Hammurabi. Therefore, most scholars (except for Margalith, who does not discuss the philological counterarguments) categorically conclude that it is philologically impossible that Amraphel in fact could be the same name as Hammurabi.[94]

The discussion about the identity of Amraphel outlined above, however, has taken place within a strict historical and philological paradigm. To me, it seems too categorical to completely rule out the possibility that the biblical name Amraphel is a reflex of the name Hammurabi, found, among other places, in Babylon and Ugarit. If the Second Temple period author of Genesis 14* learned about this particular name as a result of close or superficial contact with other peoples and their historical traditions, one should not expect his rendition of the name in question to be philologically 'correct' — according to the standards of modern comparative philology. A glimpse at early medieval literature written in Norse may illustrate how a name can be modified. King Sigurd I Magnusson (1090–1130) of Norway got the byname 'Jorsalfar' (= 'Jorsal-traveller') because of his crusade to Jerusalem, which in Norse was called *Jorsal* — a Norse adaption of the name. There is still a possibility for Amraphel

---

91   See 7.2.5 below, The World of Diaspora Communities Evident in Ezra 4: The Historical Background for the Construction of the Coalition of Chedorlaomer, Tidal, Amraphel and King Arioch

92   See Astour, 'Amraphel', *ABD* 1:217–18.

93   Böhl gives priority to the LXX reading 'Amarphal' and assumes that the MT vocalization is tendentious. Rather, by analogy with many names in the Mari texts, he assumes that the original name is *Amar-pî-el*. See Böhl, 'Das Zeitalter Abrahams', 26–49, 476–79 (45).

94   In addition to Böhl, see, e.g., Sarna, 'Amraphel', *EncJud* 2:106.

being an (albeit philologically 'incorrect') adaption of Hammurabi/
Hammurapi.

Summing up, of the four invading kingdoms, two are explicitly
found in the Table of Nations in Genesis 10 (Shinar, Elam). A third name,
Goiim, possibly corresponds to the phrase אִיֵּי הַגּוֹיִם, 'the islands of the
nations', in Gen. 10:5. The fourth name, Ellasar (אֶלָּסָר), is orthographically
reminiscent of Elishah (אֱלִישָׁה) in Gen. 10:4 (and it is possible to partially
explain the differences between the spelling of the two names). These
findings agree with the hypothesis that the author of Genesis 14* used
the Table of Nations as a source. However, I have to propose another
model for the personal names of the invaders. Although the Second Temple period author might have borrowed the name Arioch from biblical
literature, he may have got the rest from contact with other peoples, such
as those living in the diaspora in Samaria.

6.3.2 The Names of the Pentapolis Kings

Of the five Pentapolis kings, four are called by a name: King Bera (בֶּרַע)
of Sodom, King Birsha (בִּרְשַׁע) of Gomorrah, King Shinab (שִׁנְאָב) of Admah,
and King Shemeber (שֶׁמְאֵבֶר) of Zeboiim. The king of Bela/Zoar is anony-
mous. None of these four are known, however, from other biblical texts.
Moreover, in some cases the textual witnesses are not consistent. The
LXX reads Βαλλα instead of Bera and Σεννααρ instead of Shinab. In addition, Shemeber is rendered שמאבד in some Samaritan manuscripts and
שמיאבד by the *Genesis Apocryphon*.

The *Genesis Rabbah* and *Targum Pseudo-Jonathan* attest that there is an
old Jewish tradition to interpret these names as 'message names' (German: *redende Namen*). Bera is described as the villain (רע + ב, 'in evil');
Birsha as the sinner (רשע + ב, 'in sin/guilt'); Shinab as father-hater (from
שׂנא[95] + אב); and Shemeber[96] as a voluptuary (the name is derived from
שׁמם piel, 'to lay waste, to ruin', and אֶבֶר, 'member, penis').[97]

It is difficult to prove, however, whether these names from the outset
are to be understood as 'message names' or whether instead this reading

---

95   Note the initial letter שׂ, not שׁ!
96   The variant שמאבד (Sam. MSS)/שמיאבד (*Genesis Apocryphon*) could be read '[my] name
     is perished / destroyed'; cf. Fitzmyer, *Genesis Apocryphon*, 234. On philological specu-
     lations in general in literature from the intertestamental period, see, e.g., R. G. Kratz,
     '"Öffne seinen Mund und seine Ohren": Wie Abraham Hebräisch lernte', in *"Abraham,
     unser Vater": Die gemeinsamen Wurzeln von Judentum, Christentum und Islam* (ed. Rein-
     hard Gregor Kratz and Tilman Nagel; Göttingen: Wallstein, 2003), 53–66.
97   See *Targ. Ps.-J.* Gen. 14:2 and *Gen. R.* 41:5–7.

reflects a later development. In addition to the problem of vocalization (to what extent does the MT convey the original vocalization?) there is a text-critical problem (which reading is original?). Still, some considerations can be made in support of the assumption that the Jewish traditional reading of them as 'message names' actually renders the author's intention. First, 'message names' do occur already in biblical literature, as is evident in Isa. 7:3; Hos. 2:1, 23. Second, in light of the aetiological narrative in Gen. 19:18–22, the fifth of the five cities—Bela/Zoar—does appear to have a name that plays on the word מִצְעָר, 'little'. According to the model of the growth of the Abraham composition and the late date for Genesis 14* for which I have argued,[98] the author of Genesis 14* probably was aware of the play on the auditory similarity between צוֹעַר and מִצְעָר in Genesis 19. Third, it simply makes sense to read at least some of the names as 'message names'. In light of Genesis 19 and the anticipation of the destruction already given in Gen. 13:10, 13, there is nothing strange about the king of Sodom being called King 'In-Evil'[99] and the king of Gomorrah being called King 'In-Sin'.

Therefore, there are reasons to assume that the names of the Pentapolis kings were conceived as 'message names' from the outset. If that is the case, some of the names are derived from the biblical material (e.g., as King Bera ['In-Evil'] of Sodom). However, others may reflect traditions that have left no other tracks in the Bible (e.g., as Shemeber ['voluptuary']).

6.3.3 The Stations along Abram's Pursuit and Return

In addition to the stations along the route of Chedorlaomer's campaign, Genesis 14* offers a handful more place names in connection with Abram's pursuit and subsequent meeting with the king of Sodom (Gen. 14:14–17, 21–24). When Abram learns that Lot has been taken captive, he sets out from the oaks of his ally, Mamre the Amorite, and goes in pursuit of Chedorlaomer and his allies as far as *Dan* (דָּן, Gen. 14:14). From there, Abram and his 318 servants pursue them farther to a place *Hobah*, which the text locates to the north of *Damascus* (עַד־חוֹבָה אֲשֶׁר מִשְּׂמֹאל לְדַמָּשֶׂק, Gen. 14:15b).[100] After Abram returns the booty Chedorlaomer and his

---

98 See chapter 4, Genesis 14* and the Composition History of the Abraham Narratives.

99 See Gen. 13:13, where it says, וְאַנְשֵׁי סְדֹם רָעִים, 'And the men of Sodom were evil. . .'. The same root perhaps recurs in the name בֶּרַע; cf. Gen. 14:2.

100 For MT וַיֶּחֱלֹק (Gen. 14:15), see Hans-Georg von Mutius, 'Die Bedeutung von *wayyechaleq* in Genesis 14,15 im Licht der komparativen Semitistik und der aramäischen Qumranschrift *Genesis Apokryphon XXII,8ff*', BN 90 (1997): 8–12.

allies have taken, the king of Sodom goes out to meet him at a certain עֵמֶק שָׁוֵה,[101] the *Valley of Shaveh*, which is identified with the *King's Valley* (עֵמֶק הַמֶּלֶךְ, 14:17b). In what follows I will argue that some of these names may be considered to reflect geographical names that were in circulation in the Second Temple period whereas others are taken from biblical lore.

Dan: For a long time it has been recognized that a reference to Dan represents an anachronism in the context of the patriarchal period. According to Judg. 18:29 the Danites fought against the city Laish (לַיִשׁ), took possession of it, and called it Dan, after their ancestor Dan.[102] This ancestor was born to Jacob *after* the death of Abraham (see Gen. 30:6). In light of the general geographical interest the author of Genesis 14* displays, he probably refers to this particular city as the traditional northern border of Israel. In the period of the united monarchy, the formula 'from Dan to Beer-sheba' represented the northern and southern boundaries, either conventionally or perhaps also in reality.[103]

Hobah: Hobah (חוֹבָה), 'which is to the left of (that is, north of) Damascus', is unattested elsewhere in the Hebrew Bible. It has been suggested that the name is identical with the cuneiform inscription *māt ú-pí*, 'the land of 'Āpu/'Ōpu (from Egyptian *'ipwm*), which occurs in several inscriptions from the second millennium BCE. This land roughly embraced modern Syria and Lebanon.[104] Although this could be the case, this suggestion does not have any relevance for dating Genesis 14. J. Simons notes that 'it is hard to explain how U-be can be located "north of DAMMESEQ", unless it is also the name of a city (of which we have no knowledge)'.[105] However, an explanation for Simons's problem could be that the author of Genesis 14* knew about Hobah as an ancient name

---

101 The Samaritan Pentateuch reads עמק השוה.

102 According to a parallel account in Josh. 19:47, this city was formerly called Leshem (לֶשֶׁם).

103 See 1 Sam. 3:20; 2 Sam. 3:10; 17:11; 24:2, 15; and 1 Kgs. 5:5. See, moreover, texts such as 1 Kgs. 12:29–30 and 2 Kgs. 10:29, where Dan and Bethel respectively represent the northern and southern extremities of the Northern Kingdom. For a literary and historical introduction to the boundaries of Israel, see Volkmar Fritz, 'Die Grenzen des Landes Israel', in *Studies in Historical Geography and Biblical Historiography: Presented to Zecharia Kallai* (ed. Gershon Galil and Moshe Weinfeld; VTSup 81; Leiden: E. J. Brill, 2000), 14–34.

104 See *HALOT* 1, *s.v* חוֹבָה, 295; and Wayne T. Pitard, 'Damascus: Pre-Hellenistic History', *ABD* 2:5–7. For a cartographic presentation, see Othmar Keel, Max Küchler, and Christoph Uehlinger, *Orte und Landschaften der Bibel: Ein Handbuch und Studien-Reiseführer zum Heiligen Land. I Geographisch-geschichtliche Landeskunde* (Zürich: Benzinger Verlag, 1984), illustrations 115 and 119.

105 J. Simons, *The Geographical and Topographical Texts of the Old Testament: A Concise Commentary in XXXII Chapters* (Leiden: E. J. Brill, 1959), § 362–3/p. 215.

somehow associated with Damascus, but did not know exactly what the original reference of the name was, which was commonly used in the second millennium BCE. The result is a historically and geographically inaccurate location.

Moreover, a corresponding name is found in the book of Judith:

> Jdt. 15:5 (NRSV): When the Israelites heard it [i.e., that the Assyrians fled in panic], with one accord they fell upon the enemy, and cut them down as far as *Choba* [*my emphasis*]. Those in Jerusalem and all the hill country also came, for they were told what had happened in the camp of the enemy. The men in Gilead and in Galilee outflanked them with great slaughter, even beyond *Damascus* [*my emphasis*] and its borders.

The place Choba mentioned in Jdt. 15:5 is written in the same way as Hobah in LXX Gen. 15:15: Χωβα.[106] In this verse, the situation is very similar to the one depicted in Gen. 14:15. Moreover, Damascus also appears in Jdt. 15:5, as is also the case in Gen. 14:15.[107] Either the book of Judith is borrowing from Genesis 14, or it gives a parallel testimony about a city called Hobah, which in the Second Temple period may have been thought to be one of Israel's northern border towns.[108]

Damascus: With two exceptions in the Pentateuch (Gen. 14:15; 15:2), the city Damascus is first mentioned in connection with the account of David's wars in 2 Samuel 8, where it is reported that David stationed garrisons in this Aramaean city whose inhabitants became tributary vassals (2 Sam. 8:5–6).

The author of Genesis 14* probably could not have borrowed the reference to Damascus from Genesis 15. Although Genesis 15 as such probably antedates Genesis 14 and probably followed immediately after Genesis 13, the clause referring to Damascus in Gen. 15:2 appears to be secondary (see 4.3.6, Did Genesis 15 Originally Continue Genesis 13 or Genesis 14?).[109] Therefore, in light of the overall similarity to narratives

---

106 In the previous verse (Jdt. 15:4) a place Chobai (Χωβαι) appears as on the border of Israel (ὅριον Ισραηλ). Despite the fact that most translations render both by Choba, I, nevertheless, do not think the two places are identical. In Jdt. 15:4 *Chobai* seems to already be under Israelite control. In Jdt. 15:5 *Choba* is one of the places to which they pursued the Assyrians.

107 However, in Gen. 14:15 Hobah is located north of Damascus. In Jdt. 15:5 nothing is said about where Choba is located in relation to Damascus.

108 The problem to identify and, consequently, locate the place Hobah seems to be reflected in the rendition of the *Genesis Apocryphon*: חלבון 'Helbon'. Helbon, which is otherwise mentioned in Ezekiel's lamentation over Tyre (Ezek. 27:18), is located ca. 24 km north of Damascus. See Fitzmyer, *Genesis Apocryphon*, 243–44.

109 The glossator who inserted Damascus into Gen. 15:2 may have known and borrowed the reference to Damascus in Genesis 14*.

from 1–2 Samuel and 1–2 Kings,[110] it is more likely that the narratives from the historical books gave the author of Genesis 14* the impetus to include the city Damascus in Abram's itinerary.

The *Valley of Shave,* the *King's Valley*: After the victory over Chedor-laomer and the kings with him, Abram and his allies return and meet the king of Sodom in *the Valley of Shave* (עֵמֶק שָׁוֵה, Gen. 14:17). This place is not mentioned in any other biblical text. However, the place is equated with the *King's Valley* (עֵמֶק הַמֶּלֶךְ), a valley mentioned in 2 Sam. 18:18 as the place where Absalom set up a pillar for himself to keep his name in remembrance.

Regardless of whether this is a secondary gloss or stems from the hand of the author of Genesis 14*, the exact location of these two places is not known today.[111] The textual witnesses give the impression that it is not certain whether שָׁוֵה is a proper name (cf. the LXX Gen. 14:17 τὴν κοιλάδα τὴν Σαυη); or a common name (cf. *Targ. Onq.* Gen. 14:17 מִישַׁר מְפַנָּא, 'the *leveled* valley'; and the Samaritan Pentateuch עמק השוה, that is, with definite article).

Although the author apparently has not connected to any known biblical tradition when speaking about שָׁוֵה [עֵמֶק], the Copper Scroll from Qumran speaks of a place called *ha-Shave'* (השוא, 3Q15 8:10, 14), apparently in conjunction with Qidron, the valley between Jerusalem and the Mount of Olives. Given that שָׁוֵה and שוא[ה] are identical,[112] then the Qumran text demonstrates that such a place was known in the late part of the Second Temple period.[113] In light of this, an explanation of the place name עֵמֶק שָׁוֵה by way of Ugaritic literature is unnecessary.[114]

---

110 See above, 6.2.1, The Narrative Framework.

111 The *Genesis Apocryphon* identifies the King's Valley with the Vale of Beth-carma (בקעת בית כרמא, 1Q20 22:14), probably identical with the biblical Beth-haccherem (בֵּית הַכֶּרֶם, Jer. 6:1; Neh. 3:14), the location of which is suggested to be some 4 km south of Jerusalem. See Randall W. Younker, 'Beth-haccherem', *ABD* 1:686–87. Moreover, *Targ. Onq.* and *Targ. Ps.-J.* both identify the valley with בית ריסא (*Targ. Onq.*)/בית רסא (*Targ. Ps.-J.*), that is 'the racecourse, the arena'.

112 א can interchange with ה in Qumran Hebrew. A non-radical א can sometimes replace ה as a *mater lectionis* representing the vowel *e*. See Elisha Qimron, *The Hebrew of the Dead Sea Scrolls* (HSS 29; Atlanta: Scholars Press, 1986), § 100.7/p. 23.

113 However, the equation of the Valley of Shaveh with the King's Valley evident in Gen. 14:17 does not harmonize with the geographical knowledge expressed in the treasure list of the *Copper Scroll*. In the latter text Absalom's memorial appears not be located in *ha-Shave'*; compare 1Q15 10:12 with 2 Sam. 18:18, which says that it was located in the *King's Valley*.

114 For such a proposal, see Margalith, 'The Riddle of Genesis 14 and Melchizedek', 501–8 (505 n. 16).

6.4 The Map Plotted in Genesis 14 and David's Empire According to 2 Samuel 8

The itineraries in Genesis 14* constitute a geographical text.[115] The narrative plots a map of the land where Abram is *de facto* in power. By defeating Chedorlaomer and his allies, Abram succeeds them as masters over the land they have invaded (see Gen. 14:1–12). In addition, Abram also appears as master over the territories that he personally takes control over when he pursues and defeats Chedorlaomer (see Gen. 14:13–17, 21–24). The plotting of the narrative map evident in Genesis 14* is comparable to the *Genesis Apocryphon's* depiction of Abram's wandering through the land in 1Q20 21:15–19[116] (see 5.2.2, The Parallel to MT Genesis 13:14–18 in the Aramaic *Genesis Apocryphon;* and 5.2.3, Excursus: The Extent of the Promised Land and the Territories of the Invading Kings in the *Genesis Apocryphon*).

Therefore, although it is not explicitly stated in the narrative, we can assume that Abram, being superior to the subduing invaders, takes control over the fruits of their campaign.[117] At the end of Genesis 14*, Abram appears as one who completed the command in Gen. 13:17 to walk through the length and breadth of the land (the *ḥazakah*)—despite his initial passivity (see Gen. 13:18) and despite the campaign of Chedorlaomer.

Moreover, the land plotted in the narrative of Genesis 14*, and which at the conclusion of the chapter finally appears as belonging to Abram, resembles the extent of David's empire as presented in 2 Samuel 8. 2 Sam. 8:1–15 presents a catalogue of David's victories. The text reports that David defeated and gained control over the Aramaeans of Zobah and Damascus, the Ammonites, Moab, Edom, the Philistines, and the Amalekites:

> 2 Sam. 8:1–15 (NRSV): Some time afterward, David attacked the Philistines and subdued them. . . . [2] He also defeated the Moabites. . . . And the Moabites became servants to David and brought tribute. [3] David also struck down King Hadadezer son of Rehob of Zobah. . . . [5] When the Arameans of Damas-

---

115 For a discussion of the three main types of geographical documents of the Bible, see Aharoni, *The Land of the Bible*, 83–92. Aharoni divides the documents into historical-geographical descriptions, territorial administrative lists, and itineraries of expeditions and conquests. He holds Genesis 14 to be a very ancient example of the last type (pp. 92, 140–42)—a conviction I do not share. Moreover, see Philip S. Alexander, 'Geography and the Bible: Early Jewish Geography', *ABD* 2:977–88.

116 Alexander, 'Geography and the Bible', *ABD* 2:977–88 (986).

117 Thus also Zecharia Kallai, 'The Campaign of Chedorlaomer and Biblical Historiography', in Kallai, *Biblical Historiography and Historical Geography: Collection of Studies* (BEAT 44; Frankfurt am Main: Peter Lang, 1998), 218–42 (239).

cus came to help King Hadadezer of Zobah, David killed twenty-two thousand men of the Arameans. [6] Then David put garrisons among the Arameans
of Damascus; and the Arameans became servants to David and brought
tribute. . . . [11] These [precious gifts] also King David dedicated to Yahweh,
together with the silver and gold that he dedicated from all the nations he
subdued, [12] from Edom, Moab, the Ammonites, the Philistines, the Amalekites, and from the spoil of King Hadadezer son of Rehob of Zobah. [13] . . .
When he returned, he killed eighteen thousand Edomites in the Valley of
Salt. [14] He put garrisons in Edom; throughout all Edom he put garrisons,
and all the Edomites became David's servants. And Yahweh gave victory
to David wherever he went. [15] So David reigned over all Israel; and David
administered justice and equity to all his people.

Apart from the Philistine territory, the territories of the ethnic groups
mentioned in 2 Samuel 8 are embraced by the itineraries of the eastern
kings (Gen. 14:5–7) and Abram (14:13–15) respectively.

Therefore, the author of Genesis 14* probably borrows from the tradition about the magnitude of King David's empire—either identical
with that reflected in 2 Samuel 8 or a tradition similar to it—when he
composed his late text about Abram's war with the four kings.[118]

6.5 Summary

I have attempted to substantiate the thesis that the author of Genesis
14* composed his narrative to a considerable extent by borrowing from
other biblical texts. Three biblical texts or text groups seem to crystallize
as the author's sources. One source is the historical books. Narratives
from these books, and especially from 1 Samuel 30, provided the author
with both style and narrative framework. Moreover, the Table of Nations
(Genesis 10) seems to have been another important source. The author
has probably drawn much of the geographical data from this text. This is
probably also the text that acquainted the author of Genesis 14* with the
merging of the originally two separate traditions about cities of destruction into a Tetrapolis (Sodom and Gomorrah + Admah and Zeboiim).
Finally, yet another important biblical source for the author is the wilderness wandering narrative (Deuteronomy 1–3; Numbers 10–21). In
this narrative the author found an itinerary that he inverted and turned
into Chedorlaomer's campaign route. In addition, he found place names

---

118 With the exception of Philistia, mentioned in 2 Sam. 8:1, and which is not explicitly
referred to in Genesis 14*.

that he personalized and turned into persons in the narrative in Genesis 14*.

Not all of the names in Genesis 14*, however, are borrowed from these biblical texts. In addition to the author's extensive borrowing from biblical literature that obviously antedate the date of composition of Genesis 14*, he must have gotten some names from other sources as well. Above, I have proposed that the multicultural environment of the Second Temple period, characterized by several diaspora communities, provided meeting places where the history and culture of different nations may have been exchanged. For instance, in light of the presence of an Elamite diaspora community in Second Temple period Samaria, it is not necessarily strange that the assumedly Jewish author of Genesis 14* refers to a King Chedorlaomer of Elam. Such an exchange of knowledge, regardless of whether it is cursory or more thorough, provides a better explanation and model for the names of the four invading kings in Genesis 14* than the hypothesis about the so-called Chedorlaomer texts as *Vorlage*.[119]

Finally, I have argued that Genesis 14*, being a geographical text, plots a map of the Promised Land. The land over which Abram appears as master resembles King David's empire as presented in 2 Samuel 8. The author of Genesis 14* probably borrowed this map when composing Genesis 14*.

---

119 See 6.3.1.1 above, Earlier Attempts to Identify the Names.

7. The Historical Motivation for the Author of Genesis 14* and the Text's Historical Meaning

I have previously shown that the composition of Genesis 14* may have been triggered by a *Leerstelle* after Gen. 13:17–18.[1] The argumentation there was literary in orientation. In the present chapter I will also pursue the same main question: Why did someone compose Genesis 14*? Whereas the approach was literarily oriented in chapter 5, the same question will be examined from a historical perspective in the present chapter (i.e., is there anything in the author's own time that can explain both *why* he composed the text and *how* he did it?). Is there anything in the general period of the author that might shed light on Genesis 14*?

In order to discuss the historical rationales that may underlie the composition of Genesis 14*, I propose a qualified estimation of the date of composition for Genesis 14*. Consequently, I will first synthesize the previous conclusions that are relevant for finding the general period in which the author of Genesis 14* did his work. As already hinted at, I argue that Genesis 14* was composed in either the Persian or the early Hellenistic period. Unfortunately, I am not able to be more precise than that (see 7.1, The Date of Composition: A Synthesis of the Different Approaches).

Next, I will focus on different trends and concepts in these periods. This work will provide important background information that might contribute to answering *why* Genesis 14* was composed and, moreover, why the composition resulted in what it did (see 7.2, Postexilic Ideas and Events as Possible Background for Genesis 14*).

Finally, at the end of the chapter I will propose some conjectures about the meaning Genesis 14* had in its original historical context. I will not use Genesis 14* as a source for the history of the period in which it was composed. On the contrary, I will attempt to use postexilic sources to shed light on Genesis 14*. Nevertheless, I will attempt to use Genesis 14* as a historical source, not for any particular period, but for the ideology of the author, asking what his message might have been (see 7.3, A

---

1   See chapter 5, Why Was Genesis 14* Composed and Inserted into the Abraham Narrative? An Attempt at a Literary Answer.

Plea for Restoration: Attempt at Some Historically Qualified Conjectures about the Historical Meaning and the Ideology of the Author).

7.1 The Date of Composition: A Synthesis of the Different Approaches

In the following, I will synthesize the conclusions I have made previously that are relevant to dating Genesis 14*.

In chapter 3, Genesis 14* and the Abraham Tradition, I discussed the sparse information about Abraham outside the Pentateuch. Although a late preexilic tradition about him is attested to (and rejected!) in Ezekiel 33, there are good reasons to assume that Abraham's status as the first and most venerable of the patriarchs is a relatively late development.

In chapter 4, Genesis 14* and the Composition History of the Abraham Narratives, I focused on the compositional history of the Abraham narratives, emphasizing the particular stage where Genesis 14* was added to the growing Abraham narratives. I concluded that Genesis 14* was added *after* the composition and insertion of Genesis 15 into the Abraham narratives. Moreover, following Christoph Levin, I concluded that it is likely that Genesis 15 is a post-Priestly text. Consequently, Genesis 14* is a post-Priestly text written for its present position immediately after Genesis 13. Moreover, this thread is continued in chapter 5, Why Was Genesis 14* Composed and Inserted into the Abraham Narrative? An Attempt at a Literary Answer. There I argued that it makes sense to read Genesis 14* as a secondary response to a *Leerstelle* at the conclusion of Genesis 13.

In chapter 6, The Literary Building Blocks of the Author of Genesis 14*, I attempted to identify the sources from which the author borrowed the literary building blocks when composing Genesis 14*. Three biblical texts/text groups crystallize as the author's sources: (1) the historical books, especially 1 Samuel 30, (2) the Table of Nations (Genesis 10), and (3) the wilderness wandering narratives (especially the résumé in Deuteronomy 1–3). At least the last two sources are relatively late. The historical books and the historical introduction to the book of Deuteronomy in Deuteronomy 1–3 are thoroughly Deuteronomistic in formulation.[2] Moreover, as for the Table of Nations, the backbone is probably a Priestly text into which older Yahwistic material has been subsequently

---

2   See, e.g., Walter Dieterich, 'Deuteronomistisches Geschichtswerk', *RGG*[4] 2, cols. 688–92 (690); Eckart Otto, 'Deuteronomium', *RGG*[4] 2, cols. 693–96 (696); and Weinfeld, *Deuteronomy 1–11*, 13–14.

inserted.[3] The author of Genesis 14* appears to have at his disposal a *later* and *expanded* version because he borrows from both the Priestly (גוים and Elam; see Gen. 10:5, 22) and the Yahwistic (Shinar, Amorites; see Gen. 10:10, 16, in addition to the Tetrapolis; see Gen. 10:19[4]) parts. Moreover, the catalogue of David's victories in 2 Samuel 8—which illustrates the extent of his empire and which I argue is echoed in Genesis 14*—is probably also a Deuteronomistic compilation.[5]

Independently of each other, the approaches above point in the same direction. The composition of Genesis 14* took place at a time *after* most of the Abraham narratives in Genesis 12–25 had been composed, *after* the composition of different Deuteronomistic texts, and also *after* the composition of the Priestly material. The so-called Deuteronomistic History was not composed by one hand but grew over time.[6] Therefore, one cannot give a single date for its composition. Moreover, there is no consensus about the date of composition of the Priestly writing. Was it composed in Babylon *during* the exile or in Judah *after* the return—or was it perhaps composed *before* the exile, as is also argued?[7] This is not the place for a discussion of the date of the Priestly writing. Nevertheless, proceeding from the premise that the author actually borrowed material from all the mentioned biblical sources, the Priestly writing most probably took place *after* the Babylonian exile. Therefore, I propose the early postexilic period as a tentative *terminus a quo* for the composition of Genesis 14*.

At the opposite end of the scale, the *terminus ante quem* cannot be later than the date of composition of the book of *Jubilees*. *Jubilees* offers the first known example of reception history of Genesis 14 (see *Jub.* 13:22–29). This book, belonging to the genre of rewritten Bible, was probably composed in the middle of the second century BCE.[8]

---

3   For more about the Priestly and Yahwistic components of the Table of Nations, see Westermann, *Genesis 1–11*, 498–501.

4   Westermann argues that Admah and Zeboiim probably were subsequently added to the Yahwistic part of the Table of Nations; see Westermann, *Genesis 1–11*, 524.

5   So Peter Kyle McCarter, *II Samuel: A New Translation with Introduction, Notes and Commentary* (AB 9; New York: Doubleday, 1984), 251. Moreover, Hans Joachim Stoebe also holds the compilation in 2 Samuel 8 to be 'relativ jung' but not necessarily Deuteronomistic; see Stoebe, *Das zweite Buch Samuelis* (KAT 8.2; Gütersloh: Gütersloher Verlagshaus, 1994), 28, 46, 245–46.

6   See McCarter, *II Samuel*, 6–8; and Dieterich, 'Deuteronomistisches Geschichtswerk', *RGG*[4] 2, cols. 688–92 (689).

7   See Erich Zenger et al., *Einleitung in das Alte Testament* (4th ed.; Studienbücher Theologie 1,1; Stuttgart: W. Kohlhammer, 2001), 152–53.

8   According to James C. VanderKam, between ca. 163–161 BCE on the one hand and ca. 140 BCE on the other; see VanderKam, *Textual and Historical Studies in the Book of Jubilees* (HSM 14; Missoula, MT: Scholars Press for Harvard Semitic Museum, 1977), 283.

Proceeding from the discussion above, I argue that Genesis 14* was composed either in the fifth, fourth, third, or in the first half of the second century BCE. I am not able to be more precise. However, as for the history of Judah, we know that these three and a half centuries cover the entire Persian period and the early Hellenistic period. I will build on this conclusion in the following.

7.2 Postexilic Ideas and Events as Possible Background for Genesis 14*

In order to reach a qualified conjecture about the historical reasons that the author had for writing Genesis 14*, I will first on the basis of the meagre source material reconstruct certain relevant trends and conceptions that we can infer were current among Jews in the Persian and early Hellenistic periods.[9] Among these is the function Abra(ha)m had in the biblical literature (see 7.2.1, Abram in Genesis 14*—A Model Figure). Another trend during those landless times was that the delimitation of ha-ʾareṣ continued as a literary topos, despite the fact that this was a time when Judah had suffered loss of statehood and territory (see 7.2.6, The Delimitation of ha-ʾareṣ as a Literary Topos in Postexilic Period). Yet another characteristic feature of some literature from this period is the mix of fact and fiction evident in (quasi-)historical narratives (see 7.2.7, Fact and Fiction Interwoven in Quasi-Historical Narratives from the Persian and Hellenistic Periods).

7.2.1 Abram in Genesis 14*—A Model Figure

In biblical literature outside the Pentateuch from the Persian and Hellenistic periods, Abraham probably functioned as more than simply a distant figure of the past. His observance of the law was found to be ideal (Sir. 44:19; *Jub.* 15:1 [implicitly the first on earth to observe the feast of the firstfruits of the harvest of grains; see Lev. 23:15–20]; 16:21 [explicitly the first on earth to observe the feast of booths; see Lev. 23:33–44]; CD 3:2–4

---

9   For a presentation of various aspects of Israel in the Persian period, see, e.g., Erhard S. Gerstenberger, *Israel in der Perserzeit: 5. und 4. Jahrhundert v. Chr.* (Biblische Enzyklopädie 8; Stuttgart: W. Kohlhammer, 2005).

[Abraham as God's friend]). In many ways, Abram was an ideal to be followed.[10]

Moreover, also in the Pentateuch itself, Abraham incorporates and anticipates the people of Israel. By leaving Mesopotamia (Gen. 12:1–4) Abraham already anticipates the wandering of the deported ones who returned from the Babylonian exile. Further, he seems to incorporate the people of Israel and anticipate their wandering down to and exodus out of Egypt (Gen. 12:10–20). Just as the fathers of the people of Israel went to Egypt because there was a famine in the land (Genesis 37–50), so also a famine caused Abraham to go to Egypt (Gen. 12:10). Like the people of Israel went out of Egypt with riches, so also did Abraham (Exod. 12:35–36; cf. Gen. 12:16). The similarities between the patriarch and the people in terms of destiny are not the result of pure coincidences. For instance, it has been demonstrated by means of literary criticism that the story of the endangerment of the ancestress in Gen. 12:10–20 has been placed in the Abraham composition at a relatively late stage and, moreover, that an important *Vorlage* for the author of this story was the text in Exod. 11:1–3. On this basis, Christoph Levin concludes that the story about Abram and Sarah in Egypt in Gen. 12:10–20 is post-Priestly.[11] Michael Fishbane explains the parallels between Abraham and the people of Israel (their common going down to, sojourn in, and going out of Egypt) as 'typological reshaping'; Abraham is made to prefigure the people of Israel.[12]

The book of Micah offers a controllable case where Abraham explicitly functions as a model figure for a larger corporate entity; see Mic. 7:20:

---

10   See Beate Ego, 'Abraham als Urbild der Toratreue Israels: Traditionsgeschichtliche Überlegungen zu einem Aspekt des biblischen Abrahamsbildes', in *Bund und Tora: Zur theologischen Begriffsgeschichte in alttestamentlicher, frühjüdischer und urchristlicher Tradition* (ed. Friedrich Avemaria and Hermann Lichtenberger; WUNT 92; Tübingen: J. C. B. Mohr [Paul Siebeck], 1996), 25–40.

11   See the outline of Levin's argumentation above in 4.3.3, Material Dependent on the Priestly Material. The opinion that Gen. 12:10–20 is a typological anticipation with a late date of composition is put forward by Blum, *Die Komposition der Vätergeschichte*, 309; and by Schmid, *Erzväter und Exodus*, 64.

12   By reshaping an *already exisiting narrative tradition about Abraham* (Fishbane does not say anything about what this narrative about Abraham would be like), Abraham is 'in his lifetime' made to anticipate the destiny of his decendants; see Fishbane, *Biblical Interpretation in Ancient Israel*, 375–76. However, as I see it, such a narrative tradition must either have included most of the basic framework now evident in Genesis 12 (Abraham going down *who-knows-where* and then going out from the same *who-knows-where* with riches). A much easier explanation is that the basic outline of the Exodus narrative was (re-)used to create a *new* narrative, this time with *Abraham* as the protagonist. The only preexisting narrative element would be the name 'Abraham'.

תִּתֵּן אֱמֶת לְיַעֲקֹב חֶסֶד לְאַבְרָהָם אֲשֶׁר־נִשְׁבַּעְתָּ לַאֲבֹתֵינוּ מִימֵי קֶדֶם

Micah 7:20 (NRSV): You will show faithfulness to Jacob and unswerving loyalty to Abraham, as you have sworn to our ancestors from the days of old.

Here, Abraham—alongside Jacob—functions as a representative for the speaking corporate entity. The identity of the speaking 'we' is therefore important to address the question of how Abraham functions: the name stands collectively for Israel.[13]

Micah 7:20 concludes the last of the three psalms attached to the book of Micah (Mic. 7:8–20). These psalms are postexilic.[14] In his study of the redaction history of the book of Micah, B. M. Zapff attributes these psalms to a redactional layer that in the postexilic period updates and expands its preexilic *Vorlage*. In this late layer (Zapff: *Fortschreibungsschicht*), the biblical traditions attached to the patriarch and the exodus out of Egypt each play important roles. At the same time, the author of the *Fortschreibungsschicht* is influenced by a number of prophecies of Isaiah.[15] Because this redactional layer not only reworks the book of Micah but also the entire Book of the Twelve, Zapff concludes at the outset that we are dealing here with relatively *late* adoptions. On the basis of both text-internal and text-external criteria, Zapff argues that the *Fortschreibungsschicht*—of which Mic. 7:20 and the use of Abraham as a model figure is part—can be dated to the middle of the third century BCE.[16] Although other scholars are not as precise as Zapff in terms of dating, there is nevertheless a consensus that this part of the book of Micah dates to the postexilic period.

7.2.2 The Corporate Use of Abram and the Invading Kings

Given that Genesis 14* is a postexilic text and, in addition, given that Abraham in postexilic literature functions as a model figure for the contemporary people of Israel, we may assume that Abram in Genesis 14* did not simply represent a historical figure. Rather, the author intended him to symbolize the people of Israel. So, we may assume that a postexilic reading of Genesis 14* would imply that it was the *people of Israel* who were seen fighting the invaders through their model figure, Abra(ha)m.

---

13   Rainer Kessler, *Micha* (HTKAT; Freiburg im Breisgau: Herder, 1999), 311.
14   See, e.g., Kessler, *Micha*, 47, 234.
15   See Zapff, *Redaktionsgeschichtliche Studien zum Michabuch*, 217.
16   Zapff, *Redaktionsgeschichtliche Studien zum Michabuch*, 280–85.

In light of the thesis that the people of Israel and their destiny have been projected back onto Abram, I suggest that the author intended that King Chedorlaomer of Elam should represent a contemporary hostile power, and not merely a figure of the past. However, a more precise identification of this enemy must necessarily be open to discussion. The lack of a more precise date of composition for Genesis 14* implies that there may be several candidates, provided that King Chedorlaomer of Elam actually represents a particular power.

In my opinion, the most likely proposal is that Elam (see Gen. 14:1, 9) actually stands for a concrete power, namely, Persia. Although ancient Elam had ceased to exist as an independent political entity in the post-exilic period, its ancient capital, Susa, continued to function as one of the capitals of the Persian Empire. Moreover, Elamite continued to be used as the official language. Therefore, Elam did continue to exist as a cultural entity. During the Persian period, a Jew writing from the perspective of the tiny province of Judah may have used Elam as an alias for Persia in a way comparable to how Media was closely connected to Persia.[17]

There are other examples from both late-biblical and intertestamental literature that ethnic and geographic names refer to something other than what they mean literally. For instance, the name Kittim has a rich history of reception. In the Baalam prophecy there is talk about 'ships from Kittim' (וְצִים מִיַד כִּתִּים, Num. 24:24). Kittim is usually understood as a Hebrew rendition of Cition, a city on Cyprus. Nevertheless, in a later reuse of this prophecy, the 'ships of Kittim' (צִיִּים כִּתִּים, Dan. 11:30) apparently refer to the Romans, as probably is the case in most of the references to the name in the Dead Sea scrolls (e.g., 1QM 1:2, 4, 6, 9; 11:9, 11, 15; 26:3, 6, 9).[18] Another example is the use of 'Damascus' in the *Damascus Document* (e.g., CD-A 6.5, 'the converts of Israel who left the land of Judah and lived in the land of Damascus'). In this text, the reoccurring name 'land of Damascus' has, for the most part, *not* been interpreted literally as the city itself.[19]

---

17   See Esth. 1:3 ('the army of Persia and Media'), 14, 18; 10:2 ('annals of the kings of Media and Persia'); Dan. 8:20 ('the ram that you saw with the two horns, these are the kings of Media and Persia'). Note however that Horst Seebass has argued that Elam in Genesis 14 refers to a place in the desert region south of Judah; see Seebass, 'Der Ort Elam in der südlichen Wüste und die Überlieferung von Gen. XIV', *VT* 15 (1965): 389–94.

18   See Timothy H. Lim, 'Kittim', *EncDSS* 1:469–71.

19   See Jerome Murphy-O'Connor, 'Damascus ', *EncDSS* 1:165–66.

7.2.3 Not a Concrete but a Typical Campaign?

Having proposed that the author of Genesis 14* may have used Elam as a kind of 'code name', I do not imply, however, that the campaign of King Chedorlaomer and his allies reflects a concrete historical campaign in or near the biblical Promised Land. During the period of three and a half centuries that frame the date of composition of Genesis 14*, there were several cases of local revolts that were followed by Persian penal campaigns. Also later in the Hellenistic period, Palestine was not untouched by military struggle.

Unfortunately, the history of the province of Judah in the Persian and early Hellenistic periods is obscure. As a result of the Persian victory over the Neo-Babylonian empire, the land that was a kingdom until the fall of Jerusalem in 586 BCE appeared in a new fashion as the province of Judah (Aramaic יְהוּד מְדִינְתָּא). Together with other provinces, Judah was part of the satrapy Babylon and Beyond the River (עֲבַר־נַהֲרָה)[20] — one of the twenty satrapies that the Persians organized.[21] After Alexander's victory over the last Persian king, Darius III Codommanus, at Issus in 333 BCE, Judah also continued as a province (to be sure, enjoying autonomy) under Macedonian, Egyptian/Ptolamaic, and eventually Syrian/Seleucid rule. Judah regained independence under the Hasmonaean priest-kings for approximately a century after the middle of the second century BCE.

For the last two centuries of Persian rule (that is, after Ezra and Nehemiah and before Alexander), no Judean *historical* sources for the history of this particular province are known (Herbert Donner: *das dunkle Jahrhundert*). Moreover, little is known of the history of the province under Ptolemaic rule (320–198 BCE). However, for the periods of Seleucid rule, Maccabaean revolt, and Hasmonaean kingdom we do have some sources.[22]

Nonetheless, as for the Persian Empire as a whole, we know that it suffered from both external and internal threats. As for Judah's neighbourhood, we know that Persia was occupied with struggling for control over Egypt several times. It may be that the Persian army never passed

---

20 Subsequently, Beyond the River became a satrapy of its own.
21 So Herodotus, *Histories*, 3.89–97.
22 Herbert Donner, *Geschichte des Volkes Israel und seiner Nachbarn in Grundzügen*. II *Von der Königszeit bis zu Alexander dem Grossen: mit einem Ausblick auf die Geschichte des Judentums bis Bar Kochba* (2d ed.; ATD Ergänzungsreihe 14/1–2; Göttingen: Vandenhoeck & Ruprecht, 1995), 467. Moreover, Lester L. Grabbe, *Judaism from Cyrus to Hadrian*. I *The Persian and Greek Periods* (Minneapolis, MN: Augsburg Fortress, 1992), 119, 205.

through the tiny province of Judah, located in the periphery in the Judean hill country, when it was on its way to put down revolts. There is no explicit evidence for that, either in the Bible or in any other source. Yet, one should consider it highly probable that the inhabitants of Judah were aware of the different Persian military manoeuvres in their own part of the world.[23]

For instance, Egypt ended up under Persian rule during two separate periods.[24] In connection with the first period of occupation, Herodotus reports that the Persian troops on the march against Egypt were supplied with water by Arabs when crossing the dessert.[25] In addition, there were several revolts in different satrapies in the western parts of the empire.[26]

Moreover, there is speculation about whether there is indirect evidence in the Bible for a Persian campaign in the province of Judah. According to Neh. 1:1–4, Nehemiah was shocked to hear that the wall of Jerusalem was broken down and that its gates had been destroyed by fire. According to accepted chronology, this took place in 445 BCE, more than seventy years after the rebuilding of the temple (Ezra 6:15, 'in the sixth year of the reign of King Darius', that is, 516 BCE). This has provoked the question of whether there was a Judean revolt against the Persians that has otherwise been left unrecorded; however, it would have been a revolt that ended in the destruction of the wall of Jerusalem.[27]

As for the history of Judah under Macedonian, Ptolemaic, and Seleucid rule, the situation regarding historical sources is to some extent unfortunate; much of the history of Judah remains obscure. However, it is known that Alexander the Great marched southward against Egypt along *Via Maris*[28] after having defeated Tyre in 332 BCE. However, he did not campaign in the hinterland, including Jerusalem.[29] Whereas little is known about Judah in the Ptolemaic period, the sources eventually

---

23   See Aharoni, *The Land of the Bible*, 412.

24   First Persian Occupation: 525–404 BCE; Second Persian Occupation (343/342–332 BCE).

25   Herodotus, *Histories*, 3.7–9; see Amélie Kuhrt, *The Ancient Near East: c. 3000–330 BC*. II (Routledge History of the Ancient World; London: Routledge, 1995), 661–64.

26   See Grabbe, *Judaism from Cyrus to Hadrian*, I, 125–26, 139–42.

27   Ephraim Stern considers it probable that the walls of Jerusalem were destroyed in the revolt of Megabuzus (satrap of the satrapy Beyond the River) in 448 BCE; see Stern, 'The Persian Empire and the Political and Social History of Palestine in the Persian Period', *CHJ* 1:70–87 (73–74). Moreover, see Grabbe, *Judaism from Cyrus to Hadrian*, I, 93–94, 132.

28   See Isa. 9:1, 'the way by the sea', דֶּרֶךְ הַיָּם, that is, the coastal plains.

29   Despite what the Jewish Alexander legend tells, namely that Alexander visited Jerusalem and its temple (see Josephus, *Ant.* 11.325–40). It is impossible to reconcile the claim

start to speak again in connection with the strife between the Ptolemies and the Seleucids over Palestine shortly before the middle of the second century BCE. This struggle is alluded to in Daniel 11. From the perspective of Judah, the period after Alexander must have been influenced by the continuing struggle between the Ptolemies and the Seleucids over control of southern Syria and Palestine.[30]

In summary, I have argued that Genesis 14* was composed either in the Persian or the early Hellenistic period. Although there is no evidence of any Persian military campaign in the province of Judah or its immediate surroundings in this general period, there were evidently several revolts in the western part of the Persian Empire followed by Persian attempts to put them down. Moreover, there is no reason why Jews, either in Judah or in one of the many Jewish colonies, should not have been informed about these struggles.

Therefore, the author did not necessarily have a particular campaign in mind when he composed Genesis 14*. On the contrary, an equally possible assumption is that he renders a *typical* situation in which the Empire attempts to manifest its force.

7.2.4 Genesis 14*: An Anti-Persian Text?

In most cases, the biblical literature from the Persian and Hellenistic periods demonstrates a positive Jewish attitude toward the Persians. For instance, in Deutero-Isaiah, King Cyrus is enthusiastically called Yahweh's shepherd, the executioner of his will, his anointed, and the redeemer of the exiled (Isa. 44:28; 45:1, 13). The books of Ezra and Nehemiah also seem to reflect a predominantly positive attitude. This is especially evident in the so-called Cyrus decree (Ezra 1:2–4; cf. 6:3–6).

However, Persia does not have only positive connotations in biblical and other Jewish literature from this general period. In Dan. 10:13, 20, a 'prince [of the kingdom] of Persia' (פָּרַס [מַלְכוּת] שַׂר) is an enemy of the good and celestial prince Michael.

In addition, whether it is authentic or not, the disputed letter from the people of Samaria to King Artaxerxes (Ezra 4:11–16) indirectly reveals that (re-)building the wall of Jerusalem could cause accusations against the Jews of disloyalty to the Persian king. Also, the reaction of Sanballat and Tobiah against Nehemiah's rebuilding of the wall (Neh.

---

of the legend with otherwise accepted historical knowledge. See Grabbe, *Judaism from Cyrus to Hadrian*, I, 181–82, 205–8.

30　Grabbe, *Judaism from Cyrus to Hadrian*, I, 204–5.

2:19) testifies that such a building activity—which one would expect to have been welcomed by most Jews—could potentially be seen as a hostile action against the Persian king. Therefore, based on the biblical literature, the Jewish attitude toward the Persians may well have been more ambivalent than the enthusiasm expressed in Deutero-Isaiah's proclaiming of Cyrus as Yahweh's messiah.

7.2.5 The World of Diaspora Communities Evident in Ezra 4: The Historical Background for the Construction of the Coalition of Chedorlaomer, Tidal, Amraphel, and King Arioch?

More can be said about the opposition against Judah and Benjamin summarized in Ezra 4.[31] At first glance, Ezra 4:6–24 appears to be chronologically displaced because the text is about opposition during two distinct reigns *subsequent to* Darius I (522–486 BCE), namely, those of Xerxes I (486–465/4) and of Artaxerxes I Longimanus (465/4–425). However, this apparent displacement is probably due to a compositional technique common among ancient writers; in the resumptive verse Ezra 4:24, the author reattaches to the period of King Darius the narrative sequence he left just before the summary of opposition (see Ezra 4:5).[32]

Particularly interesting is the reference to the people living in Samaria who wrote the second mentioned letter (see Ezra 4:7) to Artaxerxes concerning the building of the wall of Jerusalem:

Ezra 4:8–11 (NRSV): Rehum the royal deputy and Shimshai the scribe wrote a letter against Jerusalem to King Artaxerxes as follows [9] (then Rehum the royal deputy, Shimshai the scribe, and the rest of their associates, the judges, the envoys, the officials, the Persians, the people of Erech, the Babylonians, the people of Susa, that is, the Elamites, [10] and the rest of the nations whom the great and noble Osnappar deported and settled in the cities of Samaria and in the rest of the province Beyond the River wrote—and now [11] this is a copy of the letter that they sent): 'To King Artaxerxes: Your servants, the people of the province Beyond the River, send greeting. . .'.

It is possible that vv. 9–11aα are secondary interpolations, but that is not the concern here.[33] What is interesting here is that this text, which is evi-

---

31   See also 6.3.1.2 above, My Proposal: Borrowings from the Table of Nations (Genesis 10) and from the Foreign Population Living in Diaspora.

32   Joseph Blenkinsopp, *Ezra–Nehemiah: A Commentary* (OTL; London: SCM, 1989), 42–43.

33   Blenkinsopp, *Ezra–Nehemiah*, 112.

dently postexilic,[34] gives us a glimpse of how postexilic Jews saw their contemporary world — politically, historically and ethno-demographically.

Ezra 4 reveals that *Elamites* were among those who had been deported and settled (Aramaic נלה *haphel* and יתב *haphel*) in Samaria. This fact strengthens the assumption that the author of Genesis 14* may have had a certain working knowledge of Elamite affairs, such as Elamite historical names and name patterns. One cannot exclude the possibility that the postexilic author got to know this from written documents that are comparable to King Xerxes' trilingual foundation tablet from Persepolis in Akkadian, Persian, and Elamite.[35] However, as argued earlier (see 6.3.1.2, My Proposal: Borrowings from the Table of Nations (Genesis 10) and from the Foreign Population Living in Diaspora), the source may have been much closer, namely, Elamites such as those who had been deported to Samaria.

Therefore, Ezra 4:9–11aα demonstrates that Jews in the postexilic period could conceive of those who had been deported to the former northern kingdom Israel as their adversaries (see Ezra 4:1 צר). Nevertheless, the Jewish worldview expressed in the postexilic Ezra 4 provokes the following question: Did the postexilic author of Genesis 14* construct the coalition consisting of King Chedorlaomer of Elam, King Tidal of Goiim, King Amraphel of Shinar, and King Arioch of Ellasar (Gen. 14:1, 9) on the basis of negative first-hand experiences with deportees, comparable to the situation described in Ezra 4:9–11aα?

No definitive answer can be given. One can assume, however, that the Judeans had more regular contact with the groups that the Persians had deported and settled in Samaria than they had with their common Persian masters. Therefore, from the perspective of Judah, the deportees and their masters may have been seen as two sides of the same coin. Such a mix-up of masters and deportees may explain why it is *Elam* in the narrative of Genesis 14* that plays an otherwise typical *Persian* role, namely, that of a sovereign putting down revolts.[36]

---

34 On the basis of a comparison with Aramaic correspondence, Dirk Schwiderski concludes that the Aramaic letters of the book of Ezra are fictitious texts entirely created for a literary context. A probable date of composition for the Aramaic letter in Ezra 4 is the early Hellenistic (third century BCE); cf. Schwiderski, *Handbuch des nordwestsemitischen Briefformulars: Ein Beitrag zur Echtheitsfrage der aramäischen Briefe des Esrabuches* (BZAW 295; Berlin: W. de Gruyter, 2000), 375–82. See also Kratz, *Composition*, 61–62.

35 *ANET* 316–17.

36 For the use of 'code names' in the intertestamental period, see also the reference to 'Kittim' in 1QM (the *War Scroll*). According to Philip R. Davies, the Kittim cannot be

7.2.6 The Delimitation of *ha-ʾareṣ* as a Literary Topos
in the Postexilic Period

After the Babylonian exile, Judah was not an independent state but an autonomous province until it again became independent for a short period under Hasmonaean rule. From a geographical viewpoint it had become but a tiny province, with Jerusalem in the middle and with the most distant boundaries approximately 30–40 km away from the city. Nevertheless, the loss of statehood and territory did not cause the authors of biblical literature composed during and after the exile to refrain from dealing with geographical issues. On the contrary, the delimitation of *ha-ʾareṣ* ('the Land') continued, perhaps even more so, to be a literary topos in Jewish writing—despite the political and geographical realities.

The boundaries of the Promised Land are described in detail particularly in three biblical texts: Numbers 34, Joshua 13–19, and Ezekiel 47. Scholars commonly assume that these texts somehow are generically related to one another. As for Ezekiel 47, there is no doubt that the text was composed at a time when Judah had ceased to exist as an independent state, regardless of whether it is literarily dependent on other texts or not. In Ezek. 47:13–23, Yahweh reveals to the prophet Ezekiel the new boundaries of the land. The northern boundary is especially detailed with many geographically fixed points (vv. 15–17). The eastern (v. 18), southern (v. 19), and western (v. 20) boundaries have less fixed points.

However, there is no consensus regarding the other two texts, either with regard to the question of date or to the question of direction of borrowing.

The Priestly text in Numbers 34 offers a description almost similar to Ezekiel 47 when Yahweh describes for Moses the southern (vv. 3–5), the western (v. 6), the northern (vv. 7–9), and the eastern (vv. 10–12) boundaries of the land the Israelites shall inherit.

Moreover, Joshua 13–19 gives a description of the land that remained to be conquered (chap. 13) and defines the tribal allotment (chaps. 15–19). The areas that Joshua 13–19 defines fit into those described in Numbers 34. This causes some to suggest that Joshua 13–19 presupposes Numbers 34.[37] Others think that the chapters depend on lists from the monarchic period.[38] The question of whether the map drawn in Joshua

---

any other than the Romans; see Davies, 'War Rule', *ABD* 6:875–76.

37 So Alexander, 'Geography and the Bible: Early Jewish Geography', *ABD* 2:977–88 (985).

38 So Herbert Niehr, 'Josua', in *Einleitung in das Alte Testament*, ed. Zenger et al., 193–95.

13–19 is dependent on the one drawn in Numbers 34 or vice versa is basically a question of whether Joshua 13–19 is Priestly or not.[39] Albrecht Alt and Martin Noth considered the Joshua text to be a Deuteronomistic revision. Nevertheless, they traced the very system of tribal allotment back to the premonarchic period. However, a major weakness with their model was that it built upon the no longer accepted theory of an amphictyony in premonarchic Israel. Such an amphictyony is necessary as *Sitz im Leben* for this premonarchic system of tribal allotment. Later, the Alt–Noth position was challenged by Sigmund Mowinckel, who argued for a Priestly, postexilic author of the relevant chapters in Joshua. More recently, A. G. Auld has related Joshua 13–19 with several layers of the Deuteronomistic History. In Auld's opinion, the first edition of Joshua 13–19 composed by a nomistic Deuteronomistic author (DtrN) became the source for the first edition of Numbers 34.

The point here is that regardless of whether the description of the boundaries of the land stem from preexilic traditions or not, the issue itself did not cease to be a topic in biblical literature that dates to a period where such political boundaries no longer seem to be relevant. That is evident beyond doubt in Ezekiel, probably also in Numbers 34, and even perhaps in Joshua 13–19.[40] Moreover, regardless of their date of composition, these geographical texts continued to be handed over and perhaps also edited in times where at least their political significance had become obsolete. The delimitation of *ha-ʾareṣ* continued as a literary topos despite Judah's loss of statehood and territory. This is further confirmed by the evidently postexilic description of the tribal territories in 1 Chronicles 2–8.[41]

Moreover, the previously discussed late Deuteronomistic compilation of David's victories in 2 Samuel 8 fits into this picture.[42] Especially interesting in this context is how the text mirrors its late Deuteronomistic compiler and his concept of the geographical extension of 'Israel'. In 2 Sam. 8:15, he sums up David's many victories, saying, 'And David reigned over all Israel [עַל־כָּל־יִשְׂרָאֵל], and David executed justice and righteousness to all his people [לְכָל־עַמּוֹ]'. Given that the compiler here uses 'all Israel' as a geographical and not a demographical term, then it is his

---

39   See Noort, *Das Buch Josua*, 173–97.
40   The book of Joshua was probably composed either in the exilic or postexilic period, in any case after 586 BCE. See Herbert Niehr, 'Josua', in *Einleitung in das Alte Testament*, ed. Zenger et al., 193–95.
41   See Magnar Kartveit, *Motive und Schichten der Landtheologie in I Chronik 1–9* (ConBOT 28; Stockholm: Almqvist & Wiksell, 1989).
42   See above, 7.1, The Date of Composition: A Synthesis of the Different Approaches; and note 5.

particular view of the extent of Israel that is articulated—and that in a landless time *after* the end of the united monarchy, *after* the fall of the Northern Kingdom, and *after* the fall of the Southern Kingdom.[43] Furthermore, another example of a delimitation of the land is also evident in what probably is the work of a post-Deuteronomistic editor, namely, in Moses' vision of the land from the top of Mt. Pisgah in the land of Moab on the other side of Jordan, immediately before his death (Deut. 34:1–3). From what Yahweh shows him, it is evident that the Promised Land (according to the post-Dtr editor) stretches from Dan in the north, to the Mediterranean Sea in the west, and down to the Negeb and the Aqabah as far as Zoar in the south (see Genesis 14, in which Zoar occurs in vv. 2, 8, and Dan in v. 14). Deuteronomy 34 belongs to one of the latest (if not the latest) editorial frameworks around the core of Deuteronomy.[44]

Much later in the first century BCE, the author of the *Genesis Apocryphon* demonstrated a continuing geographical interest, perhaps inspired by the Hasmonaean interlude of independence. The land that Abram takes possession of by walking through it has taken phantastic proportions, including the whole fertile crescent, the Arabian and the Sinai peninsulas, and the land east of the Nile (see above 5.2.3, Excursus: The Extent of the Promised Land and the Territories of the Invading Kings in the *Genesis Apocryphon*).

In summary, even after the remnants of the preexilic monarchies had suffered a loss of statehood and territory (Judah) or even experienced a complete destruction (Israel), Jewish literature was concerned with issues revolving around where the boundaries of the land should be set.

---

43   See note 5 above.

44   According to Joseph Blenkinsopp, this is the result of the amalgamation of Deuteronomy with the Priestly writing, which necessitated that the commissioning of Joshua and the death of Moses be transposed from their original position in the P narrative to the end of Deuteronomy (Deut. 32:48–52; 35:1, 7–9). Moreover, this revised and relocated version of these events was subsequently 'disturbed' by the insertion of the poetic blessing of Moses (Deuteronomy 33) and 'minor expansions in the Deuteronomistic style' (Deut. 34:2–6). See Blenkinsopp, *The Pentateuch*, 229–31. Moreover, see Otto, 'Deuteronomium', *RGG*⁴ 2, cols. 693–96 (696); and Kratz, 'Der vor- und nachpriesterschriftliche Hexateuch', 295–323 (316–22).

7.2.7 Fact and Fiction Interwoven in Quasi-Historical Narratives from the Persian and Hellenistic Periods

In Jewish literature from the Persian and Hellenistic periods, there are several examples of novelistic, quasi-historical narratives. Although they differ (e.g., some written in first person, others in third person, etc.), they nevertheless have in common that they *mix fact and fiction*. On the surface, the narratives appear as authentic historical sources. However, a more thorough investigation reveals that many of the historical assertions cannot be sustained as fact. Moreover, many of these narratives have a didactic purpose in that they exhort the readers to piety, monotheism, and obedience to God's will.[45] Although this is never explicitly stated, in many if not most cases the protagonists of these narratives are role models whose example the readers are urged to follow.

The purpose here will be to briefly describe some of these novelistic, quasi-historical narratives. Could Genesis 14* also be a story 'with no serious claim to historicity but [that] aim[s] to inculcate wise teachings'?[46] (However, this question will first be discussed below, see 7.3, A Plea for Restoration: Attempt at Some Historically Qualified Conjectures about the Historical Meaning and the Ideology of the Author.)

The book of Tobit is about an exemplary person from the Northern Kingdom who, according to the preamble of the book, was deported by the Assyrian King Shalmaneser. The scene of the story is Nineveh (which fell in 612 BCE) and the narrative is in part moulded in the first person. This latter feature gives the impression that the book is written by an eyewitness, something which again indirectly gives it a veil of authenticity and historicity. However, the book was composed during a much later time. A 'conservative' opinion is that it was composed in the Persian period or possibly a little later.[47] However, there are also those who date it even later (to the last part of the third or first part of the second century BCE).[48] Regardless of the lack of consensus over the author's primary purpose, the narrative nevertheless offers several historical errors. For instance, the tribe of Naphtali was deported by Tiglath-pileser III (see 2 Kgs. 15:29) and not Shalmaneser V (so Tob. 1:2). Moreover, Sargon II, not Sennacherib, was the successor to Shalmaneser V (contra Tob. 1:3–

---

45   James C. VanderKam, *An Introduction to Early Judaism* (Grand Rapids, MI: Eerdmans, 2001), 69–88.
46   Quoting James C. VanderKam's summary of what he refers to as novelistic 'tales' from the Second Temple period. See VanderKam, *An Introduction to Early Judaism*, 69.
47   So VanderKam, *An Introduction to Early Judaism*, 70.
48   See Carey A. Moore, 'Tobit, Book of', *ABD* 6:585–94 (591).

22).[49] Therefore, Tobit is an example of literature composed in the same general period as Genesis 14* (i.e., Persian or early Hellenistic period) that reflects some historical knowledge and interest, and in which the author situates the events in a more or less distant past.

The book of Esther is probably also quasi historical. Although the events take place in a Persian court and the author obviously is aware of Persian affairs and words, there are several anachronisms and historical 'errors' in the book. The only externally verified historical figure in the book is King Ahasuerus (= Xerxes).[50]

In the book of Daniel there are also examples of fact and fiction interwoven. This is evident both in the first and earliest part of the book, the collection of court tales cast in the third person (Daniel 1–6) and also in the second and later part, the collection of four visions cast in the first person (Daniel 7–12). As for the date of composition, several examples of historical inaccuracy speak against the traditional dating of the book to the neo-Babylonian period (presupposing that it was composed by the Daniel who started interpreting Nebuchadnezzar's dreams in the second year of the latter's reign; see Dan. 2:1).[51] To begin with, the mention of a King Darius the Mede (Dan. 6:1 [Eng. trans., 5:31]; 9:1; 11:1) causes problems.[52] Except for these verses, no other source refers to such a Mede king. Moreover, in both parts of the book there are references to a King Belshazzar.[53] However, although the name as such has been documented, no king with this particular name is known from any other source.

In the prophetic literature there are also relevant examples of mixing fact with fiction (e.g., the book of Jonah). The book is about a prophet

---

49   For further examples, see Moore, 'Tobit, Book of', *ABD* 6:585–94 (587–88).

50   For instance, if Mordechai is counted among those who were deported from Jerusalem by King Nebuchadnezzar of Babylon, as probably is the meaning of אֲשֶׁר הָגְלָה מִירוּשָׁלַיִם (Esth. 2:6), that would imply that he was very old when he brought up Esther during the reign of Xerxes, more than a century after Nebuchadnezzar. Moreover, for a discussion of the historicity of the book, see Carey A. Moore, 'Esther, Book of', *ABD* 2:633–43 (especially pp. 636–39).

51   See John J. Collins, *Daniel: A Commentary on the Book of Daniel* (Hermeneia; Minneapolis: Augsburg, 1993), 30–33.

52   Klaus Koch states that '[n]irgends setzt sich das Danielbuch mit dem tatsächlichen Verlauf der Geschichte des Altertums so sehr in Widerspruch wie bei der Gestalt des medischen Königs Dareios.' See Koch, 'Darios, der Meder', in *The Word of the Lord Shall Go Forth: Essays in Honor of David Noel Freedman in Celebration of his Sixtieth Birthday* (ed. Carol L. Meyers, Michael Patrick O'Connor, and David Noel Freedman; American Schools of Oriental Research 1; Winona Lake, IN: Eisenbrauns, 1983), 287–99 (287).

53   Dan. 5:1–2, 9, 22, 29–30; 7:1; 8:1.

called Jonah, son of Amittai, whom Yahweh calls to go to Nineveh. A prophet with a similar name occurs as a contemporary of King Jeroboam II of Israel in 2 Kgs. 14:25, that is, in the first half of the eight century BCE. However, most scholars date the book later, partly on the basis of its apparent retrospective characterization of Nineveh (Jon. 3:3), which makes best sense after Nineveh's destruction in 612 BCE and Jonah's many allusions to other biblical texts.[54] Obvious fictional—or in this case the term 'legendary' is preferable—elements include the incident where the prophet is in the belly of a fish (Jonah 2) and the notion that animals are also included in the fasting (Jon. 3:7–8). But the talk of a 'king of Nineveh' (Jon. 3:6) is also not historical, as such a title is not known elsewhere.

Furthermore, I will also draw attention to the apocryphal book of Judith. Although the date of composition of this book (also?) is disputed (it has been dated to the Maccabean period[55] but also to the earlier Persian and Ptolemaic periods[56]), it nevertheless was composed in the same general period as that which I have argued for Genesis 14*. Although Judith is probably literarily dependent on, among other texts, Genesis 14 and consequently must be later that the latter text,[57] it nevertheless offers a good example of a narrative that on the surface appears historical but one in which, on closer examination, many details must be described as fictional (Ernst Haag: *freie parabolische Geschichtsdarstellung*[58]). The main character *Judith* (Greek Ιουδιθ, probably a transliteration of Hebrew יְהוּדִית, 'Jewess') is chronologically situated in the period of the reign of *Nabouchodonosor* (Greek Ναβουχοδονοσορ, variant of Hebrew נְבֻכַדְנֶאצַּר, Nebuchadnezzar), who ruled over the *Assyrians* in the great city of *Nineveh* (see Jdt. 1:1). However, in actuality Nebuchadnezzar was a Neo-Babylonian king. Moreover, when he ascended the throne in 604 BCE, Nineveh had already been destroyed for almost a decade (in 612 BCE by his predecessor Nabopolassar). In addition to the already intro-

---

54   Compare Jon. 4:2 and Exod. 14:12; 34:6–7; Jon. 2:4 and Ps. 42:8; Jon. 4:8 and 1 Kgs. 19:4, etc. Moreover, see Jonathan Magonet, 'Jonah, Book of', *ABD* 3:936–42.

55   See, e.g., Erich Zenger, *Das Buch Judit* (JSHRZ 1/6; Gütersloh: Gütersloher Verlagshaus Gerd Mohn, 1981), 431: between ca. 150 and 100 BCE. Moreover, see Helmut Engel, 'XI. Das Buch Judit', in *Einleitung in das Alte Testament* (ed. Zenger et al.), 256–66 (262), who argues that the situation described in the book reflects the distress in the Seleucid period under Antiochos IV (175–164 BCE) and Demetrios I Soter (162–150 BCE).

56   See Benedikt Otzen, *Tobit and Judith* (Guides to Apocrypha and Pseudepigrapha; Sheffield: Sheffield Academic Press, 2002), 132–35.

57   See Zenger, *Das Buch Judit*, 441.

58   Ernst Haag, *Studium zum Buche Judith: Seine theologische Bedeutung und literarische Eigenart* (Trierer Theologische Studien 16; Trier: Paulinus-Verlag, 1963), 133.

duced mix-up of historical places and peoples, the chief general of Nebu-chadnezzar, *Holofernes*, and the latter's eunuch, *Bagoas*, both have *Persian* names in the book of Judith.[59] Therefore, the book of Judith describes a scenario that at first glance appears historical but upon closer examination turns out not to agree with the information derived from histori-cal sources. According to Erich Zenger, these historical contradictions are not necessarily caused by any lack of knowledge or any flaw by the author. Rather, they are the result of his literary technique.[60]

Finally, I will also cautiously point to a biblical fragment among the Qumran discoveries: 4Q51 (4QSam^a) 11.X–2, 7–12. This fragment offers an entire paragraph that is completely missing in all of the other tex-tual witnesses (MT, LXX, etc.). The addition, which consists of three and a half lines, is placed between 1 Sam. 10:27^a and 27^b and is about Nahash, king of the Ammonites, and his gouging out of the right eyes of the Gadites and Reubenites. Because Josephus also attests this passage,[61] Frank Moore Cross[62] and later Emanuel Tov[63] have argued that the plus represents an original part of the text that for some reason has been left out by the received textual witnesses. Consequently, the NRSV transla-tion has incorporated this plus into its translation.[64] Vis-à-vis this view, Alexander Rofé argues that the extra passage is an aggadic interpolation with no consequence whatsoever for the history of Israel in the eleventh century BCE. On the contrary, he argues that 'it submits extremely impor-tant evidence for the *intrusion of late legend into the biblical manuscripts.*'[65]

In summary, there are several examples of quasi-historical narra-tives of different lengths and types in the Jewish literature from the Per-

---

59   See Sidnie Ann White, 'Bagoas', *ABD* 1:567–68; and Albert Pietersma, 'Holofernes', *ABD* 3:257.

60   Zenger, *Das Buch Judit*, 434.

61   Josephus, *Ant.*, 6.68–71.

62   Frank Moore Cross, 'The Ammonite Oppression of the Tribes of Gad and Reuben: Missing Verses from 1 Samuel 11 Found in 4QSamuel^a', in *The Hebrew and Greek Texts of Samuel: 1980 Proceedings IOSCS-Vienna* (ed. Emanuel Tov; Jerusalem: Academon, 1980), 105–9 [reprinted in *History, Historiography and Interpretation: Studies in Biblical and Cuneiform Literatures* (ed. H. Tadmor and M. Weinfeld; Jerusalem: Magnes, 1983), 148–58 (not consulted)]. Moreover, the NRSV translation has incorporated this pas-sage into its Bible translation.

63   Tov, *Textual Criticism of the Hebrew Bible*, 342–44.

64   See also Martin Abegg, Peter Flint, and Eugene Ulrich, eds., *The Dead Sea Scrolls Bible: The Oldest Known Bible Translated for the First Time into English by Martin Abegg, Jr., Peter Flint and Eugene Ulrich* (San Francisco: HarperSan Francisco, 1999), 224–25.

65   Alexander Rofé, 'From Tradition to Criticism: Jewish Sources as an Aid to the Critical Study of the Hebrew Bible', in *Congress Volume: Cambridge 1995* (ed. John A. Emerton; VTSup 66; Leiden: E. J. Brill, 1997), 235–47 (243–44, my emphasis).

sian and Hellenistic periods. They have in common that they *mix fact and fiction*. Although at first sight they appear historical, a more thorough investigation reveals that many of the historical facts cannot be sustained. These examples provide analogies that strengthen the thesis that Genesis 14* represents a quasi-historical narrative from the Persian or Hellenistic period.

7.3 A Plea for Restoration: Attempt at Some Historically Qualified Conjectures about the Historical Meaning and the Ideology of the Author

Although it is not possible to be much more precise than to say that the author of Genesis 14* lived either in the Persian or the early Hellenistic period, one can nevertheless state that he lived in a time when the remnants of the preexilic kingdom of Judah had suffered not only territorial losses but also loss of statehood. At some point in the Persian period, Judah was partly reestablished—not as a sovereign state but as a semi-autonomous province ruled by a governor (פֶּחָה) appointed or approved by the Persians.

Although the world had not yet seen anything comparable to the size of the Persian Empire (see Esth. 1:1, 'from India to Ethiopia'), the empire was nevertheless frequently occupied with putting down internal revolts. Many of these revolts took place in the western parts of the empire. Later, after the Persian defeat at Issus, Palestine became the frontline between the Ptolemaic rulers in Egypt and the Seleucids in Syria. So, regardless of exactly when in the Persian or early Hellenistic period the author of Genesis 14* lived, he may have had several military campaigns as historical models when portraying local revolt followed by a military quelling of the same revolt (see Gen. 14:4–7). However, if he had a particular event as a model, it is not possible to pinpoint which one because the date of composition is not narrow enough (see 7.1, The Date of Composition: A Synthesis of the Different Approaches). Moreover, as suggested, it is equally possible that he renders a typical situation (7.2.3, Not a Concrete but a Typical Campaign).

When the author spoke about 'Abram the Hebrew', he probably did that with the expectation that the readers—that is, the postexilic people of Israel who considered Abram their father—would identify themselves with this person. Using Abra(ha)m as a model figure was nothing that the author himself invented. On the contrary, a comparable case from the same general period of a collective use of the patriarch is found in the prayer at the end of the book of Micah. In Mic.

7:20, there is no doubt that Abraham, together with Jacob, represents collectively the speaking postexilic 'we'. Moreover, in other Abraham stories in the Pentateuch there are cases of narratives where the destiny of the patriarch and the destiny of his descendants (the people of Israel) coincide. Both Abraham and the people went out of Egypt with riches, and both Abraham and the postexilic people of Israel went out from Mesopotamia to Canaan.

Moreover, the premise that the author of Genesis 14* intended that 'Abram the Hebrew' should represent the text's intended audience (i.e., the postexilic Jews) suggests that the four invaders in a similar way also function symbolically as figures of identification. If one takes the narrative at face value, it is indisputable that the invaders do not represent any friendly power from the perspective of the patriarch.

However, I have previously proposed that the diaspora communities in the Persian period, as well as those in Samaria (see Ezra 4), could have been the source for the (cursory) historical knowledge of the author of Genesis 14* (see 6.3, Literary Building Blocks Partly Borrowed from Biblical Sources, Partly Borrowed from Other Sources, or Invented by the Author). In addition, I have argued that there is a possibility that the indigenous population of Judah considered those deported and settled by the Persians and the Persian masters as two sides of the same coin (see 7.2.5, The World of Diaspora Communities Evident in Ezra 4: The Historical Background for the Construction of the Coalition of Chedorlaomer, Tidal, Amraphel, and King Arioch?).

Therefore, it is possible that the author's purpose in Genesis 14* was to encourage contemporary readers to follow their father Abraham's example and pursue the invaders beyond the boundaries of the land. These boundaries coincide with the idealistic boundaries of the land established by King David according to 2 Samuel 8.

Following the line of interpretation in which Abram the Hebrew in Genesis 14* represents the postexilic people of Israel and the four invading kings represent the adversaries of the postexilic people of Israel, I suggest that this model also applies to the Pentapolis kings. A possibility is that they stand for neighbouring provinces that also are subject to either the Persian or subsequent Hellenistic rulers. The reason for this idea is obvious: like the Pentapolis, some of the real subject provinces and satrapies actually rebelled against their sovereign (see 7.2.3, Not a Concrete but a Typical Campaign). For instance, around the middle of the fourth century BCE, Cyprus and Phoenician cities revolted together (named the Tennes Rebellion after Tennes, king of Sidon) before they

eventually were defeated.[66] The message of the author of Genesis 14*
to his contemporary readers may have been that they should follow
Abram's example when dealing with neighbouring peoples and provinces. Abram refrained from accepting an offer from the king of Sodom
that would have made him dependent (Gen. 14:21–24).

Nevertheless, in the narrative, Abram the Hebrew and his 318 men
eventually defeated the four invading kings, who at first appeared to
be stronger. With this twist of fate for Abram, the postexilic author of
Genesis 14* may have wanted to give a message of hope for the people
of Israel in a landless time. *They*, the postexilic Jews, could get rid of their
oppressors and restore the nation territorially according to the ideal evident in King David's empire in 2 Samuel 8.

In the above discussion, I have attempted to read Genesis 14* as a
cultural artefact, meaning that the text reflects trends and concepts of
the period in which it was composed. However, because I am not able to
narrow down the potential date of composition more than to argue that
it was sometime in the Persian or early Hellenistic period, I have been
reluctant to point out concrete events as the author's historical motivation and inspiration. Genesis 14* cannot be a source for the history of
postexilic Judah. Despite this, I have indirectly argued that Genesis 14*
is a source for its author's world.[67] One must assume that this text, like
other texts, reflects that which can be termed the ideology of its author,
that is, the set of beliefs and ideas on which he bases his work.[68]

In principle, ideology is neither good nor bad. On the contrary, it
is something everyone has, regardless of its quality and regardless of
whether one is conscious of it or not. However, an ideological document,
something which Genesis 14* then is, must not necessarily suppress or
repress social conflicts.[69] On the contrary, in many cases it is more probable that an ideology put down in a text reflects a substantial general

---

66   Grabbe, *Judaism from Cyrus to Hadrian.* I, 99–100.

67   Borrowing Yairah Amit's statement about Chronicles as a historical source, see Amit,
    History and Ideology: An Introduction to Historiography in the Hebrew Bible (trans. Yael
    Lotan; Sheffield: Sheffield Academic Press, 1999), 105.

68   Marc Zvi Brettler renders a definition of 'ideology' by Althusser/Deby. Accord-
    ingly, ideology is 'a system possessing its own logic and structure of representations
    (images, myths, ideas or concepts) existing and playing a historical role within a
    given society.' See Marc Zvi Brettler, *The Creation of History in Ancient Israel* (London:
    Routledge, 1995), 12–14.

69   See, e.g., David J. A. Clines, *Interested Parties: The Ideology of Writers and Readers of
    the Hebrew Bible* (JSOTSup 205; Gender Culture Theory 1; Sheffield: Sheffield Aca-
    demic Press, 1995), chapter 3, 'Haggai's Temple, Constructed, Deconstructed and
    Reconstructed'.

consensus.[70] Nevertheless, as for the political nationalism that I (hope-fully on the basis of transparent and verifiable grounds) conjecture is reflected in Genesis 14*, the sources from the postexilic period are too meagre. They do not allow us to examine thoroughly the internal Jewish discussions concerning the political realities, namely, that the remnant of the Promised Land had been turned into one among dozens of prov-inces. Such discussions may have been the historical context in which Genesis 14* was composed.

Nonetheless, because Genesis 14* does not seem to express hope for transcendent help (after all, it is Abram and his men who defeat Chedor-laomer and his allies!),[71] I suggest that the author of Genesis 14* was a Jewish militant nationalist of some kind—unlike those Jews who hoped that God himself or someone commissioned by him in the latter days would restore the faith of Israel. Yet, despite this, the relation of Abram the Hebrew toward local Amorite foreigners who were reported to be his allies suggests that the author pleaded for a more realistic and less exclu-sive nationalism than the view reflected in Deuteronomy and Ezra. In Deut. 20:17, the Amorites were among those who were to be put under

---

70 James Barr, *History and Ideology in the Old Testament: Biblical Studies at the End of a Millennium* (Oxford: Oxford University Press, 2000), 135. Moreover, Barr demon-strates how problematic an ideological-critical approach can be (that is, to *deconstruct* a text in order to reveal a potential underlying social conflict and the groups that are 'silenced' and 'marginalized'). Barr criticizes David J. A. Clines, who argues that biblical texts are ideological documents that serve some particular interest (David J. A. Clines, 'Possibilities and Priorities of Biblical Interpretation in an International Per-spective', *Biblical Interpretation* 1 [1993]: 67–87 [84].) For instance, Clines asks in which group's interest the ten commandments are, and what kind of social conflict between different groups is alluded to in them (p. 85). In response, Barr, however, dissatisfied by the lack of answer from Clines on the questions he himself has raised, asks who the groups behind the commandments really are. On the basis of the commandment 'Thou shalt not steal', Barr asks polemically:

> Are we to believe that there was a Pro-Stealing class or party whose interests were oppressed or silenced by the Anti-Stealing party, which latter group were victors in this conflict? Who were the Pro-Stealing people? Thieves? Hardly, because thieves are distinctly anti-stealers, considering it absolutely wrong for other thieves to steal the property that they have themselves stolen. Who then had an interest in the continuance of stealing? We need to know, because these people are the 'silenced', the 'marginalized', from whom the real message of the text is to come.

71 As pointed out many times, I consider the Melchizedek episode in Gen. 14:18–20 to be a secondary interpolation. If this is so, then Melchizedek's interpretation of Abram's victory (v. 20 'blessed be El Elyon who delivered your enemies into your hand') is equally secondary. See above, 2.2.1, The Melchizedek Episode (= ME) in Genesis 14:18–20: A Secondary Interpolation.

ban (חרם) by the Israelites. Moreover, in Ezra 9:1–2, the people of Israel were accused of not having separated themselves from the people of the lands, among them the Amorites.

Because the author of Genesis 14* seems to have modelled his narrative on an earlier biblical text and because he also seems to have borrowed many of the details, I suggest that he was well versed in many of the scriptures that modern scholars refer to as the Hebrew Bible.

By creating a retrospective narrative, in part by biblical borrowings and in part by using situations assumed to have been typical for both his and his readers' time as models, this Second Temple period author in fact made a plea for a restoration of the land under the control of the descendants of Abraham.

Part III: The Melchizedek Episode (= ME) in Genesis 14:18–20

8. Preliminaries

In Part III, I will address the origin and purpose of the Melchizedek episode (Gen. 14:18–20, referred to as the 'ME'). This atomistic approach to one of the units of the narrative in the received text of Genesis 14 is justified by the conclusion I made earlier, namely, that the ME is a secondary interpolation.[1]

I will attempt to answer the following questions, which revolve around the problem of the origin and purpose of this episode. *When* was the episode composed? *How* was this done? *Why* was the ME composed? *How* do we relate ME and the hermeneutics that lie behind its composition to the world of Jewish literature that appears to have blossomed in the late postexilic period?

8.1 Episode: An Appropriate Term

The term 'episode' comes from the Greek noun ἐπεισόδιον, 'an addition, episode'.[2] In ancient Greek plays, the spoken dialogue between two choral singings was called an ἐπεισόδιον. However, in modern times an episode refers to a byplay or subplot that is mostly self-contained.

In light of this, it seems appropriate to characterize Gen. 14:18–20 as an *episode* that is named after its most prominent character, thus 'the Melchizedek episode'. Although it is a monologue and not a dialogue (Abram is silent), it nevertheless seems to have another plot besides the dialogue between the king of Sodom and Abram (vv. 17, 21–24) into which it appears to have been interpolated. In addition, an extra feature that sets the ME apart from the enclosing dialogue between the king of Sodom and Abram in Genesis 14* is the main character's preformative speech, that is, Melchizedek's blessing of Abram (v. 19) and of El Elyon (v. 20).

---

1   See above, 2.2.1, The Melchizedek Episode (= ME) in Genesis 14:18–20: A Secondary Interpolation.
2   So LSJ, *s.v.* ἐπεισοδιάζω, 615.

In light of the biblical Hebrew verbal system, the incident that takes place in the ME does not necessarily happen temporarily *after* the events in Gen. 14:17 ('And the king of Sodom went out to greet him. . .'). Because the ME opens with a *waw* + non-verb (see 14:18a וּמַלְכִּי־צֶדֶק . . . הוֹצִיא לֶחֶם וַיֵּ), the relationship of the clause in Gen. 14:18 to the preceding one is *disjunctive*. Consequently, the ME can be either contrastive (e.g., 'But Melchizedek . . .'), circumstantial (e.g., 'While Melchizedek . . .'), explanatory/parenthetical (e.g., 'Now, Melchizedek . . .'), or terminative/initial, indicating either the completion of one episode or the beginning of another.[3] The categories are overlapping and the semantic distinction difficult to define. Nevertheless, the syntax indicates that the ME does not necessarily take place at a time between the king of Sodom's going out to greet Abram (Gen. 14:17) and his first message spoken to Abram (Gen. 14:21).

8.2 Catchwords from Previous Research on the ME: Aetiology and Tradition History

It has often been assumed that the ME originally was conceived as an *aetiology*. However, in the history of research there has been no consensus as to exactly *what* institution the ME supposedly legitimizes—and *when* the aetiology supposedly was needed. It has been suggested that the ME legitimizes the right to receive *tithes* for both the *preexilic* priesthood[4] and the *postexilic* priesthood.[5] Slightly different proposals are that the ME was conceived as an *aetiology for the cult in Jerusalem*, a former Canaanite sanctuary (both Westermann and Albertz have argued that it was conceived in the early monarchic period, whereas Zimmerli has

---

3   See Thomas O. Lambdin, *Introduction to Biblical Hebrew* (New York: Charles Scribner's Sons, 1971), 162–65; cf. Alviero Niccacci, 'An Outline of the Biblical Hebrew Verbal System in Prose', *Liber annuus* 39 (1989): 7–26; and Gard Granerød, 'Omnipresent in Narratives, Disputed among Grammarians: Some Contributions to the Understanding of *wayyiqtol* and Their Underlying Paradigms', *ZAW* 121 (2009): 418–34.

4   So Antonius H. J. Gunneweg, *Biblische Theologie des Alten Testaments: Eine Religionsgeschichte Israels in biblisch-theologischer Sicht* (Stuttgart: W. Kohlhammer, 1993), 120.

5   So, e.g., Otto Procksch, *Die Genesis. Übersetzt und erklärt* (KAT 1; Leipzig: Deichertsche Verlagsbuchhandlung, 1924); H. H. Rowley, 'Melchizedek and Zadok (Gen 14 and Ps 110)', in *Festschrift Alfred Bertholet zum 80. Geburtstag gewidmet von Kollegen und Freunden* (ed. W. Baumgartner et al.; Tübingen: Mohr, 1950), 461–72; and Delcor, 'Melchizedek from Genesis to the Qumran Texts and the Epistle to the Hebrews', 115–35.

argued for an early postexilic date[6]), or a *court aetiology*.[7] Jan Alberto Soggin has proposed a very late date. In his view, the purpose of the ME was either to legitimate the Hasmonaeans or to support the claim of the 'ordinary' priesthood to the tithes vis-à-vis the Hasmonaeans.[8]

In part parallel to and in part overlapping with the aetiological interpretations, many of the interpretations of the ME have been based on tradition history:

- Already Gunkel, for whom the ME was a secondary addition, argued that it stems from either oral or other sources.[9]
- In Skinner's opinion, Melchizedek was 'if not a historical figure, at least a traditional figure of great antiquity, on whom the monarchy and hierarchy of Jerusalem based their dynastic and priestly rights'.[10]
- R. H. Smith claimed that there is nothing that demands a late dating of the story in Gen. 14:18–20 and attempts to prove that names and terms in it are 'quite at home in the second millennium B.C.'[11]
- According to von Rad, there were sacral concepts located at the royal court in Jerusalem that conceived of Melchizedek as *typos*, that is, a prefiguration and precursor for the Davidic monarchs.[12]
- Zimmerli, referring to H. Schmid, 'Jahwe und die Kulttraditionen von Jerusalem',[13] stated that the ME was moulded on the basis of ancient pre-Israelite Jerusalem tradition.[14]
- M. Delcor argued on the basis of analysis of Ugaritic and Canaanite texts that there were very ancient religious traditions behind Melchizedek in

---

6   See Westermann, *Genesis 12–36*, 206; Rainer Albertz, *A History of Israelite Religion in the Old Testament Period*. I *From the Beginnings to the End of the Monarchy* (OTL; trans. John Bowden; London: SCM, 1994), 300 n. 43; and Zimmerli, 'Abraham und Melchisedek', 255–64. See also Hans-Jürgen Zobel, 'Der frühe Jahwe-Glaube in der Spannung von Wüste und Kulturland', *ZAW* 101 (1989): 342–65 (359–63).

7   So Gunkel, *Genesis*, 286–87.

8   Jan Alberto Soggin, 'Abraham and the Eastern Kings: On Genesis 14', in *Solving Riddles and Untying Knots: Biblical, Epigraphic, and Semitic Studies in Honor of Jonas C. Greenfield* (ed. Ziony Zevit et al.; Winona Lake, IN: Eisenbrauns, 1995), 283–91; and idem, *Das Buch Genesis*, 234–35.

9   Gunkel, *Genesis*, 286–87.

10   Skinner, *A Critical and Exegetical Commentary on Genesis*, 270.

11   Robert Houston Smith, 'Abram and Melchizedek (Gen 14:18–20)', *ZAW* 77 (1965), 129–53 (130–31).

12   Von Rad, *Das erste Buch Mose*, 139.

13   *ZAW* 67 (1955), 168–97.

14   Zimmerli, 'Abraham und Melchisedek', 255–64; cf. Schmid, 'Jahwe und die Kulttraditionen von Jerusalem', 168–97. Schmid argues that both Gen. 14:18–20 and Psalm 110 demonstrate cultic traditions about El Elyon as the pre-Israelite god of Jerusalem; see pp. 175–76.

Gen. 14:18–20 with regard to the worship of El Elyon in Jerusalem—regardless of exactly when the ME itself was composed.[15]

- J. A. Emerton concluded that there must have been some kind of tradition underlying Gen. 14:18–20, namely, that El Elyon was the god of Jerusalem before David's conquest and that there was a great king with the name Melchizedek. However, Emerton found it impossible to get back to the tradition, beyond pointing to the names of the king (Melchizedek) and his god (El Elyon).[16]
- F. L. Horton suggested that Gen. 14:18–20 is a traditional story of indefinable origin; the person Melchizedek was probably a historical person remembered in popular traditions.[17]
- Claus Westermann agreed in seeing some kind of tradition underlying the episode, even though vv. 18–20 in his view cannot have existed independently before the episode was added to the context. However, Westermann went one step further and argued that the episode had grown out of a regular re-occurring cultic event: the exchange of priestly blessing and giving of the tithe.[18]

The traditio-historical approach is also evident in more recent contributions. The ME (often together with the linguistically enigmatic clause in Ps. 110:4) continues to be used as a source for the history of religion in pre-Israelite Jerusalem. H. D. Preuß and A. H. J. Gunneweg argue strongly, on the basis of the ME and Ps. 110:4, that other gods were worshipped in pre-Israelite Jerusalem besides El. Because of the assumed theophoric names *Melchizedek* (Gen. 14:18; Ps. 110:4), *Adoni-zedek* (Josh. 10:1, 3), and *Zadok* (2 Sam. 8:17 et al.), both scholars reckon with a god Ṣedeq. Moreover, R. Albertz uses Gen. 14:18–20 and Ps. 110:4 to support the thesis that there was an *unbroken continuity in the Jerusalem priesthood* from pre-Israelite times. He takes the priest Zadok, who seems to suddenly 'pop up' in 2 Sam. 8:17 in the vicinity of David after the latter made Jerusalem the capital of the united monarchy, to be the former Jebusite priest of Jerusalem.[19]

---

15   Delcor, 'Melchizedek from Genesis to the Qumran Texts and the Epistle to the Hebrews', 115–35 (119).

16   Emerton, 'The Riddle of Genesis XIV', 403–439 (426). Emerton writes, 'The writer's purpose would have been better served if there was already in Jerusalem a well-known tradition about a great king named Melchizedek' (p. 426). It is difficult for me to see what weight such an argument carries.

17   Horton, *The Melchizedek Tradition*, 23.

18   Westermann, *Genesis 12–36*, 206.

19   Albertz, *A History of Israelite Religion in the Old Testament Period.* I *From the Beginnings to the End of the Monarchy*, 129, 295 n. 8. So also Gunneweg, *Biblische Theologie des Alten Testaments*, 120, 127.

8.3 Some Critical Remarks about Earlier Research

It is appropriate to be sceptical of the use of the ME and Ps. 110:4 as historical sources for the pre-Israelite period. An inconsistency that I believe is evident in the argumentation of Albertz illustrates a major problem. (In chapter 1, Background, Method, Aim, and Overview, I have shown the same dichotomy in Westermann's approach to Genesis 14.) On the one hand, Albertz characterizes the ME as a relatively late text.[20] On the other hand, he considers it to be a 'special tradition' and uses the text (together with Ps. 110:4) as a keyhole which he thinks he can peek through and get a glimpse of the religious situation in Jerusalem before the city was taken by King David. Similarly, Preuß assumes that the ME stems from the monarchic period.[21] Yet, he uses it as a source for the pre-Israelite period.

As far as I can see, relatively much is said about the early history of religion in Israel on the basis of relatively little. However, in addition to the question of the quantity of the sources comes another and more important problem: the question of the quality of the sources. In general, a given text has to be thoroughly scrutinized before it can possibly be used as a historical source. Crucial questions include the following: *When* was the text composed? What is its *transmission history*? If there are multiple sources, is one of them dependent on the other or do they independently of one another reflect a common source? Eventually, what does the text actually say—and what does it *not* say?

8.4 The Terms and Concepts in the ME:
Inconclusive with Respect to the Date of the Episode

In the following I will argue that the divine names, epithets, and concepts evident in the ME are inconclusive as means for dating the ME.

---

20   See Rainer Albertz, *A History of Israelite Religion in the Old Testament Period*. II *From the Exile to the Maccabees* (OTL; trans. John Bowden; London: SCM, 1994), 649 n. 49: 'The relatively late references to Jerusalem in Gen. 14:18 ("Salem") and 22:2 ("Moria", cf. 2 Chron. 3:1) are not explicit'.

21   See Horst Dietrich Preuß, *Theologie des Alten Testaments*. I *JHWHs erwählendes und verpflichtendes Handeln* (Stuttgart: W. Kohlhammer, 1991), 192, 264; and idem, *Theologie des Alten Testaments*. II *Israels Weg mit JHWH* (Stuttgart: W. Kohlhammer, 1992), 12.

8.4.1 El's Epithets

In each of Melchizedek's blessings, the noun El has two attached epi-
thets. In Gen. 14:19, he is אֵל עֶלְיוֹן קֹנֵה שָׁמַיִם וָאָרֶץ, 'El Elyon creator of heaven
and earth', whereas in the following verse אֵל עֶלְיוֹן is אֲשֶׁר־מִגֵּן צָרֶיךָ בְּיָדֶךָ, '[he]
who delivered your [= Abram's] enemies into his [= Abram's] hand'.[22]

8.4.1.1 Elyon

'El Elyon' occurs in both blessings (so also in Gen. 14:22[23]). In the context
of the Hebrew Bible, the phrase אֵל עֶלְיוֹן is found only here and in Ps.
78:35. However, the phrase אֱלֹהִים עֶלְיוֹן is found in Ps. 57:3 and Ps. 78:56.
Moreover, עֶלְיוֹן and אֵל are found in parallelism in Balaam's fourth oracle
(Num. 24:16) and in Ps. 107:11. עֶלְיוֹן and אֱלֹהִים occur in parallelism in Pss.
46:5; 50:14. עֶלְיוֹן and יְהֹוָה occur in parallelism in Deut. 32:8–9; 2 Sam. 22:14;
and Pss. 18:14; 21:8; 91:9; 92:2; and 97:9. In addition, עֶלְיוֹן functions as
an epithet for Yahweh in Pss. 7:18; 47:3; and 83:19 (Eng. trans., 83:18).
Finally, עֶלְיוֹן occurs parallel to שַׁדַּי in Ps. 91:1.

The phrase אֱלָהָא עִלָּיָא is used frequently in the Aramaic section of the
book of Daniel. In the Dead Sea scrolls, the term עֶלְיוֹן occurs several times.
For example, the phrase אֵל עליון occurs in the Hodayot (1QH 4:31; 6:33),
and עליון and אל appear in parallelism in the Community Rule (1QS 10:12;
11:15). Moreover, the Greek counterpart ὕψιστος was frequently used in
the late postexilic period. For instance, an accumulation of epithets is
evident in Sir. 50:17: ὁ κύριος παντοκράτωρ θεός ὕψιστος. Josephus refers to
Hyrkanus as ἀρχιερέως θεοῦ ὑψίστου, 'high priest of the Most High God'
(see Ant. 16:163).[24]

There have been several attempts to explain the designation אֵל עֶלְיוֹן
in the ME as a reflection of an assumed pre-Israelite, Canaanite pantheon.[25] However, no deity known as אל עליון is attested in any of the sources

---

22 Martin Metzger argues that 'El Elyon, creator of heaven and earth' was a Canaanite
deity worshipped in Jerusalem; see Metzger, 'Eigentumsdeklaration und Schöpfungsaussage', in 'Wenn nicht jetzt, wann dann?' (ed. Hans-Georg Geyer, J. M. Schmidt, and
M. Weinrich; FS H.-J. Kraus; Neukirchen-Vluyn: Neukirchener Verlag, 1983), 37–51
(37).

23 See above, 2.2.1, The Melchizedek Episode (= ME) in Genesis 14:18–20: A Secondary
Interpolation.

24 For more references to עליון and the Greek counterpart ὕψιστος in the late biblical/early
postbiblical period, see H.-J. Zobel, 'עֶלְיוֹן', in ThWAT 6,1, cols. 131–51 (149–51).

25 So, e.g., Fritz Stolz, who presupposed/argued for a pre-Israelite Jerusalem pantheon
with El Elyon as the leading deity, using Gen. 14:18–20 as the main historical source;
see Stolz, Strukturen und Figuren im Kult von Jerusalem: Studien zur altorientalischen,
vor- und frühisraelitischen Religion (BZAW 118; Berlin: W. de Gruyter, 1970), 149–52.

that without doubt stem from either the second millennium or the first half of the first millennium BCE. On the contrary, the impression is quite clear: El and Elyon are treated as distinct deities (see the Sfire inscription from the middle of the eighth century BCE: אל ועליון, 'El *and* Elyon'[26]).

Therefore, in biblical use 'Elyon' is probably an attribute of 'El'. Consequently, the translation 'God Most High' is appropriate, which is also attested by the Greek rendering ὕψιστος. However, more important is the chronological distribution. The use of the term עֶלְיוֹן as such is spread over such a long period that it cannot give any clue as to the provenance of the ME. On the contrary, the combination אֵל עֶלְיוֹן, 'El Elyon' is elsewhere attested only in obviously late texts.

8.4.1.2 'Creator of Heaven and Earth'
In Melchizedek's first blessing (Gen. 14:19; cf. 14:22), the epithet קֹנֵה שָׁמַיִם וָאָרֶץ, 'creator of heaven and earth', is added attributively to El Elyon. In the Hebrew Bible, the comparable phrase עֹשֵׂה שָׁמַיִם וָאָרֶץ, 'maker of heaven and earth', is used attributively for Yahweh in Ps. 134:3. Behind this phrase we glimpse a theologoumenon according to which God is the creator of the entire universe—not only parts of it.

The belief in God as pantocrator[27] was irrevocably coined by the Priestly Writer (see Genesis 1). Yet, the fundamental question is whether the Priestly Writer was the first one to develop this theologoumenon or whether the idea of God having creating the entire cosmos ('heaven *and* earth') developed earlier in ancient Israel.

Several ancient Near East inscriptions from the last half of the second millennium and the first part of the first millennium BCE leave no doubt as to whether El was seen to have creative capabilities. This is probably implied in the Hebrew personal name אֶלְקָנָה, too. However, El

---

In a similar vein, H.-J. Zobel speaks of an 'El Elyon of Jerusalem'; see Zobel, 'עֶלְיוֹן', *ThWAT* 6,1, 131–51 (145–46). For a critical overview over these and other scholars who argue similarly, see Herbert Niehr, *Der höchste Gott: alttestamentlicher JHWH-Glaube im Kontext syrisch-kanaanäischer Religion des 1. Jahrtausends v. Chr.* (BZAW 190; Berlin: W. de Gruyter, 1990), 167–81.

26   See *KAI* 222 A 11. See also the much later reference to a deity 'Elioun', equated with ὕψιστος, by Sanchunyathon. Sanchunyathon is quoted by Philo of Byblos, who for his part is known only though the excerpts that the late-third/early-fourth century Eusebius quotes (*Praep. Ev.* 1:10, 15–16).

27   In the case of the book of Job, the LXX renders שַׁדַּי by παντοκράτορος. When using the term 'pantocrator' I do not refer to the translation practice evident in the LXX but to the theologoumenon that God is the sole creator of the *entire* universe.

does not appear as a pantocrator in any of these texts. On the contrary, they present him only as 'creator of earth'.

In a Hittite text from Bogazköy (thirteenth century BCE or earlier) a deity Elkunirša appears together with his consort Ašertu. The name Elkunirša is probably a borrowing from Canaanite אל קנה ארץ, 'creator of earth'.[28] Moreover, in an eighth-century inscription from Karatepe one gets a glimpse of a Phoenician pantheon, perhaps representative for all of Canaan. Here, a deity אל קן ארץ, 'El, creator of earth', is listed together with בעל שמם, 'Baal of heaven', Šamaš, etc.[29] Further, the Jerusalem ostracon (from eighth or seventh century BCE) reads [l]qn'rṣ, which according to P. D. Miller means 'El, the creator of earth' (note that Yahweh [yhw] occurs in the same context!).[30] Finally, El supplied with the epithet 'creator of earth' is also documented in texts from the first centuries CE.[31]

Rainer Albertz has proposed that the god El was worshipped only as the creator of *earth* (see Gen. 14:19b) in pre-Israelite Jerusalem. He explains the extension of El's creative power to include heaven also as the result of Babylonian influence. He argues that a precisely similar predicate (*bāni šamē u erṣitim*) is attested for Marduk in an inscription from the Cassite period.[32]

Albertz does not say anything about when the proposed influence took place. However, given that the extension of El's creative power to include heaven actually is the result of Babylonian influence, then this influence cannot have been exercised in the Cassite period, which coincides approximately with the second half of the second millennium BCE.[33] On the contrary, if such a theological concept actually was exported from Babylonia to Palestine, then it could have happened only much later,

---

28   See H. Otten, 'Ein kanaanäischer Mythus aus Bogazköy', *MIO* 1 (1953): 125–50; and E. von Schuler, 'Elkunirša', *WM* 1,1, 162–63.

29   See *KAI* 26 A III 11.18–19 (קן is a active participle).

30   P. D. Miller, Jr., 'El the Creator of Earth', *BASOR* 239 (1980): 43–46.

31   In a text from Palmyra (biblical Tadmor) from the first century CE, we (probably) read אלקונרע. According to G. L. Della Vida, this is a philological derivation of Aramaic אל קן (א)רע(א) (= Hebrew אל קן ארץ). See Della Vida, 'El ʾElyon in Genesis 14:18–20', *JBL* 63 (1944): 1–9 (8). Moreover, in a Punic inscription from Leptis Magna (second century CE), we read the phrase לארן אל קן ארץ (cf. *KAI* 129 I 1).

32   Albertz, *A History of Israelite Religion in the Old Testament Period.* I *From the Beginnings to the End of the Monarchy*, 302 n. 52.

33   See Horst Klengel, ed., *Kulturgeschichte des alten Vorderasien* (Veröffentlichungen des Zentralinstituts für Alte Geschichte und Archäologie der Akademie der Wissenschaft der DDR 18; Berlin: Akademie-Verlag, 1989), 308–26.

namely, in the first millennium BCE when Palestine politically was under Babylonian influence.[34]

Therefore, neither the biblical nor the extrabiblical materials point in the direction of an early date for the epithet 'creator of *heaven and earth*'.

8.4.1.3 '. . . Who Delivered Your Enemies into Your Hands'

In Melchizedek's second blessing (Gen. 14:20), El Elyon is supplied with the epithet אֲשֶׁר־מִגֵּן צָרֶיךָ בְּיָדֶךָ, 'who delivered your enemies into your hands'. One can find epithets that also describe God as one who has intervened in history in other texts as well.[35] Proceeding from the premise that the ME is a secondary interpolation, this clause functions as a theological interpretation. According to it, Abram's victory is at bottom Yahweh's work.[36] The idea of Yahweh giving military victory is probably a holy-war motif.[37]

However, the time of the origin of this epithet cannot be determined with certainty. The idea that military victory in the end is God's deliverance is articulated in texts that might be early and in texts that definitely are late (for the latter, see, e.g., Ezra 8:31; Jdt. 16:2, 5–6; cf. Jdt. 8:33; 1 Macc. 9:46).

8.4.2 Melchizedek's Two Blessings: A Clue to the Provenance of the ME?

Melchizedek utters two blessings, one for Abram (Gen. 14:19) and one for El Elyon (Gen. 14:20). Can the blessings possibly give any clues to the provenance of the ME? The passive participle of the verb ברך used in a speech act is found in different parts of the Hebrew Bible.[38]

---

34 Thus also W. Herrmann, 'Wann wurde Jahwe zum Schöpfer der Welt?' *UF* 23 (1991): 165–80 (180).

35 See, e.g., Exod. 18:10; 1 Sam. 17:37; and 2 Sam. 18:28.

36 According to Zimmerli, the secondarily inserted ME spiritualizes the originally 'profane' war narrative found in Genesis 14*; cf. idem, 'Abraham und Melchisedek', 255–64.

37 See 2.1.2 Absence of Metaphysical Explanations in Genesis 14*.

38 ברך (qal passive participle) used either alone or together with an imperative of היה in a speech act (i.e., in a blessing): Gen. 9:26; 14:19–20; 24:27; 27:29, 33; Exod. 18:10; Num. 24:9; Deut. 7:14; 28:3–6; 33:20, 24; Judg. 17:2; Ruth 2:19–20; 3:10; 4:14; 1 Sam. 15:13; 23:21; 25:32–33, 39; 26:25; 2 Sam. 2:5; 18:28; 22:47; 1 Kgs. 1:48; 5:21; 8:15, 56; 10:9; 1 Chr. 16:36; 29:10; 2 Chr. 2:11; 6:4; 9:8; Ezra 7:27; Ps. 18:47; 28:6; 31:22; 41:14; 66:20; 68:20, 36;

A formally similar blessing of an individual followed by a blessing of El Elyon is found in the late book of Judith.[39] However, this book is probably dependent on, among other texts, Genesis 14. Therefore, the analogy does not help to date the ME because the Judith passage probably is a literary borrowing. Judith does theoretically provide a *terminus ante quem*. In practical terms, however, this is less significant since the date of the book of Judith is itself disputed (see 7.2.7, Fact and Fiction Interwoven in Quasi-Historical Narratives from the Persian and Hellenistic Periods).

Furthermore, Melchizedek's second blessing formally refers to God in the third person. A development evident in late- and post-biblical texts is that prayers were concluded by the so-called *ḥatīmā* (חֲתִימָה), a blessing addressing Yahweh in the second person: . . . בָּרוּךְ אַתָּה יְהוָה, 'Blessed be you, O Lord . . .'.[40] The formal predecessor of the *ḥatīmā* in the Hebrew Bible is found in two evidently late texts: 1 Chr. 29:10 and Ps. 119:12; cf. the apocryphal 1 Esd. 4:60a εὐλογητὸς εἶ ὅς κτλ., 'Blessed are you, who have given me wisdom'. However, parallel to the *ḥatīmā*, the 'traditional' blessing of Yahweh in the third person continued to be used (see, e.g., 1Q33 13:2 [= the *War Scroll*]; Luke 1:68; 2 Cor. 1:3; 11:31; Eph. 1:3; 1 Pet. 1:3). Therefore, the form of the blessing of God (Gen. 14:20) is not conclusive with respect to the date of the ME.

8.4.2.1 Excursus: Is Abram Blessed 'by' or 'in Front of' El Elyon?

Melchizedek's first blessing is difficult from a grammatical point of view. The exact meaning of the preposition ל in בָּרוּךְ אַבְרָם לְאֵל עֶלְיוֹן (Gen. 14:19) is not clear. Joseph Scharbert has discussed this problem.[41] Two solutions are traditionally offered. According to the first, the ל indicates the agent

---

72:18–19; 89:53; 106:48; 115:15; 118:26; 119:12; 124:6; 135:21; 144:1; Prov. 5:18; Isa. 19:25; Jer. 20:14; Ezek. 3:12; Zech. 11:5.

39   See Jdt. 13:18 (NRSV):

> Then Uzziah said to her [= Judith], 'O daughter, you are blessed by the Most High God above all other women on earth; and blessed be the Lord God, who created the heavens and the earth, who has guided you to cut off the head of the leader of our enemies. . .'.

40   For a discussion of this, see W. Sibley Towner, '"Blessed Be YHWH" and "Blessed Art Thou": The Modulation of a Biblical Formula', *CBQ* 30 (1968): 386–99.

41   Josef Scharbert, '"Gesegnet sei Abraham *vom* Höchsten Gott"? Zu Gen 14,19 und ähnlichen Stellen im Alten Testament', in *Text, Methode und Grammatik* (ed. Walter Groß, Hubert Irsigler, and Theodor Seidl; FS Wolfgang Richter; St. Ottilien: EOS-Verlag, 1991), 387–401.

in the passive verbal action ('Blessed be Abram *by* El Elyon', thus, e.g., NRSV). According to the other proposal, the ל indicates a dative (thus, e.g., von Rad and Gunkel, 'Gesegnet sei Abram *dem Höchsten Gott* [von Rad]/*dem El 'eljon* [Gunkel], and the LXX εὐλογημένος Αβραμ τῷ θεῷ τῷ ὑψίστῳ κτλ.[42]).

Similar constructions with בָּרוּך (*qal* passive participle) and the preposition ל prefixed to a divine name are found in several other places in the Hebrew Bible.[43] However, none of them really helps solve the problem of the exact meaning. Instead, Scharbert bases his argumentation on analogies from Aramaic and Phoenician inscriptions. In many of these inscriptions it seems that the preposition ל can be replaced by the preposition קְדָם, 'in front (of)'. To me, Scharbert's arguments in favour of a spatial interpretation of the preposition ל in בָּרוּךְ אַבְרָם לְאֵל עֶלְיוֹן (Gen. 14:19) are convincing.[44]

8.4.3 Nothing in the ME Necessitates an Early Date

Summing up, the terms and concepts that we find in the ME do not suggest an early date, either with respect to the terms and concepts themselves or for the ME itself.

8.5 Is There a 'Melchizedek Tradition'— and Where?

Only two texts mention מַלְכִּי־צֶדֶק in the Hebrew Bible, either definitely or potentially: Ps. 110:4 and Gen. 14:18—and below in chapter 12 I will argue that מַלְכִּי־צֶדֶק originally did not function as a personal name in Psalm 110. In addition, מלכי צדק or the Greek Μελχισεδεκ is found in quite a few other texts from the Second Temple period.

---

42 Paraphrased by Joseph Scharbert: 'Melchisedek empfahl Abram seinem Gott, indem er Gutes über ihn sagte, ihn rühmte'. According to Scharbert, the LXX apparently proceeds from the premise that εὐλογέω simply means 'to speak well of'.

43 See Judg. 17:2; 1 Sam. 15:13; 23:21; 2 Sam. 2:5; Ps. 115:15; Ruth 2:22; 3:10.

44 Consequently, Scharbert renders Gen. 14:19 'B [= Abram] ist/sei dem Gott N.N. [= El Elyon] rühmlich empfohlen' ('May Abram be El Elyon laudably recommended'). However, he concludes his thorough discussion about how to translate by laconically remarking: 'Ob man so freilich in einer Volksbibel übersetzen soll, erscheint mir zweifelhaft.' See Scharbert, '"Gesegnet sei Abraham *vom* Höchsten Gott"? Zu Gen 14,19 und ähnlichen Stellen im Alten Testament', 387–401 (400).

8.5.1 Extrabiblical Sources

The ancient Greek translation of the Bible reads Μελχισεδεκ in both Gen.
14:18 and LXX Ps. 109:4. Moreover, in the Dead Sea scrolls, מלכי צדק
occurs in two different texts. In the Aramaic *Genesis Apocryphon* (1Q20),
an example of the genre rewritten Bible, מלכי צדק designates the priest-
king Melchizedek in a way similar to Gen. 14:18–20. However, in the
other text, the so-called *Melchizedek* document from Qumran (11Q13), it
is less clear how מלכי צדק functions.

Below, in chapter 12, עַל־דִּבְרָתִי מַלְכִּי־צֶדֶק: An Analysis of MT Psalm
110:4b, I will show that מלכי צדק in 11Q13 may have functioned as a functional and ontological characterisation of a heavenly figure. The contrast
figure was accordingly the 'king of wickedness' (מלכי רשע)/'Belial' (בליעל).
In the same chapter I will also argue that the author of the *Melchizedek*
document probably learned about מלכי צדק from either one or both of
the biblical sources mentioning מלכי צדק—although he does not explicitly refer to Gen. 14:18 and Ps. 110:4 in the known fragments. In favour
of this is the fact that he explicitly builds on other biblical texts (Lev.
25:9–12; Isa. 61:1–3).

A figure called Melchizedek also occurs in other sources from the
last part of the Second Temple period. For instance, according to Josephus, Melchizedek was the founder of Jerusalem and its temple and the
first priest of God (*War*, 6, § 438). According to the Letter to the Hebrews,
Melchizedek is 'without father, without mother, without genealogy,
having neither beginning of days nor end of life, but resembling the Son
of God', and he remains 'a priest forever' (Heb. 7:3).[45]

Additional sources mention Melchizedek, as well. However, in
many cases they are problematic with respect to their date of composition and their transmission history. For instance, the story of Abram's
meeting with Melchizedek after the former's victory over the Arme-
nians (*sic*) is reported by the historian Eupolemus, who probably lived
before the first century BCE. Unfortunately, an excerpt of Eupolemus's
works is found only in a quotation by Eusebius in *Praeparatio Evangelica* (9.17,6), written several centuries later. Further, a legend about the
birth of Melchizedek appears in *2 (Slavonic) Enoch*. However, the dating

---

45   See Gard Granerød, 'Melchizedek in Hebrews 7', *Bib* 90 (2009): 188–202. For an
     overview of the kinds of information the different postbiblical sources offer about
     Melchizedek, see Horton, *The Melchizedek Tradition*, 86 table 3.1. See also Miriam von
     Nordheim, *Geboren von der Morgenröte? Psalm 110 in Tradition, Redaktion und Rezep-
     tion* (WMANT 118; Neukirchen-Vluyn: Neukirchener Verlag, 2008), 92–93; and Victor
     Aptowitzer, 'Malkisedek: Zu den Sagen der Agada', *MGWJ* 70 (1926): 93–113.

of this pseudepigraphal work ranges from pre-Christian times to late Middle Ages, and no manuscripts earlier than the fourteenth century are known.[46]

In addition, in the Coptic tractate known as *Melchizedek*, a Gnostic document found at Nag Hammadi (IX,1 *Melchizedek*), the Melchizedek figure plays an important role. However, the tractate as a whole was completed in the third century CE, although parts of it may be earlier.[47] Eventually, besides the translations of Genesis in the Targums, Melchizedek is mentioned several times in the Talmud[48] and in other rabbinic writings.[49]

However, we should weigh the sources and not only count them. It can be stated that when referring to מלכי צדק/Μελχισεδεκ all of the extra-biblical sources mentioned above somehow are ultimately dependent on the Melchizedek material in the Hebrew Bible. This seems also to be the case with some extrabiblical sources that go a step further than the Hebrew Bible by offering extra information about Melchizedek. This is probably also the case with the *Melchizedek* text from Qumran (11Q13), which contains no explicit reference to Gen. 14:18 or Ps. 110:4. Because 11Q13 is dependent on and discusses other biblical texts, it is reasonable to assume that the author also borrowed מלכי צדק from the Bible.[50]

Summing up, it is justified to state that all of the references to מלכי צדק/ Μελχισεδεκ outside the Hebrew Bible are part of the reception history of Genesis 14 and Psalm 110. There is at least a postbiblical Melchizedek tradition.

---

46 See F. I. Andersen, '2 (Slavonic Apocalypse of) ENOCH (late first century)', *OTP* 1:94–95; cf. also Christfried Bötterich, 'The Melchizedek Story of *2 (Slavonic) Enoch*: A Reaction to A. Orlov', *JSJ* 32 (2001), 445–70; and idem, 'Die vergessene Geburtsgeschichte: Mt 1–2/Lk 1–2 und die wunderbare Geburt des Melchizedek in slHen 71–72', in *Jüdische Schriften in ihrem antik-jüdischen und urchristlichen Kontext* (ed. Hermann Lichtenberger and Gerbern S. Oegema; Studien zu den Jüdischen Schriften aus hellenistisch-römischer Zeit 1; Gütersloh: Gütersloher Verlagshaus, 2002), 222–48.

47 Birger A. Pearson, 'Melchizedek (NHC IX, 1)', *ABD* 4:688.

48 *B. Ned.* 32b; *b. Suk.* 52b (כהן צדק; Munich codex: מלכי צדק); *b. B. Bat.* 14b; *y. Ta'an.* 2a, pereq 1, halakhah 1.

49 *Pesiqta de Rab Kahana, Ha-ḥodesh* 9; *Midrash haGadol* Gen. 11:30; *Genesis Rabba* 26:3; *Seder ʿOlam Rabbah* 21; *Midrash Shir hash-Shirim* II.13.4, etc.

50 For a discussion of the references to Melchizedek outside the Bible, see also 12.6.3, Evidence Based on the Reception History.

8.5.2 A 'Melchizedek Tradition' also prior to and within the Bible?

However, is there a Melchizedek tradition within the Hebrew Bible? To answer this we have to address Ps. 110:4 and Gen. 14:18–20 in particular and the relationship between them.

This provokes several questions:

- Is מַלְכִּי־צֶדֶק really a personal name referring to an individual in both Ps. 110:4 and Gen. 14:18–20?
- On the question of the relationship between Ps. 110:4 and Gen. 14:18–20:
  - Is the use of מַלְכִּי־צֶדֶק in both texts dependent on a common source?
  - Or, is one of the texts dependent on the other, and in that case, which one comes first?

I will discuss these questions thoroughly in separate chapters below in Part III. However, I will anticipate parts of the discussion below. The preliminary observations will in turn lead to the hypotheses that I will propose with respect to the background and origin of the ME.[51]

8.5.3 Is מַלְכִּי־צֶדֶק a Personal Name in both Genesis 14:18–20 and Psalm 110:4?

The question of whether מַלְכִּי־צֶדֶק is a personal name in both Ps. 110:4 and Gen. 14:18–20 necessitates a closer look at the literary contexts in which מַלְכִּי־צֶדֶק appears. In Psalm 110, the two words מַלְכִּי־צֶדֶק appear without a narrative context. In addition, they follow immediately after another puzzling phrase, the *hapax legomonon* עַל־דִּבְרָתִי. Nevertheless, most Bible translations relate the half verse Ps. 110:4b עַל־דִּבְרָתִי מַלְכִּי־צֶדֶק to the preceding half verse 4a. In v. 4a a person is directly spoken to and given/confirmed in an eternal priesthood: נִשְׁבַּע יְהוָה וְלֹא יִנָּחֵם אַתָּה־כֹהֵן לְעוֹלָם. This reading is evident in LXX Ps. 109:4: σὺ εἶ ἱερεὺς εἰς τὸν αἰῶνα κατὰ τὴν τάξιν Μελχισεδεκ, 'You are a priest forever after the order of Melchizedek.' Most modern translations translate in a similar fashion, for example, the NRSV, 'The LORD has sworn and will not change his mind, "You are a priest forever according to the order of Melchizedek"'.

Therefore, the LXX (followed by most modern translations) seems to assume that Melchizedek's priesthood serves as a source or model for the priesthood of the person to whom Yahweh addressed the oracle in Ps. 110:4. However, as I will argue below, LXX Ps. 109:4b probably deviates

---

51   See chapter 9, Hypothesis: The Origin of the Melchizedek Episode Best Explained within the Paradigm of 'Diachronic, Inner-biblical Exegesis'. For a discussion of the circularity, see 1.3 Why a Study on Genesis 14? A Brief Epistemological Consideration.

from the Hebrew text.[52] For the time being it suffices to say that Psalm 110 does not provide any biographical or otherwise relevant information about a possible Melchizedek tradition within the Hebrew Bible—that is, with the exception of the two words מַלְכִּי־צֶדֶק. As I will show in chapter 12, it is possible to argue that מַלְכִּי־צֶדֶק originally functioned either as an ordinary nominal phrase or as a nominal clause in the psalm.

In Genesis 14 the situation is different. From the biographical information provided by the literary context it is evident that מַלְכִּי־צֶדֶק functions as a personal name. For instance, the person referred to as מַלְכִּי־צֶדֶק is presented as a contemporary of the patriarch Abraham. Further, according to the text he is מֶלֶךְ שָׁלֵם, that is, 'king of Salem' (provided that שָׁלֵם is a place name and not a common noun or an adjective[53]) and priest of El Elyon. Moreover, he brought out bread and wine to Abraham and blessed him and El Elyon. The brief episode concludes with the remark 'And he gave him tithes from everything'. (It should be pointed out that the biblical text does not specify the identity of the donor and that of the recipient.)[54]

Summing up, מַלְכִּי־צֶדֶק does function as a personal name in the episode in Gen. 14:18–20. However, in Psalm 110 that is not necessarily the case.

8.5.4 Concluding Remark

I will postpone the discussion of the nature of the relationship between the two biblical texts mentioning מַלְכִּי־צֶדֶק to subsequent chapters. Both the content of the so-called Melchizedek tradition (often referred to as the *traditum*) and the process of passing on of the *traditum* (often referred to as the *traditio*; note the relationship between the two texts) are unclear.[55] By that I mean it is unclear both what מַלְכִּי־צֶדֶק in Ps. 110:4 exactly means and what the relationship between Ps. 110:4 and Gen. 14:18–20 possibly is. Therefore, I suggest that one should be sceptical of any discussion

---

52 See chapter 12, מַלְכִּי־צֶדֶק עַל־דִּבְרָתִי: An Analysis of MT Psalm 110:4b.

53 William Foxwell Albright has proposed to correct the text to מֶלֶךְ שְׁלֹמוֹ, 'a king in alliance with him'; cf. Albright, 'Abram the Hebrew—A New Archeological Interpretation', *BASOR* 163 (1961): 36–54 (52). R. H. Smith has proposed that it means 'submissive/obsequious king'; cf. Smith, 'Abram and Melchizedek (Gen 14:18–20)', 129–53 (141ff.).

54 The usual understanding, however, is that Abram is the donor.

55 For the terminological distinction between *traditum* and *traditio*, see Fishbane, *Biblical Interpretation in Ancient Israel*, 6; idem, 'Inner-Biblical Exegesis', 33–48; and Rösel, 'Traditionskritik / Traditionsgeschichte', 732–43 (733).

regarding a tradition about the assumed Canaanite priest-king called Melchizedek that *antedates* the biblical texts in question.

8.6 Preliminary Conclusion and Point of Departure: The ME—A Doubly Late Interpolation

As I demonstrated by means of literary criticism,[56] the ME (Gen. 14:18–20) is probably an interpolation into an earlier composition, that is, Genesis 14*. The date of interpolation must be later than the date of composition of the text it was interpolated into. However, what about the date of composition of the ME itself?

Genesis 14* does not betray any cases of dependence on the ME.[57] On the contrary, Melchizedek's blessing of 'El Elyon, who has delivered your enemies into your hand!' (Gen. 14:20a) only makes sense in light of Abram's victory over the eastern kings (Gen. 14:14–16). Because the ME appears to interrupt the conversation between Abram and the king of Sodom (Gen. 14:17, 21–24), and because the ME is dependent on Genesis 14* and not vice versa, it is reasonable to assume that the date of composition of the ME is later than the date of composition of Genesis 14*.

The assumption that the interpolation is dependent on its proximate context (Genesis 14*) suggests that the date of composition and the date of interpolation into Genesis 14* more or less coincide. Therefore, it is unlikely that an assumed proto-ME ever existed independently of Genesis 14*—before it eventually was interpolated into the narrative. On the contrary, the episode was probably composed for this particular narrative at the outset.[58]

I have argued above that Genesis 14* was composed in either the Persian or the early Hellenistic period.[59] Therefore, the date of composition of Genesis 14* serves as *terminus a quo* for the date of compostion and the date of interpolation of the ME.

Moreover, the observations I made concerning the terms and concepts found in the ME fit into this picture (see 8.4, The Terms and

---

56 See 2.2.1, The Melchizedek Episode (= ME) in Genesis 14:18–20: A Secondary Interpolation.

57 As for Abram's oath to 'Yahweh, El Elyon, the creator of heaven and earth' (MT Gen. 14:22), see 2.2.1, The Melchizedek Episode (= ME) in Genesis 14:18–20: A Secondary Interpolation.

58 See also 19.2.4, The Likeliest Explanation: Both Genesis 14* and Later the ME Were Added in Connection with the Production of New Copies.

59 See 7.1, The Date of Composition: A Synthesis of the Different Approaches.

Concepts in the ME: Inconclusive with Respect to the Date of the Episode), as does the negative conclusion I made with respect to the legitimacy of speaking about a Melchizedek tradition in the context of the Hebrew Bible (see 8.5, Is There a 'Melchizedek Tradition' — and Where?). A Melchizedek tradition in a real sense is documented only in the biblical reception history.

Therefore, a point of departure for the following investigation is that the ME is late in terms of date of composition and date of interpolation. Genesis 14*, the narrative the ME has been interpolated into, is a relatively late text dating to the Persian or early Hellenistic period. Because the ME is dependent on this narrative, the episode must consequently have an even later date of composition.

9. Hypothesis: The Origin of the Melchizedek Episode Best Explained within the Paradigm of Diachronic, Inner-Biblical Exegesis

I have argued above that Genesis 14* was composed in the fifth, fourth, third, or first half of the second century BCE (see 7.1, The Date of Composition: A Synthesis of the Different Approaches). The ME is dependent on Genesis 14* and cannot be dated earlier than the latter.

There are several examples of biblical literature from the same general period whose background could be sought in early Jewish intertextuality. Perhaps the largest inner-biblical example is the composition of the Chronistic History, supposedly a rewriting of both the Torah and the so-called Deuteronomistic History.

Moreover, it was probably in the same general period that someone started connecting the biblical psalms to events in the biblical historiographic literature.

This opens the possibility of explaining the background and origin of the ME on the basis of that which I initially called the paradigm of diachronic, inner-biblical intertextuality (see 1.5, The Paradigm of Diachronic, Inner-Biblical Intertextuality: A Promising Paradigm for Exploring the Background, Origin and Purpose of Genesis 14; and 1.6, Aim, Scope, and Fundamental Hypothesis).

9.1 Psalm 110—A Poetic Version of Genesis 14*

As I will argue in a subsequent chapter,[1] sometimes—probably first in the Second Temple period—historical events mentioned in the biblical historiographical literature were related to different biblical psalms. This is evident in many of the secondary superscriptions in the book of Psalms.

Therefore, the first hypothesis I put forward is about how Psalm 110 was read in the Second Temple period. At one point before the ME was

---

1   See chapter 11, The Phenomenon of Assimilation in the Bible.

composed, someone started reading the psalm as a poetic version of the narrative about Abram's war against the eastern kings, that is Genesis 14* (note: *without* the ME in vv. 18–20).

9.2 'You' in Psalm 110 = Abraham

Parallel to and probably closely connected with the historiographical interpretation of many psalms is the interpretation of the ל in the phrase לְדָוִד (Ps. 110:1a etc.) as a ל-*auctoris*. Because the Jewish reading community conceived of King David as the author of Psalm 110, the same reading community identified David with the prophetic psalm speaker (the 'I') in the psalm. Therefore, when it was thought that David was the one communicating the oracles in Psalm 110 to a figure called אֲדֹנִי, 'my lord' (Ps. 110:1a), this figure was necessarily thought to be different from King David himself.

The second hypothesis I will attempt to substantiate is that the Second Temple period reading community — which related Psalm 110 to Genesis 14* — identified David's 'lord' (see אֲדֹנִי, 'my lord', in Ps. 110:1a) with the patriarch Abraham. A consequence of such identification was that the interpreting community understood all references to 'you'/'your' in the psalm as directed to Abraham.[2]

9.3 The Composition of the ME: The Result of a Secondary Assimilation between Genesis 14* and Psalm 110

It is possible to show that there are many terminological similarities between Genesis 14* and Psalm 110. However, at the same time there is no one-to-one similarity between them. When Psalm 110 is read as a poetic version of Abram's war, several *Leerstellen* appear in Genesis 14* vis-à-vis the psalm.

My third hypothesis is that the ME was composed to fill out these *Leerstellen* in Genesis 14*. The material which then was used was provided by the psalm, in particular the surplus information that Psalm 110 offers vis-à-vis Genesis 14*.[3]

---

2 See chapter 13. Early Intertextual Readings of Genesis 14 and Psalm 110 and chapter 14, The Result of an Assimilation of Two Texts, Both Thought to be Referring to Abram's War with the King.

3 See in particular chapter 14, The Result of an Assimilation of Two Texts, Both Thought to be Referring to Abram's War with the King.

10. Psalm 110

Before I attempt to substantiate the hypotheses formulated above about the origin of the ME, I will take a step aside and discuss Psalm 110 in particular. I have hypothesized that the ME is the result of the assimilation of Genesis 14* and Psalm 110, which was read as a poetic account of Abram's war. Therefore, it is a prerequisite for this model that it is possible to reckon a date of composition for Psalm 110 that antedates the composition of the ME.

In the history of research on Psalm 110, three different time frames for the psalm have been proposed. Whereas some have argued that the psalm is a modification of a pre-Israelite, Canaanite hymn, another—and more common—proposal has been to date it to the monarchic period. However, there are also quite a few scholars who have dated it relatively late, namely, to the postexilic period, even as late as the Maccabaean period.

Therefore, in the following I will discuss Psalm 110, focusing in particular on the date of the psalm and the criteria for drawing conclusions as to the date. I will conclude that a date in the monarchic period is likely.[1]

10.1 The Characters Speaking and Spoken to in the Psalm

Most structural analyses of Psalm 110 take their point of departure in the psalm's two oracles, the first in v. 1 and the other in v. 4. The first oracle is spoken *to* אֲדֹנִי, 'my lord' (note: *not* אֲדֹנָי 'the Lord'; see Ps. 110:5a!), and employs the motif of sitting at the right side of God and treading down one's enemies. The first oracle should be limited to v. 1. In vv. 2–3 Yahweh is probably no longer the speaker but is referred to in the third person. However, the addressee, that is, the person spoken to in vv. 2–3, appears to be identical with the addressee of the oracle in v. 1. In other

---

1   For a fuller outline of the history of research on Psalm 110, see von Nordheim, *Geboren von der Morgenröte?* 5–22.

words, the person that the phrase אֲדֹנִי, 'my lord', in v. 1 refers to and who in the same verse is told to sit at Yahweh's right is probably the one spoken to in vv. 2–3. The prophetic[2] psalm speaker who mediated between Yahweh and אֲדֹנִי, 'my lord', also addresses אֲדֹנִי in vv. 2–3, however not in the name of Yahweh but on his own behalf.

Moreover, in Ps. 110:4aβ.b, Yahweh is quoted for the second time speaking in the first person ('Yahweh has sworn and will not repent: "You are a priest . . ."'). Here, he either promises or confirms (depending on whether it is preformative or confirmative speech) eternal priesthood for the addressee of the oracle. Although the addressee is unnamed, it is common to identify him with the addressee of the oracle in v. 1, that is, the person who there is called אֲדֹנִי, 'my lord'.[3] By analogy to vv. 2–3, Yahweh ceases speaking and is instead referred to in the third person in the two verses (vv. 5–6) following immediately after the oracle in v. 4 (see v. 5a, אֲדֹנָי, 'the Lord' [*not* אֲדֹנִי, 'my lord']). Likewise, by analogy to the oracle in v. 1 and the two following verses (vv. 2–3), the addressee of the oracle in v. 4 is also the addressee of the utterances in vv. 5–6 (he is evident in the second person pronominal suffix in v. 5a: עַל־יְמִינְךָ, 'on *your* right side'.

Verse 7 does not explicitly introduce any new subject for the verbs it contains. Therefore, on formal grounds it could be argued that אֲדֹנִי, 'my lord', is also the subject here. If so, v. 7 offers an anthropomorphism because it describes Yahweh drinking from the brook and raising his head. The anthropomorphism causes many interpreters—at least modern ones[4]—to understand the addressee of the two oracles in vv. 1, 4 as

---

2   Because of the noun phrase נְאֻם יְהוָה, which is frequently found in the prophetic litera-
     ture, the mediator is probably a prophet.

3   Other proposals have been made by H. H. Rowley and Rudolf Kilian. Rowley inter-
     prets the psalm as a coronation ritual. According to him, the priest Zadok addresses
     the king in vv. 1–3, whereas the king himself replies and confirms Zadok's priestly
     rights in v. 4. Moreover, vv. 5–6 is a priestly blessing spoken *to* the king. See Row-
     ley, 'Melchizedek and Zadok (Gen 14 and Ps 110)', 461–72. Moreover, Rudolf Kilian
     argues that Psalm 110 as such is a *relecture* of ancient Egyptian enthronement rituals
     from the early monarchic period. However, in his view, v. 4 appears to be isolated in
     the context of Psalm 110. Moreover, because he follows others who have characterized
     Genesis 14 as a late midrash that has left no marks in the biblical reception history, he
     argues that Ps. 110:4 can not be an old and original part of Psalm 110. On the contrary,
     in his opinion it is a late interpolation. See Rudolf Kilian, 'Relecture in Psalm 110', in
     Kilian, *Studien zu alttestamentlichen Texten und Situationen* (SBAB 28; Stuttgart: Katho-
     lisches Bibelwerk, 1999), 237–53 (250–53).

4   As for ancient interpretations of Ps. 110:7 I do not know how the question of the sub-
     ject of the verbs in this particular verse was answered.

the grammatical subject. According to this reading, the verse is some-how loosely connected to the preceding verses, at least in a formal sense.

Summing up, Psalm 110 seems to involve at least three different per-sons: *Yahweh* (אֲדֹנָי/יְהוָה), the *prophetic psalm speaker*, and the *addressee* of the oracles in vv. 1, 4 (partly referred to in the third person [אֲדֹנִי, 'my lord'], partly in the second person ['you'/'your']).

10.2 Traditional Issues in the Research

As any query in a bibliography database will show, Psalm 110 has received much attention in biblical scholarship. One reason is probably that it is among the most frequently quoted psalms in the New Testa-ment.[5] Or to be more correct, two of the psalm's seven verses are cited by New Testament authors, whereas the remaining verses seem to have been of no interest. The first verse that is often referred to or alluded to in the New Testament is Ps. 110:1. This verse is read in a messianic context and, in addition, serves as the basis for the motif of the Son of Man's sitting at the right side of God (see Matt. 22:44 and par.; Matt. 26:64 and par., etc.). The second verse is Ps. 110:4. In the latter case, it is in particular the author of the Letter to the Hebrews who demonstrates his interest. For him, this verse serves as textual evidence for the claim that God designated Jesus 'a *high priest* according to the order of Melchize-dek' (Heb. 5:10 NRSV, my emphasis) so that the priesthood of Jesus is superior to that of Aaron.[6]

With respect to Psalm 110, one can single out three traditional loci of research: textual criticism, date of composition and royal ideology.

10.2.1 Textual Criticism

One recurring issue in the history of research is textual criticism. In particular, v. 3 has attracted much attention as the MT Ps. 110:3 differs distinctively from its Greek counterpart in LXX Ps. 109:3.[7] Whereas the

---

5   For Psalm 110 and the New Testament, see David M. Hay, *Glory at the Right Hand: Psalm 110 in Early Christianity* (SBLMS 18; Nashville: Abingdon, 1973).

6   See, e.g., Horton, *The Melchizedek Tradition*, 152–72.

7   See, e.g., Joachim Schaper, 'Der Septuaginta-Psalter. Interpretation, Aktualisierung und liturgische Verwendung der biblischen Psalmen im hellenistischen Judentum', in *Der Psalter in Judentum und Christentum* (ed. Erich Zenger; HBS 18; Freiburg: Herder, 1998), 165–84 (173–77); and Gary A. Rendsburg, 'Psalm cx 3b', *VT* 49 (1999): 548–53.

nominal clause in the MT is difficult, if not even incomprehensible, the
LXX offers a verbal clause:

MT Ps. 110:3:

עַמְּךָ נְדָבֹת בְּיוֹם חֵילֶךָ בְּהַדְרֵי־קֹדֶשׁ מֵרֶחֶם מִשְׁחָר לְךָ טַל יַלְדֻתֶיךָ

The translation of the MT in the NRSV:

> Your people will offer themselves willingly on the day you lead your forces
> on the holy mountains. From the womb of the morning, like dew, your
> youth will come to you.

LXX Ps. 109:3:

μετὰ σοῦ ἡ ἀρχὴ ἐν ἡμέρᾳ τῆς δυνάμεώς σου ἐν ταῖς λαμπρότησιν τῶν ἁγίων ἐκ
γαστρὸς πρὸ ἑωσφόρου ἐξεγέννησά σε

Brenton's LXX translation:[8]

> With thee is dominion in the day of thy power, in the splendours of thy
> saints: I have begotten thee from the womb before the morning.

The LXX Ps. 109:3 is depicting Yahweh, probably speaking in the first
person, addressing the addressee of both the oracle in v. 1 and the following v. 2. So, the clause LXX Ps. 109:3 ἐκ γαστρὸς πρὸ ἑωσφόρου ἐξεγέννησά
σε is comparable to Ps. 2:7aβ.b.[9] In other words, whereas the MT Psalm
110 only offers two oracles of Yahweh (vv. 1, 4), the LXX for its part offers
three (vv. 1, 3, 4).[10]

LXX Ps. 109:3 is easier to read and comprehend than the MT counterpart. An argument often found in favour of giving preponderance to
LXX Ps. 109:3 vis-à-vis MT Ps. 110:3 is that the former is the *lectio facilior*.
The idea, then, is that it reflects a Hebrew *Vorlage* that depicts Yahweh's
giving birth in a way comparable to Ps. 2:7. Moreover, the difficult MT,
on the contrary, is assumed to be the result of a corruption.

---

8   Lancelot C. L. Brenton, *The Septuagint with Apocrypha: Greek and English* (London:
     Samuel Bagster, 1851 [reprint, Peabody, MA: Hendrickson, 1986; and subsequent
     reprints]).
9   Ps. 2:7aβ.b (MT / LXX):

אָמַר אֵלַי בְּנִי אַתָּה אֲנִי הַיּוֹם יְלִדְתִּיךָ
κύριος εἶπεν πρός με υἱός μου εἶ σύ ἐγὼ σήμερον γεγέννηκά σε

10   Among the questions that have been asked is whether either the MT יַלְדֻתֶיךָ ('your
     youth') or the LXX ἐξεγέννησά σε (assumed to reflect a Hebrew text יְלִדְתִּיךָ*, 'I begot
     you') is the original reading. Likewise, it has been discussed which one is the original
     of the MT עַמְּךָ נְדָבֹת ('your people [is?] willing[?]') or the corresponding LXX μετὰ σοῦ ἡ
     ἀρχή (<עַמְּךָ נְדִבֹת* 'with you are the noble ones'). Another problem is the MT טַל ('dew'),
     a noun not reflected in the LXX. Finally, it is discussed whether the MT בְּהַדְרֵי (which
     the LXX is assumed to paraphrase by ἐν ταῖς λαμπρότησιν) is original or whether it
     rather should be taken as a misreading of a original בְּהַרְרֵי* 'on the mountains', a read-
     ing supported by some ancient textual witnesses (Jerome and Symmachus).

However, it could be the other way around. The MT may reflect a *Vorlage* that no longer was comprehensible at the time of the translation of the LXX. If that is the case, the LXX translators harmonized Ps. 109:3 with Ps. 2:7.[11]

The point I make here is that it can be argued that the LXX translator did the same in connection with Ps. 110:4b (= LXX Ps. 109:4b). This half verse, which plays an important role in the model of the origin of the ME that I develop in subsequent chapters, is polyvalent in the Hebrew of the MT.[12] In contrast, LXX Ps. 109:4b is quite clear:

MT Ps. 110:4:

נִשְׁבַּע יְהוָה וְלֹא יִנָּחֵם אַתָּה־כֹהֵן לְעוֹלָם עַל־דִּבְרָתִי מַלְכִּי־צֶדֶק

The translation of the MT in the NRSV:

> The Lord has sworn and will not change his mind, 'You are a priest forever according to the order of Melchizedek'.

LXX Ps. 109:4 (my emphasis):

> ὤμοσεν κύριος καὶ οὐ μεταμεληθήσεται σὺ εἶ ἱερεὺς εἰς τὸν αἰῶνα κατὰ τὴν τάξιν Μελχισεδεκ

Brenton's LXX translation (my emphasis):[13]

> The Lord sware, and will not repent, Thou art a priest for ever, *after the order of Melchisedec.*

For now, I will argue that the translation in LXX Ps. 109:4b presupposes and is dependent on the ME and the brief biographic information about the priest-king Melchizedek given there. First, the LXX translator has rendered the Hebrew *hapax legomenon* עַל־דִּבְרָתִי in terms of a (priestly) ordinal concept. Moreover, in accordance with the ME, the ambiguous Hebrew words מַלְכִּי־צֶדֶק have been rendered by an unambiguous personal name, Melchizedek.

10.2.2 Date

More relevant in this context is the second issue often discussed in the history of research: the date of Psalm 110. The wider context of this discussion is the dating of the so-called royal psalms (for more about this

---

11 So also Eberhard Bons, 'Die Septuaginta-Version von Psalm 110 (109 LXX): Text-gestalt, Aussagen, Auswirkungen', in *Heiligkeit und Herrschaft: Intertextuelle Studien zu Heiligkeitsvorstellungen und zu Psalm 110* (ed. Dieter Sänger; BThS 55; Neukirchen-Vluyn: Neukirchner Verlag, 2003), 122–45 (141); and Raymond Jacques Tournay, *Seeing and Hearing God with the Psalms: The Prophetic Liturgy of the Second Temple in Jerusalem* (JSOTSup 119; Sheffield: JSOT Press, 1991), 213.

12 I will argue for this in more detail in chapter 12, עַל־דִּבְרָתִי מַלְכִּי־צֶדֶק: An Analysis of MT Psalm 110:4b.

13 Brenton, *The Septuagint with Apocrypha.*

group, see 10.2.3, Royal Ideology). Historically, scholars have generally assumed that the royal psalms refer to historical persons. Consequently, the persons addressed in the royal psalms probably were the kings who reigned at the time the psalm was composed and (re-)used.[14] Therefore, many have dated the psalms belonging to this group (or Psalm 110 particularily) to the monarchic period.[15] However, there have been dissenting voices. On the one hand, there are those who argue that the psalm to some extent is of pre-Israelite provenance.[16] On the other hand, some have also proposed different dates for Psalm 110 in the postexilic period. Especially around the turn of the century, more than one hundred years ago, this dating was often proposed. For instance, F. Baethgen argued that the psalm was a messianic prophecy from the Hasmonaean period. And, being a messianic prophecy, it could not refer to a historical person.[17] Moreover, B. Duhm related it to the Hasmonaean Simon's installation into the office of supreme political and religious leader (see 1 Macc. 14:41ff.).[18] More recently, Herbert Donner, Ernst Axel Knauf, and Miriam von Nordheim have argued for such a dating.[19]

---

14   An alternative view is proposed by Raymond Jacques Tournay. He argues that the royal psalms are eschatological from the outset. He characterizes Psalm 110 as an 'anthological psalm with midrashic tendencies'. See Tournay, *Seeing and Hearing God with the Psalms*, 216.

15   See, e.g., Kraus, *Psalmen. II Psalmen 60–150*, 929. Moreover, see Hermann Gunkel, *Die Psalmen* (HKAT; Göttingen: Vandenhoeck & Ruprecht, 1926), 481–87; R. Kittel, *Die Psalmen* (6th ed.; KAT 13; Leipzig: Deichertsche Verlagsbuchhandlung, 1929), 7–12, 355–59; J. W. Bowker, 'Psalm CX', *VT* 17 (1967): 31–41; Geo Widengren, 'Psalm 110 und das sakrale Königtum in Israel', in *Zur neueren Psalmenforschung* (ed. P. H. A. Neumann; WdF 192; Darmstadt: Wissenschaftliche Buchgesellschaft, 1976), 185–216 (originally published in Swedish in 1941); A. Weiser, *Die Psalmen* (7th ed.; ATD, 14–15; Göttingen: Vandenhoeck & Ruprecht, 1966); M. Dahood, *Psalms III: 101–150* (Garden City, NY: Doubleday, 1970); Johannes Schildenberger, 'Der Königspsalm 110', *Erbe und Auftrag* 56 (1980): 53–59; Willem van der Meer, 'Psalm 110: A Psalm of Rehabilitation?' in Willem van der Meer and J. C. de Moor, *The Structural Analysis of Biblical and Canaanite Poetry* (JSOTSup 74; Sheffield: JSOT Press, 1988), 207–34; Th. Booij, 'Psalm cx: "Rule in the midst of your foes!"', *VT* 41 (1991): 396–407; K. Seybold, *Die Psalmen* (HAT I/15; Tübingen: Mohr, 1996); and John W. Hilber, 'Psalm cx in the Light of Assyrian Prophecies', *VT* 53 (2003): 353–66.

16   See H. G. Jefferson, 'Is Psalm 110 Canaanite?' *JBL* 73 (1954): 152–56; and H. H. Rowley, 'Melchizedek and Zadok (Gen 14 and Ps 110)', 461–72.

17   F. Baethgen, *Die Psalmen* (3d ed.; HKAT; Göttingen: Vandenhoeck & Ruprecht, 1904).

18   B. Duhm, *Die Psalmen* (2d ed.; KHC 14; Tübingen: Mohr, 1922).

19   Herbert Donner, 'Der verläßliche Prophet. Betrachtungen zu I Makk 14,41ff und zu Ps 110', in idem, *Aufsätze zum Alten Testament* (BZAW 224; Berlin: W. de Gruyter, 1994), 213–23 (originally printed in *Prophetie und geschichtliche Wirklichkeit im alten Israel: Festschrift für Siegfried Herrmann zum 65. Geburtstag* [ed. Rüdiger Liwak and Siegfried Wagner; Stuttgart: W. Kohlhammer, 1991], 89–98); Ernst Axel Knauf, 'Psalm lx und

10.2.3 Royal Ideology

Royal ideology is another catchword that has recurred in different works on the royal psalms, a group that also includes Psalm 110.[20] The particular royal ideology that scholars find expressed in the psalm is often used as a means to date the psalm.

Several questions concerning the ideology reflected in Psalm 110 in particular are answered differently. What is the specific ideology and from where have the motifs occurring in the psalm been derived? Are they *gemeinorientalisch*, Mesopotamian (see Hilber), or rather Egyptian (see Kilian)? Moreover, did the psalm originally play a role in an enthronement ceremony in the monarchic period of Judah, for example, as part of the coronation liturgy? Or is it perhaps rather an exilic/postexilic text, reflecting the merging of the royal office into the priestly (Schreiner)? Is it perhaps to be dated as late as the investiture of Simeon Maccabaeus as priest and king around 140 BCE (Donner)?

An important historical problem with immediate consequences for the dating of Psalm 110 relates to the functions of the king in preexilic Israel/Judah: Were the Davidic kings also priests (see Ps. 110:4: 'You [= the king?] are a priest . . .')?

It is evident from different texts that kings in the ancient Near East in general took part in the cult of their respective deities. The Neo-Assyrian kings officiated in the Ashur cult as the highest ranked priests. The high priest of Ashur acted in the cult on behalf of the king when the king was absent.[21] However, although the title '*šangû* of Ashur' often borne by Neo-Assyrian kings usually is translated 'priest of Ashur', it could also be rendered 'administrator of Ashur'.[22] If the latter translation proves to be correct, the title first of all reveals the understanding of the Neo-

---

Psalm cviii', *VT* 50 (2000): 55–65 (64–65); and von Nordheim, *Geboren von der Morgenröte?* 134–41. See also M. Treves, 'Two Acrostic Psalms', *VT* 15 (1965): 81–90. Finally, it should be noted that Stefan Schreiner has argued that Ps. 110:4 is a postexilic interpolation into the psalm. The purpose was to legitimize the new postexilic institution of the high priesthood. See Schreiner, 'Psalm CX und die Investitur des Hohenpriesters', *VT* 27 (1977): 216–22.

20   There is a consensus in counting Psalm 110 among the so-called royal psalms of the book of Psalms. As to the royal psalms, Psalms 2, 20, 21, 45, 72, 89, 101, 110, 132, and 144:1–11 are regarded as an irreducible minimum by most scholars; see John Day, *Psalms* (T. & T. Clark Study Guides; Sheffield: Sheffield Academic Press, 1999 [reprint, London: T. & T. Clark, 2003], 88). Moreover, this group is not defined on the basis of a common form but rather on the basis of a common theme: all are about kings; cf. Kraus, *Psalmen. I Psalmen 1–59*, 60.

21   So Klengel, ed., *Kulturgeschichte des alten Vorderasien*, 351.

22   See *CAD* 17, *s.v. šangû*, 377–82.

Assyrian king as an executive acting on behalf of Ashur, the real ruler.[23] Nevertheless, throughout the whole history of Egypt, the king acted on behalf of his subordinates as a corporate personality, and so in theory was the high priest.[24]

As for Israel and Judah, the sources—all of which are in the Hebrew Bible—reveal that the kings performed activities that may have been priestly. According to the story of the transfer of the ark to Jerusalem, David was wearing a linen ephod when the ark was brought to Jerusalem (2 Sam. 6:14).[25] Sacrifices were offered by kings (Saul: 1 Kgs. 13:9–10; David: 2 Sam. 6:13, 17–18; 24:25; Solomon: 1 Kgs. 3:4, 15; 8:5, 62–64; 9:25; Ahaz: 2 Kgs. 16:12–15; Jeroboam: 1 Kgs. 12:33; 13:1–2). In addition, David and Solomon blessed the people—according to Num. 6:22–27 and 1 Chr. 23:13, if not a priestly prerogative then at least a typical priestly activity—in the meeting tent (2 Sam. 6:18) and the temple (1 Kgs. 8:14).

Nevertheless, no Israelite or Judahite king is ever explicitly called 'priest'. Terminologically, the closest example is found in 2 Sam. 8:18b: וּבְנֵי דָוִד כֹּהֲנִים הָיוּ, 'and David's sons were priests'. Taking the Chronistic History into account, the picture gets more complicated. In the report about the deeds of King Uzziah, the king is reported to have intended to make an offering on the altar of incense in the temple of Yahweh. According to 2 Chr. 26:16–21, this was interpreted as apostasy that caused the king to become leprous and experience a lifelong expulsion from the temple community. The reason the chief priest Azariah gives is that Uzziah has trespassed (מעל); it is only the priests of Aaron's line who have been consecrated to make offering to Yahweh (v. 18).

10.3 The Notion of the Ancient Israelite–Judahite Royal Ideology and Consequences for the Dating of Psalm 110

When discussing the disputed priestly dignity of the preexilic kings, scholars have interpreted the biblical data in different ways. For instance, Horst Dietrich Preuß has claimed that the ancient Israelite-Judahite kings did not have any regular cultic or priestly function—in contrast

---

23   So Kuhrt, *The Ancient Near East: c. 3000–330 BC.* II, 507.

24   So Edward F. Wente, 'Egyptian Religion', *ABD* 2:408–12 (409).

25   However, commentators regard the passage in which 2 Sam. 6:14 occurs as secondary; see McCarter, *II Samuel*, 184; and Stoebe, *Das zweite Buch Samuelis*, 197–202. Nevertheless, according to Stoebe, David's wearing of the linen ephod was still incontestable at the time of the last redaction (p. 198).

to the surrounding kingdoms. He admits that there is a nexus between the royal and the sacral offices in Ps. 110:4. However, he explains this by saying that the (Israelite-) Judahite kings at the same time inherited a *separate office*, namely, that of being king of Jerusalem. A priestly dignity did belong to this latter office, which in principle was distinct from the other royal dignity. According to Preuß, the office of king of the city of Jerusalem took place in the succession of the priest-king Melchizedek mentioned in Gen. 14:18–20. Therefore, the office of the city king of Jerusalem offered more space for priestly activities than did the office of king of Israel/Judah.[26]

Other scholars, however, take a different position. For instance, Antti Laato, who holds Psalm 110 to be traditio-historically connected with the coronation ritual, has argued that Ps. 110:4 shows that the Davidic kings were called into a priestly office at the time of their coronation.[27]

A different position has been taken by H. H. Rowley. He suggested that the oracle concerning priesthood in Ps. 110:4 was spoken *by* the king *to* the priest Zadok. He understood the whole psalm as a coronation ritual in which the priest addressed the king in vv. 1–3, while the king in reply confirmed Zadok's priestly prerogatives in v. 4. In Rowley's opinion, vv. 5–6 offer a priestly blessing of the king. According to Rowley, priestly prerogatives were part of the royal office, and as such they did not require any specific recognition.[28]

Some scholars use the lack of explicit references in the Hebrew Bible to any Davidic king as priest as an argument for a late date for Psalm 110. On the assumption that the אֲדֹנִי, 'my lord', in Ps. 110:1 is identical with the person called priest in Ps. 110:4, Stefan Schreiner has related the psalm in its present form to Zech. 6:9–15, a text about the coronation of the high priest Joshua. He suggests the possibility that the psalm as we now have it represents a reworking of an early monarchic royal psalm whose original content and form is no longer possible to reconstruct. Schreiner, following Noth and von Rad, states that kingship and priesthood never were connected in ancient Israel, as explicitly evident in Psalm 110. On the basis of this a priori understanding, the two decisive questions for Schreiner are the following. First, is there a time in the history of Israelite religion in which the idea of an inauguration into

---

26 Horst Dietrich Preuß, *Theologie des Alten Testaments. II Israels Weg mit JHWH*, 59–60.

27 Antti Laato, *A Star Is Rising: The Historical Development of the Old Testament Royal Ideology and the Rise of the Jewish Messianic Expectations* (University of South Florida International Studies in Formative Christianity and Judaism 5; Atlanta : Scholars Press, 1997), 92–93. A similar conclusion is also reached by, e.g., John Day based on Ps. 110:4; see Day, *Psalms*, 100.

28 H. H. Rowley, 'Melchizedek and Zadok (Gen 14 and Ps 110)', 461–72.

royal and priestly offices at the same time would make sense? Second, is there any institution characterized by the essential unification of the two offices in one person? This leads Schreiner to connect Psalm 110 to the office of the high priest (*Hohenpriester*) that developed in the Second Temple period with Joshua as its first office holder. On the basis of the history of religion in Israel that he outlines, Schreiner thinks that v. 4 must be a postexilic interpolation into the psalm—an interpolation resulting in a text that basically legitimized the new high priest institution.[29]

In many ways, Herbert Donner more recently has followed the same line of thought as that of Schreiner in dating Psalm 110. However, initially he discusses the text found in 1 Maccabees 14, reporting the investiture of the Hasmonaean Simon around 140 BCE:

1 Macc. 14:41–49 (NRSV, my emphasis): "The Jews and their priests have resolved that Simon should be *their* leader and *high priest forever*, until a trustworthy prophet should arise, [42] and that he should be *governor* over them and that he should take charge of the sanctuary and appoint officials over its tasks and over the country and the weapons and the strongholds, and that he should take charge of the sanctuary, [43] and that he should be obeyed by all, and that all contracts in the country should be written in his name, and that he should be clothed in purple and wear gold.

[44] "None of the people or priests shall be permitted to nullify any of these decisions or to oppose what he says, or to convene an assembly in the country without his permission, or to be clothed in *purple* or put on a gold buckle. [45] Whoever acts contrary to these decisions or rejects any of them shall be liable to punishment."

[46] All the people agreed to grant Simon the right to act in accordance with these decisions. [47] So Simon accepted and agreed to be *high priest*, to be *commander* and *ethnarch* of the Jews and priests, and to be protector of them all. [48] And they gave orders to inscribe this decree on bronze tablets, to put them up in a conspicuous place in the precincts of the sanctuary, [49] and to deposit copies of them in the treasury, so that Simon and his sons might have them.

According to this text, an accumulation of offices takes place in the investiture. Besides being a political leader (ἡγούμενος) and high priest

---

29   Schreiner, 'Psalm CX und die Investitur des Hohenpriesters', 216–22. Erhard S. Gerstenberger, *Psalms and Lamentations*. II (FOTL 15; Grand Rapids, MI: Eerdmans, 2001), 263–70, also argues similarly. He thinks that the priestly role of the Davidic king is obvious according to Ps. 110:4, at the same time being aware that modern scholars, according to him, are cautious toward this question. The problem, therefore, is when and where to locate the merging of political and sacral offices in Judean kingship and priesthood, respectively (p. 265). He identifies thorough reworking of ancient oracles in vv. 5–6, which now, according to Gerstenberger, describe an eschatological battle. The latter is a Persian conception, so that Psalm 110 should be dated to postexilic period.

(ἀρχιερεύς) forever (εἰς τὸν αἰῶνα), he is also a governor (στρατηγός) and ethnarch (ἐθνάρχης), being allowed to wear (the royal colour?) purple and gold, among other things.

The inauguration, however, lacked legitimacy: the Hasmonaean Simon had neither a Davidic nor a Zadokite genealogy. The entrusting of the political and religious leadership to Simon is qualified by the phrase 'until a trustworthy prophet should arise' (ἕως τοῦ ἀναστῆναι προφήτην πιστόν, v. 41). Donner asks how a 'trustworthy prophet' in 1 Maccabees 14 could speak in order to legitimate Simon. His answer is: roughly as in Ps. 110:4. The oracle spoken by a prophet (who perhaps was leaning on Moses' prophecy about Yahweh's raising up a prophet 'like me' in the future; cf. Deut. 18:15, 18) would compensate for Simon's genealogical deficit. For Donner, Ps. 110:4 is the strongest proof for a Maccabaean dating of the psalm.[30]

Donner notices that scholars very often regard the Melchizedek theme of the psalm as an important support for interpreting Psalm 110 as a preexilic coronation psalm. However, he put forward several arguments against the underlying theory of a pre-Israelite, Jebusite tradition that was transferred to the Davidic kings of Jerusalem. First, he finds it striking that Melchizedek is not mentioned anywhere in the texts about kings and kingdom—except in Psalm 110. Moreover, Melchizedek is not part of the repertoire of the prophets where he, according to Donner, would fit very well. Second, Donner claims that texts that may be correlated with the Judahite enthronement ritual (he does not count Psalm 110 among them) never speak of the king having any priestly dignity or function. Third, in the Hebrew Bible there is a tendency to dissolve pre-Israelite traditions; the pre-Davidic Jerusalem did not have any *Heilsbedeutung*.[31]

However, Donner does not give any answer as to when and where Genesis 14 or at least the ME was composed. Apparently, in Donner's opinion, the ME must antedate Psalm 110. For Donner, it does not cause any historical problem to date the psalm late because he argues that the book of Psalms was still being formed as late as the last half of the second century BCE.

I have tried to show that both Schreiner and Donner argue for a late date for Psalm 110 on the basis of an a priori conviction, namely, that there was a clear distinction between the royal office on the one hand and the priestly office on the other in the monarchic period. However, is this a priori conviction historically correct?

---

30   Donner, 'Der verläßliche Prophet', 213–23 (219).
31   Donner, 'Der verläßliche Prophet', 213–23 (220–21).

Deborah W. Rooke has touched on this problem.[32] Her point of departure is what she refers to as a received scholarly wisdom: the Israelite monarchy was an example of sacral kingship, and consequently, the king had a priestly role. As the most explicit reference to the king's priestly prerogatives, she points to Ps. 110:4. According to her, the whole premise for dating the psalm to Maccabaean time fails because the idea of a sacral kingship for Israel now is widely accepted.[33] On the contrary, according to her, most scholars now think Psalm 110 stems from the early monarchic period.

It is probable that the preexilic kings of Israel/Judah had priestly functions. Rooke's question of whether the kings' priesthood differed essentially from that of non-royal priests is appropriate. She claims that priesthood has two main characteristics in the Hebrew Bible. The first characteristic is its *functional* nature: 'priesthood is primarily about *doing* things, about carrying out rituals and procedures, rather than about *being* a particular kind of person or having a particular genealogical descent'.[34] This is also evident in the word כֹּהֵן, which has the form of a participle. Although there were cultic specialists such as the Levites, it appears that anyone could function as priest in the early history of religion of Israel/Judah. The limitation of priestly rights to particular groups is a later development. The second characteristic of priesthood is its *involvement with sanctuaries*. Rooke concludes: 'It seems . . . that the normal priesthood at its root is basically a function performed by certain members of the population on behalf of the rest of the population—it is an office as opposed to a vocation'.[35] However, in her view, the priesthood of the *king* arose on a different basis. In contrast to other priests, the king mediated between Yahweh and the people as priest because of his unique position before Yahweh. Therefore, the king had an *ex officio* priestly status that arose out of the sacral nature of his kingship.[36]

---

32   Deborah W. Rooke, 'Kingship as Priesthood: The Relationship between the High Priesthood and the Monarchy', in *King and Messiah in Israel and the Ancient Near East: Proceedings of the Oxford Old Testament Seminar* (ed. John Day; JSOTSup 270; Sheffield: Sheffield Academic Press, 1998), 187–208.

33   She is aware of recent lone wolves who do not fit into this picture. In addition to M. Treves, 'Two Acrostic Psalms', 81–90, and Stefan Schreiner's article mentioned above, she also mentions G. Gerleman, 'Psalm CX', *VT* 31 (1981): 1–19; and Michael C. Astour, 'Melchizedek', *ABD* 4:684–88. Rooke does not mention Donner's article 'Der verläßliche Prophet'.

34   Rooke, 'Kingship as Priesthood', 187–208 (189).

35   Rooke, 'Kingship as Priesthood', 187–208 (191–92).

36   Rooke, 'Kingship as Priesthood', 187–208 (193).

Therefore, according to Rooke, Ps. 110:4 sums up the difference between 'ordinary' priesthood on the one side and royal, *ex officio* priesthood on the other. It should be pointed out that she does not stress a reference to Melchizedek when defining the royal priesthood, as is often done. In her opinion, the usual rendering 'after the order of Melchizedek' is a translation of the LXX Ps. 109:4 and not what the MT reads. She would rather translate v. 4b 'because of/for the sake of Melchizedek'. Consequently, the extraordinary nature of the royal priesthood is, first, that it is bestowed by divine oath (נִשְׁבַּע יְהוָה וְלֹא יִנָּחֵם) and, second, that it is eternal (לְעוֹלָם).[37]

For the sake of clarity it should be pointed out that Rooke, in contrast to the thesis that will be defended in the present study, does not discuss the philological possibility that the two words מַלְכִּי־צֶדֶק may not represent a personal name; she just renders them by the name Melchizedek.

10.4 Psalm 110—A Hellenistic Encomion?

In a recent monograph Miriam von Nordheim has argued for dating Psalm 110 to the Hellenistic period. Her argument is in part based on assumed cases in the psalm of literary dependence on earlier biblical texts and in part on the assumption that the psalm is an example of the genre of encomium. According to von Nordheim, this genre first appeared in the Hellenistic period.

As to the literary dependence, von Nordheim argues that there is remarkable agreement in terms of themes (*Motivik*) between Psalm 110 and the song of jest against the king of Babylon in Isaiah 14, an agreement that however is not synonymous but antonymous. Moreover, she also argues that the Balaam prophecy in Numbers 24, the Song of Deborah in Judges 5, and King Hezekiah's prayer concerning Sennacherib to some extent resembles Psalm 110.[38]

Furthermore, as to the genre, von Nordheim argues that Psalm 110 resembles the genre of encomium, a type of praise that originated in Alexandria in the Ptolemaic period and that is closely associated with Hellenistic Greek poets such as Callimachus and Theocrit. It is typical for an encomium that the legitimacy of the one who is praised is anchored in a historical figure. Among other things, von Nordheim argues that the reference to Melchizedek shows clear affinity to hymns and encomiums from Ptolemaic period Alexandria.

---

37   Rooke, 'Kingship as Priesthood', 187–208 (197).
38   In the following, see von Nordheim, *Geboren von der Morgenröte?* 47–141.

Von Nordheim does indeed point to intriguing similarities between Psalm 110 and other biblical texts, above all Isaiah 14. However, it is less certain that the similarities have to be explained as the result of literary dependence. And even if there is a literary dependence, the direction of borrowing has to be determined. Moreover, the argument regarding the similarity between Psalm 110 and the Hellenistic genre of encomium is circular. First, von Nordheim points to cases of similarity between the psalm and the Hellenistic genre. Second, on the basis of the similarity she establishes it as a fact that the genre of Psalm 110 is that of encomium. Third, she uses the place and date of origin of the genre of encomium as an argument for dating the composition of Psalm 110. The encomium argument is weak. Nevertheless, even more important is the premise on which von Nordheim's argumentation is based: that 'Melchizedek' in Ps. 110:4 refers to a person and a tradition — who then somehow legitimizes the king praised in the psalm. Later in this study, I will offer arguments for the thesis that מַלְכִּי־צֶדֶק in Ps. 110:4 originally did not represent the personal name Melchizedek.

The similarities between Psalm 110 and other literature, especially the nonbiblical examples, are rather vague. In any case, perhaps with the exception of Isaiah 14, the assumed similarities do not offer any accumulation of borrowings that unambiguously point in a certain direction. The presence of motifs such as enemies as one's footstool (see Ps. 110:1), words of destruction such as מָחַץ ('beat to pieces'; see Ps. 110:5), etc. all seem to be part of a literary repertoire common for cultures across the entire ancient Near East and throughout at least the last two millennia BCE. In sum, I do not find von Nordheim's arguments for dating the composition of Psalm 110 to the Hellenistic period persuasive.

10.5 Conclusion: A Date of Composition in the Monarchic Period Probable for Psalm 110

In my view, von Nordheim's attempt to date Psalm 110 to the Hellenistic period is not convincing. Moreover, it turns out that Schreiner and Donner build their argumentation on an improbable assumption when they date Psalm 110 late. The kings in ancient Israel/Judah did indeed function as priests, although they are never explicitly called priests. That is the case, however, only if we keep Psalm 110 out of the picture. The fact that Psalm 110 now appears to call the ruler a priest (see Ps. 110:1, 4) causes Schreiner to question the integrity of the psalm. Verse 4 is, in his view, a postexilic interpolation into an assumed monarchic text. Donner, on the other hand, apparently finds v. 4 to be an integrated part of the psalm. However, the fusion of the political and religious offices causes him to date the psalm altogether to the Hasmonaean period.

Those who advocate a late date for Psalm 110 on the basis of the idea that the royal and sacral offices were kept strictly apart in the monarchic period have the biblical material against them.[39] The kings obviously took part in the cult, as did also kings in the smaller and larger neighbouring kingdoms. Given that the ruler in v. 1 (אֲדֹנִי, 'my lord') really is the king, and given that it is the same king who is called 'priest' in v. 4,[40] the probable date for Psalm 110 therefore is the monarchic period. The reference to Zion (v. 2) speaks in favour of a southern, that is, Judahite or Jerusalemite, provenance.

For the sake of clarity, I will here briefly point out something that I will develop more thoroughly in subsequent chapters. After the end of monarchy, Psalm 110 was interpreted differently. I will argue that the psalm started being read *historiographically* and the person in the psalm referred to as אֲדֹנִי, 'my lord', gradually was identified with the patriarch *Abraham*.[41]

---

39   I subscribe to John Day's common sense argument against late dating of royal psalms in general. It is most natural to read these psalms as relating to real individual kings; see Day, *Psalms*, 90.

40   There is nothing in the text that suggests that the person to whom the oracle in v. 1 was addressed is different from the person to whom the oracle in v. 4 was addressed. In my opinion, H. H. Rowley, who assumes that a shift of speaking person takes place between v. 1 (the priest speaks to the king) and v. 4 (the king speaks to the priest), in fact reads this shift *into* the text; see H. H. Rowley, 'Melchizedek and Zadok (Gen 14 and Ps 110)', 461–72.

41   See 12.7, Psalm 110:4: Synthesis and Conclusion; chapter 13, Early Intertextual Readings of Genesis 14 and Psalm 110; and chapter 14, The Result of an Assimilation of Two Texts, Both Thought to be Referring to Abram's War with the King.

11. The Phenomenon of Assimilation in the Bible

I have hypothesized that the originally monarchic Psalm 110 started being read as a historical psalm in the Second Temple period. At some point it started to be read as a poetic account of Abram's war, a war for which Genesis 14* offered a narrative account.[1] Moreover, I have hypothesized that this early case of intertextual reading functioned as a catalyst for a subsequent assimilation of the poetic and narrative accounts of Abram's war. The result of this subsequent assimilation was the ME.

In order to strengthen this hypothesis, I will in what follows show that there are other more or less documented cases of assimilation between two texts, not only in early extrabiblical literature but even in the Bible itself. First, I will give examples of how historical narratives prompted the interpolation of secondary information *into poetic texts*.[2] Then, I will offer cases where poetic texts have caused assimilations to be interpolated *into historical narratives*.[3] Finally, I will argue that the hermeneutical principle that was called *gezerah shawah* by the rabbis (see the *Seven Rules of Hillel*) in fact existed as early as the last centuries BCE.[4]

In the context of the present work, the argumentative thrust of this chapter is to prepare the ground for the thesis regarding the origin of the ME that I will argue for in a subsequent chapter.[5]

---

1   Later on, the phenomenon of relating the psalms to the history continued in rabbinic literature. See Gerhard Bodendorfer, 'Zur Historisierung des Psalters in der rabbinischen Literatur', in *Der Psalter in Judentum und Christentum* (ed. Erich Zenger; HBS 18; Freiburg: Herder, 1998), 215–34.
2   See 11.1, Historiography Assimilating into Poetry.
3   See 11.2, Poetry Creating Historiography.
4   See 11.3, The Rabbinic Hermeneutical Principle 'Gezerah Shawah' and Its Biblical Predecessor.
5   See chapter 14, The Result of an Assimilation of Two Texts, Both Thought to be Referring to Abram's War with the King.

11.1 Historiography Assimilating into Poetry

One type of assimilation is evident in the many secondary psalm super-scriptions that relate some psalms to events in David's life. For instance, Psalm 3, a psalm of lament, is situated to a particular time: בְּבָרְחוֹ מִפְּנֵי אַבְשָׁלוֹם בְּנוֹ, 'when he [David] fled from Absalom, his son' (Ps. 3:1; cf. 2 Sam 15:13–31). Psalm 7, also a psalm of lament, opens with the clause 'A Shig-gaion of David, which he sang to Yahweh because of Cush, a Benjami-nite'. Here, the historical background referred to is admittedly less clear. A Cushite is mentioned as the messenger who brings David the news about Absalom's death (2 Sam. 18:21, 23, 31–32).[6] Psalm 18, formally a psalm of thanksgiving but also counted among the royal psalms, is situated to the day when Yahweh delivered David from the hand of all his enemies and from the hand of Saul (Ps. 18:1; cf. 2 Samuel 22). The thanksgiving reappears almost verbatim in 2 Samuel 22. Moreover, Psalm 34 is, according to the superscription in v. 1, spoken by David when he feigned madness before Abimelech 'so that he drove him out, and he went away'. The historical situation probably referred to is found in 1 Sam. 21:12–15, where Achish of Gath, and not Abimelech, is David's opponent. Likewise, Psalm 51 is connected to David's affair with Bath-sheba (see 2 Samuel 12), Psalm 52 to the notice that Doeg the Edomite brought an intelligence report to Saul about David's meeting with the priest Ahimelech (1 Sam. 22:9–10), and so on.[7]

It is not always possible for a modern reader to pinpoint precisely what the authors or editors had as their rationale for adding the super-scriptions. An inner relationship between the psalms and the historical texts is not apparent in every case. Nevertheless, the superscriptions demonstrate that poetry and historiography were correlated and, more-over, that this correlation created the possibility of editing the text so that the assumed similarity between the two texts became even clearer. That which was found to be an original relationship between narrative and poetry by the editor functioned as a catalyst for the secondary composi-tion of the superscriptions.

---

6   However, Kraus does not find this comprehensible. Instead, he suggests that the author of this editorial note may have had a tradition in mind that is not reflected in the Bible; see Kraus, *Psalmen. I Psalmen 1–59*, 193.

7   Compare Psalm 54 and 1 Sam. 23:19–20; Psalm 56 and 1 Sam. 21:10–16; Psalm 57 and 1 Samuel 22–24; Psalm 59 and 1 Sam. 19:11–17; Psalm 60 and 2 Samuel 8; Psalm 63 and 1 Sam. 23:14; 24:1–23; and finally, Psalm 142 and 1 Samuel 22–24.

11.2 Poetry Creating Historiography

The examples above illustrate that information moves from historical to poetic texts. However, there are also examples of movement in the other direction, namely, where poetry creates historiography. Yair Zakovitch gives several examples.[8] For instance, Psalm 105 adds a detail to the story of the life of Joseph that is not attested in the Joseph novella in Genesis: 'His feet were hurt with fetters, his neck was put in a collar of iron' (Ps. 105:18 NRSV). Genesis 39 agrees in that Joseph was detained: 'And Joseph's master took him and put him into the prison, the place where the king's prisoners were confined; he remained there in prison' (Gen. 39:20 NRSV). But there is no talk about fetters and an iron collar. However, in the pseudepigraphic *Testament of Joseph*, the psalm's surplus information about the treatment of Joseph is integrated into the autobiographical narrative put in the mouth of Joseph (*T. Jos.* 1:5–6).

Moreover, in the book of Judges there are two versions of Sisera's battle, a narrative in Judges 4 and a poetic account in the song of Deborah in Judges 5. The latter contains a surplus of information vis-à-vis the former. However, in Josephus's paraphrase of the narrative version (i.e., Judges 4), he integrates the surplus found in Judges 5 (see *Ant.* 5.205–9).

Furthermore, in connection with the song of Deborah (Judges 5) one can perhaps find a further example of how poetry creates historiography. In this case, secondarily created historiographical information has been added to the Bible itself, namely, in Judg. 3:31: 'After him came Shamgar son of Anath, who killed six hundred of the Philistines with an oxgoad. He too delivered Israel'. The problem with this brief note is that it appears dislocated in its narrative context. In the fifteen verses preceding the note about Shamgar in Judg. 3:31 it is the judge Ehud who is in focus. Moreover, in the verse following immediately after the note about Shamgar, Ehud appears again: 'The Israelites again did what was evil in the sight of the Lord, after Ehud died' (Judg. 4:1 NRSV).

In the Bible Shamgar is mentioned for the second (and last) time in the song of Deborah (Judg. 5:6): 'In the days of Shamgar son of Anath, in the days of Jael, caravans ceased and travelers kept to the byways' (Judg. 5:6).

---

8   See Yair Zakovitch, 'Poetry Creates Historiography', in *"A Wise and Discerning Mind"*: *Essays in Honor of Burke O. Long* (ed. Saul M. Olyan and Robert C. Culley; BJS 325; Providence, RI: Brown Judaic Studies, 2000), 311–20.

Zakovitch has suggested that the brief historiographical note about the judge Shamgar found in Judg. 3:31 was secondarily created in order to solve the mystery of this otherwise unknown judge, referred to in the song of Deborah.[9] Moreover, as to the date of composition of the note in Judg. 3:31, Zakovitch tentatively suggests that the adding of the assumed secondary note in Judg. 3:31 took place *after* the Deuteronomistic redaction of the book of Judges since the note lacks both the common Deuteronomistic editorial formulas and the dedication of Shamgar's victory to God.

Finally, whereas it is not possible to completely verify Zakovitch's proposal concerning the origin of the apparently dislocated historiographical note in the case of Judg. 3:31, he does offer a controllable case on how a piece of information from a psalm has been interpolated into a narrative. The story about King Amaziah's victory over the Edomites is offered in two versions. In the assumed original version of this story, Amaziah is simply reported to have 'killed ten thousand Edomites in the Valley of Salt' and to have taken Sela by storm (2 Kgs. 14:7 NRSV). However, the elaborated version found in the Chronistic History is much more detailed and—from the perspective of a modern reader—horrible:

> 2 Chr. 25:11–12 (NRSV): [11] Amaziah took courage, and led out his people; he went to the Valley of Salt, and struck down ten thousand men of Seir. [12] The people of Judah captured another ten thousand alive, took them to the top of Sela, and threw them down from the top of Sela, so that all of them were dashed to pieces.

Here, the source for the Chronicler's additional information is probably a psalm:

> Ps. 137:7–9 (NRSV): [7] Remember, O LORD, against the Edomites the day of Jerusalem's fall, how they said, "Tear it down! Tear it down! Down to its foundations!" [8] O daughter Babylon, you devastator! Happy shall they be who pay you back what you have done to us! [9] Happy shall they be who take your little ones and dash them against the rock!

This last example enables us to see the original version into which new historical information has been added and, moreover, probably also the poetic source from which the new historical information has been derived.

---

9   Zakovitch, 'Poetry Creates Historiography', 311–20 (314–15).

11.3 The Rabbinic Hermeneutical Principle *Gezerah Shawah* and Its Biblical Predecessor

The methodological conception that underlies the assimilation of texts evident in the Bible itself and in early extrabiblical literature was probably that which later was formalized in the rabbinic hermeneutical rule *gezerah shawah* (גְּזֵרָה שָׁוָה, 'similar decision'). This rule created the possibility for analogical deductions. The rule presupposed that the interpreter recognized certain similarities between two texts, for example, the presence of a common term. The hermeneutical rule is explicitly mentioned in early rabbinic sets of hermeneutical rules for the interpretation of the Bible, namely, the *Seven Rules of Hillel* and the *Thirteen Rules of Rabbi Ishmael*. Hillel the Elder lived in the second half of the first century CE and Ishmael in the second century CE. However, scholars assume that Hillel did not himself create the rules that are associated with his name. On the contrary, Hillel's name probably only points to the approximate time of their acceptance.[1]

An explicit example of this rule is found in the Mishnah. In *Naz.* 9:5, the late-second-century rabbi Nehorai concludes that Samuel must have been a nazirite, although he is not called that in the MT. In 1 Sam. 1:11, Samuel's mother Hannah is quoted as swearing 'no razor shall touch his head'. In the story of Samson, who is explicitly called a nazirite, precisely the same oath occurs (Judg. 13:5). Therefore, inferring from analogy, Rabbi Nehorai states that Samuel must have been a nazirite too.

The hermeneutical rule *gezerah shawah* is, as mentioned, first found formalized in the first century CE. However, it is possible to demonstrate indirectly that the underlying hermeneutical technique is older. Now, if we stick to the idea about Samuel being a nazirite that is evident in *Naz.* 9:5, then we can see that the same idea has also been expressed in texts earlier than the Mishnah. In LXX, a nazirite prohibition has been added to 1 Sam. 1:11: καὶ οἶνον καὶ μέθυσμα οὐ πίεται, 'and he [= Samuel] shall drink no wine or strong drink.' This is a nazirite prohibition that is found in MT Num. 6:3 and Judg. 13:4, 7, 14. Moreover, a similar understanding of Samuel being a nazirite is documented in 4QSam[a] (4Q51), which adds to 1 Sam. 1:22, 'I will dedicate him as a nazirite forever. . .'.

Therefore, the LXX and the Qumran discoveries indirectly testify to the existence of a hermeneutical technique already used in the last

---

1   Rivka Kern-Ulmer, 'Hermeneutics, Techniques of Rabbinic Exegesis', *EncMidr* 1:268–92 (271–72, 274–76). See also Fishbane, *Biblical Interpretation in Ancient Israel*, 249 nn. 48–49.

centuries BCE that is comparable to and probably the predecessor of one of the rules that were formalized by Hillel, namely, *gezerah shawah*.[2]

11.4 Conclusion

I have shown above that there are cases where psalms have been subject to subsequent interpolation with the intention of assimilating the psalms into historiographic texts. Moreover, I have shown cases where poetry has caused the interpolation of new historical information into historical texts. In addition, on the basis of evidence in early textual versions of the Bible, I have shown that *gezerah shawah* was used in the last centuries BCE. The hermeneutical technique allowed for the possibility of assimilating texts. Therefore, the phenomenon of assimilation is not limited to the reception history but, on the contrary, is also found in the Hebrew Bible itself.

As an interlude to the discussion I will present in the following chapters, I direct attention to Zakovitch's words:

> [Biblical] texts serve as building blocks for the elaboration of other texts, and even for the creation of new ones. Sometimes the elaboration is motivated by the need to bring two parallel (and even neighboring) traditions, one prose and one poetic, into agreement. In other cases, the linguistic association with an otherwise unrelated poem may stimulate the elaboration. We also find cases when the historiographer's ideology necessitates the creation of a new piece of narrative, the materials for which he collects from a well-known biblical poem.[3]

---

2   Also Fishbane suggests that forebears of the rabbinic principle of גְּזֵרָה שָׁוָה are present in the books of Chronicles; see Fishbane, *Biblical Interpretation in Ancient Israel*, 157 n. 36.
3   Zakovitch, 'Poetry Creates Historiography', 311–20 (320).

עַל־דִּבְרָתִי מַלְכִּי־צֶדֶק 12.
An Analysis of MT Psalm 110:4b

In Christian scholarship and its more or less secular aftermath, the MT Ps. 110:4b has, almost without exception, been rendered in accordance with the LXX Ps. 109:4: σὺ εἶ ἱερεὺς εἰς τὸν αἰῶνα κατὰ τὴν τάξιν Μελχισεδεκ, 'Thou art a priest for ever, after the order of Melchisedec'[1]—a reading which in turn has been reflected in the New Testament (see Heb. 5:6; 6:20; 7:17). An exception among modern translations is the JPS TANAKH translation,[2] which renders the Hebrew by 'You are a priest forever, a rightful king by My decree'.

In this chapter I will discuss the phrase עַל־דִּבְרָתִי מַלְכִּי־צֶדֶק. I will argue that the traditional (Christian) rendering of the Hebrew (e.g., the one found in the NRSV, 'You are a priest forever according to the order of Melchizedek') probably is wrong and only possible when the Hebrew text is translated via the interpretation offered in LXX Ps. 109:4 and the subsequent New Testament quotations of the same verse.

The thesis will be that in Ps. 110:4, מַלְכִּי־צֶדֶק does not represent a personal name but either a nominal phrase or a nominal clause. The relevance for the overall hypothesis of the origin of the ME will be pointed out below in subsequent chapters.[3] For the sake of clarity, I will anticipate the conclusion. I will propose that the reference to מַלְכִּי־צֶדֶק in Gen. 14:18–20 indeed is to a *person*, that is, 'Melchizedek'. This, however, is probably the result of a secondary personification of the clause/phrase מַלְכִּי־צֶדֶק found in Ps. 110:4.

---

1   Quoted from Brenton, *The Septuagint with Apocrypha*, ad loc.
2   Jewish Publication Society of America: Philadelphia, PA, 1985 [2d ed. 1999].
3   See chapter 13, Early Intertextual Readings of Genesis 14 and Psalms 110; chapter 14, The Result of an Assimilation of Two Texts, Both Thought to be Referring to Abram's War with the King, chapter 15, What Has Happened to the Words מַלְכִּי־צֶדֶק on the Way from Psalm 110 to the Melchizedek Episode?, and chapter 17, A Critical Assessment of the 'Assimilation Model'.

12.1 Two Assumptions Shared
by the Majority of Scholars

Despite the extraordinary scholarly interest Psalm 110 has attracted and the diverging opinions about it, the majority of scholars seem to share two assumptions. First, most scholars assume that the *hapax legomenon* עַל־דִּבְרָתִי has a modal meaning. That is, the majority thinks that the phrase עַל־דִּבְרָתִי indicates *in what way* the person spoken to in v. 4 is a priest.[4] Second, an even greater majority assumes that the two words מַלְכִּי־צֶדֶק in Ps. 110:4b are the proper name Melchizedek.[5]

12.2 Alternative Voices Concerning עַל־דִּבְרָתִי and
מַלְכִּי־צֶדֶק in the History of Research

During the last century or so there have been different attempts to approach the puzzling phases עַל־דִּבְרָתִי and מַלְכִּי־צֶדֶק in Ps. 110:4b in a fresh way. In my view, some have argued thoroughly and others more cursorily. Before I continue with the discussion proper, I will first outline some proposals that have been made with respect to this difficult half verse.

I will begin with עַל־דִּבְרָתִי. J. A. Fitzmyer has argued that it is an alternative form of עַל־דְּבַר.[6] To this form, an obsolete case ending has been attached. Although עַל־דְּבַר otherwise means 'for the sake of', the context of Psalm 110, in Fitzmyer's opinion, does not suit this causal sense.

---

4   Thus, most recently von Nordheim, who renders Ps. 110:4b 'Du bist Priester in Ewigkeit *in Nachahmung* Melchizedeks'. She is building on the premise that מַלְכִּי־צֶדֶק cannot be anything but a personal name; see von Nordheim, *Geboren von der Morgenröte?* 30–31, 44 (my emphasis). Moreover, the NRSV translation and the German Lutherbibel are two other typical examples; the former reads, 'according to the order of Melchizedek'; the latter, 'nach der Weise Melchisedeks'. An forceful argument in favour of such a reading is also offered by L. C. Allen, *Psalms 101–150* (WBC 21; Waco, TX: Word, 1983), 81. In his view, the phrase implies *succession* of some kind.

5   Thus recently von Nordheim, *Geboren von der Morgenröte?* 30–31, 44, and in particular 91–99. This is also the case in Martin Noth's monograph on Hebrew personal names; see Noth, *Die israelitischen Personennamen im Rahmen der gemeinsemitischen Namengebung* (BWANT III, 10; Stuttgart: W. Kohlhammer, 1928 [repr. Hildesheim: Georg Olms, 1980]), 114, 161 n. 4. In Noth's opinion, מַלְכִּי־צֶדֶק contains a theophoric element of Canaanite origin, namely, מַלְך. Noth assumes that it is an ancient name. Therefore, he takes the element צדק to be predicative, and not to be the name of a god.

6   Joseph A. Fitzmyer, '"Now this Melchizedek . . ."', in idem, *Essays on the Semitic Background of the New Testament* (Sources for Biblical Study 5; London: G. Chapman, 1971), 221–43 (225–26) (originally published in *CBQ* 25 [1963], 305–21).

This is the reason, he says, why ancient and modern translations rather favour a modal sense.

V. Hamp has however argued that עַל־דִּבְרָתִי has a causal meaning.[7] He reaches this conclusion by comparing the phrase with עַל־דְּבַר, עַל־דִּבְרֵי, and עַל־דִּבְרַת, all of which are variants of the Aramaic bureaucratic term עַל־דְּבַר and, more important, all of which have a causal sense in the Hebrew Bible. The usual modal translation 'nach der Weise' is derived from the LXX, Vulgate, and Peshitta translations.

J. G. Gammie has changed the vocalization of MT Ps. 110:4b and reads 'Thou are a priest forever // *Because I have spoken righteously, my king*' (my emphasis).[8] He renders the preposition עַל causally and understands דברתי as a finite verb, that is, the *qatal* form of דבר. He reads מַלְכִּי as vocative and צֶדֶק as adjective, here with an adverbial function.

Stefan Schreiner has translated v. 4aβb 'Du bist (oder: sollst sein) Priester für immer, meiner Zusage gemäß (ein) Malki-Zedek'.[9] Behind דִּבְרָתִי he finds the noun דִּבְרָה, which refers to Yahweh's oath and to which the first person pronominal suffix has been attached.

J. M. Baumgarten, who considers Psalm 110 to be spoken *to* Melchizedek, has reached a similar conclusion: דִּבְרָתִי in v. 4 is the suffixed form of the noun דִּבְרָה, which is also found in Job 5:8.[10] If so, דִּבְרָתִי may refer to Yahweh's pronouncement concerning Melchizedek's eternal priesthood, as Rowley also has argued (see 10.3, The Notion of the Ancient Israelite–Judahite Royal Ideology and Consequences for the Dating of Psalm 110).

More recently, D. W. Rooke has concluded—without any argumentation, as far as I can see—that 'because of' or 'for the sake of' should be the preferred translation of עַל־דִּבְרָתִי.[11]

As for מַלְכִּי־צֶדֶק, several alternatives to the more common interpretation of it as a personal name have been proposed. T. H. Gaster translated v. 4aβb 'Thou art a priest for ever, // A king rightfully appointed, // In accordance with Mine order!'[12] According to Gaster's approach, מַלְכִּי־צֶדֶק is a title. However, he gives scarcely any arguments.

Moreover, H. E. Del Medico has translated the *whole* clause עַל־דִּבְרָתִי מַלְכִּי־צֶדֶק in v. 4b by a series of finite verb forms: 'attaque, ai-je

---

7   Vinzenz Hamp, 'Psalm 110,4b und die Septuaginta', in *Neues Testament und die Kirche* (FS R. Schnackenburg; Freiburg: Herder, 1974), 519–29 (519–21).

8   John G. Gammie, 'A New Setting for Psalm 110', *ATR* 51 (1969), 4–17 (13 n. 27).

9   Schreiner, 'Psalm CX und die Investitur des Hohenpriesters', 216–22 (217, 221 n. 6).

10   Joseph M. Baumgarten, 'The Heavenly Tribunal and the Personification of Ṣedeq in Jewish Apocalyptic', *ANRW* 2.19/1 (Berlin: W. de Gruyter, 1979), 219–39 (222 n. 11).

11   Rooke, 'Kingship as Priesthood', 187–208 (197).

12   T. H. Gaster, 'Psalm 110', *JMEOS* 21 (1937): 37–44 (40–41).

ordonné, fais régner la justice!'[13] (= 'attack, I ordered, make reign justice!'). According to Del Medico, the imperative clause מלכי צדק has been personalized in the LXX Ps. 109:4.

Furthermore, M. Dahood has read מַלְכִּי־צֶדֶק as a noun phrase.[14] In his view, it is a construct chain. In addition, he argues that the archaic *third* (*sic*) person singular pronominal suffix ־י has been interposed: 'His legitimate king'.[15]

Paul J. Kobelski's approach to the discussion of the form and meaning of Melchizedek is by observing that מלכי צדק is written as two words in the *Melchizedek* text from Qumran (11Q13) and in the Targumic tradition.[16] On the basis of this observation he has suggested that the two-word form 'during this period' perhaps betrays the popular-etymology explanation of the name as 'the righteous king' or 'king of righteousness', as reflected in the works of Philo (*Leg. All.* 3.79–82), Josephus (*Ant.* 1.179–181; *War* 6.438), and in Heb. 7:2. As for the reference to מלכי צדק/ מלכיצדק in the Aramaic *Genesis Apocryphon* (1Q20 22:14), he says 'there appears to be a very slight space between *yod* of *mlky* and the *ṣade* of *ṣdq*, but it is not large enough to say definitely that the name has been written as one word there'.[17] Furthermore, Kobelski argues that the formative ־י in מַלְכִּי is the first person pronominal suffix, not a *compaginis* suffix. As proof he offers an analogy attested in Ebla, *Ré-ì-na-Adad*, 'Adad is our shepherd', where the suffix *na* is first person plural pronominal suffix.

Finally, P. J. Nel has briefly discussed v. 4aβb עַל־דִּבְרָתִי מַלְכִּי־צֶדֶק.[18] In his own translation of Psalm 110 he writes, '[You are a priest forever] in the order of Melchizedek'. However, in the following discussion and commentary he says that 'later traditions have historicized מלכי צדק', and he translates the same expression as 'in the order of the righteous king'. He does not discuss the meaning of עַל־דִּבְרָתִי, nor does he flesh out what he really means when speaking about a noun phrase having been 'historicized'.

---

13   H. E. Del Medico reads עַל as an ancient variant of the imperative of the verb עלה and דברתי as a verb in *qatal* form; see Del Medico, 'Melchisédech', *ZAW* 69 (1957): 160–70 (166, 169).

14   Dahood, *Psalms III: 101–150*, 117.

15   Dahood argues that the pronominal suffix ־י in this case denotes third person singular and gives a cross reference to n. 7 in relation to Ps. 102:24.

16   Paul J. Kobelski, *Melchizedek and Melchireša*ᶜ (CBQMS 10; Washington, D.C.: Catholic Biblical Association of America, 1981), 55–56.

17   Nevertheless, I cannot see how Kobelski considers the fact that the two-word form is also evident in the two occurrences in the MT. Neither in the case of Psalm 110 nor in Genesis 14 are there textual witnesses to the Hebrew text deviating from this two-word form.

18   Nel, 'Psalm 110 and the Melchizedek Tradition', 1–14 (3, 6–7).

12.3 The Common View: Following LXX Psalm 109:4b

Despite the differing voices discussed above, most scholars and translations appear to stand in the LXX and New Testament tradition in rendering the Hebrew עַל־דִּבְרָתִי by a phrase similar to the Greek κατὰ τὴν τάξιν
found in LXX Ps. 109:4. The LXX prepositional phrase clearly denotes the
mode of the priesthood of the person addressed in v. 4. A phrase with κατά
and a subsequent noun in the accusative may mark equality, similarity,
or example.[19] Further, τάξις can among other things mean 'an arrangement of things in sequence' (fixed succession/order), 'an assigned sta-
tion or rank' (position, post), or 'an arrangement in which someone or
something functions' (arrangement, nature, manner, condition, outward
aspect)[20] and simply, 'a class of men'.[21] As evident from the Letter to
the Hebrews, LXX Ps. 109:4b was understood as an expression denoting
comparison or similarity; cf. Heb. 7:15: καὶ περισσότερον ἔτι κατάδηλόν
ἐστιν, εἰ κατὰ τὴν ὁμοιότητα Μελχισέδεκ ἀνίσταται ἱερεὺς ἕτερος, NRSV:
'It is even more obvious when another priest arises, *resembling* Melchizedek . . .' (my emphasis).

The only parallel to the phrase κατὰ τὴν τάξιν in a Jewish/Christian
text in Greek is found in the pseudepigraphic *Life of Adam and Eve* (first
century CE).[22] In *LAE* 38.2 God gave order that the angels should convene
before him, 'each according to his rank'.[23]

In the case of the translation of Ps. 110:4 found in the Peshitta, the
Old Testament in Syriac, the translation has moved even further away
from the Hebrew *hapax legomenon* עַל־דִּבְרָתִי than LXX Ps. 109:4 did with its
reading κατὰ τὴν τάξιν. When the Peshitta reads *bdmuth dmlkyzdq*, 'in the
likeness [cf. Hebrew דְּמוּת] of Melchizedek', it is the result of an assimilation with Heb. 7:15, κατὰ τὴν ὁμοιότητα Μελχισέδεκ.[24]

Moreover, despite proposals such as those described above,[25] the vast
majority of scholars and Bible translations render the Hebrew מַלְכִּי־צֶדֶק in
Ps. 110:4b by the name Melchizedek. The reason for this common opinion is probably twofold. First, LXX Ps. 109:4 reads Μελχισέδεκ, a reading

---

19 So BAA, *s.v.* κατά, col. 827.

20 So BAA, *s.v.* τάξις, col. 1603.

21 So LSJ, *s.v.* τάξις, 1756.

22 So Bons, 'Die Septuaginta-Version von Psalm 110 (109 LXX): Textgestalt, Aussagen,
    Auswirkungen', 122–45 (138).

23 Translation of M. D. Johnson, *OTP* 2:249–95 (my emphasis).

24 See Michael Weitzmann, *The Syriac Version of the Old Testament: An Introduction* (Uni-
    versity of Cambridge Oriental Publications 56; Cambridge: Cambridge University
    Press, 1999), 278.

25 See 12.2, Alternative Voices Concerning עַל־דִּבְרָתִי and מַלְכִּי־צֶדֶק in the History of Research.

that is unequivocally a personal name. Second, in the MT itself there is an *additional* text where one finds two words מַלְכִּי־צֶדֶק: in Gen. 14:18. In the latter text where the context is a narrative one, the two words unequivocally function as a personal name, Melchizedek. In other words, in Gen. 14:18 the Hebrew phraseology necessitates that מַלְכִּי־צֶדֶק מֶלֶךְ שָׁלֵם has to mean 'King Melchizedek of Salem', just as אֲדֹנִי־צֶדֶק מֶלֶךְ יְרוּשָׁלַם in Josh. 10:1, 3 has to mean 'King Adoni-zedek of Jerusalem'.

12.4 Objections against the Common View

There are reasons to dispute the established tradition of rendering Ps. 110:4 along the line of LXX Ps. 109:4. First, regarding the semantics of עַל־דִּבְרָתִי, I raise objections on methodological grounds against the common modal translation that probably follows the LXX. Second, I also put forward historical, orthographical, and grammatical arguments in addition to arguments based on the earliest nonbiblical reception history against the common opinion that the two words מַלְכִּי־צֶדֶק in Ps. 110:4b are a personal name.

12.5 The Prepositional Phrase עַל־דִּבְרָתִי in Psalm 110:4b

12.5.1 Methodology for Describing the Semantics of a *hapax legomenon*

I will start with discussing the *hapax legomenon* עַל־דִּבְרָתִי. In general, the meaning of a *hapax legomenon* in any language should preferably be derived from the context in which it occurs. If this approach does not help, then one should, if possible, consult cognate phrases in the source language and in sources that have some proximity (temporal, cultural, religious, etc.) to the source in which the *hapax legomenon* occurs. Cognate in this sense refers to form and not meaning, since it is precisely the meaning of the *hapax legomenon* we seek. Therefore, possible cognate expressions must have some kind of formal similarity with the *hapax legomenon*. Only when the above procedures either have not shed light on the semantics of the *hapax legomenon*, or if no cognate expressions are found, should one then consult other translation(s) of the expression. The closer these translations are to the source and the source language in terms of chronology and cultural competence, the more weight they carry.

12.5.2 The Semantics of עַל־דִּבְרָתִי

As for עַל־דִּבְרָתִי in particular, the context in Ps. 110:4 does not contribute much to its semantics. Partly because it belongs to a poetic genre, and partly because the particular immediate context, that is, מַלְכִּי־צֶדֶק, is likewise puzzling, it is not possible to derive the meaning of the prepositional phrase from its context. From a syntactical point of view we can state that the prepositional phrase functions as adverbial. As adverbial, however, it is not clear which syntactic slot it modifies. Does it modify the preceding word כֹּהֵן [subject predicative] or לְעוֹלָם [adverbial of time]? Or, does it modify the subsequent expression, מַלְכִּי־צֶדֶק?[26] Moreover, it is not clear what kind of modification עַל־דִּבְרָתִי represents. Is it an adverbial of time, of cause, of mode, etc.?

In sum, the context of עַל־דִּבְרָתִי does not shed much light on its semantics. Therefore, we will let formally cognate expressions shed light on the *hapax legomenon*. The Hebrew Bible offers three potential cognates: עַל־דְּבַר, עַל־דִּבְרֵי, and עַל־דִּבְרַת. All three are prepositional phrases constituted by an עַל, which in each case is followed by a word derived from the root דבר. These phrases are found both in Biblical Hebrew and Biblical Aramaic, as well as in Middle Hebrew, Imperial Aramaic, and postbiblical Aramaic.

עַל־דְּבַר is used thirteen times in the Hebrew Bible with an unequivocal causal meaning, as, for example, in Gen. 12:17, עַל־דְּבַר שָׂרָי 'because of Sarai'.[27] In addition, the phrase is used four times in contexts where a more general reference is possible ('as to, concerning') alongside a causal rendering.[28] A sidelong glance at the LXX demonstrates that it never renders עַל־דְּבַר with a Greek modal expression. On the contrary, it translates the expression by περί + genitive, ἕνεκεν + genitive, ἕνεκα + genitive, διά + accusative, παρά + accusative, ὑπέρ + genitive, or ὅτι. These prepositional phrases have either a causal or a final meaning, in any case, never a modal. The rendering of the Vulgate fits very well into this picture as it offers 'propter', 'per', 'pro', 'super', 'quia', and 'quod'.

עַל־דִּבְרֵי is used five times with a potential adverbial function.[29] However, the picture is not as clear as in the case of עַל־דְּבַר. In all five instances,

---

26 The last point is even more intriguing if מַלְכִּי־צֶדֶק is in fact a nominal phrase ('king of righteousness'), or even a nominal clause (e.g., 'my king is righteous'). See 12.6 The Two Words מַלְכִּי־צֶדֶק in Psalm 110:4b.

27 The thirteen occurrences are Gen. 12:17; 20:11, 18; 43:18; Exod. 8:8 [Eng. trans., 8:12]; Num. 17:14 [Eng. trans., 16:49]; 31:16; Deut. 22:24 (x 2); 23:5 [Eng. trans., 23:4]; 2 Sam. 13:22; Ps. 45:5; 79:9.

28 Num. 25:18 (2x); 2 Sam 18:5; 1 Chr. 10:13.

29 2 Sam. 3:8; 2 Chr. 32:8; Ps. 7:1; Jer. 7:22, 14:1.

a literal translation of דִּבְרֵי by 'word, matter(s)' is possible. Accordingly, the Vulgate translates דִּבְרֵי literally. Being a little more differentiated, the LXX renders עַל־דְּבַר by περί + genitive in Jer. 7:22 (περὶ ὁλοκαυτωμάτων καὶ θυσίας, 'concerning burnt offerings and sacrifices', and in Jer. 14:1 (περὶ τῆς ἀβροχίας, 'concerning the drought').

The prepositional phrase עַל־דִּבְרַת is used only three times in Biblical Hebrew (Eccl. 3:18; 7:14; 8:2) and twice in Biblical Aramaic (Dan. 2:30; 4:14 [Eng. trans., 4:17]). In Eccl. 3:18, the LXX reads περὶ λαλιᾶς υἱῶν τοῦ ἀνθρώπου ('concerning the speech of the sons of man'), which appears to be a literal rendering of the consonantal text of MT Eccl. 3:18 עַל־דִּבְרַת בְּנֵי הָאָדָם. In this case the Vulgate simply reads 'de filiis hominum', 'with regard to human beings'. In Eccl. 7:14, עַל־דִּבְרַת is used in connection with the relative particle שֶׁ and the negation לֹא (עַל־דִּבְרַת שֶׁלֹּא). In this case the LXX seems to offer a mixture of a literal and an idiomatic translation of a consonantal text: περὶ λαλιᾶς ἵνα μή. The Vulgate contents itself with the conjunction 'ut' with final meaning and a negation 'ut non' ('[so] that not'). Finally, as for Eccl. 8:2b, the LXX offers a causal reading, but at the same time probably renders דִּבְרַת literally by λόγου: περὶ λόγου ὅρκου θεοῦ ('because of the word of the oath of God'). In this case, the Vulgate reads עַל דִּבְרַת as a direct object ('Ego os regis observo et *praecepta iuramenti Dei*', 'I observe the mouth of the king, and *the commandments of the oath of God*'). In Biblical Aramaic the expression עַל־דִּבְרַת דִּי is used twice. The LXX parallel to עַל־דִּבְרַת דִּי in MT Dan. 2:30 is ἀλλ' ἕνεκεν + τοῦ + δηλωθῆναι (passive infinitive of δηλόω, 'make clear, show; indicate; inform') and expresses *purpose* ('but for the sake of making known'[30]). As for the MT עַד־דִּבְרַת דִּי[31] in Dan. 4:14 [Eng. trans., 4:17], Theodotion-Daniel 4:17 has the final conjunction ἵνα. The LXX text of Daniel 3–6 diverges extensively from the MT, so scholars think that the LXX and MT do not reflect the same *Vorlage* for these texts. In this case the Vulgate has the conjunction 'donec' ('as long as, until'); its translator must have read עַד not as an assimilated עַל but as the preposition עַד with a temporal meaning.

In sum, the parallel readings of the ancient textual witnesses to the MT עַל־דְּבַר, עַל־דִּבְרֵי and עַל־דִּבְרַת are, unfortunately, not subject to a constant rendering—given that they reflect a consonantal text identical to that transmitted in the MT. Nevertheless, it still seems reasonable to state that the ancient textual witnesses in most cases support the claim that these prepositional phrases either carry a causal or at least a final notion. In no

---

30   So Brenton, *The Septuagint with Apocrypha*, ad loc.
31   עַד־דִּבְרַת דִּי יִנְדְּעוּן חַיַּיָּא, 'so that the living ones shall know'. עַד־דִּבְרַת: *'addibrat* < *'al-dibrat*; see Franz Rosenthal, *A Grammar of Biblical Aramaic* (5th ed.; Porta linguarum orientalium: NS 5; Wiesbaden: Harrassowitz, 1983), 38 / § 86.

case has it been proved that the MT עַל־דָּבָר, עַל־דִּבְרֵי and עַל־דִּבְרַת have been understood to have a modal notion.

This impression is supported by the extrabiblical occurrences of cognate phrases. In Lachish ostracon no. 4 (sixth century BCE), the phrase על דבר is found, probably with the meaning 'concerning, with regard to'.[32] Moreover, the phrase על דברת is found twice in Qumranic Aramaic in the *Targum of Job* (in 11Q10 1:7 perhaps with a causal meaning and in 11Q10 34:4 as an introduction to a telic clause). Moreover, in the Cambridge manuscript of the *Aramaic Levi Document*—whose date of composition perhaps is in the third or very early second century BCE[33]—the phrase על דברת די introduces a causal clause (CTLevi ar, *Cambridge Col.* a, 16). Neither in these cases nor in any of the other cases where the phrases על דבר or על דבתר occur in Northwest Semitic texts and inscriptions[34] is the meaning modal, contrary to what LXX Ps. 109:4 κατὰ τὴν τάξιν, 'according to the order [of]' and, for example, *HALOT* suggest.[35]

The survey indicates that the Hebrew phrase עַל־דִּבְרָתִי in Ps. 110:4b carries a causal[36] or telic notion. Most probably, the phrase expresses cause, result, or purpose. Below I will argue that the suffixed *yod* is a pronominal suffix, although other explanations are also possible.

12.5.3 The Formative *yod* in עַל־דִּבְרָתִי

Given that the MT עַל־דִּבְרָתִי represents the original reading, the formative י– needs an explanation because it is precisely this formative that makes the phrase a *hapax legomenon*. Principally, the suffixed *yod* can be one of three things. The first possibility is that the formative י– is an archaic Semitic case ending marking a genitive.[37] Probably until the last half of the second millennium BCE, Northwest Semitic dialects made use of case

---

32 See *KAI* 194.5.

33 See Michael E. Stone, 'Levi, Aramaic', *EncDSS* 1:486–88 (486); and Kugler, *From Patriarch to Priest*, 23.

34 See J. Hoftijzer and K. Jongeling, *Dictionary of the North-West Semitic Inscriptions. I* ʾ–*l* (Handbuch der Orientalistik 1. Abteilung, Der Nahe und Mittlere Osten 21; Leiden: E. J. Brill, 1995), s.v. *dbr₃*, 239–40.

35 See *HALOT* 1, s.v. דִּבְרָה, 212. The article suggests that the word דִּבְרָה in the phrase עַל־דִּבְרָתִי (Ps. 110:4) means 'manner'.

36 The tendency to understand it causally is also the case in the Talmud. In *b. Ned.* 32b, על דברתי in Ps. 110:4 is said to mean 'on account of the word of Melchizedek' (על דיבורו של מלכי צדק).

37 See *IBHS*, 127; and Rudolf Meyer, *Hebräische Grammatik. II Formenlehre, Flexionstabelle* (3d ed.; de Gruyter Studienbuch; Berlin: W. de Gruyter, 1992), 47–48 / § 45.1–2.

ending vowels.[38] Subsequently, this system more or less disintegrated. Gradually, the grammatical slots started becoming marked in other ways, for example, by means of the particle אֵת as the object marker. Nevertheless, if ־ִי in דִּבְרָתִי actually is an archaic *דִּבְרָה[39] in the genitive case, then there is no semantic difference between the עַל־דִּבְרָתִי (fem. sing., with genitive case ending) of Psalm 110 and the עַל־דִּבְרַת of Eccl. 3:18; 7:14; and 8:2. Both serve as *nomen regens* for the subsequent noun phrase.

The second possibility is that the formative ־ִי simply is a *yod compaginis*.[40] In this case, the *yod* simply functions as an auxiliary vowel without any semantic or syntactical significance. It follows, then, that there is no difference between the two forms עַל־דִּבְרָתִי and עַל־דִּבְרַת.

The third possibility is that the formative ־ִי is the first person singular pronominal suffix. The noun phrase דִּבְרָתִי could then be split up into *דִּבְרָה in construct state (= דִּבְרַת) and the first person singular pronominal suffix.

12.5.4 Conclusion

It is evident that we cannot tell from the form what particular kind of *yod* we are dealing with. The problem is probably best solved by means of statistics. Of the three potential candidates presented above, it is not likely that the *yod* is an archaic Northwest Semitic case ending vowel marking a genitive. This is not to deny that there are remnants of the archaic Northwest Semitic case system in Biblical Hebrew, but these remnants are not found frequently. When found, they predominantly occur in frozen forms of certain nouns and adverbs.[41] Moreover, the problem with the category *yod compaginis* is that it consists of accompanying *yods*

---

38   Angel Sáenz-Badillos, *A History of the Hebrew Language* (trans. John Elwolde; Cambridge: Cambridge University Press, 1993), 45. Cf. *IBHS* 126.

39   *DCH* 2, *s.v.* דִּבְרָה, 412, suggests 'cause, reason, manner'. Here, Ps 110:4 is listed as the *only* occurrence where the meaning 'manner' is proposed. Likewise, *HALOT* 1, *s.v.* דִּבְרָה, 212 offers the meaning 'manner', with Ps 110:4 as the only place where this meaning is assumed to be found. However, the rendering of the noun in both lexicons is, from my point of view, coined by the LXX τάξις.

40   Meyer, *Hebräische Grammatik. II Formenlehre, Flexionstabelle*, 50–51 / § 45.3.e.

41   It is widely accepted that the genitive *yod* appears in the construct state of nouns such as father (אָב/אֲבִ) and brother (אָח/אֲחִי). Further, remnants of the case system are often found attached to adverbs; see לַיְלָה (< *לֵיל + accusative *a*), יוֹמָם (< יוֹם + accusative *a* + mimation), etc. See Meyer, *Hebräische Grammatik. II Formenlehre, Flexionstabelle*, 47–51 / § 45.1–3. Theoretically, it is possible that our form עַל־דִּבְרָתִי is an archaic adverb. This would, however, be more probable if there were additional instances of this archaic form *besides* Ps. 110:4.

we cannot really account for; they definitely are suffixed to the word, but apparently without any significance (see, e.g., Deut. 33:16, שֹׁכְנִי סְנֶה, usually understood as a construct chain, 'the one who is dwelling in the bush').[42] Using Ockham's razor, it seems that the most readily available explanation is that the *yod* in the phrase עַל־דִּבְרָתִי is the first person singular pronominal suffix.

Therefore, inferring from the similarly constructed prepositional phrases עַל־דְּבַר and עַל־דִּבְרַת (and perhaps in some cases עַל־דִּבְרֵי, too), we can assume that the phrase עַל־דִּבְרָתִי found in Ps. 110:4 has a causal or possibly telic notion. Moreover, proceeding from the premise that the formative ־ִי is the first person singular pronominal suffix, then a possible translation of the phrase is 'because of me' or 'for my sake'.

12.6 The Two Words מַלְכִּי־צֶדֶק in Psalm 110:4b

12.6.1 Lack of Historical Evidence

As anticipated above, there are various arguments against the traditional view that the two words מַלְכִּי־צֶדֶק in Ps. 110:4b together represent the agglutinated personal name 'Melchizedek'. First, a historical counterargument is that only two—as for me, I would say only one[43]—biblical source(s) mention(s) the alleged name. In the ME in Genesis 14, the two words מַלְכִּי־צֶדֶק without doubt function as a full-fledged personal name, as is evident from the apposition מֶלֶךְ שָׁלֵם and the overall narrative context. The other possible occurrence is Psalm 110. Herbert Donner's argument referred to above (see 10.3, The Notion of the Ancient Israelite–Judahite Royal Ideology and Consequences for the Dating of Psalm 110) is convincing. If the tradition of a pre-Israelite king of Jerusalem really was an ancient and integrated part of the royal ideology in ancient Israel, then it is striking that no biblical texts connected[44] to kingship ever mention him (that is, with the exception of Psalm 110!). Moreover, Melchizedek is not

---

42 Meyer calls it a 'Hilfsvokal'; see Meyer, *Hebräische Grammatik. II Formenlehre, Flexionstabelle*, 51/§ 45.3.e. In my opinion, 'vocal of confusion' would be a more suitable term.

43 Thus, anticipating the conclusion in 12.7, Psalm 110:4: Synthesis, namely, that the words מַלְכִּי־צֶדֶק in Ps. 110:4b do not represent an agglutinated personal name ('Melchizedek') but either a nominal phrase or a nominal clause.

44 By 'connected', I mean being about kings, the kingdom, or in some other way dealing positively or negatively with royal ideology.

part of the prophetic repertoire, where he, in Donner's opinion, would fit very well.[45]

Donner's historical argument is, of course, *ex nihilo*. The absence of sources mentioning Melchizedek is after all only a proof of absence of sources mentioning Melchizedek—not counterevidence against the possibility that such a tradition ever existed. Yet, we can turn the whole picture and require from those who argue in favour of the existence of an ancient Melchizedek tradition that they put forward positive evidence. After all, in light of the few and meagre sources, *they* have the burden of proof. What we actually see is that scholars who attempt to support this theory refer to Gen. 14:18–20 and Ps. 110:4.[46] As argued in the present study, these two texts do not carry any weight as historical evidence for the existence of a Melchizedek tradition in ancient Israel's royal ideology. The ME is a late interpolation into Genesis 14* (see 2.2.1, The Melchizedek Episode (= ME) in Genesis 14:18–20: A Secondary Interpolation).

12.6.2 Orthographic Counterevidence

Yet another argument supporting the hypothesis that מַלְכִּי־צֶדֶק originally was not a proper name involves orthography. Hebrew compound names are normally written as *one* word.

There are other possible compound proper names in the Hebrew Bible that are not written as one word. One group has in common that the word בֶּן, 'son', makes up the first element.[47] Mostly, בֶּן refers to a literal or figurative sonship. For instance, בֶּן־זוֹחֵת (1 Chr. 4:20) is son of זוֹחֵת.

---

45 Whether this would apply to the messianic prophecies of some kind or rather as an impetus to prophetic scorn toward the royal institution is another question.

46 For the sake of brevity I choose to let John Day's short and concise argumentation stand (or suffer?) vicariously for all scholars who draw hasty conclusions from Genesis 14 and Psalm 110; see Day, *Psalms*, 100:

> In Ps. 110:4 we read the following words in connection with the king: 'The Lord has sworn and will not change his mind, "You are a priest for ever after the order of Melchizedek"'. This is the one place in the Psalter where the king is explicitly called a priest. The reference here must be to the king, since it is the king who is addressed elsewhere in the psalm. Moreover, Melchizedek is mentioned in Genesis 14 as the pre-Israelite Jebusite priest *and* king in Jerusalem (Salem), so it is clearly a royal priesthood that is being inherited. . . . *We have evidence here of the fusion of the Jebusite and Israelite royal ideologies, and this is most naturally understood as having occurred soon after David's conquest of the Jebusite city of Jerusalem.* [my emphasis]

47 1 Kgs. 15:18, 20; 20:1–2, 5, 9–10, 12, 16–17, 20, 26, 30, 32–34; 2 Kgs. 6:24; 8:7, 9, 14; 13:3, 24–25; 2 Chr. 16:2, 4; Jer. 49:27; Amos 1:4.

The father of the Aramaean king Ben-hadad (בֶּן־הֲדַד), however, is not Hadad but Tibrimmon (1 Kgs. 15:18).[48] Moreover, בֶּן can also indicate that the person referred to has a share of a certain quality or is member of a certain group. For instance, בֶּן־חַיִל (2 Chr. 17:7) may mean something like 'one having power'. Further, בֶּן־אוֹנִי, 'son of my sorrow' (Gen. 35:18), is the name Rachel gave Benjamin before she died in the birth bed. Common for all these names is that it is questionable to what extent they were conceived of as 'real' names at the time of those who were called by them. Likewise, it is questionable to what extent the names given by the prophets Hosea and Isaiah to their children were real names: לֹא עַמִּי (Hos. 1:9; 2:23), לֹא רֻחָמָה (Hos. 1:6, 8; 2:23); and מַהֵר שָׁלָל חָשׁ בַּז (Isa. 8:1, 3). In a similar way it is possible to understand קֶרֶן הַפּוּךְ (Job 42:14) — perhaps 'horn of eye make-up' — as a literary device or a figure of speech; its bearer is one of the daughters Job received *after* Yahweh restored his fortune.

Another group of compound names not written as one word are the names of Assyrian, Babylonian, and Persian kings and officials, that is, נֵרְגַל אֱוִיל מְרֹדַךְ (2 Kgs. 25:27; Jer. 52:31), מְרֹדַךְ בַּלְאֲדָן (2 Kgs. 20:12[49]; Isa. 39:1), שַׂר־אֶצֶר (Jer. 39:3, 13), סַמְגַּר־נְבוּ (Jer. 39:3), שְׁתַר בּוֹזְנַי (Ezr. 5:3, 6; 6:6, 13), תִּגְלַת פִּלְאֶסֶר (2 Kgs. 15:29; 16:7, 10), and תִּלְגַת פִּלְנְאֶסֶר (1 Chr. 5:6, 26; 2 Chr. 28:20).

Without pretending to present the complete picture of compound names in the Hebrew Bible that are not written as one word, we also find אֲבִי־עַלְבּוֹן (2 Sam. 23:31), בֶּן־גֶּבֶר (1 Kgs. 4:13), בֶּן־חָנָן (1 Chr. 4:20), בֶּן־חוּר (1 Kgs. 4:8), יִשְׁבִּי בְּנֹב (2 Sam. 21:16 *qere*), יֹשֵׁב בַּשֶּׁבֶת (2 Sam. 23:8), יוֹשֵׁב חֶסֶד (1 Chr. 3:20), מֵי זָהָב (Gen. 36:39; 1 Chr. 1:50), מְרִיב בַּעַל (1 Chr. 8:34; 9:40), נְתַן־מֶלֶךְ (2 Kgs. 23:11), נֵרְגַל שַׂר־אֶצֶר (Jer. 39:3, 13), עֹבֵד־אֱדוֹם (2 Sam. 6:10–12; 1 Chr. 13:13–14; 15:18, 21, 24–25; 16:5, 38; 26:4, 8, 15; 2 Chr. 25:24), עֶבֶד־מֶלֶךְ (Jer. 38:7–8, 10–12; 39:16), פֹּכֶרֶת הַצְּבָיִים (Ezr. 2:57; Neh. 7:59), טוֹב אֲדוֹנִיָּה (2 Chr. 17:8), תּוּבַל־קַיִן (Gen. 4:22), and צָפְנַת פַּעְנֵחַ (Gen. 41:45).

Various reasons for why these compound personal names are not written as one word may be given. Further, we may also discuss to what extent these compound names really are ordinary personal names. Nevertheless, we can consider it as a fact that compound names in the Hebrew Bible normally are contracted to one word, as in נַבְרִיאֵל Gabriel, אֱלִיעֶזֶר Eliezer, אֱלִימֶלֶךְ Elimelech, etc.

Therefore, the spelling of מַלְכִּי־צֶדֶק suggests that we originally are not dealing with a personal name. This is, however, only a possibility

---

48   Other examples of similarly constructed names — at least understood to be names by the NRSV — are בֶּן־גֶּבֶר (1 Kgs. 4:13), בֶּן־חַיִל (2 Chr. 17:7); בֶּן־חָנָן (1 Chr. 4:20), בֶּן־חוּר (1 Kgs. 4:8) and בֶּן־אוֹנִי (Gen. 35:18).

49   The MT reads בְּראדַךְ בַּלְאֲדָן.

because there are cases where biblical compound names are not written as one word: מַלְכִּי־צֶדֶק in Gen. 14:18 and אֲדֹנִי־צֶדֶק in Josh. 10:1, 3 count among them.[50] In these two cases, it is difficult not to translate the Hebrew expression as a personal name. In both cases, the phrase is followed by an apposition, 'king of (Jeru)Salem'.[51]

12.6.3 Evidence Based on the Reception History

The early history of reception of Psalm 110 and the Qumran literature containing מלכי צדק are ambiguous because they treat מַלְכִּי־צֶדֶק both as a name and as an appellative. As already touched upon, the LXX Ps. 109:4 clearly offers a personal name when rendering its *Vorlage* in Greek by Μελχισεδεκ. For Josephus, this name carried a meaning that suited the person called by this name. In *Ant.* 1.180, he writes that Melchizedek signifies 'the righteous king'. In *Bell.* 6.438, he identifies the first temple builder as a Canaanite, 'who in our own tongue [is] called [Melchizedek], the Righteous King'.[52] Philo also understands the name to mean βασιλεὺς δίκαιος, 'righteous king'.[53] The author of the Letter to the Hebrews interprets it as βασιλεὺς δικαιοσύνης, 'king of righteousness' (Heb. 7:2).

The *Melchizedek* document from Qumran (11Q13) offers no explicit reference to Psalm 110 or to Genesis 14. That is, its main protagonist, מלכי צדק, is not explicitly connected with the only two biblical texts that contain the identical words. However, 11Q13 is a work that bases itself heavily on biblical material, especially Lev. 25:9–12 and Isa. 61:1–3.[54] Therefore, it is unlikely that the author came up with the character of מלכי צדק independently and without knowledge of the two biblical texts that contain מַלְכִּי־צֶדֶק.[55] According to Kobelski, the similarities between Psalm 110 and 11Q13 are too numerous and too basic to the interpreta-

---

50 Perhaps also אֲדֹנִי־בֶזֶק in Judg. 1:5–7 is a name: 'Adoni-bezek'. However, it can also be argued that it is a title, 'lord of [the city of] Bezek' since 'Bezek' is the name of the city (Judg. 1:4–5). In the latter case, *yod* would either have to be a genitive case ending vowel or a *yod compaginis*.

51 Josh. 10:1a וַיְהִי כִשְׁמֹעַ אֲדֹנִי־צֶדֶק מֶלֶךְ יְרוּשָׁלַ͏ִם 'And it came to happen when King Adoni-zedek of Jerusalem heared . . .'; cf. Gen. 14:18a וּמַלְכִּי־צֶדֶק מֶלֶךְ שָׁלֵם 'And King Malchi-zedek of Salem. . .'.

52 Quoted from Flavius Josephus, *The New Complete Works of Josephus* (trans. William Whiston; commentary by Paul L. Maier; rev. and expanded ed.; Grand Rapids, MI: Kregel, 1999), ad loc.

53 *Leg. All.* 3.79, 82.

54 See, e.g., George J. Brooke, 'Melchizedek (11QMelch)', *ABD* 4:687–88; and Gareth Lee Cockerill, 'Melchizedek or "King of Righteousness"?' *EvQ* 63 (1991), 305–12.

55 Kobelski, *Melchizedek and Melchireša*, 51 n. 8.

tion of each document to be coincidental. The occurrence of that which Kobelski thinks of as the *name* Melchizedek in Ps. 110:4 strongly suggests that the Melchizedek presented in 11Q13 was consciously modeled after the character addressed as אֲדֹנִי, 'my lord', in Ps. 110:1. Kobelski assumes that the author of 11Q13 read Psalm 110 as oracles spoken *to Melchizedek*. In this way, there are similarities between the war motifs in Ps. 110:2–3, 5–6 on the one hand, and the eschatological battle motifs in 11Q13 on the other. Likewise, the priestly concern of the author of 11Q13 — perhaps the priestly dignity of the figure of מלכי צדק — is a common motif in Psalm 110 and 11Q13. Therefore, it is legitimate to state that 11Q13 is a text belonging to the history of reception of Psalm 110.

This leads us, first, to how the equivalent to MT מַלְכִּי־צֶדֶק is written in 11Q13, and, second, to how it functions. As already mentioned, Melchizedek is written in two words in 11Q13, מלכי צדק. Now, as demonstrated above (in 12.6.2, Orthographic Counterevidence), this observation alone only hints at the possibility of מַלְכִּי־צֶדֶק *not* being a personal name.

However, another figure called מלכי רשע appears in 4QᶜAmramᵇ 2:3 and 4Q280 2. In the latter text (4Q280 2), the character called מלכי רשע is cursed. Moreover, in another Qumran text, 4Q286 10 2:1–13, Belial (בליעל) is cursed in a similar way. Therefore, we may assume that מלכי רשע and בליעל are identical in the Qumran literature.

This leads us back to 11Q13. In this text, מלכי רשע does not appear. However, בליעל (Belial) appears as the main opponent. It is from the hands of בליעל (Belial) that מלכי צדק will rescue the community of the covenant (see 11Q13 2.25). Kobelski demonstrates that the motif of two heavenly opponents struggling for the control of persons is employed in 11Q13. Because מלכי רשע probably is identical with בליעל in the Qumran literature, we may therefore have indirect evidence in 11Q13 allowing us to assume that מלכי צדק did not function as a personal name in this particular text. On the contrary, the fact that his opponent בליעל (Belial) may also have been called מלכי רשע suggests that the stress was put on the literal meaning of מלכי צדק in 11Q13 and perhaps the entire Qumran literature. The phrase מלכי רשע, 'king of evil', is probably derived from the phrase מלכי צדק, 'king of justice'.[56]

Therefore, in 11Q13 it seems that מלכי צדק was used as a *functional and ontological characterisation* of a heavenly figure, and not simply a personal name. It was the function and nature as צדק, 'righteous[ness]', and not רשע, 'evil, wicked', that was decisive.

Summing up, ancient extrabiblical texts show that the two words מַלְכִּי־צֶדֶק did not unequivocally function as a personal name. The interest

---

56   Kobelski, *Melchizedek and Melchirešaᶜ*, 33.

in the semantics of the words evident in the texts discussed may be explained as an expression of a general interest in etymology at the time of their composition. But, the etymological interest may also betray that an assumed original understanding of the word sequence צדק מלכי in Ps. 110:4b was still extant.

In the following, I will proceed from the premise that the words מַלְכִּי־צֶדֶק originally did not represent a personal name in Ps. 110:4b and that the reading of them as the name Melchizedek represents a later development. Consequently, I will discuss the form and meaning of מַלְכִּי־צֶדֶק.

12.6.4 Form and Meaning of מַלְכִּי־צֶדֶק

As for the MT, we notice that the two words מַלְכִּי־צֶדֶק are compounded by means of a *maqqeph*: -. This small stroke is part of the Tiberian Masoretic system of accents. The *maqqeph* is the most conjunctive of the accents because it makes the word(s) preceding proclitic, that is, without a primary stress. The result is that the group of words knit together by means of it form a phonetic unit.[57] Being a conjunctive accent, the *maqqeph* does not have any semantic significance.

Morphologically, three elements constitute מַלְכִּי־צֶדֶק: first, **malk*; second, the formative *ī*; and third, *ṣedeq*. The first element **malk* is no doubt the noun מֶלֶךְ in construct state.[58] The last element *ṣedeq* is no doubt the noun צֶדֶק. However, the formative ־י interposed between the nouns is problematic. Formally, three potential explanations are possible. The first alternative is that it is a *yod compaginis*. The second alternative is that

---

57   See J–M, § 13/pp. 58–59.

58   Del Medico's proposal to read it as an imperative is not convincing; see 12.2, Alternative Voices Concerning עַל־דִּבְרָתִי and מַלְכִּי־צֶדֶק in the History of Research. As analogy, he refers to Judg. 9:10:

וַיֹּאמְרוּ הָעֵצִים לַתְּאֵנָה לְכִי־אַתְּ מָלְכִי עָלֵינוּ

Then the trees said to the fig tree, 'You come and reign over us.' (NRSV)

Here, מָלְכִי is a form which probably has preserved the more ancient and original Semitic vowel *a*. According to the law of attenuation, the vowel *a* in a closed, unstressed syllable changes to *i* (see J–M, § 29aa/p. 98). Therefore, the form in question is formally identical with the form קִטְלִי, which is the more usual feminine imperative form in Biblical Hebrew. But, as the Hebrew quotation shows, the fig tree (תְּאֵנָה) is *feminine*. Therefore, it does not provide any support for Del Medico's proposal to read מָלְכִי in מַלְכִּי־צֶדֶק as an imperative. His assumed imperative מָלְכִי would then be feminine. However, צֶדֶק is *masculine*.

the formative is an archaic genitive case ending. The third alternative is that it is the first person singular pronominal suffix.

If the puzzling formative ־ִי is either the first alternative, a *yod compaginis*, or the second alternative, a genitive case ending, the result is that מַלְכִּי־צֶדֶק in Ps. 110:4b is a noun phrase, 'king of righteousness'.[59] However, if the formative ־ִי turns out to be the third alternative, a pronominal suffix, מַלְכִּי־צֶדֶק is a nominal clause, 'my king is righteous[ness]'[60].

How, then, do we determine which one of the three alternatives is expressed by means of the formative ־ִי in מַלְכִּי־צֶדֶק in Ps. 110:4b? We can also argue along the lines drawn above in connection with עַל־דִּבְרָתִי. When we encounter cases where a formative ־ִי is suffixed to a noun, it is in most cases a pronominal suffix. This is not to deny that there are instances in the Hebrew Bible where the same formative should be identified as a *yod compaginis* or as a genitive case ending. But, the pronominal suffix should on the basis of statistics be given priority as a possible solution before one considers the two other, just as I argued in connection with עַל־דִּבְרָתִי. For the same reason, Dahood's proposal to read ־ִי as *third* person masculine pronominal suffix is farfetched.[61]

Given that the words מַלְכִּי־צֶדֶק in Ps. 110:4b originally were conceived as appellatives, I conclude that the formative ־ִי probably marks a pronominal suffix. Consequently, the words מַלְכִּי־צֶדֶק constitute a nominal clause in Ps. 110:4. As a clause they should be rendered 'my king [is] righteousness'.

12.6.5 Reminiscences of a Canaanite God 'Ṣedeq' in the מַלְכִּי־צֶדֶק of Psalm 110?

The word צֶדֶק has a relatively broad semantic field. The following main entries are found in *HALOT*: 1. 'accuracy, what is correct'; 2. 'equity, what is right'; 3. 'communal loyalty, conduct loyal to the community'; 4. 'salvation, well-being'; 5. 'צֶדֶק in connection with the king (Messiah)'; and 6. a theophoric element in Ugaritic, Phoenician, and Old South Arabian names, as well as a theophoric element in the biblical names אֲדֹנִי־צֶדֶק and מַלְכִּי־צֶדֶק.[62]

---

59 Because here I primarily discuss the function of the formative ־ִי, I choose for the sake of simplicity to use 'righteousness' as a translation of צֶדֶק. However, below I will discuss what particular segment of the semantic field of צֶדֶק one should use (see 12.6.5, Reminiscences of a Canaanite God 'Ṣedeq' in the מַלְכִּי־צֶדֶק of Psalm 110?).

60 See note above. Here I tentatively suggest that the noun צֶדֶק functions adjectively.

61 Dahood, *Psalms III: 101–150*, 117.

62 See *HALOT* 3, s.v. צֶדֶק, 1004–5.

Although one cannot rule out the possibility that צֶדֶק is a theophoric element, this theory nevertheless suffers from a lack of clear and indisputable evidence. צֶדֶק appears independently as a god *sydyk* together with his brother *mismor* in the *Phoenician History* of Philo of Byblos (ca. 70–160 CE). This source is known only through later excerpts and quotations by Eusebius of Caesarea (ca. 260–340 CE) in *Praeparatio Evangelica*. Otherwise, those who argue for the existence of an originally pre-Israelite, Jebusite god Ṣedeq find support in Ugaritic personal names from around 1400 BCE and, finally, in the two biblical names Adoni-zedek (אֲדֹנִי־צֶדֶק) and Melchizedek (מַלְכִּי־צֶדֶק) (*sic*).[63] What is more, Preuß uses the apparent tendency in the biblical psalms to let צֶדֶק appear as a person as support for צֶדֶק originally being a god of Jebus, who in the meantime has been subordinated and incorporated to Yahweh.[64]

Even though it is not impossible that there has been a god Ṣedeq, the lack of ancient texts with explicit evidence makes it a loosely founded assumption that he was worshipped in pre-Israelite Jebus. It is equally unlikely to think of צֶדֶק in 'Melchizedek' as a theophoric element, referring to this god Ṣedeq, presumably worshipped in Jerusalem. On the contrary, in the case of מַלְכִּי־צֶדֶק in Ps. 110:4b it is simply an easier explanation that צֶדֶק is an appellative, a common noun.

Therefore, the remaining semantic field of צֶדֶק as proposed in *HALOT* demonstrates that the word is used both in forensic and more general contexts. In light of this, it could be argued that one should, for the sake of simplicity, choose to render the word as 'righteousness'. This can be supported by biblical texts. According to Isa. 1:21–27 Zion is closely associated with 'righteousness' (v. 21: '. . . righteousness lodged in her'; v. 26: 'Afterward you shall be called the city of righteousness. . .'). Jeremiah 23:5–6 offers a pun on the name of the unrighteous king Zedekiah. The coming king will be called 'Yahweh is our righteousness' (יְהוָה צִדְקֵנוּ). According to Isa. 11:4–5, the king that will come will judge the poor with righteousness. Righteousness shall be the belt around his waist.

However, in various Aramaic inscriptions from the eighth, seventh, and fifth–fourth centuries BCE, there are analogies to the typical ancient Near Eastern political situation that Ps. 110:4 reflects, namely, that most kings in fact were vassal kings. These analogies suggest that צֶדֶק might have a political meaning in Psalm 110:4b. In these inscriptions, צדק has a political notion, referring to the 'loyalty' of a vassal king (or high priest)

---

63 Above all, see R. A. Rosenberg, 'The God Ṣedeq', *HUCA* 36 (1965): 161–77. In addition, see K. Koch, "צדק," *THAT* 2, cols. 507–30 (509).

64 Preuß, *Theologie des Alten Testaments. I JHWHs erwählendes und verpflichtendes Handeln*, 198–200.

as servant (עֶבֶד) vis-à-vis the Assyrian suzerain (or his personal god) as his master.[65] Equally, it can be argued that a similar master–servant relationship is reflected in Psalm 110 between the (vassal) king spoken to on the one hand and the speaking suzerain Yahweh on the other.

12.7 Psalm 110:4: Synthesis and Conclusion

I have argued above that עַל־דִּבְרָתִי is a prepositional phrase with an adverbial function. Moreover, in light of cognate Biblical Hebrew and Aramaic phrases, I have argued that the *hapax legomenon* carries a causal or telic connotation. Furthermore, I have argued that the formative ־ִי probably represents a pronominal suffix in first person singular.

Moreover, I have argued that the words מַלְכִּי־צֶדֶק in MT Ps. 110:4 do not have to represent a personal name but, on the contrary, are words that make up an integral part of the text. Further, I have argued that מַלְכִּי־צֶדֶק is a nominal clause. In this clause, מַלְכִּי, 'my king', functions as subject and צֶדֶק, 'loyalty', functions as predicative.

Summing up the discussion concerning Ps. 110:4b thus far, I propose that the meaning of Ps. 110:4 was the following around the time of its composition, that is, in the monarchic period:

Yahweh has sworn and will not repent:

'You are[66] a priest forever.

For my sake my king is loyal'.[67]

---

65   See Klaus Koch, "צדק," *THAT* 2, cols. 507–30 (508) and *KAI* 215.11, 19; 216.4–5; 217.3, 5; 219.4; 226.2 and 228A.15. For instance, in *KAI* 215.11, the clause בחכמתה ובצדקה פי אחז בכנף מראה מלך אשור is rendered 'Auf Grund seiner Weisheit und *auf Grund seiner Loyalität* ergriff er [i.e., Panamuwa, the father of Barrākib] den Gewandsaum [i.e., a phrase expressing the vassal relationship, also found in Akkadian] seines Herrn, des Königs von Assyrien' (my emphasis).
66   The time reference of the Hebrew nominal clause is open. If v. 4 is preformative speech, the recipient 'will be' a priest from the time of speaking to eternity (עוֹלָם). If v. 4 is a confirmation of the recipient's already existent priesthood, then we should instead use a durative verb form, e.g., like English present tense: 'you are [still] a priest'.
67   Although צֶדֶק is a noun, it nevertheless functions as a substitute for an adjective. See J-M, § 141a/p. 521. Even though it has been argued that the formative ־ִי most plausibly marks a pronominal suffix, the possibility that it represents either a *yod compaginis* or a genitive case ending cannot be entirely excluded. If it should turn out that the formative is one of the these two options, then מַלְכִּי־צֶדֶק in Ps. 110:4b is a *noun phrase*, 'king of righteousness'. If that is the case, the phrase מַלְכִּי־צֶדֶק functions as a vocative:

'You are a priest forever,
    for my sake / because of me, O king of righteousness.'

In other words, Yahweh's oracle in Ps. 110:4 contains two lines. The first seems to be addressed directly to the king ('you are a priest forever'). In the second, Yahweh—perhaps addressing a wider audience—accounts for his opinion concerning the king ('for my sake my king is loyal').

* * *

Regardless of what the meaning of Ps. 110:4 was in the monarchic period, I will for the sake of clarity anticipate the theses I will argue for in subsequent chapters:[68] *In the Second Temple period, Psalm 110 started being interpreted as a historiographical psalm.* The phrase לְדָוִד was understood as an author designation. Moreover, אֲדֹנִי, 'my lord' (see Ps. 110:1), was identified with the patriarch Abraham. And, because אֲדֹנִי was identified with Abraham, who was involved in war activities in the psalm, the psalm was associated with the only story in the patriarchal narratives where Abraham fights a war, namely, Genesis 14* (that is, *without* the secondarily interpolated ME).

As a consequence of the intertextual reading established between Psalm 110 and Genesis 14*, it became evident that the former text contained extra material not to be found in Genesis 14*, or to put it another way, a *Leerstelle* emerged in Genesis 14* vis-à-vis Psalm 110.

The ME was composed and interpolated into Genesis 14* in order to fill out the *Leerstelle* that emerged vis-à-vis Psalm 110. In the process of the composition of the ME, the extra material in Psalm 110 vis-à-vis Genesis 14* seems to have served as the literary building blocks that the author used when composing the ME.

Moreover, the ME has influenced the traditional interpretation of the oracle in Ps. 110:4. When Ps. 110:4 was translated into Greek, the translation of the oracle was harmonized with the content of the ME. As a consequence of the oracle in Ps. 110:4 being read in light of the ME, the ancient Greek translation reads a personal name (Melchizedek) and reflects the concept of a certain priestly line ('after the order of'): σὺ εἶ ἱερεὺς εἰς τὸν αἰῶνα κατὰ τὴν τάξιν Μελχισεδεκ, 'you are a priest forever *according to the order* of Melchizedek' (LXX Ps. 109:4).

The majority of translations follow the LXX—whose translation has been coined by the ME—in the translation of the Hebrew מַלְכִּי־צֶדֶק and the *hapax legomenon* עַל־דִּבְרָתִי (see, e.g., the NRSV: 'The LORD has sworn and will not change his mind, "You are a priest forever according to the order of Melchizedek"'.).

---

68   See chapter 13, Early Intertextual Readings of Genesis 14 and Psalm 110, and chapter 14, The Result of an Assimilation of Two Texts, Both Thought to be Referring to Abram's War with the King.

13. Early Intertextual Readings of Genesis 14 and Psalm 110

In a previous chapter, I demonstrated that there are several examples of two or more texts having been assimilated.[1] In the following I will argue that assimilation is the key to explaining the origin of the ME, that is, *why* and *how* the episode was composed and interpolated into Genesis 14*. The thesis I will attempt to substantiate is that Genesis 14* (note: *without* the ME) and Psalm 110 were subject to an intertextual reading that resulted in the composition of the ME.

13.1 The 'Abrahamic' Interpretation of Psalm 110 and Other Cases of Early Intertextual Readings of Genesis 14 and Psalm 110

Having proposed the fundamental assumptions that

- Psalm 110 has an earlier date of composition than the ME (Gen. 14:18–20)[2] and furthermore,
- that the two words מַלְכִּי־צֶדֶק in Ps. 110:4b probably originally were appellatives (and not the personal name Melchizedek),[3]

I now return to the question of the joint origin of the ME and the Melchizedek tradition. In order to substantiate the theory of an early intertextual reading between Genesis 14* and Psalm 110, it is appropriate, first, to discuss the term 'intertextuality' as it is used here, and second, to draw attention to the early history of interpretation of Genesis 14 and Psalm 110.

Julia Kristeva was the first scholar to introduce the term intertextuality. She used the term to describe every discourse, written or spoken. For Kristeva, the basic force of intertextuality was to problematize those

---

1   See 7.1, The Date of Composition: A Synthesis of the Different Approaches; and chapter 11, The Phenomenon of Assimilation in the Bible.
2   See 10.5, Conclusion: A Date of Composition in the Monarchic Period Probable for Psalm 110.
3   See 12.6, The Two Words מַלְכִּי־צֶדֶק in Psalm 110.4b.

lines of demarcation that allow the reader to talk about the meaning, subject, or origin of a given text.[4]

However, in the meantime, the term has taken on a life of its own, resulting in a wide range of different definitions and applications. Although I risk stirring up a hornet's nest by using such a highly debated term, I still find it appropriate as long as I define my understanding of the term. Kisten Nielsen writes: 'Each and every text forms part of a network of texts from which it derives its meaning'.[5] This is a statement about how meaning is created in general. We may assume that networks of texts also existed earlier, in our case in the Second Temple period. The texts involved could be directly dependent on each other, that is, one as the *Vorlage* of the other. However, even without any original relationship, texts must have been thought to be part of textual networks. A more or (in the Second Temple period probably) less formalized network of texts was subsequently considered as the biblical canon.

When I propose that Psalm 110 and Genesis 14* were read intertextually at a certain point in the Second Temple period, I assume that the two texts reciprocally constituted important parts of each other's network of texts, without denying that other texts could be part of this network. Yet, when interpreted as 'Abrahamic' (i.e., assuming that Yahweh's oracles in the psalm were addressed to Abraham), Psalm 110 appears to be a poetic résumé of a battle in which Abram takes part. In the patriarchal narratives, since Genesis 14* is the only text where Abram makes war, it as an obvious member of the psalm's network.

Different text corpora demonstrate that the two texts actually were read intertextually in the last part of the Second Temple period. However, it should be noted that in the majority of these cases it was apparently the shared use of the two words מַלְכִּי־צֶדֶק in Genesis 14 and Psalm 110 that motivated the intertextual reading. This is undoubtedly the case in the discussion of the status of Jesus in Hebrews 7 (ca. 60–90 CE), where there are explicit references to Gen. 14:18–20 and implicit references to Ps. 110:4 in the same context. Moreover, even earlier intertextual readings of Genesis 14 and Psalm 110 may be found. Anders Aschim suggests that the author of the book of *Jubilees* (ca. second century BCE[6]) describes the elevation of Levi to the priesthood by means of Melchizedekian phraseology. In particular, Aschim focuses on *Jub.* 32:1, which

---

4   Timothy K. Beal, 'Glossary', in *Reading between Texts: Intertextuality and the Hebrew Bible* (ed. Danna Nolan Fewell; Literary Currents in Biblical Interpretation; Louisville, KY: Westminster/John Knox Press, 1992), 21–24 (22–23).

5   Nielsen, 'Intertextuality and Hebrew Bible', 17–31 (17).

6   See chapter 16, The Date of the Melchizedek Episode.

seems to borrow from both Genesis 14 and Psalm 110: 'Levi dreamed that he had been appointed and ordained *priest of the Most High God* [cf. Gen. 14:18–20], he and his sons *forever* [cf. Ps. 110:4]'.[7] After this, Levi rises and gives a 'tenth of everything' [*Jub*. 32:2; cf. Gen. 14:20b]. The author of *Jubilees* seems to have used the two biblical texts that mention Melchizedek in his elevation of Levi to priesthood, despite the fact that *Jubilees* does not mention Melchizedek at all.[8] Furthermore, there may be similar terminological borrowings from both Genesis 14 and Psalm 110 in 4Q213b 5–6 (= the *Aramaic Levi Document*). Here, Levi says that his father Jacob tithes (him?), and further, that

> I [= Levi] was first at the head of the priesthood and to me of his sons he gave a gift of . . . to God, and he invested me in the priestly garb and he conse-crated me and I became a priest of the God of eternity.[9]

In addition, Aschim suggests that the portraying of Melchizedek in 11Q13 is the result of creative exegesis of Genesis 14 and Psalm 110.[10]

The texts referred to above have in common that their intertextual readings of Genesis 14 and Psalm 110 seem to have their 'lowest common denominator' in Melchizedek. The ME (Gen. 14:18–20) and the oracle in Ps. 110:4 together seem to have served as a point of departure for the intertestamental texts mentioned above that were combining excerpts from the Torah and Psalm 110.

However, the hypothesis that I propose is that the ME is an inter-polation *based on* Ps. 110:4. A prerequisite for this hypothesis is that an intertextual reading of Genesis 14* and Psalm 110 already existed before the ME was composed. Consequently, the texts discussed so far have no value as proof texts for my hypothesis because their 'lowest common denominator' is the ME and Ps. 110:4. Instead, I will explore another

---

7   Anders Aschim, 'Melchizedek and Levi', in *The Dead Sea Scrolls: Fifty Years after Their Discovery: Proceedings of the Jerusalem Congress, July 20–25, 1997* (ed. Lawrence H. Schiff-man, Emanuel Tov, and James C. VanderKam; Jerusalem: Israel Exploration Society, 2000), 773–88 (774–75). The translation is that of O. S. Wintermute, *OTP* 2:35–142 (116, my emphasis).

8   In the passage where one would expect *Jubilees* to offer its parallel to the dialogue between Abram and Melchizedek (Gen. 14:18–20), it has instead a law of the tithe (*Jub*. 13:25–27).

9   Aschim, 'Melchizedek and Levi', 773–88 (775–76).

10   See Anders Aschim, 'Verdens eldste bibelkommentar? Melkisedek-teksten fra Qum-ran', *TTK* 2 (1995): 85–103; idem, 'Melchizedek the Liberator: An Early Interpretation of Genesis 14?' in *Society of Biblical Literature 1996 Seminar Papers* (Society of Biblical Literature Seminar Papers 35; Atlanta: Scholars Press, 1996): 243–58; and idem, 'The Genre of 11QMelchizedek', in *Qumran between the Old and New Testaments* (ed. Fred-erick H. Cryer and Thomas L. Thompson; JSOTSup 290; Copenhagen International Seminar 6; Sheffield: Sheffield Academic Press, 1998), 17–31.

path, that is, a rabbinic tradition of interpretation of Genesis 14 and Psalm 110:

In the eleventh century, the Jewish Bible commentator Rashi wrote concerning Ps. 110:1: 'Our rabbis interpreted [my lord] as a reference to Abraham, our father . . .'.[11] In this way Rashi gives a good summary of the *early* rabbinic interpretation of this psalm.[12] Admittedly, the sources also suggest other possible interpretations of the psalm. For instance, according to Justin Martyr, the Jew Trypho ventured to expound Psalm 110 as if it referred to King Hezekiah.[13] However, no trace of such an interpretation is found elsewhere. Moreover, in later rabbinic texts, there is an interpretation that applies the psalm to David.[14] Nevertheless, as a rule of thumb, the early rabbis interpreted Psalm 110 as 'Abrahamic'. This implies that they assumed that David was the speaker of the psalm and that David identified אֲדֹנִי, 'my lord', with Abraham.

This identification of אֲדֹנִי in Ps. 110:1 is found in the Talmud. In *b. Ned.* 32b, the third/fourth-century R. Zechariah speaks in the name of the first/second-century R. Ishmael and gives an explanation of why the priesthood was taken from Melchizedek (by the rabbis identified with Shem, the son of Noah) and given to Abraham:

> Immediately he gave it [the priesthood] to Abraham, as it is said, *The Lord said to my Lord, 'Sit on my right hand until I shall set your enemies as a stool for your feet'* (Ps. 110:1), and after this it is written, *The Lord has sworn and will not repent. You are a priest forever* עַל דִּבְרָתִי *Melchizedek* (Ps. 110:4), that is, on account of what Melchizedek had said (עַל דִּיבּוּרוֹ שֶׁל מַלְכִּי צֶדֶק). This corresponds to what is written, *And he was priest to El Elyon. He* was priest, but his descendants were not priests.[15]

Likewise, R. Hana b. Liwai (date uncertain) identifies אֲדֹנִי with Abraham in *b. Sanh.* 108b:

---

11   Mayer Irwin Gruber, *Rashi's Commentary on Psalms* (Brill Reference Library of Judaism 18; Leiden: E. J. Brill, 2004), 645.

12   So Gerhard Bodendorfer, 'Abraham zur Rechten Gottes: Der Ps 110 in der rabbinischen Tradition', *EvT* 59 (1999): 252–66 (264).

13   Justin Martyr, *Dialogue with Trypho*, chaps. 32–33, 83.

14   See *Midr. Ps.* 110 § 5 (233b; cf. Str–B 4, 'Achtzehnter Exkurs: Der 110. Psalm in der altrabbinischen Literatur', 452–65 [456]); and *Targ. Pss.* 110 (see David M. Stec, *The Targum of Psalms: Translated, with a Critical Introduction, Apparatus, and Notes* [The Aramaic Bible 16; London: T. & T. Clark, 2004], 202–3; and Michael Tilly, 'Psalm 110 zwischen hebräischer Bibel und Neuem Testament', in *Heiligkeit und Herrschaft: Intertextuelle Studien zu Heiligkeitsvorstellungen und zu Psalm 110* [ed. Dieter Sänger; BThS 55; Neukirchen-Vluyn: Neukirchener Verlag, 2003], 146–70 [148]).

15   Translation of M. McNamara, in idem, 'Melchizedek: Gen 14,17–20 in the Targums, in Rabbinic and Early Literature', *Bib* 81 (2000): 1–31 (11).

R. Ḥana b. Liwai said: Shem, [Noah's] eldest son, said to Eliezer[16] [Abraham's servant], 'When the kings of the east and the west attacked you, what did you do?'—He replied, 'The Holy One, blessed be He, took Abraham and placed him at His right hand, and they [God and Abraham] threw dust which turned to swords, and chaff which turned to arrows, as it is written, *A Psalm of David. The Lord said unto my master, Sit thou at my right hand, until I make thine enemies thy footstool;* and it is also written, *Who raised up the righteous man* [sc. Abraham] *from the east, called him to his foot, gave the nations before him, and made him rule over kings? He made his sword as the dust and his bow as driven stubble.*[17]

There are other examples as well that all have in common the use of the phrase אֲדֹנִי n Ps. 110:1 as a reference to the patriarch Abraham.[18] However, the quoted *b. Sanh.* 108b—unlike the above-mentioned Hebrews 7, *Jubilees* 32, Aramaic Levi Document, 11Q13, and *b. Ned.* 32b—bears witness to an intertextual reading of Genesis 14 and Psalm 110 (and Isa. 41:2–13 as the *Haftarah*[19] to the Torah text in the synagogue reading) that is *not* dependent solely on the common use of the name Melchizedek (or in the case of *Jub.* 32:1, the 'Melchizedekean' priestly terminology).

13.2 The Origin of the Intertextual Reading of Genesis 14 and Psalm 110 Independent of מַלְכִּי־צֶדֶק

It is evident from the sources mentioned above that at least some rabbis a short time after the destruction of the Second Temple understood Genesis 14 and Psalm 110 as separate texts referring to an identical event: Abram's war with the kings. Now, the crucial questions are as follows: At what time did someone start relating these two texts to each other? Is it possible that the intertextual reading of these two texts started even before the ME was composed and interpolated? In other words, when did the historiographical reading of Psalm 110 as a poetic account of Abram's war with the four kings first emerge?

---

16   This Talmud passage identifies Abram's 318 men (see Gen. 14:14) with Eliezer (see Gen. 15:2) on the basis of a *gematria*. See 4.3.6, Did Genesis 15 Originally Continue Genesis 13 or Genesis 14?; and, in particular, note 119 in part II above.

17   Quoted after Isidore Epstein, ed., *Hebrew–English Edition of the Babylonian Talmud* (18 vols.; London: Soncino, 1961), ad loc.

18   The following references are collected from Bodendorfer, 'Abraham zur Rechten Gottes: Der Ps 110 in der rabbinischen Tradition', 252–66 (255–60): *Ag. Ber.* 19; *Gen. R.* 39:8; 46:5; 55:6; 56:10; *Deb. R.* 2:7; *Mek.* Shirata 16; *PRE* 8; *S. 'Ol. R.* 21; *Tanḥ. B* Lekh 4 (30b–31a), Vayera 4 (3b); *Tanḥ.* Lekh 13; *Tanḥ.* Beshalla 16; *Vay. R.* 25:6.

19   That is, a synagogue lectionary from the Prophets.

I have already argued that historiography and poetry were already correlated in biblical times.[20] However, as far as I am concerned, the closest instance in the history of research of a discussion touching on the questions I have raised in the paragraph above is the question of whether the rabbi's 'Abrahamic' interpretation of Psalm 110 was an anti-Christian reaction or not. Did the rabbis react to the first Christians' christological interpretation of the psalm, which was important for the formulation of the dogma of the elevation of Christ to the Father's right side,[21] by identifying אֲדֹנִי, 'my lord', with Abraham instead of Messiah?

One view, expressed in Str–B, is that a messianic interpretation of Psalm 110 was known in pre-Christian Jewish circles (although no proof texts dating to the pre-Christian period are mentioned in this connection). Accordingly, the traditional messianic interpretation was initially abandoned as part of an anti-Christian, antichristological reaction:

> R. Jischmaʾel [first part of the second century CE; see *b. Ned.* 32b above[22]] [hat] die traditionelle messianische Deutung unseres Psalms ausschließlich aus christentumsfeindlichen Tendenzen aufgebeben u[nd] durch die Deutung auf Abraham ersetzt. . . .[23]

According to this view, the Jews again returned to the Messianic interpretations of the old days after ca. 250 CE, that is, *after* the schism between the synagogue and church became irrevocable.[24]

However, David M. Hay has criticized the logic in the argumentation of Str–B. Nevertheless, Hay allows for the possibility that a messianic interpretation was current the first-century Judaism. However, he states that one cannot know how widely it was accepted. As for the 'Abrahamic' interpretation of the psalm and the psalm's connection with Genesis 14 as evident in, for example, *b. Ned.* 32b,[25] Hay suggests that this pattern of exegesis was moulded by the synagogue lectionary of the Sec-

---

20 See chapter 11, The Phenomenon of Assimilation in the Bible.
21 See Matt. 26:64 par.; cf. Ps. 110:1; see Martin Hengel, 'Psalm 110 und die Erhöhung des Auferstandenen zur Rechten Gottes', in *Anfänge der Christologie: Feschschrift für Ferdinand Hahn zum 65. Geburtstag* (ed. Cilliers Breytenbach and Henning Paulsen; Göttingen: Vandenhoeck & Ruprecht, 1991), 43–73; Gerhard Dautzenberg, 'Psalm 110 im Neuen Testament', in idem, *Studien zur Theologie der Jesustradition* (SBAB 19; Stuttgart: Verlag Katholisches Bibelwerk, 1995), 63–97; and Manfred Görg, 'Thronen zur Rechten Gottes: Zur altägyptischen Wurzel einer Bekenntnisformel', *BN* 81 (1996): 72–81.
22 See 13.1, The 'Abrahamic' Interpretation of Psalm 110 and Other Cases of Early Intertextual Readings of Genesis 14 and Psalm 110.
23 Str–B 4, 460.
24 Str–B 4, 458, 460.
25 See 13.1, The 'Abrahamic' Interpretation of Psalm 110 and Other Cases of Early Intertextual Readings of Genesis 14 and Psalm 110.

ond Temple period.[26] Hay finds support for this thesis in Jacob Mann's study, published in 1940, on the cycle of readings in the old synagogue.[27] According to Mann, the eleventh *seder* in the triennial Torah reading cycle began with Gen. 14:1 and continued to 15:1.

Like Hay, Gerhard Bodendorfer has also traced the origin of the 'Abrahamic' interpretation of Psalm 110 to the synagogue lectionary. Taking Mann's theory of a triennial reading cycle as a point of departure, Bodendorfer assumes that Genesis 14 was combined with Psalm 110 (and Isaiah 41 as *Haftarah*) in the synagogue lectionary because of their close conceptual and linguistic proximity.

In connection with a passage in *Mekilta de Rabbi Ishmael* (Shirata 6 Lauterbach II 45) — a passage resembling *b. Sanh.* 108b, which was quoted above[28] because of its intertextual reading of Genesis 14 and Psalm 110 *without any mention of Melchizedek* — Bodendorfer comments:

> Munstergültig liegt hier [i.e., in *Mekilta de Rabbi Ishmael*] ein Beispiel des hermeneutischen Prinzips der Intertextualität vor, das die rabbinische Exegese besonders auszeichnet: Sie bedeutet auf einen Nenner gebracht, daß *alle Texte der Bibel in einem Dialog stehen.*[29]

According to Bodendorfer, the rabbinic interpretation of the psalm was not guided by anti-Christian tendencies but, on the contrary, by inner-Jewish hermeneutics.

However, Mann's study of the cycles of readings in the old synagogue has been criticized and perhaps may not provide any support for Hay's and Bodendorfer's suggestion that the early synagogue lectionary formed the intertextual reading of Genesis 14 and Psalm 110 that is evident in early rabbinic literature. In his prolegomenon to the second edition of Mann's *The Bible as Read and Preached in the Old Synagogue*, B. Z. Wacholder questions Mann's main hypothesis. He states that it is surprising how little we know of the ancient Palestinian sabbatical readings of the Scripture. Moreover, according to him, Mann failed to prove his hypothesis of the antiquity of the so-called Triennial Cycle of the Torah reading.[30]

---

26 Hay, *Glory at the Right Hand*, 27–30.

27 Jacob Mann, *The Bible as Read and Preached in the Old Synagogue: A Study in the Cycles of the Readings from Torah and Prophets, as well as from Psalms, and the Structure of the Midrashic Homilies* (Cincinnati, OH: Union of American Hebrew Congregations, 1940).

28 See 13.1, The 'Abrahamic' Interpretation of Psalm 110 and Other Cases of Early Intertextual Readings of Genesis 14 and Psalm 110.

29 Bodendorfer, 'Abraham zur Rechten Gottes: Der Ps 110 in der rabbinischen Tradition', 252–66 (254, my emphasis); cf. also 264–66.

30 Ben Zion Wacholder, 'Prolegomenon', in Jacob Mann, *The Bible as Read and Preached in the Old Synagogue: A Study in the Cycles of the Readings from Torah and Prophets, as well as*

Therefore, direct textual evidence for an intertextual reading of Genesis 14 and Psalm 110, where the texts have been read as different versions of the same event, is — I must say unfortunately — first found in the early Christian period. However, that does not have to mean that such a historiographical, 'Abrahamic' reading of Psalm 110 first emerged in the early Christian period. On the contrary, as both Hay and Bodendorfer have pointed out, the identification of the person called אֲדֹנִי, 'my lord', in Ps. 110:1 with Abraham did not come as a result of anti-Christian polemic. On the contrary, it was rooted in the Jewish hermeneutics of intertextuality. And the Jewish hermeneutics of intertextuality is, of course, independent of and earlier than the Christian creed — as I demonstrated above in connection with the hermeneutical rule *gezerah shawah*.[31]

The fact that the guiding hermeneutical principle behind the rule which was later called *gezerah shawah* dates back to the Second Temple period, of course, does not prove my theory. Yet, despite the lack of textual evidence, I will maintain as a working hypothesis that Genesis 14* and Psalm 110 were read as parallel versions of the same event before the ME was composed and interpolated into Genesis 14*.

The potential legitimacy of this thesis is its explanatory force: To what extent does it show itself capable of solving problems concerning the date and motivation of the interpolation? Can it give an answer to *when* the interpolation took place, *how* the interpolator worked, and *what motivation* he may have had? Further, is the proposal in accordance with what we know about the Second Temple period (social-political conditions, hermeneutics, the transition from the text genesis of the Hebrew Bible to the dawn of Bible interpretation, etc.)?

---

from Psalms, and the Structure of the Midrashic Homilies (2 vols.; New York: Ktav, 1966, 1971), xi-li (xii). Moreover, see Günter Stemberger, 'Psalmen in Liturgie und Predigt der rabbinischen Zeit', in *Der Psalter in Judentum und Christentum* (ed. Erich Zenger; HBS 18; Freiburg: Herder, 1998), 199–213.

31   See 11.3, The Rabbinic Hermeneutical Principle 'Gezerah Shawah' and Its Biblical Predecessor.

14. The Result of an Assimilation of Two Texts, Both Thought to Be Referring to Abram's War with the King

In the present chapter, I will discuss the following questions: Why did an interpolator create the ME, and how did he do it?

Despite the lack of explicit textual evidence, I will nonetheless attempt to reconstruct an intertextual reading of Genesis 14* and Psalm 110 that *antedates* the composition and interpolation of the ME into Genesis 14*. I will do this in order to examine the explanatory force of the working hypothesis that the ME was composed in order to assimilate Genesis 14* and Psalm 110. Admittedly, this is an enterprise loaded with methodological problems. Consequently, the model will necessarily be conjectural. Yet, I believe this is appropriate in light of other, more conjectural approaches (e.g., models of the background and origin of the ME that take refuge in tradition history and consequently often evade transparency and verification, especially when dealing with assumed pre-literate stages of narratives, motifs, etc.).

14.1 A Historiographical Reading of Psalm 110

The idea that David was the author of many biblical psalms is broadly attested. In the New Testament, David is taken to be the author of Psalm 110: 'For David himself says in the book of Psalms, "The Lord said to my Lord . . ."' (Luke 20:42 NRSV). Moreover, in a prose section in 11QPsalms^a (= 11Q5), David is said to have composed 3,600 psalms and many songs to be sung on different occasions in the Temple cult, in all, 4,050 psalms and songs. According to the Qumran author, David spoke all of these psalms and songs through prophecy (בנבואה) that was given to him from the Most High (עליון) (11QPs^a 27:2–11).

Therefore, when someone who read biblical psalms in the Second Temple period understood לְדָוִד as a description of the psalm author, then one can expect that this reader inferred that David himself was the prophetically inspired psalm speaker who raised his voice in Ps. 110:1 (see נְאֻם יְהוָה). Besides the prepositional phrase לְדָוִד, the psalm speaker reveals himself in the pronominal suffix in לַאדֹנִי, 'to *my* lord'. Therefore, one can assume that the Second Temple period psalm reader read Psalm 110 as if David himself uttered the words 'The oracle of Yahweh to my lord' (Ps. 110:1).

Proceeding from the premise that the Second Temple period reader took David to be the speaker of Psalm 110, what reasons may they have had for considering the patriarch Abraham to be identical with the person whom David called אָדֹון, 'lord' (see Ps. 110:1 נְאֻם יְהוָה לַאדֹנִי)? Given that this identification of אָדֹון with Abraham took place *before* the ME was composed and interpolated into Genesis 14*, what were the criteria for such an identification?

First, one must take for granted that for the ideal figure David, only a rather limited number of candidates were potentially qualified to be addressed as 'lord' by him, at least according to the expectations of a Jew in the Second Temple period. One person explicitly addressed as 'lord' on several occasions by David is Saul (1 Sam. 24:7, 9, 11; 26:15, etc.). Rabbinic literature likewise in some cases identifies the אֲדֹנִי, 'my lord', in Ps. 110:1 with Saul.[1] However, Jews in the Second Temple period would probably find the patriarch *Abraham* to be a more appropriate candidate for enjoying the honour of being called 'my lord' by David (see Ps. 110:1). Second Temple period readers, reading the biblical history consecutively beginning with the Torah and continuing through the Neviʾim (including the story about David's rise to power), probably would find Abraham to be a more important figure than Saul. From a canon-historical point of view, such a reading must have been possible in, at least, the second half of the Second Temple period. The general impression given by the Torah and Neviʾim that Abraham is by far more important than Saul may have been supported by yet another observation of Second Temple period readers. In the patriarchal narratives, the noun אָדֹון/אָדֹן is most frequently used about Abraham, only once about Isaac, and never about Jacob.[2]

If Genesis 14* and Psalm 110 were read as two versions of the same event already before the ME was composed and interpolated into Genesis 14*, I must account for why such an intertextual reading could potentially take place before a common mention of the two words מַלְכִּי־צֶדֶק could have motivated it.

1　For references, see Str–B 4, 452–65 (456).

2　*Abraham*: Gen. 18 (v. 12, by Sarah) and 24 (several times by his servant). In Gen 24:65 *Isaac* is called אֲדֹנִי (by Abraham's servant). Moreover, in the Joseph novella *Joseph* is called lord several times: Gen. 42:10, 30, 33; 43:20; 44:8, 16, 18, 19, 20, 22, 24, 33 (by his brothers); Gen. 44:5 (by his steward); Gen. 45:8, 9 (by himself/Yahweh?); Gen. 47:18, 25 (by the Egyptians).

14.2 *Leerstellen* in Genesis 14* vis-à-vis Psalm 110

In the table below, I will point out several resemblances between the two texts that may have been recognized by a reader before the ME was composed and interpolated. There are words and motifs that are shared by both texts. Many *dramatis personae*, words, and events in the one text find a correspondence in the other:

Psalm 110 Verse	Possible correspondence	Genesis 14* (except vv. 18–20) Verse
1aβ אֲדֹנִי	≈	13ff. אַבְרָם הָעִבְרִי
1b, 2aβ, 4aα אֲדֹנָי; יְהוָה		∅[3]
1bα אֹיְבֶיךָ	≈	1, 5–7, 17 אַרְיוֹךְ, אַמְרָפֶל, תִּדְעָל and כְּדָרְלָעֹמֶר
2aβ מִצִּיּוֹן		∅
2a.b *War terminology* (רְדֵה; מַטֵּה־עֻזְּךָ)	≈	14–17, 21–22 *War terminology* (נכה; רדף; [עַד])
3aα עַמְּךָ	≈	14, 22 חֲנִיכָיו יְלִידֵי בֵיתוֹ (v. 14), הָאֲנָשִׁים אֲשֶׁר הָלְכוּ אִתִּי עָנֵר אֶשְׁכֹּל וּמַמְרֵא (v. 22)
3aβ יַלְדֻתֶיךָ	≈	14 חֲנִיכָיו יְלִידֵי בֵיתוֹ
4aβ אַתָּה־כֹהֵן לְעוֹלָם עַל־דִּבְרָתִי מַלְכִּי־צֶדֶק ('You [read: Abraham] are priest...')		∅
5bβ מְלָכִים	≈	17 כְּדָר־לָעֹמֶר וְאֶת־הַמְּלָכִים אֲשֶׁר אִתּוֹ
5a.b *War terminology* (יוֹם־אַפּוֹ; מחץ)	≈	14–15 *War terminology* (נכה; רדף [עַד])
6aα יָדִין	≈	14bβ עַד־דָּן[4]

---

3   Without the Melchizedek episode, the war narrative in Genesis 14* is 'profane', i.e., Abram's pursuit is not depicted as a holy war.

4   There is consonance and assonance between יָדִין (Ps. 110:6) and דָּן (Gen. 14:14). In addition, the possibility should be considered that דָּן in the phrase עַד־דָּן started

6aα	גּוֹיִם	≈	1bβ,	וַתִּדְעָל מֶלֶךְ גּוֹיִם
			14–15,	(v. 1bβ),
			17	כְּדָר־לָעֹמֶר וְאֶת־הַמְּלָכִים
				אֲשֶׁר אִתּוֹ (v. 17a)
7a.b	*Drinking motif,*		∅	
	elevation of head			

The tabular presentation of the words and motifs that may have caused the assumed intertextual reading of Psalm 110 and Genesis 14* also demonstrates that readers may have recognized a surplus of information in Psalm 110 vis-à-vis Genesis 14*. In the table above, the symbol ∅ is used in the right column to indicate the pieces of information that appear to be lacking in Genesis 14* vis-à-vis a historiographical, 'Abrahamic' reading of Psalm 110. In other words, the symbol ∅ indicates the assumed *Leerstellen* one could locate in Genesis 14* when the narrative was read intertextually with Psalm 110.

In the table above, I have identified four cases of surplus information in Psalm 110 vis-à-vis Genesis 14*. The first case is the psalm's notion of Yahweh as active subject of the acts of war (Ps. 110:1bα, 2aβ, 5bα, 6bα). Although the person spoken to in the psalm seems to be participating (see Ps. 110:2b רְדֵה בְּקֶרֶב אֹיְבֶיךָ, 'rule in the midst of your enemies!'), it is nonetheless Yahweh who is the real agent. In contrast, in Genesis 14* the contending parties are, on the one side, the patriarch and, on the other, the four kings (see Gen. 14:14–15).

The second case of surplus information in Psalm 110 vis-à-vis Genesis 14* is the phrase מִצִּיּוֹן, 'from Zion' (Ps. 110:2aβ). In Psalm 110, Zion is the place from which Yahweh comes to provide aid for the benefit of the person spoken to (who, again, was understood to be Abraham). On the contrary, in Genesis 14* there are no traces of Zion.

The third case of surplus information consists of a whole clause, namely, Ps. 110:4. In this particular verse, a person called 'you' is granted an everlasting priesthood. Above, I have discussed what its meaning possibly was in the monarchic period.[5] At that time, the

---

(erroneously) being interpreted as a verb: 'until he [= Abram] executed judgment'. This would be the meaning, given that דָּן was read as a finite verb (a *qatal* form of the root דין) and not a toponym. Similarly constructed phrases with עַד followed by a finite verb are found in Josh. 2:22, עַד־שָׁבוּ הָרֹדְפִים 'until the pursuers returned'; Ps. 110:1, עַד־אָשִׁית 'until I put'; Prov. 8:26, עַד־לֹא עָשָׂה 'until he not made' meaning 'before he had made', etc.

5   See chapter 10, Psalm 110.

prepositional phrase עַל־דִּבְרָתִי probably had a causal meaning. Moreover, the two words מַלְכִּי־צֶדֶק were probably, from the outset, common
nouns that either constituted a noun phrase or (more probably) a nominal clause. However, no matter what the original, preexilic meaning
of the puzzling half-verse was in the monarchic period, one should
nevertheless expect that a Jew reading the psalm in the Second Temple
period would have identified the person referred to as 'you' in Ps. 110:4
with the person whom David, the psalm speaker, called אֲדֹנִי 'my lord'
in Ps. 110:1. In other words, when Ps. 110:4 is read along the lines noted
above, then it is the patriarch Abraham who would have been the one
who was granted priesthood in the clause אַתָּה־כֹהֵן לְעוֹלָם, 'You are a priest
forever. . .'.[6]

A fourth case of surplus information in Psalm 110 vis-à-vis Genesis
14* is found in the concluding verse of the psalm (Ps. 110:7). In this enigmatic verse, someone drinks (water?) מִנַּחַל בַּדֶּרֶךְ, 'from the wadi by the
road', and because of this he raises his (?) head.[7]

14.3 Hypothesis: The ME Was Composed to Fill Out the *Leerstellen* in Genesis 14*

In other words, the historiographical 'Abrahamic' reading of Psalm 110
as a poetic version of the narrative found in Genesis 14* about Abram's
war leaves Genesis 14* with certain *Leerstellen* vis-à-vis the psalm. I propose that the author of the ME composed it in order to fill out these
Leerstellen. For, in Genesis 14*, Yahweh fails to appear as the real subject
of the war and no reference to Zion is found. Moreover, in Genesis 14*,
no parallel to the enigmatic verse Ps. 110:4 is evident. Genesis 14* does
not report any installation of Abraham to priesthood as Ps. 110:4 would
imply when interpreted as 'Abrahamic',[8] nor does it offer anything that
reminds one of the cryptic clause עַל־דִּבְרָתִי מַלְכִּי־צֶדֶק. In addition, Ps. 110:7
does not have any parallel in Genesis 14*.

---

6   See 14.6.1, Excursus: Abraham, a Priest According to the ME?
7   The ME does not tell whose head it is. Moreover, it is difficult to determine the iden-
     tity of the grammatical subject in Ps. 110:7. See 10.1, The Characters Speaking and
     Spoken to in the Psalm.
8   See 13.1, The 'Abrahamic' Interpretation of Psalm 110 and Other Cases of Early Inter-
     textual Readings of Genesis 14 and Psalm 110.

14.4 First Case of Psalm Surplus Crystallizing in the ME

Most of the surplus of Psalm 110 vis-à-vis Genesis 14* seems to crystallize in the ME. The first case of crystallization is that the psalm's holy war motif is evident in the interpolated ME. The blessing put in the mouth of the priest-king Melchizedek interprets Abram's victory as a divine act. This is evident from the relative clause in the last blessing: 'Blessed be El Elyon, *who has delivered your enemies into your hand!*' (Gen. 14:20a). The clause אֲשֶׁר־מִגֵּן צָרֶיךָ בְּיָדֶךָ resembles the proclamation of the ban so often found in the historical books of the Bible.[9]

14.5 Second Case of Psalm Surplus Crystallizing in the ME

The second case of crystallization is that Yahweh's abode in Zion (see Ps. 110:2) reoccurs in the mention of 'Salem' (thus the traditional rendering of שָׁלֵם) in the ME. Here, it is not necessary to discuss the historical identity of the place Salem.[10] It suffices to say that the place names 'Salem' and 'Zion' occur in parallelism in Ps. 76:3 (Eng. trans., 76:2). The parallelism shows that it has been possible to use them as alternative designations for the same place.

14.6 Third Case of Psalm Surplus Crystallizing in the ME

The third case is that the whole verse Ps. 110:4 crystallizes in the ME. The most obvious is of course the common occurrence of the two words מַלְכִּי־צֶדֶק. Whereas above I have suggested that they originally functioned as appellatives in Ps. 110:4b,[11] they no doubt function as the personal name Melchizedek in Gen. 14:18a. Moreover, if we assume that it was possible for Second Temple period readers to interpret Psalm 110 as Abrahamic, as argued above,[12] Ps. 110:4a was probably understood as

---

9   For a list, see von Rad, *Der Heilige Krieg im alten Israel*, 7–8.
10   See, e.g., John A. Emerton, 'The Site of Salem, the City of Melchizedek (Genesis XIV 18)', in *Studies in the Pentateuch* (ed. John A. Emerton; VTSup 41, Leiden: E. J. Brill, 1990), 45–71; and Aschim, 'Melchizedek and Levi', 773–88 (783–84).
11   See 12.6, The Two Words מַלְכִּי־צֶדֶק in Psalm 110.4b.
12   See 13.1, The 'Abrahamic' Interpretation of Psalm 110 and Other Cases of Early Intertextual Readings of Genesis 14 and Psalm 110.

a priestly installation of Abraham: 'You [read: Abraham] are a priest forever'. My proposal is that the ME in fact describes Abram as priest because *he* [*sic*] receives tithes from Melchizedek.

14.6.1 Excursus: Abraham, a Priest According to the ME?

Now, the literal reading of Gen. 14:20b מִכֹּל מַעֲשֵׂר לוֹ וַיִּתֶּן, 'And he [= Melchizedek] gave him [= Abram] a tithe of everything', needs an explanation because it contradicts the majority reading of this half verse. Most Bible translations and exegetes identify the donor in this action with Abram. Moreover, some translations even articulate this view by inserting the name Abram as the subject. For instance, the NRSV reads, 'And Abram [*sic*] gave him one tenth of everything'.

However, contrary to this identification, which is based on an a priori understanding of the events taking place, the most natural reading is to follow the Hebrew text, which merely says, 'And he gave . . .'. In my opinion, it is likely that one should identify the donor with Melchizedek and the receiver with Abram. The reason for this is that Melchizedek is also the subject of the verbal actions, that is, the blessing, in the two preceding verses. Because no shift of grammatical subject is indicated between vv. 18–19 on the one hand and v. 20a on the other, the most natural reading is that Melchizedek, in the capacity of being the last-mentioned person, also is the subject of וַיִּתֶּן, 'and he gave'.[13]

Having argued that Melchizedek is the subject and Abram the receiver of the tithing in Gen. 14:20, it can be argued that the ME demonstrates that Abram is a priest עַל־דִּבְרָתִי מַלְכִּי־צֶדֶק in the meaning 'because of Melchizedek'. In other words, Melchizedek's tithing to Abram in the ME fills a *Leerstelle* in Genesis 14* that becomes evident as soon as the narrative is intertextually related to Psalm 110. Abram is a priest because of Melchizedek, that is, because Melchizedek blesses him and, above all, gives him a tithe.[14]

---

13   MT Gen. 14:20bβ מִכֹּל מַעֲשֵׂר לוֹ וַיִּתֶּן is supported by the LXX, the Vulgate, the Peshitta, *Targ. Onq.* and *Targ. Neof.* However, it contradicts a rendering found already in 1Q20 22:17: 'He gave him a tithe of all the wealth of the king of Elam and his allies'. According to the *Genesis Apocryphon*, Abraham must be the one who gives. A similar understanding is evident in *Targ. Ps.-J.*: 'And he gave him a tithe of all that he had brought back'.

14   Above, I have argued that the *hapax legomenon* עַל־דִּבְרָתִי originally had a causal (and not modal!) meaning: 'because of', 'for the sake of'. See 12.5.2, The Semantics of עַל־דִּבְרָתִי.

In the following I will discuss why one can argue that Melchizedek's tithing to Abram in the context of Second Temple period theology furnishes the latter with priestly dignity.

In the Second Temple period, the receiving of the tithes was a priestly prerogative. However, this prerogative was the result of a historical development of the theology of the tithes in Israel. In the monarchic period, kings were probably entitled to levy tithes, at least according to Samuel's warning against the people of Israel's demand for a king (see 1 Sam. 8:15, 17). Moreover, tithes were not brought exclusively to Jerusalem. Tithes were carried to both Bethel and Gilgal (see Gen. 28:22 and Amos 4:4), that is, to the clergy there. Further, in Deuteronomy two new features are probably evident vis-à-vis earlier texts. First, the tithes seem to have been a philanthropic phenomenon. It is above all the *persona miserae* who benefit from it, such as Levites, aliens, orphans, and widows (Deut. 26:12). Second, somehow the giving of the tithes was centralized to one sanctuary, the place chosen by the LORD (see Deut. 12:6, 11, 17; 14:22–23, 26, 28). Nevertheless, it is evident from all the texts that date to the Second Temple period that the receiving of tithes was clearly understood to be a priestly prerogative.[15] Moreover, the close association of the right to receive tithes and the status as priest seems confirmed in 4Q213b (4Q Aramaic Levi^c).

In light of this, then, it is plausible that Second Temple Jews could associate Abram with the priesthood when they read about his receiving of tithes. Not only did someone who already was called priest (according to the ME, *Melchizedek*, who was priest of El Elyon) give a tithe to the patriarch. What is more, it all took place close to Salem, which in the Second Temple period may have been identified with Jerusalem (see Ps. 76:3 [Eng. trans., 76:2]).

In other words, when Psalm 110 is read as Abrahamic, Abraham turns out to be a priest, according to the enigmatic clauses in Ps. 110:4. This piece of information does not have any parallel in Genesis 14*. However, according to the secondary ME, it can be argued that Abram is a priest 'because of Melchizedek', that is, because Melchizedek gives him a tithe. The idea of Abram's priesthood is attested in *b. Ned.* 32b mentioned

---

15 According to Hendrik Jagersma, the biblical texts from the postexilic period are Lev. 27:30ff.; Num. 18:21, 24, 26, 28; Mal. 3:8, 10; Neh. 10:37–38, 12:44, 13:5, 12; 2 Chr. 31:5–6, 12); see Jagersma, 'The Tithes in the Old Testament', *OTS* 21 (1981): 119–22. In addition, there are relevant texts such as Tob. 1:6–8; Judith 11:13; Sir. 7:31; *Jub.* 13:25–27; 32:10–15. Moreover, perhaps also relevant as historical sources for the Second Temple period are later texts such as *Ma'as.* 1:1 and *Yeb.* 86b. The latter text explains why the Levites lost the right to receive tithes: They hesitated in returning from Babylon (see Ezra 2:40; 8:15–20).

above and other rabbinic texts, too. In all cases, Ps. 110:4 is understood
to be addressed *to Abram* (*Gen. R.* 46:5 [in a comment on Genesis 17, discussing the circumcision], 55:6 [in a comment on the 'binding of Isaac',
Genesis 22], and *Lev. R.* 25:6).

Somewhere, sometime, and somehow on the trajectory *from* the originally preexilic Psalm 110 *to* the postexilic and interpolated ME, the two
words מַלְכִּי־צֶדֶק were subject to a transformation. Whereas the two words
originally were probably common nouns in the psalm, they have been
turned into a personal name in the ME. This phenomenon, which I tentatively call 'personification', will be discussed below.[16] However, if my
assumption concerning the original meaning of מַלְכִּי־צֶדֶק should be wrong
after all and that מַלְכִּי־צֶדֶק has been a personal name in Ps. 110:4 from the
outset, then it could be argued that the ME has attached a legendary
biography to it.

14.7 A Possible Fourth Case of Psalm
Surplus Crystallizing in the ME

There is possibly a fourth instance of surplus material from Psalm 110
that may have been crystallized in the interpolated ME. Psalm 110:7, a
verse not easily integrated into the psalm context, reads, 'He drinks from
the wadi by the road. Therefore he lifts up [his?] head'. This verse, or at
least the verse's drinking motif, may recur in the drinking of wine in
Gen. 14:18a ('Melchizedek . . . brought out bread and wine'). However,
the only thing in common is the drinking. Therefore, I consider this case
to be much weaker that the other three discussed above.

---

16   See chapter 15, What Has Happened to the Words מַלְכִּי־צֶדֶק on the Way from Psalm 110
     to the Melchizedek Episode?

15. What Has Happened to the Words מַלְכִּי־צֶדֶק on the Way from Psalm 110 to the Melchizedek Episode?

I have argued above for the possibility that Yahweh's oracle in Ps. 110:4 originally (i.e., in the monarchic period) meant something like the following:[1]

> Yahweh has sworn and will not repent:
> 'You are a priest forever.
> For my sake (עַל־דִּבְרָתִי) *my king is loyal* (מַלְכִּי־צֶדֶק)'.

According to the model I have proposed of how the ME came into being, מַלְכִּי־צֶדֶק has been subject to a transfer of its semantic value: the words מַלְכִּי־צֶדֶק in Ps. 110:4b have been personified to become the personal name Melchizedek. In the following, I will point out analogies to the phenomenon of personification.[2]

Nevertheless, although there are analogical cases where appellatives have been personified, I cannot completely rule out the possibility that מַלְכִּי־צֶדֶק was a personal name (Melchizedek) in Psalm 110 from the outset (i.e., in the monarchic period). Given that the ME is an interpolation from the Second Temple period, then Ps. 110:4 is the only source from the monarchic period referring to a person with this name. In this case, the ME reflects the creation of a legendary biography such as happens in the Enoch literature.[3]

15.1 Personification

In the case of a personification, there is a transfer of the semantic value; when a common noun is personified, the noun possesses characteristics typical of a personal being. Generally speaking, when a concept is treated as if it were an individual being, it has been personified.

---

1   See 12.7, Psalm 110:4: Synthesis and Conclusion.
2   See 15.1, Personification.
3   See 15.2, Alternative Explanation: Creation of Legendary Biographies and New Narrative Roles.

Personification is a phenomenon found in both biblical and — probably more often — in Jewish extrabiblical literature from the Second Temple period. For instance, in Ps. 85:11 [Eng. trans., 85:10], steadfast love (חֶסֶד) and faithfulness (אֱמֶת) *meet*, and righteousness (צֶדֶק) and peace (שָׁלוֹם) *kiss* each other. Moreover, in Job 28:22, the underworld (אֲבַדּוֹן) and death (מָוֶת) *speak*.[4] In these and other cases it could be argued that the personification simply functions as a figure of speech, that is, a kind of metaphor. Then we only have to deal with a poetic personification. However, in other cases the sources do not allow us to content ourselves with speaking about a poetic speech figure. This is the case with חָכְמָה as the personal being Lady Wisdom in Proverbs 8. Not only does she claim to be the first that Yahweh acquired — possibly created[5] — (Prov. 8:22). In addition, she claims she was his coworker when he created the world.[6] The personification of חָכְמָה is further developed in Sirach 24, a text apparently composed with the monologue of Lady Wisdom in Proverbs 8 in mind. Here, Lady Wisdom is a member of the assembly of the Most High (Sir. 24:2) and is eventually identified with the Torah (Sir. 24:23).[7]

Another example of an appellative that has been transformed into a personal name is הַשָּׂטָן, 'the accuser/slanderer/adversary', and שָׂטָן with the meaning 'Satan'. In the Bible, both terrestrial and celestial beings are called הַשָּׂטָן. In 1 Sam. 29:4, David is called שָׂטָן by the Philistine commander. In 2 Sam. 19:23, David accuses the sons of Zeruiah of being שָׂטָן to him. In these and other cases as well, שָׂטָן designates a terrestrial opponent.[8]

Moreover, there are several texts in the Hebrew Bible where a celestial being is called שָׂטָן. With a single exception, the noun שָׂטָן is determined in all of these cases. In Num. 22:22, 32, an angel of Yahweh (מַלְאַךְ יְהוָה) stands on the road לְשָׂטָן, 'as adversary' (NRSV), against Balaam. Here, it is evident that being שָׂטָן is an occasional task for the angel of Yahweh. The task was caused by Balaam's action and Yahweh's subsequent wrath. More-

---

4   See also Mark E. Biddle, 'The Figure of Lady Jerusalem: Identification, Deification and Personification of Cities in the Ancient Near East', in *The Biblical Canon in Comparative Perspective* (ed. K. Lawson Younger, William W. Hallo, and Bernard Frank Batto; Scripture in Context 4; Ancient Near Eastern Texts and Studies 11; Lewiston, NY: Edwin Mellen, 1991), 173–94.

5   The verb קנה can mean both; see *HALOT* 3, *s.v.* קנה, 1111–13. However, Bruce Vawter argues that קֹנֵה שָׁמַיִם וָאָרֶץ simply acknowledges the *lordship* of the deity El Elyon, as reflected in the *Genesis Apocryphon*'s rendition of the phrase in Aramaic by the noun מרה 'lord' (1Q20 22:16). See Vawter, 'Yahweh: Lord of the Heavens and the Earth', *CBQ* 48 (1986): 461–67 (463–64).

6   See Roland E. Murphy, 'Wisdom in the OT', *ABD* 6:920–31.

7   See also Bar. 3:9–4:4; and 4Q525 2 II.2–8.

8   See 1 Kgs. 5:17; 11:14, 23, 25; and probably Ps. 109, where שָׂטָן stands in parallelism with רָשָׁע, 'wicked man'.

over, the frame narrative of the book of Job is located in Yahweh's court assembly. Here, the sons of God (בְּנֵי הָאֱלֹהִים) presented themselves before Yahweh. One of the sons of God is referred to as הַשָּׂטָן (Job 1:6–9, 12; 2:1–7). With Yahweh's explicit approbation, the son called הַשָּׂטָן causes one tragedy after another to affect Job before Job himself is inflicted with loathsome sores. Furthermore, in Zechariah's fourth vision the prophet sees the high priest Joshua standing before an angel of Yahweh and with an additional being present: וְהַשָּׂטָן עֹמֵד עַל־יְמִינוֹ לְשִׂטְנוֹ, 'and הַשָּׂטָן was standing on his right side to accuse/slander him/be his adversary'. Finally, in 1 Chr. 21:1 a being referred to by the *undetermined* noun שָׂטָן incites David to count Israel. In the parallel account in 2 Sam. 24:1, which probably is the Chronicler's *Vorlage*, it is *Yahweh's wrath* that incites David to count the people.

It has long been suggested that the undetermined noun שָׂטָן in 1 Chr. 21:1 is an example of an originally common name that has secondarily assumed the character of a proper name.[9] This is, however, not necessarily the case, as one could also translate the clause in 1 Chr. 21:1 'and a *śāṭān* [meaning: 'slanderer' or 'accuser'] stood up against . . .'.[10] Whatever the correct opinion might be, the phrase שָׂטָן appears to function as a *person* in extrabiblical literature (e.g., Sir. 21:27; *1 En.* 53:3; perhaps *Jub.* 10:11; 23:29; and *T. Mos.* 10:1).

Additional examples of names that probably are personified nouns are Mastema and Adam. The chief of the spirits is called Mastema in *Jubilees* 10:7 (here identified with Satan); 11:5; 19:28; 1QM 13:11; and CD 16:5. The name is probably from the abstract noun מַשְׂטֵמָה ('persecution') found only in Hos. 9:7–8.[11] Eventually, in the creation narratives in Genesis 1–5, אָדָם is used both as a common noun meaning 'human being, mankind' (e.g., Gen. 1:26) and as the personal name Adam (e.g., 4:25; Gen. 5:1a, 3–5). As the personal name of the first forefather אָדָם/Adam, it is used in 1 Chr. 1:1, Hos. 6:7; Job. 31:33; Deut. 4:32; and Sir. 49:16.[12]

15.2 Alternative Explanation: Creation of Legendary Biographies and New Narrative Roles

If the hypothesis I have put forward regarding the transformation of the two words מַלְכִּי־צֶדֶק found in Ps. 110:4b into the personal name Melchizedek in the ME should turn out to be incorrect, one can still explain what takes

---

9   So already GKC, § 125f./p. 402.
10   So Victor P. Hamilton, 'Satan', *ABD* 5:985–89.
11   See *HALOT* 2, *s.v.* מַשְׂטֵמָה, 640–41.
12   See, e.g., Howard N. Wallace, 'Adam', *ABD* 1:62–64.

place in the ME on the basis of Second Temple period biblical hermeneutics. In this case, Psalm 110 is still the earlier text. Therefore, the mention of Melchizedek in the ME represents a later reference. If this is correct, the ME has secondarily furnished with fictional biographical data the marginal character Melchizedek known only from Psalm 110.

Enoch, son of Jared, probably represents an analogy to the phenomenon of a marginal biblical character that has attracted disproportionately much interest in postbiblical literature. In Gen. 5:18–24, we learn that he had the son Methuselah at the age of sixty-five, that he had other children, and that he 'walked with God after the birth of Methuselah three hundred years'. Quite exceptional is what we read in v. 24: 'Enoch walked with הָאֱלֹהִים. And he was no more, because אֱלֹהִים took him'. In the book of *Jubilees*, this short notice has been expanded with a story about his stay in heaven (*Jub.* 4:16–26). Being credited as the first one to learn writing and also the first one to write 'testimonies', Enoch is reported to have experienced a unique communication with the angels of God 'for six jubilees of year' as the latter showed him everything that is on earth and in the heavens, the dominion of the sun (*Jub.* 4:21–22). An attempt to close a gap in the Pentateuch is also present in the corpus of literature ascribed to Enoch, son of Jared.[13] *First (Ethiopic) Enoch* opens with Enoch saying, '(This is) a holy vision from the heavens which the angels showed me. . .' (*1 En.* 1:2), a passage that probably fills out the clause 'אֱלֹהִים took him' (Gen. 5:24). The Bible allows for the possibility that Enoch did not have a normal death (see Heb. 11:5). On the contrary, God or the angels—depending on the meaning of (הָ)אֱלֹהִים—took him to heaven. Likewise, the longer version of *2 (Slavonic) Enoch* opens with the phrase 'The story of Enoch: how the LORD took him to heaven'.[14] Finally, the tradition about Enoch's unique communication with God's angels is probably also reflected in the *Genesis Apocryphon*.[15]

Also relevant is probably עֲזָאזֵל, a term found in the Hebrew Bible only in Leviticus 16. Here, the meaning of the term is far from clear. According to David P. Wright,[16] four main interpretations—both modern and

13 See, e.g., Sidnie White Crawford, 'The Use of the Pentateuch in the *Temple Scroll* and the *Damascus Document* in the Second Century B.C.E.', in *The Pentateuch as Torah: New Models for Understanding Its Promulgation and Acceptance* (ed. Gary N. Knoppers and Bernhard M. Levinson; Winona Lake, IN: Eisenbrauns, 2007), 301–17 (306).

14 *2 En.* 1:1 translated by F. I. Andersen in *OTP* 1.

15 See 1Q20 2:20b–21a: 'For he (Enoch) is beloved and a fa[vourite of God, and with the Holy Ones] is his lot apportioned; and they make everything known to him'. The restored noun קדישׁיא, 'Holy Ones' (thus both Fitzmyer, *The Genesis Apocryphon of Qumran Cave 1 [1Q20]*, and Florentino García Martínez and Eibert J. C. Tigchelaar, eds., *The Dead Sea Scrolls Study Edition* on the other) must refer to the angels.

16 David P. Wright, 'Azazel', *ABD* 1:536–37.

ancient—are attested. According to one interpretation, the term is a geographical designation meaning 'precipitous place' or 'rugged cliff'.[17] A
second—and modern—interpretation is that עֲזָאזֵל is an abstract noun
meaning 'entire removal'.[18] A third interpretation is that עֲזָאזֵל is a compound made by עֵז, 'goat', and אָזֵל, a participle of a verb meaning 'go
away'.[19] According to a fourth interpretation, already attested in the late
Second Temple period, עֲזָאזֵל is a proper name designating a personal
being, namely, the demon Azazel.[20]

It is beyond the scope of the discussion here to determine which
of the four main interpretations understands the 'original meaning' of
Leviticus 16 most correctly. Nevertheless, Jewish literature from the Second Temple period demonstrates an interest in a demon Azazel *not pro-
portional* to the number of appearances of the phrase עֲזָאזֵל in the Hebrew
Bible. Whereas עֲזָאזֵל is found only four times in the Bible—and that in a
single chapter—Azazel is frequently mentioned in the pseudepigrapha,[21]
in Qumran literature,[22] and in rabbinic literature. In extrabiblical texts,
he is a fallen archangel who has become the archdemon.

If the phrase עֲזָאזֵל is a name from the outset, then the extrabiblical interest attached to him illustrates that a legendary biography has
been created for him. In Leviticus 16, he has no biography, whereas he
appears as an archdemon in the history of reception. However, if the
phrase עֲזָאזֵל originally did *not* function as a personal name in Leviticus
16, but instead was a common noun (or a term that combines two common nouns), then the extrabiblical literature provides us with additional
examples of what I refer to as personification (see 15.1, Personification).

There are also examples in Jewish extrabiblical literature where the
biblical stories have been legendarily reshaped through the adding of
new roles. For instance, in the *Genesis Apocryphon's* version of the story
about Abram and Sarai in Egypt, two *dramatis personae* appear who are
not found in the biblical account: Hyrcanus, a minister of Pharaoh, and

---

17　According to Wright, 'Azazel', *ABD* 1:536–37, the geographical interpretation is found
　　in *Sifra*, Aḥare Mot 2:8; and *Tg. Ps.-J.* Lev. 16:10, 22.
18　See BDB, *s.v.* עֲזָאזֵל, 736.
19　This understanding is in part reflected in the LXX renderings derived from the verb
　　ἀποπέμπω, 'send away' (LXX Lev. 16:8, 10) and ἄφεσις 'dismissal'. Moreover, it is sup-
　　ported by the existence of an Arabic root ġzl, 'to remove'. It is also reflected in the
　　English term 'scapegoat'. 'Scape' is short for 'escape'; see Walter W. Skeat, *A Concise
　　Etymological Dictionary of the English Language* (Oxford: Clarendon, 1882).
20　This interpretation is evident from, e.g., *1 En.* 8:1; 9:6; 10:4–8; 13:1; cf. 54:5–6; 55:4; 69:2;
　　Apoc. Abr. 13:6–14; 14:4–6; 20:5–7; 22:5; 23:11; 29:6–7; 31:5.
21　See, e.g., *1 En.* 6–13; *T. Sol.* 7:7 ('Azael' probably = 'Azazel'); *Apoc. Abr.* 13:6–14; 14:4–6;
　　20:5–7; 22:5; 23:11; 29:6–7; 31:5.
22　See, e.g., 11Q19–20 (*Temple Scroll*) 26:4, 13: עזאזל > עזזאל.

Lot, Abram's nephew (1Q20 19:10–20:32; cf. Gen. 12:10–20). Moreover, it is also possible to observe another example of the adding of new roles by comparing the MT version of the story of Saul's birth and dedication with its LXX counterpart. Whereas MT 1 Sam. 1:14 reads וַיֹּאמֶר אֵלֶיהָ עֵלִי, 'And Eli said to her . . .', the LXX adds an additional character: καὶ εἶπεν αὐτῇ τὸ παιδάριον Ἡλί 'And the *servant* of Eli said to her . . .'.[23]

15.3 Evaluation: Personification or the (Secondary) Creation of a Legendary Biography?

The weakness of both the idea of personification and that of creation of a legendary biography is the quality and amount of the textual evidence. After all, the way Ps. 110:4 actually was read and comprehended around the time it presumably was composed (i.e., probably in the preexilic period) suffers from a lack of control. Modern interpreters do not have access to the author of Psalm 110, who potentially could have clarified what he meant when using the words מַלְכִּי־צֶדֶק.

One of the arguments against the traditional view that מַלְכִּי־צֶדֶק in Ps. 110:4 is a personal name is an *ex nihilo* argument; elsewhere in the biblical material, a person with the name Melchizedek is mentioned only in Gen. 14:18–20 (= ME). But, as I have argued above, the ME is probably dependent on Psalm 110 and stems from a much later period. For those reasons, the ME does not carry any weight as to what the meaning of מַלְכִּי־צֶדֶק in Ps. 110:4 was in the monarchic period. Therefore, the fact that this person is not mentioned elsewhere in the early sources speaks against the view that Ps. 110:4 refers to a person called Melchizedek.

On the other hand, the lack of any reference to an assumed person called Melchizedek outside Psalm 110 and the ME, which is dependent on the former source, does not exclude entirely the possibility that מַלְכִּי־צֶדֶק in Psalm 110 at the outset was meant as a personal name.

Taking all the circumstances discussed previously into consideration,[24] I nevertheless am inclined to give preponderance to personification, that is, that the personal name Melchizedek evident in the ME is the result

---

23   The texts mentioned are discussed by Alexander Rofé, 'The Methods of Late Biblical Scribes as Evidenced by the Septuagint Compared with the Other Textual Witnesses', in *Tehillah le-Moshe: Biblical and Judaic Studies in Honor of Moshe Greenberg* (ed. Mordechai Cogan, Barry L. Eichler, and Jeffrey H. Tigay; Winona Lake, IN: Eisenbrauns, 1997), 259–70 (266). According to him, the creation of new roles is a characteristic *aggadic* feature.

24   See, in particular, 12.6, The Two Words מַלְכִּי־צֶדֶק in Psalm 110:4b.

of a personification of the words מַלְכִּי־צֶדֶק found in Ps. 110:4. Although it is speculative to conjecture about exactly when the words מַלְכִּי־צֶדֶק from Psalm 110 became personified, I consider it most probable that it happened in connection with the very composition and interpolation of the ME. The alternative is that the words מַלְכִּי־צֶדֶק from Psalm 110 were personified *after* the composition of Psalm 110 but *before* the composition of the ME. However, against this position one could put forward the same arguments as against tradition history, that it is beyond transparency and control.

15.4 Assimilation—In the Form of an Aggadah?

The model I have proposed for explaining how and why the ME was composed implies that the interpolation was caused by a desire to assimilate two biblical texts. The interpolator understood Psalm 110 as a poetic version of Abram's war with the four kings as narrated in Genesis 14*. The intertextual reading resulted in the existence of additional information in Psalm 110 vis-à-vis Genesis 14*. The ME, then, is the result of an attempt to smooth out the tension between these two texts. The author of the ME used the psalm's surplus information as 'textual raw material' when he composed the ME.

The best technical term for describing the proposed development behind the ME is probably the already frequently used term 'assimilation'. However, if one dares to point out a term drawn from the vocabulary of Jewish hermeneutics, then I am inclined to characterize the ME as an early example of *aggadic exegesis*[25] that has found its way into the very text it interprets, namely, Genesis 14*. Because the ME does not seem to prescribe for the reader how he should conduct his life, it is *not* halakhic.[26] On the contrary, it appears to be a piece of nonbehavioural exegesis. This observation, together with the observation that it all takes place in a narrative, nonlegal text corpus, suggests that the ME is an early example of an *aggadah* that has found its way into the very text it comments on, namely, Genesis 14*.

---

25 By 'aggadic exegesis' I mean exegesis with a nonbehavioural purpose. Its typical antithesis is halakhic exegesis, which is behavioural and aims at prescribing how to behave. See, e.g., Burton L. Visotzky, 'Hermeneutics, Early Rabbinic', *ABD* 3:154–55.

26 This is the implication of a literal reading of, in particular, Gen. 14:20b. If we proceed from the premise that it is Melchizedek who gives tithes to Abram and not vice versa, then it does not make sense to speak of Abram's giving of the tithes to the priest in (Jeru-)Salem as a paradigm for subsequent generations. See 14.6.1, Excursus: Abraham, a Priest According to the ME?

16. The Date of the Melchizedek Episode

I have already argued that the date of composition of the ME and the date of its interpolation into Genesis 14* coincide. Consequently, the date of composition of Genesis 14* serves as *terminus a quo* for the date of composition *and* the date of interpolation of the ME. However, in terms of actual chronology I have not been able to date Genesis 14* more precisely than to either the Persian or the early Hellenistic period.[1]

Yet, there are several textual witnesses from the last centuries BCE that either indirectly or directly reveal knowledge of the ME. Indirectly, the Hebrew *Melchizedek* scroll from Qumran (11Q13) might reflect the ME—given, of course, that it is the result of creative exegesis of both Genesis 14 (presumably containing the ME) and Psalm 110.[2] Scholars disagree about the exact date of the scroll. Whereas A. S. van der Woude dates it to the first half of the first century CE,[3] Paul J. Kobelski argues for a somewhat earlier date, the second half of the first century BCE.[4]

The pseudepigraphic book of *Jubilees*, however, may indirectly reflect knowledge of the ME. This reflection is not in the passage where one would expect it, namely, in the rewritten account of Abram's war in Genesis 14 (*Jub.* 13:22–29). Rather, *Jubilees* has a law of the tithe (*Jub.* 13:25b–27). Moreover, it has been proposed that the description of Levi's elevation to priesthood (*Jub.* 32:1) is formulated by means of phraseology drawn from the two Bible texts that mention Melchizedek, that is, the ME and Psalm 110.[5] Although the textual history of *Jubilees* is complicated (the only surviving virtually complete text is in Geez, which presumably is a translation from Greek; the Greek version is for its part assumed to be a translation of a Hebrew original), scholars nevertheless

---

1 See 8.6, Preliminary Conclusion and Point of Departure: The ME—A Doubly Late Interpolation.
2 See 13.1, The 'Abrahamic' Interpretation of Psalm 110 and Other Cases of Early Intertextual Readings of Genesis 14 and Psalm 110.
3 A. S. van der Woude, 'Melchisedek als himmliche Erlösergestalt in den neugefundenen eschatologischen Midraschim aus Qumran Höhle XI', *OTS* 14 (1965): 354–73 (356–57).
4 Kobelski, *Melchizedek and Melchireša*ᶜ, 3.
5 See 13.1, The 'Abrahamic' Interpretation of Psalm 110 and Other Cases of Early Intertextual Readings of Genesis 14 and Psalm 110.

date it to the second century BCE.[6] On the basis of (a) the oldest fragments from Qumran, which are dated to ca. 125–120 BCE, (b) assumed
borrowings in *Jubilees* from the Enochic *Book of Dreams* (*1 En.* 83–90), and
(c) allusions to Maccabean history, James C. VanderKam sets the date of
composition to around the middle of the second century BCE.[7]

Moreover, as I have shown previously,[8] it has also been proposed
that 4Q213b reflects the ME. The script of the particular fragment, which
is part of a composition referred to as *Aramaic Levi*, resembles those typical of the late Hasmonean or early Herodian period.[9]

However, the drawback to arguing from all the possible relevant
texts noted above is that they, at best, only indirectly testify to the existence of the ME. On the other hand, there is an obvious text that *directly*
renders the ME, the LXX. In principle, the LXX offers the most readily
available *terminus ante quem* for the date of the ME.

Unfortunately, what is uncomplicated in theory is more complicated
in practice. The pseudepigraphic *Letter of Aristeas* presents the story of
the translation of the Jews' sacred lawbooks as having taken place during the reign of Ptolemy II (285–246 BCE). Moreover, in the fragments of
the works of the Jewish apologete Aristobulus quoted by later antique
authors, Aristobulus argues that philosophers such as Pythagoras and
Plato took their best ideas from earlier, partial versions of the Mosaic
law.[10]

Today it is acknowledged that each of the translations and original
compositions that eventually constituted the LXX has its own history
and character.[11] Although it has often been assumed that the book of
Genesis was the first Hebrew biblical book to be translated into Greek,
there is absolutely no external proof for this.[12] Nevertheless, according
to Jennifer Dines, most scholars opt to date the translation of the Pentateuch to early or mid-third century BCE, in accordance with the *Letter of
Aristeas*. To make the whole picture even more complicated, Giovanni
Garbini argues on the basis of the evidence from Aristobulus that one
can infer that before the third century BCE there were various Greek ver-

---

6   See O. S. Wintermute, 'Jubilees (Second Century B.C.)', *OTP* 2:35–142 (43–44).
7   See Wintermute, 'Jubilees (Second Century B.C.)', *OTP* 2:35–142 (44); and VanderKam,
     An Introduction to Early Judaism, 97.
8   See 13.1, The 'Abrahamic' Interpretation of Psalm 110 and Other Cases of Early Inter-
     textual Readings of Genesis 14 and Psalm 110.
9   See Michael E. Stone, 'Levi, Aramaic', *EncDSS* 1:486–88 (486).
10   See Yarbro Collins, 'Aristobulus (Second Century B.C.)', *OTP* 2:831–42 (839–41).
11   See Dines, *The Septuagint*, 13.
12   Dines, *The Septuagint*, 14.

sions of Jewish writings corresponding approximately to what we call the Hexateuch—but with the exclusion of Genesis![13]

Although the LXX version of Genesis 14 is relevant for establishing a *terminus ante quem*, the exact date of the translation into Greek is difficult to determine. If the overall dating argued for in the *Letter of Aristeas* actually is correct, then the ME cannot have been interpolated into Genesis 14* later than in the early or mid-third century BCE.

In the paragraphs above I have not considered the possibility that the ME was added secondarily to an earlier Greek translation of Genesis. Yet, no direct, external proof for such a secondary harmonization of the Greek translation vis-à-vis its Hebrew *Vorlage* exists. One can speculate whether or not the lack of a parallel to the ME in *Jubilees* could indirectly support this theory.[14]

---

13 Giovanni Garbini, *History and Ideology in Ancient Israel* (trans. John Bowden; London: SCM, 1988), 136.
14 See chapter 17, A Critical Assessment of the 'Assimilation Model'.

17. A Critical Assessment of the Assimilation Model

The model developed in the preceding chapters explaining the *when, why,* and *how* of the ME suffers from the lack of external proof. I cannot document that Psalm 110 was read historiographically as a poetic version of Abram's war and, as such, was intertextually related to Genesis 14* (note: *without* vv. 18–20) *before* the ME was interpolated into the latter narrative. In other words, I cannot refer to sources that explicitly prove that an intertextual reading of Psalm 110 and Genesis 14* functioned as a catalyst for the composition and interpolation of the ME. At the bottom line, the strength of the assimilation model is its explanatory force, that is, its ability to provide the best possible answer to the question of the background of the ME and the purpose of the interpolation into Genesis 14*.

First, there are analogical cases in the Bible itself and in early inter-testamental literature of the phenomenon of (secondary) assimilation of two texts that were conceived as parallel accounts. This is not to deny the methodological problem of the assimilation model; the methods and techniques of the assumed author of the ME are *not* handed down to us along with the ME. With regard to another late-biblical author, namely, the Chronicler, Isaac Kalimi concludes that his historiographical methods and literary techniques are elusive and that the scholar must ferret them out through close literary examination of the text.[1] In the case of Chronicles and the Chronicler, one does have access to his sources, above all the books of Samuel–Kings, to the background of which the methods and techniques of the Chronicler can be contrasted. As for the assimilation model concerning the ME, the situation is not completely comparable to the book of Chronicles. Nevertheless, the model is able to account for the assumed source of the ME (i.e., Psalm 110, and in particular v. 4). Therefore, it is possible to make qualified conjectures and ferret out the methods and techniques of the author of the ME.

Second, the assimilation model does explain the origin of the ME better than traditio-historical theories. Although there are nuances

---

1   Isaac Kalimi, *The Reshaping of Ancient Israelite History in Chronicles* (Winona Lake, IN: Eisenbrauns, 2005), 404.

among these theories, they all seem to assume that the content of the ME (its *traditum*) ultimately stems from pre-Israelite Jerusalem (the name Melchizedek, that he was a Canaanite priest of El[-Elyon]). However, proceeding from the conclusion that the ME has been interpolated into Genesis 14* in the Second Temple period, that is, much later, such theories must hypothesize a *Sitz im Leben* for the content of the ME. Then many questions arise. In what part of ancient Israel was the content of the ME passed on for centuries? Why did the passing on (*traditio*) of this *traditum* take place parallel to but without connection to the *traditio* of the biblical stories and motifs before it eventually had its literary setting in Genesis 14*, a text from either the Persian or early Hellenistic period?

Third, according to the assimilation model, it is possible to read the ME (in particular Gen. 14:20b) literally; *Abra(ha)m* is the one who receives the tithe.[2] Moreover, on the basis of what we can infer from other relatively late texts (biblical and nonbiblical alike), we can make two conclusions. First, it was considered a priestly prerogative to receive tithes in the late-biblical period. Second, the question of priestly genealogy and ordination became urgent. At the time of the meeting with Melchizedek, Abra(ha)m had already built three altars (Gen. 12:7, 8; 13:18) and invoked the name of Yahweh twice (Gen. 12:8; 13:4). Later on in the Abraham stories, he was about to offer his son Isaac (Genesis 22). Yet, Abra(ha)m does not have any priestly genealogy nor do the patriarchal narratives report any installation of him to priesthood. Therefore, it can be argued that the author who composed and probably also interpolated ME into Genesis 14* solved the potential problem of the discrepancy between Abra(ha)m's obvious priestly functions on the one hand and Abra(ha)m's lack of any priestly genealogy/priestly ordination on the other. According to Gen. 14:20b, Abram is a priest *because of Melchizedek* (see Ps. 110:4b), that is, because Melchizedek gives him a tithe and in doing so recognizes his priestly status. The idea that Abraham was a priest is evident in both the Talmud (*b. Ned.* 32b, quoted above[3]) and the rabbinic exegetical literature (the author of *Genesis Rabbah* can point to

---

2   This reading has already been done by Immanuel Benzinger. He, however, suggests that by tithing to Abram, Melchizedek recognizes the former's legal claim on Canaan; see Benzinger, 'Zur Quellenscheidung in Gen 14', in *Vom Alten Testament: Karl Marti zum siebzigsten Geburtstage* (ed. Karl Budde; FS K. Marti; BZAW 41; Gießen: Töpelmann, 1925), 21–27.

3   See 13.1, The 'Abrahamic' Interpretation of Psalm 110 and Other Cases of Early Intertextual Readings of Genesis 14 and Psalm 110.

Abraham's priesthood in connection with Genesis 22 and the 'binding of Isaac'[4]).

There are no texts in the Bible that explicitly call Abra(ha)m a priest. However, given that Abra(ha)m functioned as a model figure for the Jews in the Second Temple period,[5] we may speculate as to whether or not the puzzling verse Exod. 19:6a provided another problem that needed to be solved:

> Exod. 19:6a: 'And you shall be (תִּהְיוּ) for me a kingdom of priests
> (מַמְלֶכֶת כֹּהֲנִים) and a holy nation'.

It is possible to read this half verse as a descriptive clause.[6] Moreover, its reception history demonstrates that it has provoked many interpretations.[7] The ME perhaps offers a comment to the question of *why* the Israelites, according to Exod. 19:6a, were priests. The answer, according to the ME, would be *because the Israelites are the descendants of Abraham, whose priesthood was recognized by Melchizedek.*

A probably stronger case demonstrating how lack of a priestly genealogy became an urgent problem in the Second Temple period is found

---

4   See *Gen. R.* 55:6 (quoted from Isidore Epstein, ed., *Hebrew–English Edition of the Babylonian Talmud,* ad loc.):

> Now Abraham said HERE AM I—ready for priesthood, ready for kingship, and he attained priesthood and kingship. He attained priesthood, as it says, *The Lord hath sworn, and will not repent: Thou art a priest for ever after the manner of* Melchizedek (Ps. CX, 4); kingship: *Thou art a mighty prince among us* (Gen. XXIII, 5). . . .

Moreover, see *Gen. R.* 46:5; *Lev. R.* 25:6; and 14.6.1 above, Excursus: Abraham, a Priest According to the ME?

5   See, e.g., how 'Abraham' and 'Jacob' function in Mic. 7:20.

6   Here, upon the arrival at Sinai, Yahweh commands Moses to communicate these words to the Israelites. Syntactically, Exod. 19:6a, וְאַתֶּם תִּהְיוּ־לִי מַמְלֶכֶת כֹּהֲנִים, is usually related to the conditional clause in the preceding verse. In Exod. 19:5a, the protasis stipulates the conditions: 'If (אִם) you really obey my voice and keep my covenant. . . .' The conditioned result is given in the apodosis in the last half (Exod. 19:5bα): '[*then*] you shall be (וִהְיִיתֶם) for me a personal property out of all the peoples'. In Bible translations, Exod. 19:6a is often taken to represent a second part of the apodosis: 'And [*then*] you shall be for me a kingdom of priests. . .'. Accordingly, if Exod. 19:6a is part of the conditional clause that starts in the preceding verse, then the temporal reference of the verb תִּהְיוּ is future: 'you shall be . . .'. Moreover, in this case, the Israelites' priestly status depends on their ability to comply with the stipulations in the protasis in Exod. 19:5a: ('If [אִם] you really obey my voice and keep my covenant . . .').

However, a short clause separates the two apodoses: 'For (כִּי), the whole earth is mine' (Exod. 19:5bβ). Therefore, in my view it is possible to read Exod. 19:6a וְאַתֶּם תִּהְיוּ־לִי מַמְלֶכֶת כֹּהֲנִים as a *syntactically independent* and *descriptive* clause: 'You [= the Israelites] are a kingdom of priests'.

7   See Kugel, *Traditions of the Bible,* 671–74.

in a text from 1 Chronicles and its assumed *Vorlage*. In 1 Chr. 5:34 (Eng. trans., 6:8; cf. 6:35–38 [Eng. trans., 6:50–53]), one finds probably the first text according to which David's priest Zadok is made an Aaronite priest: 'And Ahitub begot Zadok, and Zadok begot Ahimaaz'.

The Chronicler's assumed *Vorlage* in 2 Sam 8:17 probably originally read 'Zadok and Abiathar, son of Achimelech son of Ahitub'.[8] According to this reconstruction of the assumed *Vorlage* by Julius Wellhausen, which has been accepted by most scholars, Zadok does not have an Aaronitic origin. We can therefore infer that the Chronicler solved the problem of Zadok's (lacking) genealogy by secondarily creating one. Moreover, whereas Zadok suddenly appears alongside David without any further introduction in 2 Sam 8:17, the Chronicler portrays Zadok as one of David's warriors already at the time of David's mustering of his troops *in Hebron*, that is, before he captured Jerusalem (1 Chr. 12:29 [Eng. trans., 12:28]).

Fourth, given that the composition and interpolation of the ME into Genesis 14* took place relatively late in the period that I have argued for above,[9] then this may explain why the book of *Jubilees* does not contain any explicit parallel to the ME. At the place where one would expect *Jubilees* to offer its rewritten version of the ME, it instead offers a law on the tithe (*Jub.* 13:25–27). Perhaps the ME was not an integral part of the *Vorlage* the author of *Jubilees* used? On the other hand, if it is correct that *Jub.* 32:1 actually reflects both Ps. 110:4 and the ME,[10] then the author of *Jubilees* must have been familiar with the aggadah reflected in the ME, albeit not from the *Vorlage* he had constant access to when composing *Jubilees* but from another manuscript.[11]

Therefore, the assimilation model explains the *when*, *why*, and *how* of the ME better than the various traditio-historical approaches that all attempt to solve the problems by taking refuge in a postulated ancient tradition, a tradition that ultimately stems from the assumed pre-Israelite cult of El in Jebus/Jerusalem.

---

8   See Lester L. Grabbe, *Priests, Prophets, Diviners, Sages: A Socio-Historical Study of Religious Specialists in Ancient Israel* (Valley Forge, PA: Trinity Press International, 1995), 60–62.

9   See chapter 16, The Date of the Melchizedek Episode.

10   See 13.1, The 'Abrahamic' Interpretation of Psalm 110 and Other Cases of Early Intertextual Readings of Genesis 14 and Psalm 110.

11   Below, in 19.2.4, The Likeliest Explanation: Both Genesis 14* and Later the ME Were Added in Connection with the Production of New Copies, I argue that the ME probably was added to the biblical text in connection with the production of a new copy of the Torah. It is likely also that the *composition* of the ME took place closely related to this.

18. Summary of Part III

The ME is a secondary insertion into Genesis 14*, on which it is also dependent. Genesis 14* itself should be dated to the Persian or early Hellenistic period. Therefore, the date of composition of the ME must be later than that of Genesis 14*. Moreover, texts from the last centuries BCE betray knowledge of the ME. On the basis of this, I have proposed a qualified conjecture as to the date of composition of the episode: around the middle of the Second Temple period or perhaps earlier.

The date of composition and the date of insertion of the ME probably coincide. The ME has probably never had a 'past life' that is independent of Genesis 14*.

Furthermore, I argue that it is possible to explain the composition of the ME as the result of an attempt to assimilate two texts. At some point, Psalm 110 started to be read as a poetic version of Abram's war with the four kings (see Genesis 14*). The similarities between the texts functioned as a catalyst for an additional assimilation, the concrete result of which was the ME. The figure called Melchizedek in the ME is the result of a personification of the words מַלְכִּי־צֶדֶק in Ps. 110:4. Alternatively, the מַלְכִּי־צֶדֶק originally signified a personal name in Ps. 110:4. In the latter case, the ME is the result of the creation of a legendary biography that has been attached to an originally marginal biblical character.

The ME can perhaps be called an early example of an *aggadah*, which in addition has been incorporated into the biblical text itself.

Part IV: The Addition of Genesis 14*
and the Melchizedek Episode in Perspective

19. The Addition of Genesis 14 to the Torah in Light of Second Temple Period Book Production

19.1 Aim and Scope

Identifying fractures, unevenness, internal inconsistencies, etc., all suggesting that a given literary composition has grown over time, is one thing.[1] Another, however, is explaining how the growth technically has taken place in light of the available knowledge about how and in what kind of milieu books were produced in ancient Israel and Judah.

Is it possible to say something about how Genesis 14* and the ME concretely became part of the biblical manuscript that today is reflected in the received biblical text? Moreover, can the technical aspect of the incorporation of these texts into the biblical text provide additional information about the authors of Genesis 14* and the ME respectively, supplementing the conjectures I made above in chapter 7 (especially in 7.3, A Plea for Restoration: Attempt at Some Historically Qualified Conjectures about the Historical Meaning and the Ideology of the Author)? Besides discussing these questions, I will also attempt to relate my observations in chapter 6 to recent discussions about the interplay of orality and textuality as a backdrop to the production of biblical texts in the Second Temple period. I will conclude with a brief, yet fundamental, discussion of the implications of phenomena such as expansions and reworking of biblical literature for our understanding of the status of the Bible in Second Temple period Judaism. When a text was expanded and othewise reworked again and again, what does this say about the text?

In the following, the overall aim will be to put the discussions in Part II and Part III, regarding Genesis 14* and the secondary Melchizedek episode (Gen. 14:18–20), respectively, in perspective.

---

1   See 2.2, The Textual Integrity of Genesis 14; chapter 4, Genesis 14* and the Composition History of the Abraham Narratives; and 8.6, Preliminary Conclusion and Point of Departure: The ME—A Doubly Late Interpolation.

19.2 The Technical Aspect

The late dates of composition and interpolation that I have proposed for Genesis 14* and the ME, respectively, need to be related to the physical facts. How concretely did Genesis 14* and later the ME become part of a manuscript, a manuscript that for its part at some point apparently has become part of the chain of manuscripts that today's received text continues?

19.2.1 Book Format: Scrolls

On the basis of both internal biblical evidence[2] as well as the findings of biblical texts around the Dead Sea and the Judean Desert we can assume that the scroll format was used for long-duration texts such as biblical books.[3] The codex format was first introduced at the beginning of the Christian era. In general, two sorts of material were used for producing scrolls: sheets of papyrus glued together or sheets of leather that either were stitched or glued together. It is assumed that the use of papyrus scrolls was gradually supplanted by leather scrolls in the Second Temple period.[4]

Therefore, for the period in which Genesis 14* and subsequently the ME were composed and added—that is in the Persian or early Hellenistic period[5]—we can take for granted that the scroll format was used for the ascendant Mosaic Torah. However, this raises a technical question: How can we best explain the technical aspect of the incorporation of Genesis 14* and subsequently the ME into the Torah?

19.2.2 Genesis 14 Added by Filling
an Open Space or by Writing in the Margin?

Were Genesis 14* and the ME added to the Torah scroll either by filling in an open space or by writing in the margin of an already existing Torah scroll?

---

2   Ps. 40:8; Jer. 36:2, 4, 6, 14, 20–21, 23, 25, 27–29, 32; Ezek. 2:9; 3:1–3; Zech. 5:1–2; cf. Luke 4:17, 20.
3   See André Lemaire, 'Writing and Writing Materials', *ABD* 6:999–1008; and Tov, *Textual Criticism of the Hebrew Bible*, 201–7.
4   See Menahem Haran, 'Book-Scrolls at the Beginning of the Second Temple Period: The Transition from Papyrus to Skins', *HUCA* 54 (1983): 111–22; and Tov, *Textual Criticism of the Hebrew Bible*, 202.
5   See above, 7.1, The Date of Composition: A Synthesis of the Different Approaches; and chapter 16, The Date of the Melchizedek Episode.

In general, the Dead Sea scrolls attest that texts were divided into sections and textual units already in the centuries before the Christian Era. Moreover, the Dead Sea scrolls attest that this was done in a way comparable to the paragraphing named *parashiyyot* in the MT. Although the Dead Sea scrolls and the MT differ with respect to where the major and minor divisions were noted, a major division in the Dead Sea scrolls was, as in the MT, denoted by means of a space extending from the last word in the line to the end of the line (in Masoretic terminology: פרשה פתוחה, 'open section'). Equally, a minor division was noted by means of a space in the middle of the line (פרשה סתומה, 'closed section').[6]

Given that the practice of marking the internal division in the biblical texts antedates the Dead Sea scrolls—and there is nothing speaking against this assumption—and, moreover, given that the scroll format actually was used for the Torah at the time Genesis 14* was composed, we can make the following assumption. There would probably not have been sufficient space between Genesis 13 on the one side and Genesis 15 on the other for adding such a long narrative as Genesis 14*. Moreover, the size of Genesis 14* excludes the possibility that it originally was added in the margin of a copy of the Torah. The ME consists of 110 to 120 letters. Therefore, this episode is also probably too long to have been added either in the space dividing Genesis 13 and Genesis 15 or in the margin.

19.2.3 Needlework?

According to Emanuel Tov, there are examples both in Qumran and in Samaritan manuscripts of scrolls that literally have been subject to needlework. In some cases, text segments have been replaced by patches that have been stitched onto the parchment.[7]

Although I cannot exclude the possibility that Genesis 14* was written on a separate sheet of leather that someone stitched onto an already existing copy of the Torah at a certain point in the Second Temple period, I do not think this explanation is likely. If a sheet of leather containing Genesis 14* were stitched onto an earlier manuscript, we should expect that there was a text underneath the patch. However, no traces of such a physically hidden and suppressed text can—as far as I see—be found in

---

6   See Tov, *Textual Criticism of the Hebrew Bible,* 50–51, 210–11.
7   Tov, *Textual Criticism of the Hebrew Bible,* 206. Moreover, Tov also shows that such 'needlework practice' on biblical scrolls is attested by early rabbinic literature.

any of the different types of textual witnesses of the Bible or in any of the early examples of biblical reception history.[8]

In addition, as far as I am concerned, there is no analogy in any ancient manuscript to patches of a size that would be needed for Genesis 14*.

Nevertheless, whereas the 'needlework model' probably does not explain how Genesis 14* became part of the Torah, the model could potentially explain the difference between the ME in the received biblical text on the one hand and the quite different 'Law of the Tithes' in *Jub.* 13:28–29 on the other. Although it is highly conjectural, it is nonetheless intriguing to speculate whether or not the 'Law of the Tithes' in *Jubilees* represents such an earlier text that subsequently has been 'hidden' by way of the ME having been stitched onto it. Admittedly, the 'Law of the Tithes' can with a higher degree of probability be explained as the result of a general tendency of the author of *Jubilees* to antedate the Mosaic laws and regulations to the patriarchal period.[9]

19.2.4 The Likeliest Explanation: Both Genesis 14* and Later the ME Were Added in Connection with the Production of New Copies

In light of the potential alternatives it seems most plausible to assume that Genesis 14* and subsequently the ME were added to the biblical text in connection with the production of a new copy of the Torah. This raises further questions concerning the relationship between the copyists and the authors of Genesis 14* and the ME. For instance, can we assume that the author of Genesis 14* is identical with the copyist who produced the new Torah scroll? If the answer is yes, can we assume that he[10] already had composed the narrative before he started producing the new copy or did he compose it *ad hoc* when he reached the latter part of Genesis 13?

No definite answer can be given as to whether the author and the copyist were one and the same person. Nevertheless, regardless of this, we can assume that the incorporation of Genesis 14* into the new copy

---

8   Here, I refer to the Masoretic and Samaritan witnesses in addition to the biblical texts found in Qumran. Moreover, other witnesses are the ancient translations of the Bible (the LXX, the Targums, the Peshitta, etc.) and the early examples of the genre 'rewritten Bible' (*Jubilees*, the Aramaic *Genesis Apocryphon*).

9   See, e.g., VanderKam, *An Introduction to Early Judaism*, 98.

10   I intentionally use the masculine pronoun 'he'. On the basis of the relatively little we know about literacy and the scribal culture in biblical Israel, we may with a relatively high degree of probability assume that those involved in the production of literary texts were men, not women. See Carr, *Writing on the Tablet of the Heart*, 11–12.

was accepted by, anchored in, and even promoted by the milieu in which the copyist worked. Likewise, we can assume that the incorporation of the ME into the new copy was accepted by, anchored in, and even promoted by the milieu in which the copyist worked. Conversely, had the community with which the copyists were associated not accepted the interpolation of Genesis 14* into the Torah and subsequently the interpolation of the ME into Genesis 14*, then it is difficult to explain how the (new) scrolls containing Genesis 14* and the ME could serve as *Vorlagen* for later copies of the Torah.

19.3 The Milieu of the Authors and Copyists

19.3.1 The Centre of Jewish Literary Culture in the Second Temple Period

The question of the milieu of the author who composed Genesis 14* and the copyist who produced the first scroll to include the narrative can be further illuminated by means of the following question. Where in Second Temple period Judaism were biblical texts copied?

This is basically a question about the extent of literacy and the nature of the literary culture in ancient Israel. These issues have been discussed more extensively in recent works by, for example, Martin S. Jaffee[11] and David M. Carr.[12] Both point to the priestly circles as the main environment for the Jewish literary culture in the Second Temple period.

As for the Second Temple period, Carr says that '[t]he priests of Israel became the main repository for both priestly and nonpriestly traditions transmitted earlier'.[13] Those who are depicted as writing are all some sort of official, both in this period but also earlier in the monarchic period.[14] In the Second Temple period, the primary employer of literary scribes was the Jerusalem Temple itself. The Temple serves not only as the cultic centre. In addition, it was the political and economic centre of the land. Although it is not possible to rule out the possibility that there were lay scribes, it is, however, on economical grounds unlikely that there were nonpriestly literary communities beyond the reach of

---

11 Martin S. Jaffee, *Torah in the Mouth: Writing and Oral Tradition in Palestinian Judaism, 200 BCE–400 CE* (New York: Oxford University Press, 2001).

12 Carr, *Writing on the Tablet of the Heart: Origins of Scripture and Literature* (Oxford: Oxford University Press, 2005).

13 Carr, *Writing on the Tablet of the Heart*, 169.

14 Carr, *Writing on the Tablet of the Heart*, 116.

the Temple.[15] The literary culture was not a 'popular' culture; on the contrary, it was rooted in the work of scribal professionals associated with the Temple.[16] Admittedly, the Qumran community provides an early example of a nontemple literary community. However, this group also appears to have been guided by (dissenting) priests from the Jerusalem priesthood. The 'teacher of righteousness' was described as a priest in the *Psalms Pesher* from Qumran cave 4 (4Q171 3:15) and the *Habakkuk Pesher* (1QpHab 2:8–9; 7:4–5).[17]

Because we can assume that the composition and interpolation of Genesis 14* into the book of Genesis took place in the Persian or early Hellenistic period, we can for that reason assume that the milieu in which it happened was a priestly one, closely associated with the Jerusalem Temple, the centre of Judah's literary culture.

19.3.2 Priestly Provenance: Implications for Understanding the ME?

In chapter 7, I argued for the possibility that the author of Genesis 14* wanted to make a plea for the restoration of the land under the control of Abraham's descendants. In light of the discussion above concerning the centre of Jewish literary culture, it is suggested that the restorative-nationalistic aspiration possibly evident in Genesis 14* was rooted in some sort of priestly circles. Moreover, the discussion above about Jew-

---

15   Jaffee, *Torah in the Mouth*, 20–22. R. G. Kratz argues for an alternative view of the relationship between the Torah and the temple; see Kratz, 'Temple and Torah: Reflections on the Legal Status of the Pentateuch between Elephantine and Qumran', in *The Pentateuch as Torah: New Models for Understanding its Promulgation and Acceptance* (ed. Gary N. Knoppers and Bernhard M. Levinson; Winona Lake, IN: Eisenbrauns, 2007), 77–103. Kratz contends that the levelling of the differences between the Torah and the temple was a slow process that began in the late Persian period and continued into Hellenistic times. Perhaps triggered by the Samaritan competition, it was intensified by the pressure of Hellenization on Judaism. He argues that there are no external proofs for the assumption that the circles that handed down the Torah and kept it sacred consisted of the priests in the Jerusalem temple. In Kratz's opinion, the evidence from Elephantine and Qumran supports the suggestion that the circles responsible for the composition and distribution of the Pentateuch were not or were not longer affiliated with the ruling class at the temple. Moreover, he proposes that the incipient connection of temple and Torah reached its official status in the Hasmonaean kingdom with the high priest Jonathan.

16   Jaffee, *Torah in the Mouth*, 20, 26.

17   Carr, *Writing on the Tablet of the Heart*, 216.

ish literary culture suggests that the later interpolation found in the ME also originated in a priestly milieu.

As I will show in the brief outline below, we can infer from various sources that there were rivalries between different priestly lines in the Second Temple period. Is it possible to relate the ME to these rivalries? Before I discuss the question I will first have to account for a few observations concerning the priesthood during the period in question.

Scholars agree that it is difficult to outline the history of the priesthood in ancient Israel.[18] Nevertheless, on the basis of several biblical sources, we can infer that there must have been tensions and factional rivalries between different priestly lines such as the Levites, the Aaronites, and the Zadokites in both preexilic and postexilic times.

Scholars speak of a Zadokite hegemony in the postexilic priesthood. For instance, in Ezekiel 40–48, a vision that cannot antedate the so-called Babylonian Exile, the Zadokites are the highest ranked priests. Moreover, whereas David's priest Zadok does not have a genealogy in 2 Samuel 8 (he apparently pops up from nowhere in v. 17), most scholars think he has been supplied with a secondary Aaronitic genealogy in the later Chronistic History (1 Chr. 5:34 [Eng. trans., 6:8]; see 6:35–38 [Eng. trans., 6:50–53]), as accounted for above.[19] Parallel to this, most scholars believe that the male members of the tribe of Levi at some point lost the traditional right to serve as priests.[20] In the Chronistic literature, one can observe that the Levites have an inferior position vis-à-vis other cultic functionaries. According to the Chronicler, the duty of the Levites was to assist the descendants of Aaron in the service of the Temple (1 Chr. 23:28, 32; cf. 1 Chr. 6:33 [Eng. trans., 48]; 9:14–34; 2 Chr. 24:5–6; 34:9).[21]

---

18   For a survey and discussion of the sources for the history of priesthood in ancient Israel, see, e.g., Aelred Cody, *A History of Old Testament Priesthood* (Analecta Biblica 35; Rome: Pontifical Biblical Institute, 1969); idem, 'An Excursus on Priesthood in Israel', in idem, *Ezekiel, with an Excursus on Old Testament Priesthood* (Wilmington, DE: Michael Glazier, 1984), 256–63; Julia M. O'Brien, *Priest and Levite in Malachi* (SBL Dissertation Series 121; Atlanta: Scholars Press, 1990), 1–23; Richard D. Nelson, *Raising up a Faithful Priest: Community and Priesthood in Biblical Theology* (Louisville, KY: Westminster/ John Knox, 1993), 5–11; Preuß, *Theologie des Alten Testaments*. II *Israels Weg mit JHWH*, 56–71; and Menahem Haran, Menahem Stern, and Gerald Y. Blidstein, 'Priests and Priesthood', *EncJud* 16:513–26.

19   See chapter 17, A Critical Assessment of the 'Assimilation Model'; and Grabbe, *Priests, Prophets, Diviners, Sages*, 60–62.

20   The Priestly writing is probably the first to describe this shift, irrespective of its date of composition. See O'Brien, *Priest and Levite in Malachi*, 22–23.

21   See also Gary N. Knoppers, 'Hierodules, Priests, or Janitors? The Levites in Chronicles and the History of the Israelite Priesthood', *JBL* 118 (1999): 49–72.

However, in contrast to the clerical hierarchy with the Zadokites on top, there are other voices more or less clearly elevating other priestly lines. A relatively late biblical source is Malachi. It has been suggested that a restoration only of the Levites (בְּנֵי־לֵוִי) and not the priests (הַכֹּהֲנִים) is put forth in Mal. 3:3. A presupposition for this view is that there is a distinction between the priests on the one hand and the Levites (בְּנֵי־לֵוִי) on the other in Malachi. If that is the case, Mal. 3:3 may bear witness to a struggle between Zadokites and Levites.[22] Moreover, more explicit alternative voices are pseudepigraphic texts such as the *Jubilees*, the *Testament of Levi*, and the so-called *Aramaic Levi Document*, all having the legitimation of the Levitic priesthood as an apologetic goal.[23] Eventually, to add complexity to the issue, the books of Maccabees and the works of Josephus show that the Zadokite line was challenged by the emergence of the Hasmonean dynasty in the second century BCE.[24]

In sum, despite meagre sources, we nevertheless know that there were rivalries among the various priestly lines. Therefore, it is tempting to ask whether or not the author of the ME conceived it with such a rivalry as a backdrop. Did he originally write the ME as a sort of comment on this? Provided that the author of the ME actually wanted the name 'Melchizedek' to symbolize the Zadokite priests, then the answer is probably yes. To be sure, it is impossible to control such a presumably intended connection between 'Zadok' and 'Melchizedek'. Nevertheless, if we pursue this train of thought, then—again—the question of the exact meaning of Gen. 14:20b becomes urgent: Who was the donor of the tithe and to whom was the tithe given? Or, in other words, whom does the author of the ME portray as superior and whom does he portray as subordinate?

I have already demonstrated that the right to receive tithes developed and became a priestly prerogative.[25] Presuming that I am correct in proposing that the author of the ME depicted Melchizedek as giv-

---

22 Karl William Weyde, *Prophecy and Teaching: Prophetic Authority, Form Problems, and the Use of Traditions in the Book of Malachi* (BZAW 288; Berlin: W. de Gruyter, 2000), 302–4, 398. In Mal. 2:1–9 the priests (הַכֹּהֲנִים) are even condemned and abolished before all the people.

23 See John C. Endres, *Biblical Interpretation in the Book of Jubilees* (CBQMS 18; Washington, DC: Catholic Biblical Association of America, 1987), 204; James Kugel, 'Levi's Elevation to the Priesthood in the Second Temple Writings', *HThR* 86 (1993): 1–64; Kugler, *From Patriarch to Priest*; and Cara Werman, 'Levi and Levites in the Second Temple Period', *DSD* 4 (1997): 211–25.

24 See Donner, *Geschichte des Volkes Israel und seiner Nachbarn in Grundzügen.* II, 483–88; and Tessa Rajak, 'Hasmonean Dynasty', *ABD* 3:67–76.

25 See 14.6.1, Excursus: Abraham, a Priest According to the ME?

ing a tithe *to Abra(ha)m*,[26] then it is possible to make some additional conjectures about what the author-intended meaning of the ME might have been.

One possibility is that the author of the ME, by depicting Melchizedek as the donor of the tithe to Abra(ha)m, *eo ipso* degraded the Zadokite line, presumably represented by the priest-king Melchizedek. It is an open question whom Abram possibly represents, except that he obviously is a non-Zadokite in the ME. However, being Levi's great grandfather, a possible guess is that he represents the Levites. Admittedly, this proposal also lacks control. Yet, the ME may have been composed in the same general period as the pro-Levi texts shown above. Moreover, the same texts that elevate Levi to priesthood do, as later rabbinic texts also do, attest the idea that Abra(ha)m was a priest.[27]

The safest conclusion is that the author of the ME belonged to some sort of priestly milieu. Moreover, provided that the readings I have proposed are correct (and for the time being it is possible neither to sanction nor to turn them down), then the author was probably a non-Zadokite.

19.4 Echoes of Earlier Texts in Genesis 14 and the Role of Literary Templates for the Production of New Texts

In recent times, there has been a trend in scholarship to emphasize the intricate interplay of orality and textuality behind the production of books in ancient Near Eastern societies.[28] For instance, Martin S. Jaffee has pointed to the practical limitations of the scroll format for information purposes. As he says, unless one wanted to read a book from beginning to end, the scroll was virtually useless as a handy source of information; one potentially had to scroll through great lengths of text to consult a particular passage. In light of this physical fact, then, he argues that the most effective use of the scroll for information retrieval was avail-

---

26 See 14.6, Third Case of Psalm Surplus Crystallizing in the ME; and 14.6.1, Excursus: Abraham, a Priest According to the ME?

27 See Kugel, 'Levi's Elevation to the Priesthood in the Second Temple Writings', 1–64 (17–19) and the references to *Jubilees* there.

28 See, e.g., Werner H. Kelber, 'Orality and Biblical Studies: A Review Essay', *Review of Biblical Literature* (December 2007), URL: http://www.bookreviews.org/pdf/2107_6748.pdf [accessed on September 7, 2009]. Moreover, see Stefan Schorch, 'Die Rolle des Lesens für die Konstituierung alttestamentlicher Texte', in *Was ist ein Text? Alttestamentliche, ägyptologische und altorientalistische Perspektiven* (ed. Ludwig D. Morenz and Stefan Schorch; BZAW 362; Berlin: W. de Gruyter, 2007), 108–22.

able only to scribes who were so familiar with the text that they would know more or less where in the scroll to find what they needed. Therefore, those who were best able to use the scroll would be people who in a basic sense already knew its contents through approximate memorization.[29] According to David M. Carr, the written documents (in Israel the standard texts were the growing biblical texts) constituted a sort of curriculum in the educational system of memorization and recitation that shaped the minds of students.[30] Moreover, he proposes that Israelite authors educated accordingly had been trained from the outset to write by building on literary templates provided by earlier texts.[31]

Carr's model provides an explanation for the observation that Genesis 14* seems to echo several earlier texts. The templates, or literary building blocks, which is the expression that I use, were found in the curriculum of standard texts that the author-scribe, who perhaps but not necessarily was identical with the copyist, once had been versed in.

19.5 Expansion and Reworking: Sign of the High Estimation of the Reworked Text

Finally, my model, which seeks to explain how, when, and why Genesis 14 was composed, raises a fundamental question. What status did a text have in those communities that altered its structure and/or made additions to it?

There are several scholarly contributions devoted to the techniques applied in ancient biblical interpretation,[32] to the question of when biblical interpretation started,[33] and to the question of what the authors of Deuteronomy, for example, intended by their work in relation to the literary compositions that preceded it.[34]

---

29   Jaffee, *Torah in the Mouth*, 16–17.
30   Carr, *Writing on the Tablet of the Heart*, 8–9.
31   Carr, *Writing on the Tablet of the Heart*, 159.
32   See above all Fishbane, *Biblical Interpretation in Ancient Israel*; and more recently Kalimi, *The Reshaping of Ancient Israelite History in Chronicles*.
33   See, e.g., Timo Veijola, 'Die Deuteronomisten als Vorgänger der Schriftgelehrten: Ein Beitrag zur Entstehung des Judentums', in idem, *Moses Erben: Studien zum Dekalog, zum Deuteronomismus und zum Schriftgelehrtentum* (BWANT 149; Stuttgart: W. Kohlhammer, 2000), 192–240.
34   See Bernard M. Levinson, *Deuteronomy and the Hermeneutics of Legal Innovation* (New York: Oxford University Press, 1997). Levinson also discusses the *intention* of the Chronicler (p. 154). In his view, the late editors, by including both the Deuteronomis-

In an introductory chapter to his anthology of texts from the Bible's earliest reception history, James L. Kugel discusses what Scripture and its meaning was conceived to be in the eyes of the ancient postbiblical interpreters.[35]

According to Kugel, the rise of interpreters of biblical texts as such took place not merely because of an antiquarian interest. On the contrary, the interpretation of Scripture could provide support for political leaders and programmes. In addition, it would influence the application of the divine laws to daily life.[36] Kugel identifies four fundamental assumptions about Scripture that in his view characterize ancient interpreters of the Bible.[37] First, they all seem to have assumed that the Bible was a cryptic document whose secrets had to be revealed by way of interpretation. Second, all ancient interpreters seem to have assumed that Scripture constituted one great Book of Instruction. As such, it was conceived of as a fundamentally relevant text. Third, all ancient interpreters worked on the assumption that Scripture is perfect and perfectly harmonious. In their eyes, there were no mistakes in it, and anything that might have looked like a mistake had to be an illusion that could be clarified by proper interpretation. The fourth assumption was that all Scripture was conceived of as divinely sanctified, of divine provenance, or divinely inspired. Kugel, however, argues that this fourth assumption is chronologically later than the three preceding ones because the subject of divine provenance does not seem to have been addressed by the most ancient interpreters.

I have argued for a late date of composition for both Genesis 14* and the ME.[38] Moreover, although I have not been able to give any absolute dates, I nevertheless argue that many of the interpreters of the Bible that Kugel is dealing with come from the same general period as Genesis 14* and the ME.[39] Because of this concourse, it is difficult to draw once and for all the line between the literary growth of the biblical text on the one hand and its history of reception on the other.

---

tic History and the Chronicler's work, contradicted the intentions of the Chronicler. The latter wanted probably for his part to replace the earlier Deuteronomistic History.

35 Kugel, *Traditions of the Bible*.
36 Kugel, *Traditions of the Bible*, 9.
37 In the following, see Kugel, *Traditions of the Bible*, 14–19.
38 See 7.1, The Date of Composition: A Synthesis of the Different Approaches; and chapter 16, The Date of the Melchizedek Episode.
39 Kugel's sources are the so-called Old Testament pseudepigrapha, the Septuagint (including the deuterocanonical/apocryphal literature), the Dead Sea Scrolls, in addition to the later works of Philo and Josephus, the New Testament, and the Targums. See Kugel, *Traditions of the Bible*, 30–35.

For the same reason, it can be argued that Kugel's discussion, which primarily is devoted to ancient *postbiblical* interpreters, has relevance for Genesis 14, too.

To conclude this case study, then, I propose that Genesis 14 is situated at the point of transition between the growth of the Bible on the one hand and the subsequent transmission and reception of it on the other. When all is said and done, the narrative was added to the Abraham narratives in the evolving Torah because the latter was considered important. The importance of the Torah did not mean that it was considered to be a fixed and static book. On the contrary, the high estimation of it repeatedly generated new reworkings and expansions.[40]

---

40   At some point, the same high estimation of the Torah started functioning in quite the opposite way. The ideal became to hand the text faithfully over to the next generation without any changes. However, that is another story. . . .

Part V: Bibliography

Abbreviations of Periodicals, Reference Works, Serials, etc.

AASOR Annual of the American Schools of Oriental Research
AB Anchor Bible
ABD David Noel Freedman, ed. *The Anchor Bible Dictionary*. 6 vols.; New York: Doubleday, 1992.
ANET James B. Pritchard, ed. *Ancient Near Eastern Texts Relating to the Old Testament*. 3d ed. with supplements; Princeton: Princeton University Press, 1969.
ANRW Hildegard Temporini and Wolfgang Haase, eds. *Aufstieg und Niedergang der römischen Welt: Geschichte und Kultur Roms im Spiegel der neueren Forschung*. Berlin: W. de Gruyter, 1972–.
ARW *Archiv für Religionswissenschaft*
ATD Das Alte Testament Deutsch
ATR *Anglican Theological Review*
BAA Walter Bauer, Kurt Aland and Barbara Aland, *Griechisch-deutsches Wörterbuch zu den Schriften des Neuen Testaments und der frühchristlichen Literatur*. 6th ed.; Berlin: W. de Gruyter, 1988.
BARev Biblical Archaeology Review
BASOR Bulletin of the American Schools of Oriental Research
BDB Francis Brown, S.R. Driver and Charles A. Briggs, *A Hebrew and English Lexicon of the Old Testament*. Oxford: Clarendon Press, 1907.
BEAT Beiträge zur Erforschung des Alten Testaments und des antiken Judentums
BeO *Bibbia e Oriente*
BETL Bibliotheca ephemeridum theologicarum lovaniensium
Bib *Biblica*
BibOr Biblica et orientalia
BJS Brown Judaic Studies
BKAT Biblischer Kommentar: Altes Testament
BN *Biblische Notizen*
BTAVO Beihefte zum Tübinger Atlas des Vorderen Orients, Reihe B [Geisteswissenschaften]
BThS Biblisch-theologische Studien
BWANT Beiträge zur Wissenschaft vom Alten und Neuen Testament
BZ *Biblische Zeitschrift*
BZAW Beihefte zur *ZAW*

CAD   Ignace J. Gelb, John A.Brinkman et al., eds. *The Assyrian Dictionary of
           the Oriental Institute of the University of Chicago*. 19 vols., Chicago, IL:
           Oriental Institute, 1956–.
CBQ   *Catholic Biblical Quarterly*
CBQMS   *Catholic Biblical Quarterly*, Monograph Series
CHJ   W. D. Davies and Louis Finkelstein, eds. *The Cambridge History of
           Judaism*. 4 vols.; Cambridge: Cambridge University Press, 1984–2006.
ConBOT   Coniectanea biblica, Old Testament
DCH   David J. A. Clines, Philip R. Davies and John W. Rogerson, eds. *The
           Dictionary of Classical Hebrew*. Sheffield: Sheffield Academic Press,
           1993–.
DSD   *Dead Sea Discoveries*
EdF   Erträge der Forschung
EncDSS   Lawrence C Schiffman and James C. VanderKam, eds. *Encyclopedia of
           the Dead Sea Scrolls*. 2 vols.; Oxford: Oxford University Press, 2000.
EncJud   Michael Berenbaum and Fred Skolnik, eds. *Encyclopaedia Judaica*. 22
           vols.; 2d ed.; Detroit: Macmillan Reference USA, 2007.
EncMidr   Jacob Neusner, Alan J. Avery-Peck et al., eds. *Encyclopaedia of
           Midrash: Biblical Interpretation in Formative Judaism*. 2 vols.; Leiden:
           E. J. Brill, 2005.
EvQ   *Evangelical Quarterly*
EvT   *Evangelische Theologie*
FAT   Forschungen zum Alten Testament
FzB   Forschung zur Bibel
FOTL   The Forms of the Old Testament Literature
FRLANT   Forschungen zur Religion und Literatur des Alten und Neuen
           Testaments
GKC   Wilhelm Gesenius, *Gesenius' Hebrew Grammar*. Edited by E.
           Kautzsch; revised and translated by A. E. Cowley; Oxford: Claren-
           don Press, 1910.
HALOT   Ludwig Koehler and Walter Baumgartner et al., eds. *The Hebrew and
           Aramaic Lexicon of the Old Testament*. Leiden: E. J. Brill, 1994–2000.
HAT   Handbuch zum Alten Testament
HBOT   Magne Sæbø, ed. *Hebrew Bible/Old Testament: The History of its Inter-
           pretation*. 3 vols.; Göttingen: Vandenhoeck & Ruprecht, 1996–.
HBS   Herders Biblische Studien
HKAT   Handkommentar zum Alten Testament
HSM   Harvard Semitic Monographs
HSS   Harvard Semitic Studies
HThR   Harvard Theological Review
HTKAT   Herders Theologischer Kommentar zum Alten Testament
HUCA   *Hebrew Union College Annual*
IBHS   Bruce K. Waltke and Michael Patrick O'Conner, *An Introduction to
           Biblical Hebrew Syntax*. Winona Lake, IN: Eisenbrauns, 1990.
ICC   International Critical Commentary
IEJ   *Israel Exploration Journal*

Jastrow	Marcus Jastrow, *A Dictionary of the Targumim, the Talmud Babli and Yerushalemi, and the Midrashic Literature*. New York: Title Publishing, 1943, repr. Peabody, MA: Hendrickson, 2005.
JBQ	*Jewish Bible Quarterly Dor le Dor*
JBL	Journal of Biblical Literature
JJS	Journal of Jewish Studies
J–M	Paul Joüon and Takamitsu Muraoka, *A Grammar of Biblical Hebrew*. 2 vols.; Subsidia biblica, 14; Rome: Editrice Pontificio Istituto Biblico, 1991, reprinted 1993 and later with corrections.
JMEOS	*Journal of the Manchester University Egyptian and Oriental Society*
JNSL	*Journal of Northwest Semitic Languages*
JSHRZ	Jüdische Schriften aus hellenistisch-römischer Zeit
JSJ	*Journal for the Study of Judaism in the Persian, Hellenistic and Roman Period*
JSOR	*Journal of the Society of Oriental Research*
JSOT	*Journal for the Study of the Old Testament*
JSOTSup	*Journal for the Study of the Old Testament*, Supplement Series
KAI	H. Donner and W. Röllig, *Kanaanäische und aramäische Inschriften*. 3 vols.; Wiesbaden: Harrassowitz, 1962–1964.
KAT	Kommentar zum Alten Testament
KHC	Kurzer Hand-Commentar zum Alten Testament
LCL	Loeb Classical Library
LSJ	H. G. Liddell, Robert Scott and H. Stuart Jones, *Greek–English Lexicon*. 9th ed.; Oxford: Clarendon Press, 1968.
LTK	Walter Kasper and Konrad Baumgartner, eds. *Lexikon für Theologie und Kirche*. 11 vols.; 3d ed.; Freiburg: Herder, 1993–2001.
MGWJ	*Monatsschrift für Geschichte und Wissenschaft des Judentums*
MIO	*Mitteilungen des Instituts fur Orientforschung*
MT	The Masoretic Text
MVAeG	*Mitteilungen der Vorderasiatisch-ägyptischen Gesellschaft*
NBL	Manfred Görg and Bernhard Lang, eds. *Neues Bibel-Lexikon*. 3 vols.; Zürich: Benziger, 1991, 1995, 2001.
NICOT	New International Commentary on the Old Testament
NJB	*New Jerusalem Bible*
NKZ	*Neue kirchliche Zeitschrift*
NRSV	The New Revised Standard Version
NS	New Series
OBO	Orbis biblicus et orientalis
OTL	Old Testament Library
OTP	James H. Charlesworth, ed. *The Old Testament Pseudepigrapha*. 2 vols.; AB Reference Library; New York, NY: Doubleday, 1983, 1985.
OTS	*Oudtestamentische Studiën*
PTMS	Pittsburgh Theological Monograph Series
Peshitta	Peshitta Institute, ed. *The Old Testament in Syriac: According to the Peshitta version/Vetus Testamentum Syriace iuxta simplicem Syrorum*

versionem. Edited on behalf of the International Organization for the Study of the Old Testament. Leiden: E. J. Brill, 1972.

RB — Revue biblique

RGG³ — Kurt Galling, Hans Freiherr von Campenhausen et al., eds. *Die Religion in Geschichte und Gegenwart: Handwörterbuch für Theologie und Religionswissenschaft.* 6 + 1 vols.; 3d ed.; Tübingen: J. C. B. Mohr [Paul Siebeck], 1957–1965.

RGG⁴ — Hans Dieter Betz et al., eds. *Religion in Geschichte und Gegenwart: Handwörterbuch für Theologie und Religionswissenschaft.* 8 + 1 vols.; 4th ed.; Tübingen: Mohr Siebeck, 1998–2005.

Sam. — The Samaritan Pentateuch

SBAB — Stuttgarter Biblische Aufsatzbände

SBL — Society of Biblical Literature

SBLEJL — SBL Early Judaism and its Literature

SBLMS — SBL Monograph series

SBLSCS — SBL Septuagint and Cognate Studies

SBS — Stuttgarter Bibelstudien

SBU — Ivan Engnell, ed. *Svenskt bibliskt uppslagsverk.* 2 vols.; 2d ed.; Stockholm: Nordiska uppslagsböcker, 1962–1963.

SEÅ — *Svensk exegetisk årsbok*

SNTSMS — Society for New Testament Studies Monograph Series

Str–B — [Hermann L. Strack and] Paul Billerbeck, *Kommentar zum Neuen Testament aus Talmud und Midrasch.* 7 vols.; Munich: Beck, 1922–1961.

s.v. — *sub verbo*

THAT — Ernst Jenni and Claus Westermann, eds. *Theologisches Handwörterbuch zum Alten Testament.* Munich: Chr. Kaiser, 1971–1976.

ThWAT — G.J. Botterweck and H. Ringgren, eds. *Theologisches Wörterbuch zum Alten Testament.* Stuttgart: W. Kohlhammer, 1970–.

TRE — Balz, Horst, Gerhard Müller and Gerhard Krause, eds. *Theologische Realenzyklopädie.* 36 vols.; Berlin: W. de Gruyter, 1977–2006.

TTK — Tidsskrift for Teologi og Kirke

TWNT — Gerhard Kittel and Gerhard Friedrich, eds. *Theologisches Wörterbuch zum Neuen Testament.* 11 vols.; Stuttgart, Kohlhammer, 1932–1979.

UF — *Ugarit-Forschungen*

UTB — UTB für Wissenschaft: Uni-Taschenbücher

VT — *Vetus Testamentum*

VTSup — *Vetus Testamentum,* Supplements

Vul. — The Vulgate

WBC — Word Biblical Commentary

WdF — Wege der Forschung

WM — H. W. Haussig, ed. *Wörterbuch der Mythologie.* 8 vols.; Stuttgart: Klett-Cotta, 1965–2004.

WMANT — Wissenschaftliche Monographien zum Alten und Neuen Testament

WUNT — Wissenschaftliche Untersuchungen zum Neuen Testament

ZAW — *Zeitschrift für die alttestamentliche Wissenschaft*

ZB — Züricher Bibelkommentare

ZDPV — *Zeitschrift des deutschen Palästina-Vereins*

Bibliography

Abegg, Martin, Jr., Peter Flint, and Eugene Ulrich, eds. *The Dead Sea Scrolls Bible: The Oldest Known Bible Translated for the First Time into English by Martin Abegg, Jr., Peter Flint, and Eugene Ulrich.* San Francisco: HarperSan Francisco, 1999.

Abegg, Martin, Jr., James E. Bowley, Edward M. Cook, and Emanuel Tov. *The Dead Sea Scrolls Concordance.* Leiden: E. J. Brill, 2003–.

Abela, Anthony. 'The Genesis Genesis.' *Melita Theologica* 39 (1988): 155–85.

Ackroyd, Peter. 'The Jewish Community in Palestine in the Persian Period'. In *CHJ* 1:130–61.

Aharoni, Yohanan. *The Land of the Bible: A Historical Geography.* Translated by Anson F. Rainey. Second revised edition. Philadelphia: Westminster Press, 1979.

Aharoni, Yohanan, and Michael Avi-Yonah. *Der Bibel Atlas: Die Geschichte des Heiligen Landes 3000 Jahre vor Christus bis 200 Jahre nach Christus: 264 Karten mit kommentierendem Text.* Translated by Walter Hertenstein. Hamburg: Bechtermünz, 1998.

Albeck, Shalom, and Menachem Elon. 'Acquisition'. *EncJud* 1:359–63.

Albertz, Rainer. *A History of Israelite Religion in the Old Testament Period.* 2 vols. Translated by John Bowden. OTL. London: SCM, 1994.

Albright, William Foxwell. 'Abram the Hebrew—A New Archeological Interpretation'. *BASOR* 163 (1961): 36–54.

———. 'The Historical Background of Genesis XIV'. *JSOR* 10 (1926): 231–69.

———. 'The Jordan Valley in the Bronze Age'. *AASOR* 6 (1926): 13–74.

———. *Yahweh and the Gods of Canaan: A Historical Analysis of Two Contrasting Faiths.* London: Athlone, 1968.

Alexander, Philip S. 'Geography and the Bible: Early Jewish Geography'. *ABD* 2:977–88.

———. 'Retelling the Old Testament'. Pages 99–121 in *It Is Written: Scripture Citing Scripture: Essays in Honour of Barnabas Lindars,* edited by D. A. Carson, D. A. and H. G. M. Williamson. Cambridge: Cambridge University Press, 1988.

Alkier, Stefan. 'Intertextualität — Annäherungen an ein texttheoretisches Paradigma'. Pages 1–26 in *Heiligkeit und Herrschaft: Intertextuelle Studien zu Heiligkeitsvorstellungen und zu Psalm 110,* edited by Dieter Sänger. BThS 55. Neukirchen-Vluyn: Neukirchner Verlag, 2003.

Allen, Leslie C. *Psalms 101–150.* WBC 21. Waco, TX: Word, 1983.

Alt, Albrecht. 'Der Gott der Väter'. Pages 1–78 in *Kleine Schriften zur Geschichte des Volkes Israel.* I, by Albrecht Alt. Munich: Beck, 1953–1959.

Alter, Robert. *Genesis*. New York: Norton, 1996.

Amit, Yairah. *History and Ideology: An Introduction to Historiography in the Hebrew Bible*. Translated by Yael Lotan. Sheffield: Sheffield Academic Press, 1999.

Andersen, Francis I. 'Genesis 14: An Enigma'. Pages 497–508 in *Pomegranates and Golden Bells: Studies in Biblical, Jewish, and Near Eastern Ritual, Law, and Literature in Honor of Jacob Milgrom*, edited by D. P. Wright et al. Winona Lake, IN: Eisenbrauns, 1995.

———. 'The Enigma of Genesis 14 Revisited'. *Buried History: Quarterly Journal of the Australian Institute of Archaeology* 35, nos. 2–3 (1999): 62.

———. '2 (Slavonic Apocalypse of) ENOCH (late first century)'. *OTP* 1:91–222.

Andersen, Francis I., and David Noel Freedman. *Micah: A New Translation with Introduction and Commentary*. AB 24E. New York: Doubleday, 2000.

Andreasen, Niels-Erik. 'Genesis 14 in Its Near Eastern Context'. Pages 59–77 in *Scripture in Context: Essays on the Comparative Method*, edited by Carl D. Evans, William W. Hallo and John B. White. PTMS 34. Pittsburgh: Pickwick, 1980.

Aptowitzer, Victor. 'Malkisedek: Zu den Sagen der Agada'. *MGWJ* 70 (1926): 93–113.

Aschim, Anders. 'Melchizedek the Liberator: An Early Interpretation of Genesis 14?' Pages 243–58 in *Society of Biblical Literature 1996 Seminar Papers*. Society of Biblical Literature Seminar Papers 35. Atlanta: Scholars Press, 1996.

———. 'Melchizedek and Levi'. Pages 773–88 in *The Dead Sea Scrolls: Fifty Years after Their Discovery: Proceedings of the Jerusalem Congress, July 20–25, 1997*, edited by Lawrence H. Schiffman, Emanuel Tov, and James C. VanderKam. Jerusalem: Israel Exploration Society, 2000.

———. 'The Genre of 11QMelchizedek'. Pages 17–31 in *Qumran between the Old and New Testaments*, edited by Frederick H. Cryer and Thomas L. Thompson. JSOTSup 290. Copenhagen International Seminar 6. Sheffield: Sheffield Academic Press, 1998.

———. 'Verdens eldste bibelkommentar? Melkisedek-teksten fra Qumran'. *TTK* 2 (1995): 85–103.

Asmussen, P. 'Gen 14, ein politisches Flugblatt'. *ZAW* 34 (1914): 36–41.

Astour, Michael C. 'Amraphel'. *ABD* 1:217–18.

———. 'Chedorlaomer'. *ABD* 1:893–95.

———. 'Goiim'. *ABD* 2:1057.

———. 'Melchizedek'. *ABD* 4:684–88.

———. 'Political and Cosmic Symbolism in Genesis 14 and in Its Babylonian Sources'. Pages 65–112 in *Biblical Motifs: Origins and Transformations*, edited by Alexander Altmann. Brandeis University Studies and Texts 3. Cambridge, MA: Harvard University Press, 1966.

———. 'Siddim, Valley of'. *ABD* 6:15–16.

———. 'Tidal'. *ABD* 6:551–52.

Avemaria, Friedrich, and Hermann Lichtenberger, eds. *Bund und Tora: Zur theologischen Begriffsgeschichte in alttestamentlicher, frühjüdischer und urchristlicher Tradition*. WUNT 92. Tübingen: J. C. B. Mohr [Paul Siebeck], 1996.

Baethgen, F. *Die Psalmen*. Third edition. HKAT. Göttingen: Vandenhoeck & Ruprecht, 1904.

Bail, Ulrike. 'Psalm 110: Eine intertextuelle Lektüre aus alttestamentlicher Perspektive'. Pages 94–121 in *Heiligkeit und Herrschaft: Intertextuelle Studien zu Heiligkeitsvorstellungen und zu Psalm 110*, edited by Dieter Sänger. BThS 55. Neukirchen-Vluyn: Neukirchner Verlag, 2003.

Balz, Horst. 'Melchisedek: III. Neues Testament'. *TRE* 22:420–23.

Baltzer, Klaus. 'Jerusalem in den Erzväter-Geschichten der Genesis? Traditionsgeschichtliche Erwägungen zu Gen 14 und 22'. Pages 3–12 in *Die hebräische Bibel und ihrer zweifache Nachgeschichte*, edited by Erhard Blum and Rolf Rendtorff. FS R. Rendtorff. Neukirchen-Vluyn: Neukirchener Verlag, 1990.

Barr, James. *History and Ideology in the Old Testament: Biblical Studies at the End of a Millennium*. Oxford: Oxford University Press, 2000.

Barton, John. 'Intertextuality and the "Final Form"'. Pages 33–37 in *Congress Volume Oslo 1998*, edited by André Lemaire and Magne Sæbø. VTSup 80. Leiden: E. J. Brill, 2000.

Bauer, Walter, Kurt Aland, and Barbara Aland. *Griechisch-deutsches Wörterbuch zu den Schriften des Neuen Testaments und der frühchristlichen Literatur*. Sixth edition. Berlin: W. de Gruyter, 1988.

Baumgarten, Joseph M. 'The Heavenly Tribunal and the Personification of Ṣedeq in Jewish Apocalyptic'. *ANRW* 2.19/1 (Berlin: W. de Gruyter, 1979), 219–39.

———. 'On the non-literal use of * maʿăśēr/dekatē*'. *JBL* 103, no. 2 (1984): 245–61.

Beal, Timothy K. 'Glossary'. Pages 21–24 in *Reading between Texts: Intertextuality and the Hebrew Bible*, edited by Danna Nolan Fewell. Literary Currents in Biblical Interpretation. Louisville, KY: Westminster/John Knox Press, 1992.

Benzinger, Immanuel. 'Zur Quellenscheidung in Gen 14'. Pages 21–27 in *Vom Alten Testament: Karl Marti zum siebzigsten Geburtstage*, edited by Karl Budde. FS K. Marti. BZAW 41. Gießen: Töpelmann, 1925.

Berenbaum, Michael and, Fred Skolnik, eds. *Encyclopaedia Judaica*. Second edition. 22 vols. Detroit, MI: Macmillan Reference, 2007.

Berger, Klaus. 'Abraham: II. Im Frühjudentum und Neuen Testament'. *TRE* 1:372–82.

Bergsma, John Sietze. 'The Jubilee: A Post-Exilic Priestly Attempt to Reclaim Lands?' *Bib* 84 (2003): 225–46.

Bernhardt, Karl-Heinz. 'Melchisedek: I. Altes Testament'. *TRE* 22:414–17.

Berlin, Adele. 'On the Use of Traditional Jewish Exegesis in the Modern Literary Study of the Bible'. Pages 173–83 in *Tehilla le-Moshe: Biblical and Judaic Studies in Honor of Moshe Greenberg*, edited by Mordechai Cogan, Barry L. Eichler and Jeffrey H. Tigay. Winona Lake, IN: Eisenbrauns, 1997.

Bernstein, Moshe J. 'The Contribution of the Qumran Discoveries to the History of Early Biblical Interpretation'. Pages 215–38 in *The Idea of Biblical Interpretation: Essays in Honor of James L. Kugel*, edited by Hindy Najman and

Judith H. Newman. Supplements to the Journal for the Study of Judaism 83. Leiden: E. J. Brill, 2004.

BibleWorks 7: Software for Biblical Exegesis and Research. Norfolk, VA: BibleWorks, 2006.

Bickerman, Elias J. 'The Diaspora: B. The Babylonian Captivety'. *CHJ* 1:342–57.

Biddle, Mark E. 'The Figure of Lady Jerusalem: Identification, Deification and Personification of Cities in the Ancient Near East'. Pages 173–94 in *The Biblical Canon in Comparative Perspective,* edited by K. Lawson Younger, William W. Hallo and Bernard Frank Batto. Scripture in Context 4. Ancient Near Eastern Texts and Studies 11. Lewiston, NY: Edwin Mellen, 1991.

Bird, Chad L. 'Typological Interpretation within the Old Testament: Melchizedekian Typology'. *Concordia Journal* (January, 2000): 36–52.

Blenkinsopp, Joseph. *Ezra–Nehemiah: A Commentary*. OTL. London: SCM, 1989.

———. 'The Pentateuch'. Pages 181–97 in *The Cambridge Companion to Biblical Interpretation,* edited by John Barton. Cambridge: Cambridge University Press, 1998.

———. *The Pentateuch: An Introduction to the First Five Books of the Bible*. AB Reference Library. New York: Doubleday, 1992.

Blum, Erhard. 'Abraham: I. Altes Testament'. *RGG*⁴ 1, cols. 70–74.

———. *Die Kompostion der Vätergeschichte*. WMANT 57. Neukirchen-Vluyn: Neukirchener Verlag, 1984.

———. *Studien zur Komposition des Pentateuch*. BZAW 189. Berlin: W. de Gruyter, 1990.

Bodendorfer, Gerhard. 'Zur Historisierung des Psalters in der rabbinischen Literatur'. Pages 215–34 in *Der Psalter in Judentum und Christentum,* edited by Erich Zenger. HBS 18. Freiburg: Herder, 1998.

———. 'Abraham zur Rechten Gottes: Der Ps 110 in der rabbinischen Tradition'. *EvT* 59 (1999): 252–66.

Bodendorfer, Gerhard, and Matthias Millard, eds. *Bibel und Midrasch: zur Bedeutung der rabbinischen Exegese für die Bibelwissenschaft*. FAT 22. Tübingen: Mohr Siebeck, 1998.

Böhl, Franz Marius Theodor de Liagre. 'Amraphel'. *RGG*³ 1, cols. 332–33.

———. 'Das Zeitalter Abrahams'. Pages 26–49, 476–79 in *Opera Minora: Studies en bijdragen op assyrologisch en oudtestamentisch terrein,* by Franz Marius Theodor de Liagre Böhl. Groningen and Djakarta: J. B. Wolters, 1953.

Bons, Eberhard. 'Die Septuaginta-Version von Psalm 110 (109 LXX): Textgestalt, Aussagen, Auswirkungen'. Pages 122–45 in *Heiligkeit und Herrschaft: Intertextuelle Studien zu Heiligkeitsvorstellungen und zu Psalm 110,* edited by Dieter Sänger. BThS 55. Neukirchen-Vluyn: Neukirchner Verlag, 2003.

Booij, Th. 'Psalm cx: "Rule in the midst of your foes!"'. *VT* 41 (1991): 396–407.

Bötterich, Christfried. 'Die vergessene Geburtsgechichte: Mt 1–2/Lk 1–2 und die wunderbare Geburt des Melchizedek in slHen 71–72'. Pages 222–48 in *Jüdische Schriften in ihrem antik-jüdischen und urchristlichen Kontext,* edited by Hermann Lichtenberger and Gerbern S. Oegema. Studien zu den Jüdischen Schriften aus hellenistisch-römischer Zeit, Bd. 1. Gütersloh: Gütersloher Verlagshaus, 2002.

————. 'The Melchizedek Story of 2 *(Slavonic) Enoch*: A Reaction to A. Orlov'. *JSJ* 32 (2001): 445–70.

Bowker, J. W. 'Psalm CX'. *VT* 17 (1967): 31–41.

Braude, William G. *The Midrash on Psalms*. 2 vols. Yale Judaica Series 13. New Haven, CT: Yale University Press, 1959.

Brenton, Lancelot C. L. *The Septuagint with Apocrypha: Greek and English*. London: Samuel Bagster & Sons, 1851. Reprint: Peabody, MA: Hendrickson, 1986 and subsequent reprints.

Brettler, Marc Zvi. *The Creation of History in Ancient Israel*. London: Routledge, 1995.

Brodsky, Harold. 'Did Abram Wage a Just War?' *JBQ* 31, no. 3 (2003): 167–73.

Brooke, George J. 'Melchizedek (11QMelch)'. *ABD* 4:687–88.

Brown, W. P. 'A Royal Performance: Critical Notes on Psalm 110:3aγ-b'. *JBL* 117 (1998): 93–96.

Brueggemann, Walter. *The Land*. Overtures to Biblical Theology. Philadelphia: Fortress, 1977.

Cancik, Hubert. *Grundzüge der hethitischen und alttestamentlichen Geschichtsschreibung*. Abhandlungen des deutschen Palästinavereins. Wiesbaden: Otto Harrassowitz, 1976.

Carr, David M. 'Intratextuality and Intertextuality—Joining Transmission History and Interpretation History in the Study of Genesis'. Pages 97–112 in *Bibel und Midrasch: Zur Bedeutung der rabbinischen Exegese für die Bibelwissenschaft*, edited by Gerhard Bodendorfer and Matthias Millard. FAT 22. Tübingen: Mohr Siebeck, 1998.

————. *Reading the Fractures of Genesis: Historical and Literary Approaches*. Louisville, KY: Westminster/John Knox Press, 1998.

————. *Writing on the Tablet of the Heart: Origins of Scripture and Literature*. Oxford: Oxford University Press, 2005.

Cassuto, Umberto. *A Commentary on the Book of Genesis*. 2 vols. Translated by Israel Abrahams. Jerusalem: Magnes, 1961–1964.

————. 'Berešit'. Pages 318–35 in *ʾEnṣiqlopediya miqraʾit*, II. Jerusalem: Mosad Bialiq, 1954.

Charlesworth, James H., ed. *The Old Testament Pseudepigrapha*. 2 vols. AB Reference Library. New York: Doubleday, 1983, 1985.

Charpin, Dominique. '"Ein umherziehender Aramäer was mein Vater": Abraham in Lichte der Quellen aus Mari'. Pages 40–52 in '*Abraham, unser Vater': Die gemeinsamen Wurzeln von Judentum, Christentum und Islam*, edited by Reinhard Gregor Kratz and Tilman Nagel. Göttingen: Wallstein, 2003.

Clines, David J. A. 'Possibilities and Priorities of Biblical Interpretation in an International Perspective'. *Biblical Interpretation* 1 (1993): 67–87.

————. *Interested Parties: The Ideology of Writers and Readers of the Hebrew Bible*. JSOTSup, 205. Gender Culture Theory 1. Sheffield: Sheffield Academic Press, 1995.

Clines, David J. A., Philip R. Davies, and John W. Rogerson, eds. *The Dictionary of Classical Hebrew*. Sheffield: Sheffield Academic Press, 1993–.

Cockerill, Gareth Lee. 'Melchizedek or "King of Righteousness"?' *EvQ* 63 (1991): 305–12.

Cody, Aelred, *A History of Old Testament Priesthood*. Analecta biblica 35. Rome: Pontifical Biblical Institute, 1969.

———. *Ezekiel, with an Excursus on Old Testament Priesthood*. Wilmington, DE: Michael Glazier, 1984.

Cohen, Chaim. 'Genesis 14—An Early Israelite Chronographic Source'. Pages 67–107 in *The Biblical Canon in Comparative Perspective*, edited by K. Lawson Younger, William W. Hallo, and Bernard Frank Batto. Scripture in Context 4. Ancient Near Eastern Texts and Studies 11. Lewiston, NY: Edwin Mellen, 1991.

Collins, John J. *Daniel: A Commentary on the Book of Daniel*. Hermeneia. Minneapolis MN: Augsburg Fortress, 1993.

Collins, Yarbro. 'Aristobulus (Second Century B.C.)'. *OTP* 2:831–42.

Cornelius, Friedrich. 'Genesis XIV'. *ZAW* 72 (1960): 1–7.

Cornill, C. H. 'Genesis 14'. *ZAW* 34 (1914): 150–51.

Crawford, Sidnie White. 'The Use of the Pentateuch in the *Temple Scroll* and the *Damascus Document* in the Second Century B.C.E'. Pages 301–17 in *The Pentateuch as Torah: New Models for Understanding Its Promulgation and Acceptance*, edited by Gary N. Knoppers and Bernhard M. Levinson. Winona Lake, IN: Eisenbrauns, 2007.

Cross, Frank Moore. 'The Ammonite Oppression of the Tribes of Gad and Reuben: Missing Verses from 1 Samuel 11 Found in 4QSamuel^a'. Pages 105–9 in *The Hebrew and Greek Texts of Samuel: 1980 Proceedings IOSCS-Vienna*, edited by Emanuel Tov. Jerusalem: Academon, 1980. Reprinted on pp. 148–59 of *History, Historiography and Interpretation: Studies in Biblical and Cuneiform Literatures*, edited by H. Tadmor and M. Weinfeld. Jerusalem: Magnes, 1983.

Dahood, Mitchell. *Psalms*. 3 vols. AB 16–17. Garden City, NY: Doubleday, 1966–73.

Dandamayev, M. 'The Diaspora: A. Babylonia in the Persian Age'. *CHJ* 1:326–341.

Daube, David, *Studies in Biblical Law*. Cambridge: Cambridge University Press, 1947. Reprint, New York: Ktav, 1969.

Dautzenberg, Gerhard. 'Psalm 110 im Neuen Testament'. Pages 63–97 in *Studien zur Theologie der Jesustradition*, by Gerhard Dauzenberg. SBAB 19. Stuttgart: Verlag Katholisches Bibelwerk, 1995.

Davies, Philip R. 'War Rule (1QM)'. *ABD* 6:875–76.

Davies, W. D., and Louis Finkelstein, eds. *The Cambridge History of Judaism*. Cambridge: Cambridge University Press, 1984.

Day, John. *King and Messiah in Israel and the Ancient Near East: Proceedings of the Oxford Old Testament Seminar*. JSOTSup 270. Sheffield: Sheffield Academic Press, 1998.

———. *Psalms*. Sheffield: Sheffield Academic Press, 1992. Reprint, London: T. & T. Clark International, 2003.

———. 'The Canaanite Inheritance of the Israelite Monarchy'. Pages 72–90 in *King and Messiah in Israel and the Ancient Near East: Proceedings of the Oxford*

Old Testament Seminar, edited by John Day. JSOTSup 270. Sheffield: Sheffield Academic Press, 1998.

Delamarter, Steve, and James H. Charlesworth. *A Scripture Index to Charlesworth's The Old Testament Pseudepigrapha.* Sheffield: Sheffield Academic Press, 2002.

Delcor, M. 'Melchizedek from Genesis to the Qumran Texts and the Epistle to the Hebrews'. *JSJ* 2 (1971): 115–35.

Delitzsch, Franz. *Neuer Commentar über die Genesis.* Fifth edition. Leipzig: Dörffling und Franke, 1887.

Della Vida, G. L. 'El ‚Elyon in Genesis 14:18–20'. *JBL* 63 (1944): 1–9.

Delling, Gerhard. 'ὕμνος κτλ. B II. Zu den Liedern des Alten Testaments und des Judentums'. *TWNT* 8:498–501.

Del Medico, H. E. 'Melchisédech'. *ZAW* 69 (1957): 160–70.

Derovan, David, Gershom Scholem, and Moshe Idel. 'Gematria'. *EncJud* 7: 424–27.

Dieterich, Walter. 'Deuteronomistisches Geschichtswerk'. *RGG*⁴ 2, cols. 688–92.

Dillmann, August. *Die Genesis.* Sixth edition. Kurzgefasstes exegetisches Handbuch zum Alten Testament 11. Leipzig: Hirzel, 1892.

Dines, Jennifer M. *The Septuagint.* Understanding the Bible and Its World. London: T. & T. Clark, 2004.

Donner, Herbert. 'Der verläßliche Prophet. Betrachtungen zu I Makk 14,41ff und zu Ps 110'. Pages 213–33 in *Aufsätze zum Alten Testament,* by Herbert Donner. BZAW 224. Berlin: W. de Gruyter, 1994. Originally printed in Rüdiger Liwak and Siegfried Wagner, eds., *Prophetie und geschichtliche Wirklichkeit im alten Israel: Festschrift für Siegfried Herrmann zum 65. Geburtstag.* Stuttgart: W. Kohlhammer, 1991, 89–98.

———. *Geschichte des Volkes Israel und seiner Nachbarn in Grundzügen.* 2 vols. Second edition. ATD Ergänzungsreihe 14/1–2. Göttingen: Vandenhoeck & Ruprecht, 1995.

Donner, Herbert, Wolfgang Röllig, and O. Rössler, *Kanaanäische und aramäische Inschriften.* Third edition. Wiesbaden: Harrassowitz, 1971.

Driver, S. R., *The Book of Genesis.* Fourth edition. London: Methuen, 1905.

Duhm, Bernhard. *Die Psalmen.* Second edition. KHC 14. Tübingen: Mohr, 1922.

Ego, Beate. 'Abraham als Urbild der Toratreue Israels: Traditionsgeschichtliche Überlegungen zu einem Aspekt des biblischen Abrahamsbildes'. Pages 25–40 in *Bund und Tora: Zur theologischen Begriffsgeschichte in alttestamentlicher, frühjüdischer und urchristlicher Tradition,* edited by Friedrich Avemaria and Hermann Lichtenberger. WUNT 92. Tübingen: J. C. B. Mohr [Paul Siebeck], 1996.

Eißfeldt, Otto, *Einleitung in das Alte Testament: Unter Einschluß der apokryphen und Pseudepigraphen sowie der apokryphen- und pseudepigraphenartigen Qumrān-Skriften: Entstehungsgeschichte des Alten Testaments.* Third revised edition. Neue theologische Grundrisse. Tübingen: Mohr, 1964.

Elgavish, D. 'The Encounter of Abram and Melchizedek King of Salem: A Covenant Establishing Ceremony'. Pages 495–508 in *Studies in the Book of Gen-*

esis. Literature, Redaction and History, edited by André Wénin. BETL 155. Leuven: Leuven University Press, 2001.

Emerton, John A. 'Some False Clues in the Study of Genesis XIV'. *VT* 21 (1971): 24–47.

———. 'Some Problems in Genesis XIV'. Pages 73–102 in *Studies in the Pentateuch,* edited by John A. Emerton. VTSup 41. Leiden: E. J. Brill, 1990.

———. 'The Riddle of Genesis XIV'. *VT* 21 (1971): 403–39.

———. 'The Site of Salem, the City of Melchizedek (Genesis XIV 18)'. Pages 45–71 in *Studies in the Pentateuch,* edited by John A. Emerton. VTSup 41. Leiden: E. J. Brill, 1990

Endres, John C., S.J. *Biblical Interpretation in the Book of Jubilees.* CBQMS 18. Washington, DC: Catholic Biblical Association of America, 1987.

Engel, Helmut. 'XI. Das Buch Judit'. Pages 256–66 in *Einleitung in das Alte Testament,* edited by Erich Zenger et al. Fourth edition. Kohlhammer-Studienbücher Theologie, 1,1. Stuttgart: W. Kohlhammer, 2001.

Engnell, Ivan, ed. *Svenskt bibliskt uppslagsverk.* 2 vols. Second edition. Stockholm: Nordiska uppslagsböcker, 1962, 1963.

Epstein, Isidore, ed. *Hebrew–English Edition of the Babylonian Talmud.* 18 vols. London: Soncino, 1961.

Evans, Craig A. 'Abraham'. *EncDSS* 1:2–4.

Fabry, Heinz-Josef. 'Melchisedek'. *LTK* 7, cols. 79–81.

Fewell, Danna Nolan, ed. *Reading between Texts: Intertextuality and the Hebrew Bible.* Literary Currents in Biblical Interpretation. Louisville, KY: Westminster/John Knox Press, 1992.

Fishbane, Michael. *Biblical Interpretation in Ancient Israel.* Oxford: Clarendon, 1985.

———. 'Inner-Biblical Exegesis'. *HBOT* 1:33–48.

———. 'Types of Biblical Intertextuality'. Pages 39–44 in *Congress Volume Oslo 1998,* edited by André Lemaire and Magne Sæbø. VTSup 80; Leiden: E. J. Brill, 2000.

Fitzmyer, Joseph A. *Essays on the Semitic Background of the New Testament.* Sources for Biblical Study 5. London: G. Chapman, 1971.

———. 'Further Light on Melchizedek from Qumran Cave 11'. *JBL* 86 (1967): 25–41. Reprinted in Joseph A. Fitzmyer, *Essays on the Semitic Background of the New Testament.* Sources for Biblical Study 5. London: G. Chapman, 1971, 245–67.

———. 'Melchizedek in the MT, LXX and the NT'. *Bib* 81 (2000): 63–69.

———. '"Now this Melchizedek. . ."'. *CBQ* 25 (1963): 305–21. Reprinted in Joseph A. Fitzmyer, *Essays on the Semitic Background of the New Testament.* Sources for Biblical Study 5. London: G. Chapman, 1971, 221–43.

———. *The Genesis Apocryphon of Qumran Cave 1 (1Q20).* Third edition. BibOr 18/B. Rome: Editrice Pontificio Istituto Biblico, 2004.

Freedman, H., and Maurice Simon, *The Midrash Rabbah.* 5 vols. Foreword by I. Epstein. London, Jerusalem, and New York: Soncino, 1977.

Friedman, Richard, and Shawna Overton. 'Pentateuch'. *EncJud* 15:730–53.

Fritz, Volkmar. 'Die Grenzen des Landes Israel'. Pages 14–34 in *Studies in Historical Geography and Biblical Historiography: Presented to Zecharia Kallai*, edited by Gershon Galil and Moshe Weinfeld. VTSup 81. Leiden: E. J. Brill, 2000.

Frumkin, Amos, and Yoel Elitzur. 'The Rise and Fall of the Dead Sea'. *BARev* (Nov./Dec., 2001): 42–50.

Füglister, Notker. 'Die Verwendung und das Verständnis der Psalmen und des Psalters um die Zeitwende'. Pages 319–84 in *Beiträge zur Psalmenforschung: Psalm 2 und 22*, edited by Josef Schreiner. FzB 60. Würzburg: Echter, 1988.

Gadamer, Hans-Georg. *Gesammelte Werke. II Hermeneutik II: Wahrheit und Methode*. UTB 2115. J. C. B. Mohr [Paul Siebeck]: Tübingen, 1986/1993.

Gall, August Freiherr von Gall. *Der hebräische Pentateuch der Samaritaner*. 5 vols. Giessen: Alfred Töpelmann, 19141–1918. Reprint, Berlin: Alfred Töpelmann, 1966.

Garbini, Giovanni. *History and Ideology in Ancient Israel*. Translated by John Bowden. London: SCM, 1988.

Gammie, John G. 'A New Setting for Psalm 110'. *ATR* 51 (1969): 4–17.

———. 'Loci of the Melchizedek Tradition of Genesis 14:18–20'. *JBL* 90 (1971): 385–96.

Gaster, T. H. 'Psalm 110'. *JMEOS* 21 (1937): 37–44.

Gelb, Ignace J., John A. Brinkman, et al., eds. *The Assyrian Dictionary of the Oriental Institute of the University of Chicago*. 19 vols. Chicago: Oriental Institute, 1956–.

Gerleman, Gillis. 'Psalm CX'. *VT* 31 (1981): 1–19.

Gerstenberger, Erhard S. *Israel in der Perserzeit: 5. und 4. Jahrhundert v. Chr.* Biblische Enzyklopädie 8. Stuttgart: W. Kohlhammer, 2005.

———. *Psalms and Lamentations: Part 2*. FOTL 15. Grand Rapids, MI: Eerdmans, 2001.

Gertz, Jan Christian. 'Abraham, Mose und der Exodus: Beobachtungen zur Redaktionsgeschichte von Gen 15'. Pages 63–81 in *Abschied vom Jahwisten: Die Komposition des Hexateuch in der jüngsten Diskussion*, edited by Jan Christian Gertz, Konrad Schmid, and Markus Witte. BZAW 315. Berlin: W. de Gruyter, 2002.

Gertz, Jan Christian, Konrad Schmid, and Markus Witte, eds. *Abschied vom Jahwisten: Die Komposition des Hexateuch in der jüngsten Diskussion*. BZAW 315. Berlin: W. de Gruyter, 2002.

Gese, Hartmut. 'Die Komposition der Abrahamserzählung'. Pages 29–51 in *Alttestamentliche Studien*, by Hartmut Gese. Tübingen: Mohr [Siebeck], 1991.

Gesenius, Wilhelm, *Gesenius' Hebrew Grammar*. Edited by E. Kautzsch. Revised and translated by A. E. Cowley. Oxford: Clarendon, 1910.

Gesenius, Wilhelm, Frants Buhl, et al., eds. *Hebräisches und Aramäisches Handwörterbuch über das Alte Testament*. Berlin: Springer, 1962 [= reprint of the seventeenth edition, 1915].

Gevirtz, S. 'Abram's 318'. *IEJ* 19, no. 2 (1969): 110–13.

Ginsburger, Moses. *Pseudo-Jonathan: Thargum Jonathan ben Usiel zum Pentateuch: Nach der Londoner Handschrift herausgegeben von Moses Ginsburger*. Berlin: Calvary, 1903. Reprint, Hildesheim: Georg Olm, 1971.

Ginzberg, Louis, *Legends of the Jews*. 2 vols. JPS Classic Reissues. Translated by Henrietta Szold and Paul Radin. Foreword by David Stern. Philadelphia: Jewish Publication Society, 2003.

Giversen, S., and A. Pearson, Melchizedek (IX,1). In *The Nag Hammadi Library in English*, edited by James M. Robinson. Fourth revised edition. Leiden: E. J. Brill, 1996.

Görg, Manfred. 'Thronen zur Rechten Gottes: Zur altägyptischen Wurzel einer Bekenntnisformel'. *BN* 81 (1996): 72–81.

———, and Bernhard Lang, eds. *Neues Bibel-Lexikon*. 3 vols. Zürich: Benziger, 1991, 1995, 2001.

Gosse, Bernard. 'Melchisédek et le messianisme sacredotal'. *BeO* 38 (1996): 79–89.

Grabbe, Lester L. *Judaism from Cyrus to Hadrian*. 2 vols. Minneapolis, MN: Augsburg Fortress, 1992.

———. *Priests, Prophets, Diviners, Sages: A Socio-Historical Study of Religious Specialists in Ancient Israel*. Valley Forge, PA: Trinity Press International, 1995.

Granerød, Gard. 'Melchizedek in Hebrews 7'. *Bib* 90 (2009): 188–202.

———. 'Omnipresent in Narratives, Disputed among Grammarians: Some Contributions to the Understanding of *wayyiqtol* and Their Underlying Paradigms'. *ZAW* 121 (2009): 418–34.

Grossfeld, Bernhard. *The Targum Onqelos to Genesis: Translated, with a Critical Introduction, Apparatus, and Notes*. The Aramaic Bible 6. Edinburgh: T. & T. Clark, 1989.

Gruber, Mayer Irwin. *Rashi's Commentary on Psalms*. Brill Reference Library of Judaism 18. Leiden: E. J. Brill, 2004.

Gunkel, Hermann. *Ausgewählte Psalmen*. Fourth edition. Göttingen: Vandenhoeck & Ruprecht, 1917.

———. *Die Psalmen*. HKAT. Göttingen: Vandenhoeck & Ruprecht, 1926.

———. *Genesis*. HKAT, Abteilung 1: Die historischen Bücher 1. Göttingen: Vandenhoeck & Ruprecht, 1917 [fourth edition] = 1910 [third edition].

Gunneweg, Antonius H. J. *Biblische Theologie des Alten Testaments: Eine Religionsgeschichte Israels in biblisch-theologischer Sicht*. Stuttgart: W. Kohlhammer, 1993.

Haag, Ernst. *Studium zum Buche Judith: Seine theologische Bedeutung und literarische Eigenart*. Trierer Theologische Studien 16. Trier: Paulinus, 1963.

Habel, N. '"Yahweh, Maker of Heaven and Earth": A Study in Tradition Criticism'. *JBL* 91 (1972): 321–37.

Hamilton, Victor P. 'Satan'. *ABD* 5:985–89.

———. *The Book of Genesis: Chapters 1–17*. NICOT. Grand Rapids, MI: Eerdmans, 1990.

Hamp, Vinzenz. 'Psalm 110,4b und die Septuaginta'. Pages 519–29 in *Neues Testament und die Kirche*, edited by Joachim Gnilka. FS Rudolf Schnackenburg. Freiburg: Herder, 1974.

Haran, Menahem. 'Book-Scrolls at the Beginning of the Second Temple Period: The Transition from Papyrus to Skins'. *HUCA* 54 (1983): 111–22.

———, Menahem Stern, and Gerald Y. Blidstein. 'Priests and Priesthood'. *EncJud* 16:513–26.

Hauser, Alan J., and Duane F. Watson, eds. *A History of Biblical Interpretation.* Grand Rapids, MI: Eerdmans, 2003–.

Hay, David M. *Glory at the Right Hand: Psalm 110 in Early Christianity.* SBLMS 18. Nashville: Abingdon, 1973.

Hengel, Martin. 'Psalm 110 und die Erhöhung des Auferstandenen zur Rechten Gottes'. Pages 43–73 in *Anfänge der Christologie: Feschschrift für Ferdinand Hahn zum 65. Geburtstag,* edited by Cilliers Breytenbach and Henning Paulsen. Göttingen: Vandenhoeck & Ruprecht, 1991.

Herodotus. *The Histories: With an Introduction and Notes by Donald Lateiner.* Translated by G. C. Macaulay. Revised throughout by Donald Lateiner. New York: Barnes & Nobles Classics, 2004.

Herrmann, W. 'Wann wurde Jahwe zum Schöpfer der Welt?' *UF* 23 (1991): 165–80.

Hertzberg, Hans Wilhelm. 'Die Melkisedek-Tradition'. Pages 36–44 in *Beiträge zur Traditionsgeschichte und Theologie des Alten Testaments,* by Hans Wilhelm Hertzberg. Göttingen: Vandenhoeck & Ruprecht, 1962.

Hilber, John W. 'Psalm cx in the Light of Assyrian Prophecies'. *VT* 53 (2003): 353–66.

Hillers, Delbert R. *Micah: A Commentary on the Book of the Prophet Micah.* Hermeneia. Philadelphia: Fortress, 1984.

Hoerth, Alfred J., Gerald L. Mattingly, and Edwin Yamauchi, eds. *Peoples of the Old Testament World.* Cambridge: Lutterworth [first edition] and Grand Rapids, MI: Baker Books [second edition], 1996.

Hoftijzer, J., and K. Jongelin., *Dictionary of the North-West Semitic Inscriptions.* 2 vols. Handbuch der Orientalistik 1. Abteilung, Der Nahe und Mittlere Osten 21. Leiden: E. J. Brill, 1995.

Holzinger, H. *Genesis.* KHC 1. Freiburg i. B.: Mohr, 1898.

Hommel, Fritz. *Die altisraelitische Überlieferung in inschriftlicher Beleuchtung: Ein Einspruch in gegen die Aufstellung der modernen Pentateuchkritik.* Munich: G. Franz'sche Hofbuchhandlung, 1897.

Horowitz, Wayne. 'The Isles of the Nations: Genesis X and Babylonian Geography'. Pages 35–43 in *Studies in the Pentateuch,* edited by John A. Emerton. VTSup 41. Leiden: E. J. Brill, 1990.

Horton, Fred L. *The Melchizedek Tradition: A Critical Examination of the Sources to the Fifth Century A.D. and in the Epistle to the Hebrews.* SNTSMS 30. Cambridge: Cambridge University Press, 1976.

Hurvitz, Avi, Jacob Milgrom, David P. Wright, and David Noel Freedman, eds. *Pomegranates and Golden Bells: Studies in Biblical, Jewish, and Near Eastern Ritual, Law, and Literature in Honor of Jacob Milgrom.* Winona Lake, IN: Eisenbrauns, 1995.

Iser, Wolfgang, *Der Akt des Lesens: Theorie ästhetischer Wirkung.* Uni-Taschenbücher 636. Munich: Fink, 1976.

Jacob, Benno. *Das erste Buch der Tora: Genesis.* Berlin: Schocken, 1934. English trans., *The First Book of the Torah: Genesis.* New York: Ktav, 1974.

Jaffee, Martin S. *Torah in the Mouth: Writing and Oral Tradition in Palestinian Judaism, 200 BCE–400 CE.* New York: Oxford University Press, 2001.

Jagersma, Hendrik. 'The Tithes in the Old Testament'. *OTS* 21 (1981): 116–28.

Japhet, Sara. *I & II Chronicles*. OTL. London: SCM, 1993.

Jastrow, Marcus. *A Dictionary of the Targumim, the Talmud Babli and Yerushalemi, and the Midrashic Literature*. New York: Title Publishing, 1943. Reprint, Peabody, MA: Hendrickson, 2005.

Jefferson, H. G. 'Is Psalm 110 Canaanite?' *JBL* 73 (1954): 152–56.

Jenni, Ernst, and Claus Westermann, eds. *Theologisches Handwörterbuch zum Alten Testament*. Munich: Chr. Kaiser, 1971–76.

Jeppesen, Knud. *Jesajas Bog fortolket*. Copenhagen: Det danske Bibelselskap, 1988.

Jeremias, Alfred. 'Die sogenannten Kedorlaomer-Texte'. *MVAeG* 21, no. 1 (1917): 69–97.

Johnson, M. D. 'Life of Adam and Eve'. *OTP* 2:249–95.

Josephus, Flavius. *Josephus: With an English Translation*. 13 vols. LCL. London: Heinemann, 1926–2004.

———. *The New Complete Works of Josephus*. Translated by William Whiston. Commentary by Paul L. Maier. Revised and expanded edition. Grand Rapids, MI: Kregel, 1999.

Joüon, Paul, and Takamitsu Muraoka. *A Grammar of Biblical Hebrew*. 2 vols. Subsidia biblica 14. Rome: Editrice Pontificio Istituto Biblico, 1991. Reprinted 1993 and later with corrections.

Kaiser, Otto. 'The Pentateuch and the Deuteronomistic History'. Pages 289–322 in *Text in Context: Essays by the Members of the Society for the Old Testament Study*, edited by A. D. H. Mayes. Oxford: Oxford University Press, 2000.

Kalimi, Isaac. *The Reshaping of Ancient Israelite History in Chronicles*. Winona Lake, IN: Eisenbrauns, 2005.

Kallai, Zecharia. 'The Campaign of Chedorlaomer and Biblical Historiography'. Pages 218–42 in *Biblical Historiography and Historical Geography: Collection of Studies*, by Zecharia Kallai. BEAT 44. Frankfurt am Main: Peter Lang, 1998.

———. 'The Wandering Traditions from Kadesh-Barnea to Canaan: A Study in Biblical Historiography'. *JJS* 33 (1982): 175–18. Reprinted in Zecharia Kallai, *Biblical Historiography and Historical Geography: Collection of Studies*. BEAT 44. Frankfurt am Main: Peter Lang, 1998, 165–74.

Kartveit, Magnar. *Motive und Schichten der Landtheologie in I Chronik 1–9*. ConBOT 28. Stockholm: Almqvist & Wiksell, 1989.

———. 'Names and Narratives: The Meaning of Their Combination in 1 Chronicles 1–9'. Pages 59–80 in *Shai le-Sara Japhet: Studies in the Bible, Its Exegesis and Its Language*, edited by Moshe Bar-Asher et al. Jerusalem: Bialik Institute, 2007.

Kasper, Walter, and Konrad Baumgartner, eds. *Lexikon für Theologie und Kirche*. 11 vols. Third edition. Freiburg: Herder, 1993–2001.

Kautzsch, E. *Die Heilige Schrift des Alten Testaments: I Mose bis Ezechiel*. Third revised edition. Tübingen: J. C. B. Mohr [Paul Siebeck], 1909.

Keel, Othmar, *Die Welt der altorientalischen Bildsymbolik und das Alte Testament*. Fifth edition. Göttingen: Vandenhoeck & Ruprecht, 1996.

————, Max Küchler, and Christoph Uehlinger. *Orte und Landschaften der Bibel: Ein Handbuch und Studien-Reiseführer zum Heiligen Land.* 4 vols. Zurich: Benzinger, 1984–.

Kegler, Jürgen, and Matthias Augustin. *Synopse zum Chronistischen Geschichtswerk.* Beiträge zur Erforschung des Alten Testaments und des antiken Judentums 1. Frankfurt am Main: Peter Lang, 1984.

Keil, Carl Friedrich. *Die Bücher Moses.* Third edition. Biblischer Commentar über das Alte Testament 1/1. Leipzig: Dörffling und Franke, 1878.

Keil, Carl Friedrich, and Franz Delitzsch. *Genesis.* Commentary of the Old Testament in Ten Volumes 1. Translated by James Martin. Fifth edition. Grand Rapids, MI: Eerdmans, 1978.

Kelber, Werner H. 'Orality and Biblical Studies: A Review Essay'. *Review of Biblical Literature* (December 2007). URL: http://www.bookreviews.org/pdf/2107_6748.pdf [accessed August 25, 2009].

Kern-Ulmer, Rivka. 'Hermeneutics, Techniques of Rabbinic Exegesis'. *EncMidr* 1:268–92.

Kessler, Rainer. *Micha.* HTKAT. Freiburg im Breisgau: Herder, 1999.

Kilian, Rudolf. 'Relecture in Psalm 110'. Pages 237–53 in *Studien zu alttestamentlichen Texten und Situationen,* edited by Rudolf Kilian. SBAB 28. Stuttgart: Katholisches Bibelwerk, 1999.

Kirkland, J. R. 'The Incident at Salem: A Re-examination of Genesis 14:18–20'. *Studia Biblica et Theologica* 7 (1977): 3–23.

Kister, Menahem. 'Observations on Aspects of Exegesis, Tradition, and Theology in Midrash, Pseudepigrapha, and Other Jewish Writings'. Pages 1–34 in *Tracing the Threads: Studies in the Vitality of Jewish Pseudepigrapha,* edited by John C. Reeves. SBLEJL 6. Atlanta: Scholars Press, 1994.

Kitchen, Kenneth A. 'Genesis 1–50 in the Near Eastern World'. Pages 67–92 in *He Swore an Oath: Biblical Themes from Genesis 12–50,* edited by Richard S. Hess, Gordon J. Wenham, and Philip E. Satterthwaite. Second edition. Carlisle, PA: Paternoster, 1994.

Kittel, R. *Die Psalmen.* KAT 13. Sixth edition. Leipzig: Deichertsche Verlagsbuchhandlung, 1929.

Kittel, Gerhard, and Gerhard Friedrich, eds. *Theologisches Wörterbuch zum Neuen Testament.* 11 vols. Stuttgart: W. Kohlhammer, 1932–79.

Klein, Ralph W. *1 Samuel.* WBC 10. Waco, TX: Word, 1983.

Klengel, Horst, ed., *Kulturgeschichte des alten Vorderasien.* Veröffentlichungen des Zentralinstituts für Alte Geschichte und Archäologie der Akademie der Wissenschaft der DDR 18. Berlin: Akademie-Verlag, 1989.

Knauf, Ernst Axel. 'Israel. II. Geschichte. 1. Allgemein und biblisch'. *RGG*⁴ 4, cols. 284–93.

————. 'Psalm lx und Psalm cviii'. *VT* 50 (2000): 55–65.

Knight, Douglas A. 'Tradition History'. *ABD* 6:633–38.

Knoppers, Gary N. 'Hierodules, Priests, or Janitors? The Levites in Chronicles and the History of the Israelite Priesthood'. *JBL* 118 (1999): 49–72.

Kobelski, Paul J. *Melchizedek and Melchireša^c.* CBQMS 10. Washington, DC: Catholic Biblical Association of America, 1981.

Koch, Klaus. 'Darios, der Meder'. Pages 287–99 in *The Word of the Lord Shall Go Forth: Essays in Honor of David Noel Freedman in Celebration of his Sixtieth Birthday*, edited by Carol L. Meyers, Michael Patrick O'Connor, and David Noel Freedman. American Schools of Oriental Research 1. Winona Lake, IN: Eisenbrauns, 1983.

———. *Was ist Formgeschichte? Methoden der Bibelexegese*. Fifth and revised edition. Neukirchen-Vluyn: Neukirchener Verlag, 1989.

———. 'צדק'. *THAT* 2, col. 509.

Köckert, Matthias. 'Die Geschichte der Abrahamüberlieferung'. Pages 103–28 in *Congress Volume: Leiden 2004*, edited by André Lemaire. VTSup 109. Leiden: E. J. Brill, 2006.

Koehler, Ludwig, and Walter Baumgartner et al., eds. *The Hebrew and Aramaic Lexicon of the Old Testament*. Leiden: E. J. Brill, 1994–2000.

König, Eduard. *Die Genesis*. Second and third revised edition. Gütersloh: Bertelsmann, 1925.

Kratz, Reinhard Gregor. 'Die Redaktion der Prophetenbücher'. Pages 9–28 in *Rezeption und Auslegung im Alten Testament und in seinem Umfeld: Ein Symposium aus Anlass des 60. Geburtstags von Odil Hannes Steck*, edited by Reinhard Gregor Kratz and Thomas Krüger and Odil Hannes Steck. OBO 153. Freiburg: Universitätsverlag, 1997.

———. 'Der vor- und nachpriesterschriftliche Hexateuch'. Pages 295–323 in *Abschied vom Jahwisten: Die Komposition des Hexateuch in der jüngsten Diskussion*, edited by Jan Christian Gertz, Konrad Schmid, and Markus Witte. BZAW 315. Berlin: W. de Gruyter, 2002.

———. 'Innerbiblische Exegese und Redaktionsgeschichte im Lichte empirischer Evidenz'. Pages 126–56 in *Das Judemtum im Zeitalter des Zweiten Tempels,*by Reinhard Gregor Kratz. FAT 42. Tübingen: Mohr Siebeck, 2004.

———. '"Öffne seinen Mund und seine Ohren": Wie Abraham Hebräisch lernte'. Pages 53–66 in *'Abraham, unser Vater': Die gemeinsamen Wurzeln von Judentum, Christentum und Islam*, edited by Reinhard Gregor Kratz and Tilman Nagel. Göttingen: Wallstein, 2003.

———. 'Redaktionsgeschichte/Redaktionskritik'. *TRE* 28:367–78.

———. *Reste hebräischen Heidentums am Beispiel der Psalmen*. Nachrichten der Akademie der Wissenschaften zu Göttingen. I. Philologisch-historische Klasse. Göttingen: Vandenhoeck & Ruprecht, 2004.

———. 'Temple and Torah: Reflections on the Legal Status of the Pentateuch between Elephantine and Qumran'. Pages 77–103 in *The Pentateuch as Torah: New Models for Understanding Its Promulgation and Acceptance*, edited by Gary N. Knoppers and Bernhard M. Levinson. Winona Lake, IN: Eisenbrauns, 2007.

———. *The Composition of the Narrative Books of the Old Testament*. Translated by John Bowden. London: T. & T. Clark, 2005.

———, Thomas Krüger, and Konrad Schmid, eds. *Schriftauslegung in der Schrift: Festschrift für Odil Hannes Steck zu seinem 65. Geburtstag*. BZAW 300. Berlin: W. de Gruyter, 2000.

———, and Tilman Nagel, eds. *'Abraham, unser Vater': Die gemeinsamen Wurzeln von Judentum, Christentum und Islam*. Göttingen: Wallstein, 2003.

Kraus, Hans-Joachim. *Psalmen*. 3 vols. Fifth edition. BKAT 15. Neukirchen-Vluyn: Neukirchener Verlag, 1978–79.

Kroeze, Jan Hendrik. *Genesis veertien: Een exegetisch-historische studie*. Hilversum: J. Schipper Jr., 1937.

Kuenen, Abraham. *An Historico-Critical Inquiry into the Origin and Composition of the Hexateuch (Pentateuch and Book of Joshua)*, Translated by Philip H. Wicksteed. London: MacMillan, 1886.

Kugel, James L. 'Levi's Elevation to the Priesthood in the Second Temple Writings'. *HThR* 86 (1993): 1–64.

———. *Traditions of the Bible: A Guide to the Bible as It Was at the Start of the Common Era*. Cambridge, MA: Harvard University Press, 1998.

Kugler, Robert A. *From Patriarch to Priest: The Levi-Priestly Tradition from Aramaic Levi to Testament of Levi*. SBLEJL 9. Atlanta: Scholars Press, 1996.

Kuhrt, Amélie. 'Israelite and Near Eastern Historiography'. Pages 257–79 in *Congress Volume Oslo 1998*, edited by André Lemaire and Magne Sæbø. VTSup 80. Leiden: E. J. Brill, 2000.

———. *The Ancient Near East: C. 3000–330 BC*. Routledge History of the Ancient World. London: Routledge, 1995.

Kutsch, E. 'Melchisedek. 1. Im AT'. *RGG*[3] 4, cols. 843–44.

Laato, Antti. *A Star Is Rising: The Historical Development of the Old Testament Royal Ideology and the Rise of the Jewish Messianic Expectations*. University of South Florida International Studies in Formative Christianity and Judaism 5. Atlanta: Scholars Press, 1997.

Lambdin, Thomas O. *Introduction to Biblical Hebrew*. New York: Charles Scribner's Sons, 1971.

Lemaire, André. 'Writing and Writing Materials'. *ABD* 6:999–1008.

———, and Magne Sæbø, eds. *Congress Volume Oslo 1998*. VTSup 80. Leiden: E. J. Brill, 2000.

Levin, Christoph. 'Jahwe und Abraham im Dialog: Genesis 15'. Pages 237–57 in *Gott und Mensch im Dialog: Festschrift für Otto Kaiser zum 80. Geburtstag*, edited by Markus Witte. BZAW 345. Berlin: W. de Gruyter, 2004.

Levinson, Bernard M. *Deuteronomy and the Hermeneutics of Legal Innovation*. New York: Oxford University Press, 1997.

Lim, Timothy H. 'Kittim'. *EncDSS* 1:469–71.

Lust, J., K. Hauspie, and Erik Eynikel, eds. *A Greek–English Lexicon of the Septuagint*. 2 vols. Stuttgart: Deutsche Bibelgesellschaft, 1992, 1996.

Magonet, Jonathan. 'Jonah, Book of'. *ABD* 3:936–42.

Maher, Michael. *Targum Pseudo-Jonathan: Genesis: Translated, with Introduction and Notes*. The Aramaic Bible 1B. Edinburgh: T. & T. Clark, 1992.

Mann, Jacob. *The Bible as Read and Preached in the Old Synagogue: A Study in the Cycles of the Readings from Torah and Prophets, as well as from Psalms, and the Structure of the Midrashic Homilies*. Cincinnati, OH: Union of American Hebrew Congregations, 1940.

———. *The Bible as Read and Preached in the Old Synagogue: A Study in the Cycles of the Readings from Torah and Prophets, as well as from Psalms, and the Structure of the Midrashic Homilies*. 2 vols. New York: Ktav, 1966, 1971.

Margalith, Othniel. 'The Riddle of Genesis 14 and Melchizedek'. *ZAW* 112 (2000): 501–8.

Martin-Achard, Robert. 'Abraham: I. Im Alten Testament'. *TRE* 1:364–72.

Martínez, Florentino García, and Eibert J. C. Tigchelaar, eds. *The Dead Sea Scrolls Study Edition*. 2 vols. Leiden: E. J. Brill, 1997–98.

Mathews, K. A. 'The Background of the Paleo-Hebrew Texts at Qumran'. Pages 549–68 in *The Word of the Lord Shall Go Forth: Essays in honor of David Noel Freedman in Celebration of his Sixtieth Birthday*, edited by Carol L. Meyers, Michael Patrick O'Connor, and David Noel Freedman. American Schools of Oriental Research 1. Winona Lake, IN: Eisenbrauns, 1983.

Matthews, Victor H. 'Abimelech'. *ABD* 1:20–21.

Mays, James Luther. *Micah: A Commentary*. OTL. Philadelphia: Westminster, 1976.

———. *Psalms*. Interpretation. Louisville: John Knox Press, 1994.

Mazar, Benjamin. 'The Historical Background of the Book of Genesis'. Pages 49–62 in *The Early Biblical Period: Historical Studies*, by Benjamin Mazar. Edited by Shmuel Ahitub and Baruch A. Levine. Translated by Ruth and Elisheva Rigbi. Jerusalem: Israel Exploration Society, 1986.

McCarter, Peter Kyle. *II Samuel: A New Translation with Introduction, Notes and Commentary*. AB 9. New York: Doubleday, 1984.

McConville, J. Gordon. 'Abraham and Melchizedek: Horizons in Genesis 14'. Pages 93–118 in *He Swore an Oath: Biblical Themes from Genesis 12–50*, edited by Richard S. Hess, Gordon J. Wenham, and Philip E. Satterthwaite. Carlisle, PA: Paternoster, 1994.

McCullough, J. C. 'Melchizedek's Varied Role in Early Exegetical Tradition'. *Near East School of Theology Theological Review* 1/2 (1978): 52–66.

McNamara, Martin. 'Melchizedek: Gen 14,17–20 in the Targums, in Rabbinic and Early Christian Literature'. *Bib* 81 (2000): 1–31.

———. *Targum Neofiti 1: Genesis: Translated, with Apparatus and Notes*. The Aramaic Bible 1A. Edinburgh: T. & T. Clark, 1992.

Meer, Willem van der. 'Psalm 110: A Psalm of Rehabilitation?' Pages 207–34 in *The Structural Analysis of Biblical and Canaanite Poetry*, by Willem van der Meer and J. C. de Moor. JSOTSup 74. Sheffield: JSOT Press, 1988.

Meinhold, Johannes. *1. Mose 14: Eine historisch-kritische Untersuchung*. BZAW 22. Gießen: Töpelmann, 1911.

Menn, Esther. 'Inner-Biblical Exegesis in the Tanak'. Pages 55–79 in *A History of Biblical Interpretation*, edited by Alan J. Hauser and Duane F. Watson. Grand Rapids, MI: Eerdmans, 2003–.

Metzger, Martin. 'Eigentumsdeklaration und Schöpfungsaussage'. Pages 37–51 in *'Wenn nicht jetzt, wann dann?'*, edited by Hans-Georg Geyer, J. M. Schmidt, and M. Weinrich. FS H.-J. Kraus. Neukirchen-Vluyn: Neukirchener Verlag, 1983.

Meyer, Rudolf. *Hebräische Grammatik*. 4 vols. Third edition. Berlin: W. de Gruyter, 1969–72. Reprint, Berlin: W. de Gruyter, 1992.

Meyers, Carol L., Michael Patrick O'Connor, and David Noel Freedman, eds. *The Word of the Lord Shall Go Forth: Essays in honor of David Noel Freedman in Celebration of his Sixtieth Birthday*. American Schools of Oriental Research 1. Winona Lake, IN: Eisenbrauns, 1983.

Miller, P. D., Jr. 'El the Creator of Earth'. *BASOR* 239 (1980): 43–46.

Moore, Carey A. 'Esther, Book of'. *ABD* 2:633–43.

———. 'Tobit, Book of'. *ABD* 6:585–94.

Morenz, Ludwig D. 'Wie die Schrift zu Text wurde'. Pages 18–48 in *Was ist ein Text? Alttestamentliche, ägyptologische und altorientalistische Perspektiven* edited by Ludwig D. Morenz and Stefan Schorch. BZAW 362. Berlin: W. de Gruyter, 2007.

———, and Stefan Schorch. 'Was ist ein Text? Einleitung'. Pages ix–xx in *Was ist ein Text? Alttestamentliche, ägyptologische und altorientalistische Perspektiven*, edited by Ludwig D. Morenz and Stefan Schorch. BZAW 362. Berlin: W. de Gruyter, 2007.

Morgenstern, Julian. 'Genesis 14'. Pages 223–36 in *Studies in Jewish Literature: Issued in Honor of Professor Kaufmann Kohler, Ph.D. President Hebrew Union College, Cincinnati, Ohio, on the Occasion of his Seventieth Birthday May the Tenth Nineteen Hundred and Thirteen*, edited by David Philipson, David Neumark and Julian Morgenstern. Berlin: Georg Reimer, 1913.

Mras, Karl, ed. *Eusebius Werke 8. Die Praeperatio Evangelica. Erster Teil. Einleitung, Die Bücher I bis X*. Die griechischen christlichen Schriftsteller der ersten drei Jahrhunderte 43. Berlin: Akademie-Verlag, 1954.

Muffs, Yochanan. 'Abraham the Noble Warrior'. *JSJ* 33 (1982): 81–108.

Murphy, Roland E. 'Wisdom in the OT'. *ABD* 6:920–31.

Murphy-O'Connor, Jerome. 'Damascus'. *EncDSS* 1:165–66

Mutius, Hans-Georg von. 'Die Bedeutung von *wayyechaleq* in Genesis 14,15 im Licht der komparativen Semitistik und der aramäischen Qumranschrift *Genesis Apokryphon XXII,8ff*'. *BN* 90 (1997): 8–12.

Naveh, Joseph, Solomon Birnbaum, David Diringer, Zvi Federbush, Jonathan Shunary, and Jacob Maimon. 'Alphabet, Hebrew'. *EncJud* 1:689–728.

Nel, P. J. 'Psalm 110 and the Melchizedek Tradition'. *JNSL* 22 (1996): 1–14.

Nelson, Richard D. *Raising Up a Faithful Priest: Community and Priesthood in Biblical Theology*. Louisville, KY: Westminster/John Knox, 1993.

Neusner, Jacob, *The Mishnah: A New Translation*. New Haven: Yale University Press, 1988.

———, and Richard S. Sarason, eds. *Tosefta. I First Division: Zeraim (The Order of Agriculture)*. New York: Ktav, 1986.

———, Alan J. Avery-Peck et al., eds. *Encyclopaedia of Midrash: Biblical Interpretation in Formative Judaism*. 2 vols. Leiden: E. J. Brill, 2005.

Niccacci, Alviero. 'An Outline of the Biblical Hebrew Verbal System in Prose'. *Liber annuus* 39 (1989): 7–26.

Nickelsburg, George W. E., and John J. Collins, *Ideal Figures in Ancient Judaism: Profiles and Paradigms*. SBLSCS 12. Chico, CA: Scholars Press, 1980.

Niehr, Herbert. *Der höchste Gott: alttestamentlicher JHWH-Glaube im Kontext syrisch-kanaanäischer Religion des 1. Jahrtausends v. Chr.* BZAW 190. Berlin: W. de Gruyter, 1990.

———. 'Israel. II. Geschichte. 3. Religionsgeschichte'. *RGG*[4] 4, cols. 294–96.

———. 'Josua'. Pages 193–95 in *Einleitung in das Alte Testament,* edited by Erich Zenger et al. Studienbücher Theologie 1,1. Fourth edition. Stuttgart: W. Kohlhammer, 2001.

Nielsen, Kirsten. 'Intertextuality and Hebrew Bible'. Pages 17–31 in *Congress Volume Oslo 1998,* edited by André Lemaire and Magne Sæbø. VTSup 80. Leiden: E. J. Brill, 2000.

Noble, Paul R. 'Esau, Tamar, and Joseph: Criteria for Identifying Inner-Biblical Allusions'. *VT* 52 (2002): 219–52.

Nöldeke, Theodor. 'Die Ungeschichtlichkeit der Erzählung Gen. XIV'. Pages 156–72 in *Untersuchungen zur Kritik des Alten Testaments,* by Theodor Nöldeke. Kiel: Schwers, 1869.

Noort, Ed. *Das Buch Josua: Forschungsgeschichte und Problemfelder.* EdF 292. Darmstadt: Wissenschaftliche Buchgesellschaft, 1998.

Nordheim, Miriam von. *Geboren von der Morgenröte? Psalm 110 in Tradition, Redaktion und Rezeption.* WMANT 118. Neukirchen-Vluyn: Neukirchener Verlag, 2008.

North, Robert. *A History of Biblical Map Making.* BTAVO 32. Wiesbaden: Reichert, 1979.

———. 'מַעֲשֵׂר/עשׂר/עֹשֶׂר. *ThWAT,* 4, cols. 432–38.

Noth, Martin. *Die israelitischen Personennamen im Rahmen der gemeinsemitischen Namengebung.* BWANT III, 10. Stuttgart: W. Kohlhammer, 1928. Reprint, Hildesheim: Georg Olms, 1980.

———. *Überlieferungsgeschichte des Pentateuch.* Stuttgart: W. Kohlhammer, 1948.

Nyberg, H. S. 'Studien zum Religionskampf im Alten Testament'. *ARW* 35 (1938): 329–87.

Oberforcher, Robert. 'Das alttestamentliche Priestertum und die tragenden Priestergestalten: Melchizedek, Levi, Aaron'. Pages 141–60 in *Alttestamentliche Gestalten im Neuen Testament: Beiträge zur biblischen Theologie,* edited by Markus Öhler. Darmstadt: Wissenschaftliche Buchgesellschaft, 1999.

O'Brien, Julia M. *Priest and Levite in Malachi.* SBL Dissertation Series 121. Atlanta: Scholars Press, 1990.

Oded, Bustanay. 'Cyprus: Ancient Period'. *EncJud* 5:347–48.

Öhler, Markus, ed. *Alttestamentliche Gestalten im Neuen Testament: Beiträge zur biblischen Theologie.* Darmstadt: Wissenschaftliche Buchgesellschaft, 1999.

Olyan, Saul. 'Zadok's Origins and the Tribal Politics of David'. *JBL* 101 (1982): 177–93.

Orlov, Andrej. 'Melchizedek Legend of 2 (Slavonic) Enoch'. *JSJ* 31 (2000): 23–38.

Otto, Eckart. 'Deuteronomium'. *RGG*[4] 2, cols. 693–96.

———. *Jerusalem – die Geschichte der Heiligen Stadt: von den Anfängen bis zur Kreuzfahrerzeit.* Urban-Taschenbücher 308. Stuttgart: W. Kohlhammer, 1980.

———. 'Politische Theologie in den Königspsalmen zwischen Ägypten und Assyrien. Die Herrscherlegitimation in den Psalmen 2 und 18 in ihren altorientalischen Kontexten'. Pages 33–65 in *'Mein Sohn bist du' (Ps 2,7): Studien zu den Konigspsalmen,* edited by Eckart Otto and Erich Zenger. SBS 192. Stuttgart: Katholisches Bibelwerk, 2002.

Otten, H. 'Ein kanaanäischer Mythus aus Bogazköy'. *MIO* 1 (1953): 125–50.

Otzen, Benedikt. *Tobit and Judith.* Guides to Apocrypha and Pseudepigrapha. Sheffield: Sheffield Academic Press, 2002.

Pearson, Birger A. 'Melchizedek (NHC IX, 1)'. *ABD* 4:688.

———. 'Melchizedek in Early Judaism, Christianity, and Gnosticism'. Pages 176–202 in *Biblical Figures outside the Bible,* edited by Michael E. Stone and Theodore A. Bergren. Harrisburg, PA: Trinity University Press, 1998.

Petuchowski, Jakob J. 'The Controversial Figure of Melchizedek'. *HUCA* 28 (1957): 127–36.

———. 'Melchisedek—Urgestalt der Ökumene'. Pages 11–37 in *Melchisedek— Urgestalt der Ökumene,* by Jakob Petuchowski. Freiburg im Breisgau: Herder, 1979.

Philo. *The Works of Philo: Complete and Unabridged: New Updated Edition.* Translated by C. D. Yonge. Peabody, MA: Hendrickson, 1993.

Pichler, Joseph. 'Abraham'. Pages 54–74 in *Alttestamentliche Gestalten im Neuen Testament: Beiträge zur biblischen Theologie,* edited by Markus Öhler. Darmstadt: Wissenschaftliche Buchgesellschaft, 1999.

Pietersma, Albert. 'Holofernes'. *ABD* 3:257.

Pinches, Theophilus G. 'Certain Inscriptions and Records Referring to Babylonia and Elam and Their Rulers, and Other Matters'. *Journal of the Transactions of the Victoria Institute* 29 (1897): 43–90.

Pitard, Wayne T. 'Damascus: Pre-Hellenistic History'. *ABD* 2:5–7.

Porton, Gary G. 'Haggadah'. *ABD* 3:19–20.

Preuß, Horst Dietrich, *Deuteronomium.* EdF 164. Darmstadt: Wissenschaftliche Buchgesellschaft, 1982.

———. *Theologie des Alten Testaments.* 2 vols. Stuttgart: W. Kohlhammer, 1991–92.

Procksch, Otto. *Die Genesis. Übersetzt und erklärt.* KAT 1. Leipzig: Deichertsche Verlagsbuchhandlung, 1924.

Pury, Albert de. 'Gottesname, Gottesbezeichnung und Gottesbegriff. *'Elohim* als Indiz zur Enstehungsgeschichte des Pentateuch'. Pages 25–47 in *Abschied vom Jahwisten: Die Komposition des Hexateuch in der jüngsten Diskussion,* edited by Jan Christian Gertz, Konrad Schmid, and Markus Witte. BZAW 315. Berlin: W. de Gruyter, 2002.

Qimron, Elisha, *The Hebrew of the Dead Sea Scrolls.* HSS 29. Atlanta: Scholars Press, 1986.

Rad, Gerhard von. *Das erste Buch Mose: Genesis.* ATD, 2/4. Ninth edition. Göttingen: Vandenhoeck & Ruprecht, 1972.

———. 'Das judäische Königsritual'. Pages 205–13 in *Gesammelte Studien zum Alten Testament,* by Gerhard von Rad. TB 8. Third edition. Munich: Chr. Kaiser Verlag, 1965.

———. *Der Heilige Krieg im alten Israel.* Fourth edition. Göttingen: Vandenhoeck & Ruprecht, 1965.

――――. *Theologie des Alten Testaments*. 2 vols. Kaiser Taschenbücher 2–3. Tenth edition. Munich: Chr. Kaiser Verlag, 1992, 1993.

Rahlfs, Alfred, ed. *Septuaginta: Id est Vetus Testamentum Graece, iuxta LXX interpretes*. 2 vols. Stuttgart: Württembergische Bibelanstalt, 1935.

Rajak, Tessa. 'Hasmonean Dynasty'. *ABD* 3:67–76.

Rendsburg, Gary A. 'Psalm cx 3b'. *VT* 49 (1999): 548–53.

――――. *The Redaction of Genesis*. Winona Lake, IN: Eisenbrauns, 1986.

Rendtorff, R. *Das überlieferungsgeschichtliche Problem des Pentateuch*. BZAW 147. Berlin: W. de Gruyter, 1976.

――――. 'El, Baʿal und Jahwe. Erwägungen zum Verhältnis von kanaanäischer und israelittischer Religion'. *ZAW* 78 (1966): 277–92.

――――. 'The Background of the Title עליון אל in Gen XIV'. Pages 167–70 in World Congress of Jewish Studies, *Fourth World Congress of Jewish Studies: Papers: Volume I*. Jerusalem: World Union of Jewish Studies, 1967.

Rengstorf, K. H. 'Melchisedek. 2. Im NT'. *RGG*[3] 4, cols. 844–45.

Rofé, Alexander. 'From Tradition to Criticism: Jewish Sources as an Aid to the Critical Study of the Hebrew Bible'. Pages 235–47 in *Congress Volume: Cambridge 1995*, edited by John A. Emerton. VTSup 66. Leiden: E. J. Brill, 1997.

――――. *Introduction to the Composition of the Pentateuch*. The Biblical Seminar 58. Sheffield: Sheffield Academic Press, 1999.

――――. 'The Methods of Late Biblical Scribes as Evidenced by the Septuagint Compared with the Other Textual Witnesses'. Pages 259–70 in *Tehillah le-Moshe: Biblical and Judaic Studies in Honor of Moshe Greenberg*, edited by Mordechai Cogan, Barry L. Eichler and Jeffrey H. Tigay. Winona Lake, IN: Eisenbrauns, 1997.

Rooke, Deborah W. 'Kingship as Priesthood: The Relationship between the High Priesthood and the Monarchy'. Pages 187–208 in *King and Messiah in Israel and the Ancient Near East: Proceedings of the Oxford Old Testament Seminar*, edited by John Day. JSOTSup 270. Sheffield: Sheffield Academic Press, 1998.

Rösel, Martin. 'Traditionskritik/Traditionsgeschichte: I. Altes Testament'. *TRE* 33:732–43.

Rosenberg, Roy A. 'The God Ṣedeq'. *HUCA* 36 (1965): 161–77.

Rosenthal, Franz, *A Grammar of Biblical Aramaic*. Porta linguarum orientalium: NS, 5. Fifth edition. Wiesbaden: Harrassowitz, 1983.

Rowley, H. H. 'Melchizedek and David'. *VT* 17 (1967): 485.

――――. 'Melchizedek and Zadok (Gen 14 and Ps 110'. Pages 461–72 in *Festschrift Alfred Bertholet zum 80. Geburtstag gewidmet von Kollegen und Freunden*, edited by W. Baumgartner et al. Tübingen: Mohr, 1950.

Rudolph, Wilhelm. *Micha, Nahum, Habakuk, Zephanja*. KAT 13/3. Gütersloh: Gerd Mohn, 1975.

Sæbø, Magne. 'Grenzbeschreibung und Landideal im Alten Testament: Mit besonderer Berücksichtigung der min-ʿad-Formel'. *ZDPV* 90 (1974): 14–37.

————, ed. *Hebrew Bible/Old Testament: The History of its Interpretation*. 3 vols. Göttingen: Vandenhoeck & Ruprecht, 1996–.

Sáenz-Badillos, Angel. *A History of the Hebrew Language*. Translated by John Elwolde. Cambridge: Cambridge University Press, 1993.

Sanders, J. A. 'The Old Testament in 11QMelchizedek'. *JANES* 5 (1973): 373–82 [= Marcus David, ed., *The Gaster Festschrift*].

Sandmel, Samuel. 'The Haggada within Scripture'. *JBL* 80 (1961): 105–22.

Sänger, Dieter, ed. *Heiligkeit und Herrschaft: Intertextuelle Studien zu Heiligkeitsvorstellungen und zu Psalm 110*. BThS 55. Neukirchen-Vluyn: Neukirchener Verlag, 2003.

Sarna, Nahum M. 'Amraphel'. *EncJud* 2:106.

————. *Genesis: The Traditional Hebrew Text with the New JPS Translation: Commentary by Nahum M. Sarna*. JPS Torah Commentary. Philadelphia: Jewish Publication Society of America, 1989.

————, and S. Sperling. 'Genesis, Book of'. *EncJud* 7:440–47.

————, S. Sperling, Israel Ta-Shma, Hannah Kasher, Shelomo Goitein, Joseph Dan, Helen Rosenau and Bathja Bayer. 'Abraham'. *EncJud* 1:280–88.

Schaper, Joachim. 'Der Septuaginta-Psalter. Interpretation, Aktualisierung und liturgische Verwendung der biblischen Psalmen im hellenistischen Judentum'. Pages 165–84 in *Der Psalter in Judentum und Christentum*, edited by Erich Zenger. HBS 18. Freiburg: Herder, 1998.

Scharbert, Josef. '"Gesegnet sei Abraham *vom* Höchsten Gott"? Zu Gen 14,19 und ähnlichen Stellen im Alten Testament'. Pages 387–401 in *Text, Methode und Grammatik*, edited by Walter Groß, Hubert Irsigler, and Theodor Seidl. FS Wolfgang Richter. St. Ottilien: EOS, 1991.

Schatz, Werner. *Genesis 14: Eine Untersuchung*. Europäische Hochschuleschriften 23/2. Bern: Herbert Lang; Frankfurt am Main: Peter Lang, 1972.

Schiffman, Lawrence C., and James C. VanderKam, eds. *Encyclopedia of the Dead Sea Scrolls*. 2 vols. Oxford: Oxford University Press, 2000.

Schildenberger, Johannes. 'Der Königspsalm 110'. *Erbe und Auftrag* 56 (1980): 53–59.

Schmid, H. 'Jahwe und die Kulttraditionen von Jerusalem'. *ZAW* 67 (1955): 168–97.

————. 'Melchisedech und Abraham, Zadok und David'. *Kairos* 7 (1965): 148–51.

Schmid, Konrad. *Erzväter und Exodus: Untersuchungen zur doppelten Begründung der Ursprünge Israels innerhalb der Geschichtsbücher des Alten Testaments*. WMANT 81. Neukirchen-Vluyn: Neukirchener Verlag, 1999.

————. 'Innerbiblische Schriftauslegung: Aspekte der Forschungsgeschichte'. Pages 1–22 in *Schriftauslegung in der Schrift: Festschrift für Odil Hannes Steck zu seinem 65. Geburtstag*, edited by Reinhard Gregor Kratz, Thomas Krüger, and Konrad Schmid. BZAW 300. Berlin: W. de Gruyter, 2000.

Schmidt, W. H. 'רבד'. *ThWAT* 2, cols. 102–33.

Schmitz, Rolf P. 'Abraham: III. Im Judentum'. in *TRE* 1:382–85.

Schorch, Stefan. 'Die Rolle des Lesens für die Konstituierung alttestamentlicher Texte'. Pages 108–22 in *Was ist ein Text? Alttestamentliche, ägyptologische und altorientalistische Perspektiven*, edited by Ludwig D. Morenz and Stefan Schorch. BZAW 362. Berlin: W. de Gruyter, 2007.

Schreiner, Stefan. 'Psalm CX und die Investitur des Hohenpriesters'. *VT* 27 (1977): 216–22.

Schuler, E. von. 'Elkunirša'. *WM* 1,1:162–63.

Schwiderski, Dirk. *Handbuch des nordwestsemitischen Briefformulars: ein Beitrag zur Echtheitsfrage der aramäischen Briefe des Esrabuches*. BZAW 295. Berlin: W. de Gruyter, 2000.

Seebass, Horst. 'Der Ort Elam in der südlichen Wüste und die Überlieferung von Gen. XIV'. *VT* 15 (1965): 389–94.

———. *Genesis*. 3 vols. Neukirchen-Vluyn: Neukirchener Verlag, 1997–2000.

Seeligmann, I. L. 'Voraussetzungen der Midraschexegese'. Pages 150–81 in *Congress Volume: Copenhagen 1953*, edited by G. W. Anderson et al. VTSup 1. Leiden: E. J. Brill, 1953.

Seidel, Moshe. 'Parallels between the Book of Isaiah and the Book of Psalms' [Hebr.], *Sînay* 38 (1956): 149–72, 229–40, 272–80.

Sellin, E. 'Melchizedek: Ein Beitrag zur Geschichte Abrahams'. *NKZ* 16 (1905): 929–51.

Seybold, Klaus. *Die Psalmen*. HAT 1/15. Tübingen: Mohr Siebeck, 1996.

———. 'Psalmen/Psalmenbuch. I. Altes Testament'. *TRE* 27:610–24.

Simons, J. *The Geographical and Topographical Texts of the Old Testament*. Studia Scholten memoriae dicata/Nederlands instituut voor het nabije Oosten 2. Leiden: E. J. Brill, 1959.

Skeat, Walter W. *A Concise Etymological Dictionary of the English Language*. Oxford: Clarendon, 1882.

Skinner, John. *A Critical and Exegetical Commentary on Genesis*. ICC. Second edition. Edinburgh: T. & T. Clark, 1930.

Smelik, Klaas A. D. *Historische Dokumente aus dem alten Israel*. Kleine Vandenhoeck-Reihe 1528. Translated by Helga Weippert. Göttingen: Vandenhoeck & Ruprecht, 1987.

Smith, Robert Houston. 'Abram and Melchizedek (Gen 14:18–20)'. *ZAW* 77 (1965): 129–53.

Soggin, Jan Alberto. 'Abraham and the Eastern Kings: On Genesis 14'. Pages 283–91 in *Solving Riddles and Untying Knots: Biblical, Epigraphic, and Semitic Studies in Honor of Jonas C. Greenfield*, edited by Ziony Zevit et al. Winona Lake, IN: Eisenbrauns, 1995.

———. *Das Buch Genesis*. Darmstadt: Wissenschaftliche Buchgesellschaft, 1997.

Sommer, Benjamin D. 'Exegesis, Allusion and Intertextuality in the Hebrew Bible: A Response to Lyle Eslinger'. *VT* 46 (1996): 479–89.

Speiser, Ephraim A. *Genesis*. AB. New York: Doubleday, 1964.

Stec, David M. *The Targum of Psalms: Translated, with a Critical Introduction, Apparatus, and Notes*. The Aramaic Bible 16. London: T. & T. Clark, 2004.

Stemberger, Günter. 'Psalmen in Liturgie und Predigt der rabbinischen Zeit'. Pages 199–213 in *Der Psalter in Judentum und Christentum*, edited by Erich Zenger. HBS 18. Freiburg: Herder, 1998.

Stern, Ephraim. 'The Persian Empire and the Political and Social History of Palestine in the Persian Period'. *CHJ* 1:70–87.

Steudel, Annette. 'Melchizedek'. *EncDSS* 1:535–37.

Stoebe, Hans Joachim. *Das zweite Buch Samuelis*. KAT 8.2. Gütersloh: Gütersloher Verlagshaus, 1994.

Stoltz, Gerhard P. J., and A. P. B. Breytenbach. 'Genesis 14 – ‚n redaksie-kritiese ondersoek'. *Hervormde teologiese studies* 57, nos. 3–4 (2001): 1312–43.

Stolz, Fritz. *Strukturen und Figuren im Kult von Jerusalem: Studien zur altorientalischen, vor- und frühisraelitischen Religion.* BZAW 118. Berlin: W. de Gruyter, 1970.

Stone, Michael E. 'Levi, Aramaic'. *EncDSS* 1:486–88.

Sullivan, Richard D. 'Cappadocia'. *ABD* 1:870–72.

Sweeney, Marwin A. 'Glosses, Textual'. *ABD* 2:1032–33.

Thayer, Joseph H. *Thayer's Greek–English Lexicon of the New Testament.* Peabody, MA: Hendrickson, 1996.

Thompson, Thomas L. 'Israelite Historiography'. *ABD* 3:206–12.

———. *The Historicity of the Patriarchal Narratives: The Quest for the Historical Abraham.* BZAW 133. Berlin: W. de Gruyter, 1974.

Tigay, Jeffrey H. 'An Early Technique of Aggadic Exegesis'. Pages 169–89 in *History, Historiography and Interpretation: Studies in Biblical and Cuneiform Literatures,* edited by H. Tadmor and M. Weinfeld. Jerusalem: Magnes, 1984.

———. 'Conflation as a Redactional Technique'. Pages 53–96 in *Empirical Models for Biblical Criticism,* edited by Jeffrey H. Tigay. Philadelphia: University of Pennsylvania Press, 1985.

———, ed. *Empirical Models for Biblical Criticism.* Philadelphia: University of Pennsylvania Press, 1985.

———. 'The Stylistic Criterion of Source Criticism in the Light of Ancient Near Eastern and Postbiblical Literature'. Pages 53–96 in *Empirical Models for Biblical Criticism,* edited by Jeffrey H. Tigay. Philadelphia: University of Pennsylvania Press, 1985.

———. 'Summary and Conclusion'. Pages 239–41 in *Empirical Models for Biblical Criticism,* edited by Jeffrey H. Tigay. Philadelphia: University of Pennsylvania Press, 1985.

Tilly, Michael. 'Psalm 110 zwischen hebräischer Bibel und Neuem Testament'. Pages 146–70 in *Heiligkeit und Herrschaft: Intertextuelle Studien zu Heiligkeitsvorstellungen und zu Psalm 110,* edited by Dieter Sänger. BThS 55. Neukirchen-Vluyn: Neukirchener Verlag, 2003.

Tournay, Raymond Jacques. 'Les relectures du Psaume 110 (109) et l'allusion à Gédéon'. *RB* 105 (1998): 321–31.

———. *Seeing and Hearing God with the Psalms: The Prophetic Liturgy of the Second Temple in Jerusalem.* JSOTSup 119. Sheffield: JSOT Press, 1991.

Towner, W. Sibley. '"Blessed Be YHWH" and "Blessed Art Thou": The Modulation of a Biblical Formula'. *CBQ* 30 (1968): 386–99.

Treves, M. 'Two Acrostic Psalms'. *VT* 15 (1965): 81–90.

Tov, Emanuel. *Textual Criticism of the Hebrew Bible.* Second revised edition. Minneapolis, MN: Fortress, 2001.

Vallat, François. 'Elam'. *ABD* 2:423–29.

VanderKam, James C. *An Introduction to Early Judaism*. Grand Rapids, MI: Eerdmans, 2001.

———. *Textual and Historical Studies in the Book of Jubilees*. HSM 14. Missoula, MT: Scholars Press for Harvard Semitic Museum, 1977.

———. *The Book of Jubilees: A Critical Text*. Scriptores Aethiopici 87–88. Leuven: Peeters, 1989.

Vanderkam, James C., and Lawrence H. Schiffman, eds. *Encyclopedia of the Dead Sea Scrolls*. 2 vols. Oxford: Oxford University Press, 2000.

Van Seters, John. *Abraham in History and Tradition*. New Haven, CT: Yale University Press, 1975.

———. *The Pentateuch: A Social-Science Commentary*. Trajectories 1. Sheffield: Sheffield Academic Press, 1999.

Vaux, Roland de. *Ancient Israel: Its Life and Institutions*. Translated by John McHugh. Biblical Resource Series. Grand Rapids, MI: Eerdmans; Livonia, MI: Dove, 1997 [= London: Darton, Longman & Todd, 1961].

———. *Die Hebräischen Patriarchen und die modernen Entdeckungen*. Düsseldorf: Patmos, 1961.

———. 'Les Hurrites de l'Histoire et les Horites de la Bible'. *RB* 74 (1967): 481–503.

———. *The Early History of Israel: To the Exodus and Covenant of Sinai*. Translated by David Smith. London: Darton, Longman & Todd, 1978.

Vawter, Bruce. 'Yahweh: Lord of the Heavens and the Earth'. *CBQ* 48 (1986): 461–67.

Veijola, Timo. 'Die Deuteronomisten als Vorgänger der Schriftgelehrten: Ein Beitrag zur Entstehung des Judentums'. Pages 192–240 in *Moses Erben: Studien zum Dekalog, zum Deuteronomismus und zum Schriftgelehrtentum*, by Timo Veijola. BWANT 149. Stuttgart: W. Kohlhammer, 2000.

Vielhauer, Roman. *Das Werden des Buches Hosea: Eine redaktionsgeschichtliche Untersuchung*. BZAW 349. Berlin: W. de Gruyter, 2007.

Visotzky, Burton L. 'Hermeneutics, Early Rabbinic'. *ABD* 3:154–55.

Wacholder, Ben Zion. 'Historiography of Qumran: The Sons of Zadok and Their Enemies'. Pages 347–77 in *Qumran between the Old and New Testaments*, edited by Frederick H. Cryer and Thomas L. Thompson. JSOTSup 290. Copenhagen International Seminar 6. Sheffield: Sheffield Academic Press, 1998.

———. 'Prolegomenon'. Pages xi–li in volume 1 of *The Bible as Read and Preached in the Old Synagogue: A Study in the Cycles of the Readings from Torah and Prophets, as well as from Psalms, and the Structure of the Midrashic Homilies*, by Jacob Mann. 2 vols. New York: Ktav, 1966, 1971.

Waldman, Nahum M. 'Genesis 14—Meaning and Structure'. *Dor le-dor* 16 (1987–1988): 256–62.

Wallace, Howard N. 'Adam'. *ABD* 1:62–64.

Waltke, Bruce K., and Michael Patrick O'Conner. *An Introduction to Biblical Hebrew Syntax*. Winona Lake, IN: Eisenbrauns, 1990.

Weinfeld, Moshe. *Deuteronomy 1–11: A New Translation with Introduction and Commentary*. AB 5. New York: Doubleday, 1991.

————. 'The Extent of the Promised Land—The Status of Transjordan'. Pages 59–75 in *Das Land Israel in biblischer Zeit: Jerusalem-Symposium 1981*, edited by Georg Strecker. Göttinger Theologische Arbeiten 25. Göttingen: Vandenhoeck & Ruprecht, 1983.

Weiser, A. *Die Psalmen*. ATD 14–15. Seventh edition. Göttingen: Vandenhoeck & Ruprecht, 1966.

Wellhausen, Julius. *Die Composition des Hexateuchs und der historischen Bücher des Alten Testaments*. Fourth unrevised edition. Berlin: W. de Gruyter, 1963 [= third revised edition, 1899].

————. *Prolegomena zur Geschichte Israels*. Sixth edition. Berlin: W. de Gruyter, 2001.

Welten, Peter. *Geschichte und Geschichtsdarstellung in den Chronikbüchern*. WMANT 42. Neukirchen-Vluyn: Neukirchener Verlag, 1973.

Wenham, Gordon J. *Genesis 1–15*. WBC 1. Waco, TX: Word, 1987.

Wente, Edward F. 'Egyptian Religion'. *ABD* 2:408–12.

Werman, Cara. 'Levi and Levites in the Second Temple Period'. *DSD* 4 (1997): 211–25.

Westermann, Claus. *Genesis 1–11*. Translated by John J. Scullion. Minneapolis, MN: Fortress, 1994.

————. *Genesis 12–36*. Translated by John J. Scullion. Minneapolis, MN: Augsburg, 1985.

————. *Genesis 12–50*. EdF 48. Darmstadt: Wissenschaftliche Buchgesellschaft, 1975.

Wewers, John William, ed. *Genesis*. Septuaginta: Vetus Testamentum Graecum/ auctoritate Academiae scientiarum Gottingensis editum 1. Göttingen: Vandenhoeck & Ruprecht, 1971.

Weitzmann, Michael. *The Syriac Version of the Old Testament: An Introduction*. University of Cambridge Oriental Publications 56. Cambridge: Cambridge University Press, 1999.

Weyde, Karl William. 'Inner-Biblical Interpretation: Methodological Reflections on the Relationship between Texts in the Hebrew Bible'. *SEÅ* 70 (2005): 287–300.

————. *Prophecy and Teaching: Prophetic Authority, Form Problems, and the Use of Traditions in the Book of Malachi*. BZAW 288. Berlin: W. de Gruyter, 2000.

White, Sidnie Ann. 'Bagoas'. *ABD* 1:567–68.

Widengren, Geo. 'Psalm 110 und das sakrale Königtum in Israel'. Pages 185–216 in *Zur neueren Psalmenforschung*, edited by P. H. A. Neumann. WdF 192. Darmstadt: Wissenschaftliche Buchgesellschaft, 1976.

Willi, Thomas. 'Melchisedek: II. Judentum'. *TRE* 22:417–20.

Wilson, J. Chr. 'Tithe'. *ABD* 6:578–80.

Wintermute, O. S. 'Jubilees (Second Century B.C.)'. *OTP* 2:35–142.

Witte, Markus, ed. *Gott und Mensch im Dialog: Festschrift für Otto Kaiser zum 80. Geburtstag*. BZAW 345. Berlin: W. de Gruyter, 2004.

Wolff, H. W. *Dodekapropheton 4: Micha*. BKAT 14/4. Neukirchen-Vluyn: Neukirchener Verlag, 1982.

Woude, A. S. van der. 'Melchisedek als himmliche Erlösergestalt in den neugefundenen eschatologischen Midraschim aus Qumran Höhle XI'. *OTS* 14
(1965): 354–73.

Wright, Addison G. 'The Literary Genre Midrash'. *CBQ* 28 (1966): 105–38.

Wright, David P. 'Azazel'. *ABD* 1:536–37.

Wünsche, Aug. *Der Midrasch Bereschit Rabba: das ist die haggadische Auslegung der
Genesis*. Leipzig: Otto Schulze, 1881.

Younker, Randall W. 'Beth-haccherem'. *ABD* 1:686–87.

Zapff, Burkard M. *Redaktionsgeschichtliche Studien zum Michabuch im Kontext des
Dodekapropheton*. BZAW 256. Berlin: W. de Gruyter, 1997.

Zakovitch, Yair. 'Assimilation in Biblical Narratives'. Pages 175–96 in *Empirical
Models for Biblical Criticism*, edited by in Jeffrey H. Tigay. Philadelphia:
University of Pennsylvania Press, 1985.

———. 'Juxtaposition in the Abraham Cycle'. Pages 509–24 in *Pomegranates and
Golden Bells: Studies in Biblical, Jewish, and Near Eastern Ritual, Law, and
Literature in Honor of Jacob Milgrom*, edited by Avi Hurvitz, Jacob Milgrom,
David P. Wright and David Noel Freedman. Winona Lake, IN: Eisen-
brauns, 1995.

———. 'Poetry Creates Historiography'. Pages 311–20 in *'A Wise and Discerning
Mind': Essays in Honor of Burke O. Long*, edited by Saul M. Olyan and Robert C. Culley. BJS 325. Providence, RI: Brown Judaic Studies, 2000.

Zenger, Erich. *Das Buch Judit*. JSHRZ 1/6. Gütersloh: Gütersloher Verlagshaus
Gerd Mohn, 1981.

———. 'Königpsalmen'. *NBL* 2:510–13.

Zenger, Erich et al. *Einleitung in das Alte Testament*. Fourth edition. Studienbücher
Theologie 1,1. Stuttgart: W. Kohlhammer, 2001.

Ziemer, Benjamin. *Abram — Abraham: Kompositionsgeschichtliche Untersuchung zu
Genesis 14, 15 und 17*. BZAW 350. Berlin: W. de Gruyter, 2005.

Zimmerli, Walther. 'Abraham und Melchisedek'. Pages 255–64 in *Das nahe und
das ferne Wort*, edited by Fritz Maaß. FS Leonard Rost. BZAW 105. Berlin:
W. de Gruyter, 1967.

———. *Grundriß der alttestamentlichen Theologie*. Sixth edition. Theologische Wissenschaft 3,1. Stuttgart: W. Kohlhammer, 1989.

———. *1. Mose 12–25: Abraham*. ZB 1.2. Zurich: Theologischer Verlag, 1976.

Zobel, Hans-Jürgen. 'Der frühe Jahwe-Glaube in der Spannung von Wüste und
Kulturland'. *ZAW* 101 (1989): 342–65.

———. 'עֶלְיוֹן'. *ThWAT* 6,1, cols. 131–51.

Index of Ancient Names, Deities, Personifications

Index of Modern Authors

Index of Passages